M000266481

RECONSTRUCTING
INDIVIDUALISM

AMERICAN PHILOSOPHY
Douglas R. Anderson and Jude Jones, series editors

RECONSTRUCTING INDIVIDUALISM

A Pragmatic Tradition from Emerson to Ellison

JAMES M. ALBRECHT

FORDHAM UNIVERSITY PRESS   NEW YORK   2012

Copyright © 2012 Fordham University Press

All rights reserved. No part of this publication may be reproduced, stored in a retrieval system, or transmitted in any form or by any means—electronic, mechanical, photocopy, recording, or any other—except for brief quotations in printed reviews, without the prior permission of the publisher.

Fordham University Press has no responsibility for the persistence or accuracy of URLs for external or third-party Internet websites referred to in this publication and does not guarantee that any content on such websites is, or will remain, accurate or appropriate.

Fordham University Press also publishes its books in a variety of electronic formats. Some content that appears in print may not be available in electronic books.

Library of Congress Cataloging-in-Publication Data

Albrecht, James M.
   Reconstructing individualism : a pragmatic tradition from Emerson to Ellison / James M. Albrecht.—1st ed.
      p.   cm.—(American philosophy)
   Summary: "Explores the theories of democratic individualism articulated in the works of the American transcendentalist writer Ralph Waldo Emerson, pragmatic philosophers William James and John Dewey, and African-American novelist and essayist Ralph Ellison" —Provided by publisher.
   Includes bibliographical references and index.
   ISBN 978-0-8232-4209-2 (hardback)
   1. Philosophy, American—19th century. 2. Philosophy, American—20th century. 3. Emerson, Ralph Waldo, 1803–1882—Philosophy. 4. James, William, 1842–1910—Philosophy. 5. Dewey, John, 1859–1952—Philosophy. 6. Ellison, Ralph—Philosophy. 7. Literature and society—United States. 8. Individualism—United States—History. 9. Individualism in literature. 10. Pragmatism in literature. I. Title.
B832.A345   2012
141'.40973—dc23

2011042862

Printed in the United States of America
14 13 12 5 4 3 2 1
First edition

THE
AMERICAN
LITERATURES
INITIATIVE

A book in the American Literatures Initiative (ALI), a collaborative publishing project of NYU Press, Fordham University Press, Rutgers University Press, Temple University Press, and the University of Virginia Press. The Initiative is supported by The Andrew W. Mellon Foundation. For more information, please visit www.americanliteratures.org.

For Lisa;
And for Hannah and Cecily,
Whose arrival in this world taught me the true meaning
of an Emersonian wonder at the advent of a new individual

Contents

Acknowledgments xi

Introduction. "Individualism Has Never Been Tried":
Toward a Pragmatic Individualism   1

PART I. EMERSON

1 What's the Use of Reading Emerson Pragmatically?:
   The Example of William James   25

2 "Let Us Have Worse Cotton and Better Men":
   Emerson's Ethics of Self-Culture   53

PART II. PRAGMATISM: JAMES AND DEWEY

3 Moments in the World's Salvation: James's
   Pragmatic Individualism   127

4 Character and Community: Dewey's Model of
   Moral Selfhood   191

5 "The Local Is the Ultimate Universal": Dewey on
   Reconstructing Individuality and Community   244

PART III. A TRAGICOMIC ETHICS IN THE
EMERSONIAN VEIN: KENNETH BURKE
AND RALPH ELLISON

6 Saying Yes and Saying No: Individualist Ethics
   in Ellison and Burke   281

Notes 311
Index 371

Acknowledgments

There are many persons and a few institutions to whom I owe heartfelt thanks for helping me to finish this work.

First, to friends and colleagues who have read portions of the study and provided both constructive criticism and necessary encouragement: Lisa Marcus, Erin McKenna, Doug Anderson, Joe Thomas, David Robinson, Lawrence Buell, and Michael Lopez. To John Stuhr and Richard Shusterman, who organized a National Endowment for the Humanities summer seminar on American Pragmatism and Culture that immersed me in the works of John Dewey precisely when I needed it most, and to all my fellow participants who made that summer a memorable and sustaining experience. To Al von Frank and Jana Argersinger at *ESQ*, who first provided me a venue for my work, and to Barry Tharaud at *Nineteenth Century Prose*. To Helen Tartar and Thomas Lay at Fordham University Press and to Tim Roberts and Edward Batchelder at the American Literatures Initiative, for their expert support in shepherding the book through the editorial and production process. And to all my wonderful colleagues in the Department of English and the Division of the Humanities at Pacific Lutheran University, who provide me with a vibrant community in which to pursue my vocation as teacher and scholar.

Several institutional grants also provided me with invaluable support. The National Endowment for the Humanities funded my participation in the seminar mentioned above; a generous Graves Award in the Humanities funded a semester's research leave that enabled me to write my two chapters on Emerson; and my home institution, Pacific Lutheran, supported me with two Regency Advancement Awards and a sabbatical leave.

Last, I owe a student's immense debt to the late Richard Poirier, in whose graduate seminar on pragmatism and American poetry I first became enthralled by the dizzying twists of an Emerson essay. My biggest regret at not having completed this study sooner is that I could not present him a copy with grateful thanks for his being a mentor in the best Emersonian sense.

To Lisa, Hannah, Cecily, and Maggie, I owe inestimable thanks for giving me the kind of loving home that makes work possible and meaningful. And to my parents, James L. and Phyllis Albrecht, I owe thanks for a lifetime of love and support.

Parts of this work have appeared previously in scholarly journals. Portions of chapter 2 appeared in *ESQ: A Journal of the American Renaissance* (vol. 41, no. 3; and vol. 45). Chapter 1 appeared in *Nineteenth Century Prose* (vol. 30, nos. 1–2); and chapter 6 originally appeared in *PMLA* (vol. 114). I am grateful to these journals for their permission to reprint my previous work.

RECONSTRUCTING
INDIVIDUALISM

Individualism is a mature and calm feeling, which disposes each member of the community to sever himself from the mass of his fellows and to draw apart with his family and his friends, so that after he has thus formed a little circle of his own, he willingly leaves society at large to itself. Selfishness originates in blind instinct; individualism proceeds from erroneous judgment more than from depraved feelings; it originates as much in deficiencies of mind as in perversity of heart.

Selfishness blights the germ of all virtue; individualism, at first, only saps the virtues of public life; but in the long run it attacks and destroys all others and is at length absorbed in downright selfishness. Selfishness is a vice as old as the world, which does not belong to one form of society more than to another; individualism is of democratic origin, and it threatens to spread in the same ratio as the equality of condition.

—Alexis de Tocqueville

This then is the individualistic view. . . . It means many good things: e.g. Genuine novelty; order being *won*, paid for; the smaller systems the truer; man [is greater than] home [is greater than] state or church. anti-slavery in all ways; toleration—respect of others; democracy—good systems can always be described in individualistic terms.

—William James

Because of the bankruptcy of the older individualism, those who are aware of the break-down often speak and argue as if individualism were itself done and over with. I do not suppose that those who regard socialism and individualism as antithetical really mean that individuality is going to die out or that it is not something intrinsically precious. But in speaking as if the only individualism were the local episode of the last two centuries . . . they slur over the chief problem—that of remaking society to serve the growth of a new type of individual.

—John Dewey

Individualism has never been tried.

—Ralph Waldo Emerson

"INDIVIDUALISM HAS NEVER BEEN TRIED"

Toward a Pragmatic Individualism

A merica has a love-hate relationship with individualism.[1] Many view individualism as morally and politically suspect, as a corrosive force that undermines democracy and is the source of many of our social ills. Such indictments usually focus on two main issues. First, that individualism precludes meaningful political change and is inescapably complicit with the liberal-capitalist status quo. Any ethics that asserts the morality of individualized activity risks being co-opted by the capitalist doctrine that rationalizes the pursuit of individualized wealth as a primary—and perhaps sufficient—means to the general good. Similarly, through an exaggerated emphasis on individual merit and responsibility, individualism can ignore or minimize social conditions that perpetuate inequalities of wealth and opportunity while, in political terms, engraining a laissez-faire bias against public efforts at reform that might create the conditions for a more widespread individual liberty. If individualism is seen as too complicit with the dominant capitalist beliefs of our culture, it is by the same token distrusted for challenging other opposing—and also widely held—beliefs that equate morality with altruistic self-sacrifice. Such concerns underlie the second major critique of individualism, influentially articulated by Tocqueville: that the equality of social condition and status in modern democracy leads to an increasingly narrow pursuit of self-interest that undermines the fabric of civic life and devolves into a materialistic selfishness. These are serious and fundamental concerns that proponents of democratic individualism must address. Anyone with progressive political leanings who has witnessed a proposed social reform—on health care, the environment, or issues of economic justice—become derailed by outcries against government encroachments on individual liberty would be hard-pressed to deny the force of the first charge. Anyone who has lived in, or observed, the frenetic patterns of work and consumerism in contemporary American society would be hard-pressed to dismiss the claim that a narrowly private and materialistic individualism exacerbates social isolation and fragmentation.

Yet, as the epigraph from James suggests, there are many aspects of individualism most Americans value deeply, seeing them as essential to a democratic society: a moral commitment to the intrinsic value of each individual, and to a society that provides opportunities for individuals to cultivate their potential; respect and tolerance for individual opinions and pursuits; respect for individual conscience as a safeguard against dogmatic or repressive impositions of communal morals; and the encouragement of individual imagination and initiative as a socially necessary source of creative vitality. Those of us who have been lucky enough to live in communities that uphold such individualistic values would be justly loath to do without them.

Reconstructing Individualism is offered on the conviction, forged through study of the writers explored herein, that individualism remains a necessary component of any full and healthy model of democracy, but that it must be a reconceived individualism whose conception and practice seeks to retain the ethical benefits and avoid the corrosive effects outlined above. Such a project is especially urgent, I believe, for those on the Left, who are often quickest to equate individualism with a reactionary politics: those committed to a more progressive and just society simply cannot afford to abandon the field and cede the rhetorical and cultural power of individualism to more conservative political agendas.[2] This conviction is fueled, in turn, by Dewey's insistence, voiced above, that the possibilities of what individualism might be are not limited to the historical course of what it has been, and, further, that the dominant conceptions of individualism we have inherited from that history—specifically, the classic liberal traditions deriving from Locke and Smith, but shaped by the dualisms of the broader Western philosophical tradition—have hindered us from reconceiving and intelligently pursuing a more fully democratic and morally coherent individualism.

The tradition of American pragmatism, including its Emersonian roots, constitutes a powerful resource for this task of remaking individualism: for diagnosing the false intellectual assumptions that must be rejected, and for suggesting how a more coherent conceptualization of individualism might transform our conduct—our attempts to cultivate moral selves, and our efforts to reform the varied aspects of society in order to create healthier communities and a more vital democracy. Toward this end, *Reconstructing Individualism* traces a pragmatic genealogy of individualism that has it roots in the writings of Ralph Waldo Emerson and extends through a series of writers influenced by him: the pragmatic philosophers William James and John Dewey, the cultural critic and theorist Kenneth Burke, and the novelist and essayist Ralph Ellison.

Pragmatism offers a radical alternative to traditional individualism because it critiques the tendency to treat the metaphysical dualisms of the Western philosophical tradition as rigidly exclusive, a tendency that in turn fosters false and distorting dualisms in our moral and political thought. The key to pragmatism's departure from traditional schools of thought stems from its pluralistic metaphysics and its subsequent advocacy of a thoroughgoing experimentalism in all areas of human inquiry and endeavor. The pluralist metaphysics embodied in both James's and Dewey's concepts of "experience" describes all things as existing not as isolated substances or essences, but only in and through their mutually transforming interaction—or transactions—with other things.[3] Pluralism describes a universe of process and flux, of real contingency and change: a world in which the mutually transforming interactions within experience are not determined by any transcendent power outside experience—no divine thinker, no ontological essences, or fated teleology. As James strikingly puts it:

> Truth grows up inside all of the finite experiences. They lean on each other, but the whole of them, if such a whole there be, leans on nothing. All "homes" are in finite experience; finite experience as such is homeless. Nothing outside of the flux secures the issue of it. It can hope for salvation only from its own intrinsic promises and potencies.[4]

A pluralistic universe that is genuinely moving and changing demands an experimentalist approach, a pragmatic theory of truths as not enjoying any absolute validity, but as limited human constructs derived from experience—hypotheses or beliefs—whose validity must be tested in the changing conditions of experience, and whose truth, in James's terms, becomes "verified" to the extent our acting upon them continues to yield satisfactory consequences.[5] Pragmatism thus rejects reductive correspondence or spectator theories of truth that equate knowing with the copying or apprehension of a static reality, insisting instead that knowing is inseparable from doing—a process of using ideas as tools to act in and transform our environment. Accordingly, our human purposes play an inescapable role in creating and verifying truth. Pragmatism turns away from the quest for theoretical certainty, and toward experimental inquiry into the problems to be remedied and possibilities to be realized in specific situations. While this vision of a pluralistic universe of flux and contingency appears frightening to some sensibilities, pragmatists stress that pluralism describes a reality suited to our intellectual and moral needs: a universe still in the making, which our purposes, desires, and beliefs help to create, and in which the methods of intelligence we derive from experience provide sufficient tools for the ongoing remaking of experience (or in Dewey's terminology, "reconstruction") that can render beneficial outcomes more secure and allow for a liberating growth in the quality and meaning of experience.

This pluralistic experimentalism rejects a rigidly dualistic approach to the central dichotomies of the Western philosophical tradition—such as subject versus object; knowing versus doing; reason versus passion, desire, or emotion; and, most importantly for the concept of individualism, dichotomies that set the individual and social in opposition to each other: "natural" individual liberty versus "artificial" social constraint; egoism versus altruism; and liberty versus responsibility. Entities traditionally conceived as having a transcendent essence—such as the individual or self, as well as specific human attributes like reason, conscience, or liberty—pragmatism views instead as results to be achieved within the transactions of experience. But in denying an entity like the self any transcendent status, by placing it wholly within the limits of experience, pragmatism does not degrade it, but affirms its capacity for growth—a growth, crucially, that can be directed by intelligent human choice. James's and Dewey's models of experience stress the mutually transforming relationship between human nature and its environing conditions. The natural and social conditions of our world, though resistant, remain plastic to our efforts to reform them, and the unparalleled plasticity of human nature—which James and Dewey both locate in our ability to form new habits—makes humankind, in James's terms, "*par excellence*, the *educable* animal."[6]

Accordingly, a pragmatic experimentalism is vitally concerned with education. The experimental processes of remaking environing conditions must focus on the educative power of those conditions: what habits of selfhood do present conditions foster, and what habits might be fostered by a proposed reorganization of conditions? Further, this educative relationship is not a static question of how present conditions shape habits, nor how individuals will be educated by conditions once a proposed future is attained: it is instead an inherently ongoing process. The self is a process of education or growth in which habits such as reasonable and conscientious choice are cultivated—and the liberty of intelligently choosing to remake one's own character is achieved—through ongoing participation in efforts to remake the conditions of our associated human activities.

These attitudes point toward a pragmatic reconception of democracy and individualism that finds its most comprehensive articulation in Dewey's concept of democracy-as-education and -as-community. The "moral meaning" of democracy, Dewey insists, lies in a primary commitment to educating and liberating individuality. Institutions are to be judged by "the extent to which they educate every individual into the full stature of his possibility,"[7] which full liberation, Dewey insists, can only be attained through a communal dynamic that affords all individuals an equal opportunity to participate (commensurate with their capacities) in the establishment and pursuit of common goals. So conceived, democracy cannot be limited to any specific form of government—nor to government itself; instead, Dewey insists, democracy is a "way of life"[8] to be realized in all areas of human association. It is an ideal to be pursued through an ongoing process of experimental, communal inquiry and endeavor insofar as no fixed model of human nature or social organization can be dogmatically predetermined: liberty is not conceived as an ontological possession that all individuals possess, and that necessitates a specific form of government, but as an exercise of intelligent, self-determining choice and a liberation of individual capacities achieved within the processes of communal endeavor; similarly, only experimental

inquiry into the problems of a given situation can determine what form
of social organization is then best suited to create a more democratic
dynamic. From this view, traditional political dualisms—such as "individualistic" versus "collective" approaches to reform—threaten to trap
us in a rigid dogmatism.[9] A pragmatic approach insists that either a social
scheme relying on personal initiative or one relying on more collective
means of regulation could be the most appropriate means, in a given
situation, for promoting the conditions of a more democratic individuality. The meaningful distinction, Dewey insists, is not individualistic
versus collective approaches, but experimental versus absolutist ones.
If this pragmatic reconception of democratic individuality receives its
fullest articulation in Dewey, its roots reach firmly back to Emerson's vision of man as reformer—"What is a man born for but to be a Reformer,
a Re-maker of what man has made?"[10]—and his concomitant vision of
personality as a process of growth and self-culture.

Individualisms Old and New: Classic Liberalism and the Pragmatic Alternative

To appreciate how radically pragmatism departs from dominant conceptions of individualism, one need only contrast this pluralistic and experimentalist vision to the metaphysical assumptions that underpin classic
liberal individualism, as famously articulated in Locke's *Second Treatise
on Civil Government*. Lockean liberalism is based on a foundational
myth of the state of nature in which individuals are inherently endowed
with liberty, equality, reason, and the right to private property. Society is
a "contract" into which these ontologically free individuals enter on a rational calculation of self-interest, as a regrettably necessary compromise
in which they submit to the "artificial" constraints of society in order to
preserve, as far as possible, their "natural" individual liberties. As Dewey
argues, this Lockean metaphysics is absolutist both in its vision of human
nature and its vision of the state. By granting ontological priority to an
individual with capacities of liberty, equality, and reason—allegedly possessed antecedent to any social existence—and by positing society as a
regrettable necessity into which naturally free individuals are "driven,"[11]
Lockean liberalism concludes that the only legitimate state is one limited
as far as possible to protecting individuals' preexisting liberty. In effect: a
dogmatic laissez-faire stance that the least public regulation is always the

best form of social organization. This political vision combines power-fully with the laissez-faire thrust of economic liberalism articulated by Adam Smith. The dualism between "natural" individual liberty and "artificial" social constraint, in both political and economic liberalism, promotes a distrust of any governmental regulations that limit individuals' pursuits of personal gain or limit the operation of "natural" economic laws that allegedly translate such self-interested pursuits into maximized wealth for all. Combined, these tenets of classic liberal individualism—articulated in the late seventeenth and eighteenth centuries—continue to operate as dominant and often unquestioned assumptions shaping our twenty-first-century social debates and public policies.[12]

Analyzed from the standpoint of a pragmatic pluralism and experimentalism, Dewey argues, classic liberal conceptions of individuality, human association, and liberty appear badly distorted. They are false to the basic fact that association is the fundamental context for all human conduct: no human ever lived—or achieved liberty—in a state of nature apart from association with other human beings. Classic liberalism also presents a false model of human psychology, positing an individual possessed of inherent faculties of reason and conscience, and driven by an essential impulse of acquisitive self-interest. It promotes an impoverished view of society as a regrettable necessity that constrains individual freedom rather than the necessary medium of human association in which individuals liberate their capacities and in which their experiences are enriched with socially shared meaning. It assumes a false, dualistic conflict between egoism and altruism, liberty and responsibility. And, most importantly, it posits a merely negative view of liberty as freedom from social constraints, a laissez-faire vision that precludes attention to a more positive vision of freedom as participation in liberating conditions of associated activity, *and* precludes experimental inquiry into creating such conditions.

Dewey's critique indicates how pragmatism responds to the first of the dominant critiques of traditional individualism—that individualism distracts attention from the social conditions that would empower a meaningful liberty or equality, and undermines collective efforts at reform that might be necessary to create those conditions. "No man and no mind was ever emancipated merely by being left alone," Dewey insists, and so a new individualism, one committed to "the genuinely spiritual element" of the individualistic tradition—"the ideal of equality of opportunity and of freedom for all"—would entail a commitment to the ongoing reform of social conditions so as to educate and liberate individuality.[13] So reconceived, Dewey notes, the "ethical formula" of individualism

> would be compatible with the efforts of organized society to *equalize conditions*. It would, for example, justify public action to secure to all an education which would effect a complete development of their capacities, so that they might meet one another on a plane of knowledge and trained intelligence as nearly even as possible. It would justify legislation to equalize the standing of those now at a disadvantage because of inequality in physical power, in wealth, in command of the machinery of employment. It would justify, in other words, a vast amount of so-called social legislation which the individualistic theory as usually held condemns.[14]

While a pragmatic individualism thus can embrace extensive collective efforts at reform, its commitment to experimental inquiry forbids replacing the laissez-faire dogmatism of liberal individualism with an equally dogmatic endorsement of collectivist politics. Further, the goal of social reconstruction is always to achieve a more democratic dynamic of community in which individuality plays a necessary role as both a means and end, and in which liberty, while dependent upon enabling social conditions, must always in a crucial sense remain a matter of individual responsibility, choice, and initiative.[15]

Dewey's vision of democracy-as-community provides perhaps the most comprehensive vision of what a pragmatic reconception of individualism might entail—and the most pointed statement of how a pragmatic approach rejects and revises central aspects of liberal individualism. Yet Dewey's writings are part of a broader strand of Emersonian and pragmatic thinking about the self, individuality, and democracy that constitutes an important and underappreciated alternative to the dominant liberal tradition. The individualist tradition that runs from Emerson through James and Dewey to Ellison is characterized by the following broad set of shared assumptions, attitudes, and characteristics—which, despite the undeniable differences between these writers, mark strong lines of affinity and influence:

- A pluralistic metaphysics that analyzes human activity, truth, power, and value as emerging and existing only within and against the limitations of specific conditions.
- A consequent attitude of tragic optimism that acknowledges both the limitations, losses, and exclusions that beset all human

endeavors *and* the sufficient successes we nonetheless achieve in re-making a resistant-yet-malleable world.

- A wholly relational model of the self as existing only in an individual subject's interactions with objective conditions, leading to an emphasis on selfhood as a process of education or "self-culture."

- An insistence that the self's inescapable social implication and indebtedness entails a fundamental obligation and responsibility to others. There is no inherent dualistic division between self-interest and the interests of others in our social groups. In a pluralistic society—and especially a modern society characterized by increased specialization and interdependence—our activities and identities are linked in complex and often unrecognized ways. Accordingly, a democratic model of moral selfhood requires habits of conscientious concern for and openness to the desires, pursuits, and perspectives of others.

- An insistence that the fundamental model for understanding human conduct is not a political model (á la Locke) or economic model (á la Smith), but rather the most comprehensive context of experience and association: the ongoing efforts of individuals living and working within social groups to create more satisfactory relations with their environing world.

- The affirmation of individuality as an essential means and end in these ongoing efforts to remake experience: individual purposes, desires, will, and imagination introduce a crucial element of novelty into collective efforts to propose and realize a reorganization of existing conditions, and the liberation of individual capacities remains a central standard by which the value of all human associations should be judged.

- By extension, the claim that individuality functions as a necessary means and end within the specific area of morals: individuals remain the seat of the satisfactions, dissatisfactions, and judgments that must be harmonized in moral deliberation—so that a pluralistic ethics must respect the desires and ideals of all sentient beings, and communities that would avoid a moral dogmatism require the salutary effects of individuals who conscientiously question the validity of the group's conventional standards.

- The articulation of an individualist ethics that supports this experimentalist model of inquiry by mandating two complementary

modes of individual activity: first, an assertive willingness to project and pursue one's own ideals and purposes, and to concentrate
one's efforts toward cultivating specialized areas of talent; second,
a counterbalancing respect, tolerance, and openness to the aspects
of experience beyond one's present purposes—and, crucially, to the
experiences and desires of other beings.

• An affirmation of the mutual plasticity of self and environment.
The model of experience as a relation of mutually transforming interaction implies both that the self can be remade as it engages new
conditions, and that human acts (and the ideas that inspire them)
help transform the environment. Even our most basic impulses,
pragmatism affirms, can be trained and redirected into new habits,
and even our most entrenched social institutions remain susceptible to our efforts to reform them.

• Accordingly, a balanced view of reform that affirms the real possibility of creative change, while soberly insisting that reform requires a remaking of both the habits that constitute the self and
the social conditions that educate character. To assert that human
personality *can* be remade, as changed environing conditions elicit
new capacities and form new habits, is also to insist that education
requires reform of existing conditions. Similarly, while a pluralistic universe is one where human ideas and actions help realize
new possibilities, such possibilities must emerge out of existing
conditions and overcome the strong inertia of existing customs
and institutions.

• The view that in a moving and changing world no human product—no truth or principle, and no achieved result—can provide
any ultimate or secure value. Ideas and truths must be treated as
tools in our ongoing efforts to achieve more satisfactory relations
with our environment and with each other, and each achieved end
must in turn be treated as a means to renewed and enriched activity. The most stable and primary values we enjoy as humans reside
in activity and growth: the new habits and capacities we cultivate
through action, and the growing quality and meaning that enriches
present activity when it is directed by intelligently chosen and socially shared ends.

• A consequent attitude of meliorism, which asserts that the morality
of our world—its adequacy for our moral needs and purposes—lies

not in the perfect attainment of any projected ideal, nor in any guarantee of ultimate success, but rather in the ongoing experience of limited success, progress, and growth we achieve against the resistant limits of our world.

- Finally, an assertion that even our highest and most complex human capacities—such as reason, conscience, and liberty—are not transcendent or antecedent possessions of the self, but complex habits of a democratic, moral selfhood to be achieved in experience. And the related insistence that our highest ideals—such as a belief in the moral nature of the universe, or a political ideal like democracy—are hypotheses or beliefs whose truth must be "verified" in the trials of experience by our success, when we use those ideals to guide our actions, in creating consequences that satisfy our moral and intellectual needs.

The emphasis on the *processes* of experience that underlies this pragmatic approach to individualism marks a radical departure from more traditional political theories. There is no blueprint for what a pragmatic individualism will look like: no fixed model of democratic selfhood beyond the flexible habits of reasonable, conscientious, and imaginative deliberation required by an experimentalist approach to inquiry, and no prescribed form of democratic social organization. For on the pragmatic view, the task of remaking our communities, our selves, and our democracy is by its nature ongoing and open-ended. The writers in this study offer no model of reconstructed individuality as a fixed ideal that could be fully achieved in some imagined future, but rather affirm our ability to achieve a reconstructing individuality in the present. They affirm our ability to forge new forms of democratic community, adapted to the challenges and possibilities of our changing world, that will provide individuals with meaningful opportunities to cultivate and exercise their capacities, and they affirm the practical achievement of liberty that individuals enjoy in the present as they exercise personal choice, imagination, and energy in contributing to common endeavors—remaking their selves as they engage in the collective project of remaking our world.

Individualism and Community:
Pragmatism versus Communitarianism

This emphasis on process indicates, as well, how pragmatism addresses the second major critique of individualism articulated by Tocqueville and his intellectual descendants. Surveying American society in the 1830s, Tocqueville argued that a widespread equality of status and opportunity creates citizens with "sufficient education and fortune to satisfy their own wants" who thus adopt the "habit of always considering themselves as standing alone, and . . . imagin[ing] that their whole destiny is in their own hands." The resulting tendency of each individual to "sever himself from the mass of his fellows and to draw apart with his family and his friends" both "saps the virtues of public life" and eventually "destroys all others."[16] This corrosive effect of individualism, Tocqueville argued, was mitigated by the "manners and customs" of American society: specifically, by Americans' extensive participation in local government and voluntary civic associations, and by the importance of religion in Americans' lives.[17] Such communal involvement, Tocqueville claimed, "multipl[ies] to an infinite extent opportunities of acting in concert for all the members of the community," making individuals "constantly feel their mutual dependence," so that the "habit and the taste" of "working for the good of one's fellow citizens" is "at length acquired."[18]

Tocqueville's larger theme is the transition from traditional society to modernity, within which context he articulates a very conflicted attitude toward individualism. He associates individualism with the forces of modern secularism that threaten the stability of traditional society, yet concludes, somewhat reluctantly, that the prospects for preserving social order—without succumbing to despotism—require harnessing this modern phenomenon of private self-interest:

> Do you not see that religious belief is shaken and the divine notion of right is declining, that morality is debased and the notion of moral right is therefore fading away? Argument is substituted for faith, and calculation for the impulses of sentiment. If, in the midst of this general disruption, you do not succeed in connecting the notion of right with that of private interest, which is the only immutable point in the human heart, what means will you have of governing the world except by fear?[19]

Tocqueville applauds Americans for their frank acceptance of self-interest as the primary motive of human conduct: "an enlightened regard for themselves constantly prompts them to assist one another and inclines them willingly to sacrifice a portion of their time and property to the welfare of the state"; the American thereby "sacrifice[s] some of his private interests to save the rest." While this logic of self-interest is "not a lofty one," it is "clear and sure": "if it does not lead men straight to virtue by the will," it leads them into civic participation and thereby "gradually draws them in that direction by their habits." If Tocqueville largely treats individualism as a threatening force that must be tempered by communal engagement, he more positively locates the "true advantages of democracy" in the way that such local involvement harnesses the energies of diverse individuals: "Democracy does not give the people the most skillful government, but it produces what the ablest governments are frequently unable to create; namely, an all-pervading and restless activity, a superabundant force, and an energy which is inseparable from it and which may, however unfavorable circumstances may be, produce wonders."[20]

The main contours of Tocqueville's approach have been reaffirmed in the influential communitarian critique of individualism offered by Robert Bellah and his colleagues. In the 1985 study *Habits of the Heart*,[21] Bellah argues that the local patterns of governmental and civic involvement, which Tocqueville lauded as counteracting the disintegrative forces of modernity, have been dangerously eroded by the increasingly large, impersonal, and rootless forms of social interaction that became ascendant in the twentieth century. And eroded, specifically, by individualism as a driving force in that process of modernization: American "individualism," Bellah suggests, "may have grown cancerous . . . destroying those social integuments that Tocqueville saw as moderating its more destructive potentialities." If Bellah's diagnosis is more dire, his prescribed remedy nonetheless replicates Tocqueville's: he calls for a revitalization of the American traditions of civic engagement, "those cultural traditions and practices that, without destroying individuality, serve to limit and restrain the destructive side of individualism and provide alternative models for how Americans might live." It is, Bellah argues, by reaffirming the civic-republican and biblical roots of American culture, which "see the individual in relation to a larger whole, a community and a tradition," that we can best regain an ethical framework "capable of sustaining genuine individuality and nurturing both public and private life." The "old cultural argument is not over," Bellah insists, and "all strands of our tradition are still alive and still speak to our present need."[22]

This communitarian critique that runs from Tocqueville to Bellah shares important concerns and goals with Dewey's vision of democracy-as-community: the view that liberal individualism has had corrosive effects on American life; the insistence that individuals live only in association, and that individuality, in its fullest, most meaningful sense, can only be attained within healthy communal contexts; the assertion that democracy is not simply a specific form of government, but must exist most vitally in the full range of associated activities that cultivate habits of democratic and civic selfhood; and, lastly, the assessment that the large and impersonal networks of interaction that typify corporate industrial society have undermined the traditional conditions of local community.[23]

Behind these shared concerns, however, lies a crucial difference between Bellah's communitarian vision and the pragmatic tradition typified by Dewey, a difference that resides in their opposing visions of the relation between community and individuality, and in their opposing attitudes toward modernity. For Bellah, the "old cultural argument" is essentially one between modernity and tradition. The "great problem with modernity" he insists, is that it "idolize[s]" a culture of "free inquiry" and "criticism" that is "all process and no substance." What "we need more than ever," he asserts, is "to reappropriate those great traditions to give us the substance for a genuine form of life." Bellah opposes mere "information" and "criticism," which he associates with modernity, to "meaning" and "substance," which are supplied by the communal "practices that enact . . . tradition." Citing the example of a congregation's weekly recitation of the Lord's Prayer, he notes that tradition provides not new information, but a reiterated "expression of the deepest commitment of the community that use it," "a renewed affirmation of meaning" through "an invocation of a total context."[24]

Bellah is careful occasionally to qualify the kind of stark opposition that lies at the heart of this argument, claiming, for instance, that tradition and criticism, meaning and information, are "polarities" and not "dichotomies"; that a healthy traditionalism cannot mean an impotent nostalgia for the past but requires a "self-revising" tradition that seeks to "reappropriate" valued elements from the past "in ways that respond to our present need"; and insisting that we Americans should not "abandon individualism."[25] Yet even noting such qualifications, the vision of community Bellah offers stands in marked contrast to the pragmatic attitudes toward individuality and community crystallized in Dewey's vision of democracy. For Dewey, community is not a source of substantive traditional meanings that ground an otherwise contentless individual liberty, but rather a dynamic process of participation in common efforts that use inherited ideas to transform the conditions of the present and create a different future. Emerson, James, and Dewey are united in stressing the inescapable and legitimate power of tradition—of inherited ideas, existing customs and truths. Yet they also insist that the traditions of the past cannot provide any ultimate stability or security; meaning and individuality reside in the growing quality of experience and liberated capacities we enjoy in the present as we engage in the common effort to remake our world. Hence, when Dewey in *The Public and its Problems* confronts how modern industrial capitalism has undermined local communities, he does not, like Bellah, advocate a reiterated invocation of stable meanings from the past. Rather, he insists that we can create reinvigorated local communities in which individuals could recover integrated individualities *only* by fully embracing the experimental inquiry that Bellah distrusts, in order to discover a new public defined by, and empowered to control, the modern conditions of association in which we find ourselves.[26] To hold Bellah's view of community is to distrust free inquiry and individualistic traits of selfhood as threatening the traditions that provide the substantive meaning to our lives;[27] to hold a pragmatic view of community is to affirm experimental inquiry as central to the continual reconstructing of community—and to insist that individuality is not a threat to, but an indispensable means and end within, that process.

Experimentalism, Activism, and Tragic Optimism: Pragmatism's Political Appeal

This pragmatic synthesis of individuality and community rejects the dualistic tendencies that continue to shape our dominant conceptions and critiques of individualism: rejects both a Lockean valorization of individual freedom over artificial social constraint, and the opposing tendency—evident in communitarian critiques like Bellah's and in various Marxist-inspired critiques—to valorize the communal or collective over and against an inherently corrosive individualism.

More broadly, the pluralism and experimentalism that underlie a pragmatic individualism shape a set of uniquely balanced attitudes toward reform that constitute much of pragmatism's enduring political appeal. Hence, a central concern in the chapters that follow is to trace the pragmatic attitudes toward reform that unite the writers in this study, and to defend the value of their pragmatic approach against a set of familiar criticisms that have been directed against them. These negative assessments cluster around the following themes. First, that pragmatism offers a naively optimistic worldview that lacks a sufficient sense of tragedy or evil—specifically, that it underestimates the repressive operations of power in social relations and overestimates the capacity of education to meliorate the darker impulses of human nature.[28] Second, that pragmatism's focus on means devolves into an expediency that sacrifices ideal ends, resulting in a "gradualist" politics that "acquiesces" to the status quo.[29] And, third, that to the extent writers in the pragmatic tradition embrace individualistic attitudes, they are so far precluded from a meaningful commitment to collective reform of social conditions, thereby seriously—if not fatally—limiting their political visions.

In response to the familiar charge leveled most damningly (and reductively) at Emerson, but also directed at James and Dewey—that they posit a naively optimistic metaphysics—I emphasize that the writers in this book share a pluralism that views all human efforts as subject to tragic limitations, losses, and exclusions, and that their ethical and political visions explicitly address these tragic limits of human existence. They endorse a melioristic location of value in the limited, but sufficient, growth of meaning and power that we do achieve within and against the resistant constraints of our world—a stance that, far from minimizing the evils to be remedied in our world, mandates and empowers an activist commitment to reform them. Similarly, they articulate models of moral selfhood that are commensurate with both the possibilities and exclusions of a pluralistic world. They exhort individuals to assert their insights, purposes, and energies of will—for without such individual energies many valued possibilities in our world will never come to fruition. Yet they also enjoin us to strive conscientiously against a tragic blindness to the complex ways that our actions connect and obligate us to others; to remain alert to the danger that in striving to realize our own ideals, we may be, in James's visceral phrase, "butchering" the ideals that others cherish.[30]

This balanced stance, which both affirms the creative power of human action and soberly acknowledges the stern limits upon it, is central to pragmatism's ethical vision, and political critiques of pragmatism become reductive or inaccurate insofar as they fail to acknowledge this balance. Such failure is evident in the fact that pragmatism gets accused of such contradictory sins: it optimistically overestimates the possibilities for reform, or it succumbs to a conservative gradualism; it is too committed to a mere, contentless method of inquiry that undermines the stability of traditional meanings, *or* its emphasis on existing means places too much weight on the need to accommodate existing customs, truths, and institutions. By contrast, I argue that pragmatism's enduring political appeal lies precisely in its balanced insistence on both the possibility and difficulty of reform—a balance that, again, reflects the mutually transforming interaction between human nature and its environing conditions posited by a pluralistic model of experience. A pluralistic universe is one in which human ideas and actions can help realize new possibilities, but such possibilities must emerge from existing conditions and overcome the inertia of existing customs and institutions. While critics like Lewis Mumford have derided this pragmatic focus on existing means as an expediency that "acquiesces" to the status quo, pragmatists counter that a truly activist stance toward social reform can only be achieved through tough-minded attention to the existing conditions, which contain both ills to be remedied and, in James's terms, "concretely grounded" possibilities[31] for a better future.

Pragmatism offers a similarly balanced view of the possibilities for reforming human nature, affirming that our most primal human impulses can be trained and redirected into new habits, while also insisting that the task of education is daunting—that remaking personality requires a commitment to reforming the full range of social conditions that shape the habits of character. In stressing the plasticity and educability of human impulses and habits, the value of pragmatism lies—as it typically does—in avoiding the opposing extremes of more absolutist or essentialist visions. It avoids, for instance, Lockean liberalism's overly optimistic vision of a self naturally endowed with reason and liberty, which underestimates the need to create the social conditions that will educate individuals in the habits of reasonable and conscientious choice. Conversely, it avoids the debilitating pessimism that might follow from those visions—such as Reinhold Niebuhr's theological vision or Freud's psychoanalytic one—that posit certain essential impulses as primal drivers of human behavior and, accordingly, take a far darker view than pragmatism does of the possibilities for reeducating human nature.

☙

The broad goals of this study are, thus, twofold. By exploring how the tradition of American letters that runs from Emerson to Ellison constitutes a uniquely pragmatic approach to democratic selfhood, I hope to demonstrate how pragmatism offers a powerful alternative to our dominant conceptions of individualism—that influential and contested strand within American culture. Further, I offer these writers' provocative perspectives on individuality and community, moral selfhood and reform, as examples of pragmatism's enduring political relevance and appeal.

I also hope by aligning these writers in a tradition of pragmatic individualism to provide a fresh perspective for appraising each author. The notion that Emerson is a seminal figure or precursor for American pragmatism is no longer new or controversial. Nonetheless, as I attempt to show in part 1 of this study, it is still underappreciated just how profoundly this connection can revise common assessments of Emerson's thought—of both the coherence of his philosophical vision, and his subsequent politics. For example, to place Emerson at the head of a tradition of democratic individualism that leads through Dewey—who equated democracy with "the idea of community life itself"—is to pose a serious challenge to the common view that Emersonian self-reliance exists in opposition to community.[32]

The genealogy I offer similarly contests any facile oppositions between the "individualistic" thought of Emerson and James and the more "social" pragmatism of Dewey.[33] As I argue in chapter three, such a dichotomy—especially when it pits James and Dewey against each other—oversimplifies James's politics, underestimates the broad continuity between James's thought and Dewey's (evident in the influence James's *Principles of Psychology* had on Dewey's vision of selfhood, education, and democracy), and underestimates as well how deeply committed Dewey remained to a reconstructed ideal of individualism. Further, to see how an individualist ethics follows from the pluralistic and pragmatic assumptions that James and Dewey share is to contest the assessment—offered even by critics who can be counted as proponents of pragmatism—that individualism is a regrettable limitation or flaw in the pragmatic vision. Rather, I contend that individualism is both an integral part of a pragmatic pluralism and—as James insisted—an important source of pragmatism's ethical and political appeal.

Similarly, to place Ellison at the conclusion of this genealogy—to argue that *Invisible Man* expresses a complex indebtedness to, as well as a critique of, Emersonian individualism—is not merely to set the literary record straight by challenging those interpretations that read the novel's parodic allusions as a scathing rejection of Emerson. A central theme in Ellison's writings is that if America is ever to fulfill its democratic promise, individuals must come to recognize more fully how our separate identities and lives are interconnected in our pluralistic culture. In its effort to portray a model of selfhood commensurate with these complexities, *Invisible Man* echoes and extends ethical concerns traced throughout *Reconstructing Individualism*: Emerson's complex sense of the self's social implication and indebtedness; James's concern over our blindness to the ways our ideals and purposes may repress and exclude others; and Dewey's call for conscientious attention to the ways our acts indirectly affect others. Ellison's novel has long been recognized as one of our literature's most compelling explorations of the aspirations and absurdities of democratic individuality in twentieth century America: a symbol of an American striving—within a society at once democratic and profoundly racist—to achieve a meaningful individual liberty and democratic selfhood; seeing the links between *Invisible Man* and the tradition explored in this study offers an important context for understanding Ellison's achievement.

Accordingly, I hope the readings offered in this study—of each writer individually, and of the tradition they collectively compose—will provide fresh insights even to experienced scholars. My hopes are that individualism will look different when considered in this tradition of pragmatic ethics, and that pragmatism will look different when considered in light of its commitment to reconstructing individualism. That scholars in philosophy who are likely to know James and Dewey (and probably acknowledge Emerson as an intellectual influence) will find in these pages an Emerson they are more likely to consider as a genuine philosophical forebear to the pragmatists, and will obtain a new window as well into the literary work of Ellison. That literary scholars who may know Emerson well, but not have studied James or Dewey in depth, will discover an Emerson whose "transcendentalism" appears different when read through the lens of these pragmatic successors. And that scholars who know Ellison, but have not recognized the depth of his complex indebtedness to Emerson, will come away with a heightened appreciation of how *Invisible Man* engages and extends an Emersonian debate on democratic selfhood.

Yet I also hope this book will be of value to scholars and students grappling with these great writers for the first time. I have striven to situate each writer's individualist ethics within the broader context of his overall philosophy. This has been a necessity since one cannot accurately assess Emerson's politics, for instance, without wrestling with the question of whether his metaphysics are monistic or pluralistic; similarly, one cannot accurately understand the individualism of either James or Dewey without seeing how it emerges from each writer's respective pragmatism. It has thus been necessary to discuss each writer's broad philosophical and ethical vision, and one result, I hope, is that the book offers accessible overviews of these thinkers. This project originated, years ago, in my own conviction while a graduate student that writers like Emerson and James offer visions of democracy and individuality that remain provocative and relevant, and that they are often subject to interpretations that distort and dismiss the enduring significance of their philosophies. Accordingly, nothing would please me more than if this study interests new readers in the work of these writers who remain so important to me.

As a work of cultural criticism and intellectual history, the aims of this book are as ambitious as I could manage: I offer sustained readings of four major American thinkers, arguing that they constitute an important countertradition on individualism—a central and contested facet of American democracy. And yet, the thinkers in this book would insist that the aims of a study like this are of necessity limited, for the ideas gotten from books are of value only to the extent that people can put them to use in their lives. "Thinking is a partial act," Emerson insists, while the "elemental force of living" one's truths "is a total act."[34] Ideas and principles provide us no secure or stable solution to our problems; as both James and Dewey insist, they can only serve as tools—guidelines and standards—to help us respond to the problems and possibilities of particular situations. The pragmatic theories of individualism explored in this book must be understood in this spirit: they are of value only to the extent that we can use them in experimental efforts to create more democratic communities and selves. This turn toward concrete consequences in lived experience, which lies at the heart of pragmatism, is familiar enough, but the radical import of this pragmatic turn is seldom fully appreciated. Pragmatism, for a philosophy now more than a century old, remains in many ways shockingly radical in its challenge to traditional, absolutist modes of thinking that still constrain our approach to social problems. As Dewey argues, however accustomed we have grown to an experimentalism in the natural sciences, we have never adopted a fully experimentalist attitude toward social issues; as a result, we remain trapped in formalistic conceptions of democracy and individual liberty.

This suggests one gloss on Emerson's ringing indictment, in the epigraphs to this introduction, that "individualism has never been tried." So long as we remain mired within dualisms—like "individualistic" versus "collective," or "liberty" versus "responsibility"—that hinder a thoroughly experimental approach to the task of remaking social institutions and the type of democratic individuality they cultivate, in so far has individualism never been tried, never been fully pursued as a guiding moral ideal. Indeed, the writers in this study would insist not only that individualism has "never been tried," but in a more radical sense that it will *always* remain to be tried. Individualism, like democracy, is best understood as a principle, a moral hypothesis or belief whose validity must be continually verified—"tried"—in experience, in our efforts to practice democracy as a way of life in all areas of human association. Emerson, James, Dewey, and Ellison offer no set blueprint of what a pragmatic individualism would look like, but they do affirm democracy's moral commitment to individuality. They challenge us to devote the full resources of human intelligence to creating more democratic communities, and assure us that the ideal of a socially integrated and liberated individuality-within-community, though never fully achieved, nonetheless has a living existence in the enriched quality of experience we enjoy when we strive to create more democratic communities and selves.

PART ONE

EMERSON

ONE

WHAT'S THE USE OF READING EMERSON PRAGMATICALLY?

The Example of William James

I n the opening lines of *Pragmatism*, William James approvingly quotes G. K. Chesterton's claim that "the most practical and important thing about a man is still his view of the universe"—in other words, his philosophy. In the broadest and most meaningful terms, James asserts that philosophy is "not a technical matter" but rather describes each person's "sense," consciously articulated or not, "of what life honestly and deeply means."[1] A philosophy, pragmatists such as James and Dewey argue, is in essence a belief, an attempt to describe reality and orient ourselves toward it in a manner that satisfies fundamental human needs and desires—such as the need actively to express our selves and engage our world, and the moral desire that our actions and choices should make some significant difference.[2] The way that we describe the world we inhabit has an immense practical importance, for it shapes the choices we make about how to engage that world, how to act, how to spend the energy of our lives. In other words, ethics—the "practical question of the conduct of life. How shall I live?" as Emerson puts it[3]—is inseparable from metaphysics. Indeed, one of pragmatism's central gestures is to insist that philosophical concerns like metaphysics and epistemology must be understood in terms of ethics, in terms of the difference they make for our conduct: that philosophy must turn away from the traditional concept of truth as accurately or objectively naming the nature of reality, and toward the practice of judging beliefs based on whether they direct our conduct in ways that yield beneficial outcomes. Thus, although this book is concerned with ethics, with alternative visions of individualism, it is also of necessity concerned with broader philosophical concerns. In order to understand the individualist ethics of the writers explored in this study, one must understand their pragmatic views of truth, action, value, and the nature of experience.

This is especially true in the case of Emerson. Any assessment of Emerson's ethics or politics must begin with a discussion of his metaphysics—his "view of the universe"—for there persists in Emerson studies today a profound disagreement over the basic character of his thought. Applying what James identified as the "most central" and "pregnant" of all philosophical distinctions,[4] this disagreement is most clearly framed as the question of whether Emerson is a monist, viewing reality as suffused by an absolute, ideal unity, or a pluralist, viewing reality as characterized by real diversity, particularity, and contingency. For many of Emerson's critics, from his day to our own, there has been no real debate. As Michael Lopez and Charles Mitchell have shown, the history of Emerson's critical reception records a remarkably widespread view that Emerson is an idealist of the monistic variety, whose "transcendentalist" fascination with the absolute tends to ignore or subsume the particulars of our material existence; as a result, critical debate often has been limited to assessing the value or consequences of this accepted version of Emersonianism.[5] Some have described Emerson's alleged detachment from the muddy particulars of life as a virtue, like the critics from the "genteel tradition" who, Mitchell argues, viewed Emerson's idealism as a kind of moral haven cloistered from the amoralities of Gilded Age society,[6] or like Lewis Mumford, who depicted Emerson as a Romantic champion of the imagination's power to transform the mundane facts of experience into an ideal truth.[7] Much more frequently, however, readers as diverse as Herman Melville, Henry James, George Santayana, T. S. Eliot, Van Wyck Brooks, and, more recently, Irving Howe, David Marr, John Updike, and Bartlett Giamatti, have cited Emerson's supposed commitment to an abstract idealism in order to dismiss him as philosophically obsolete, woefully out of touch with the secular empiricism of the modern world, and morally deficient, a naive optimist who blithely ignores the reality of evil and promotes a socially and politically irresponsible individualism.[8] Moreover, as both Lopez and Mitchell ably document, Emerson's defenders and detractors alike often have used the accepted portrait of Emerson as an abstract idealist to suggest that his writings themselves no longer merit any careful interpretation—if they ever did. Emerson's historical importance is almost universally acknowledged, even as his essays are dismissed as outdated in their ideas, lacking in philosophical logic, and incoherent in terms of literary form. The result has been a remarkable inattention to the very complexities of Emerson's writings that would complicate and challenge the entrenched caricature of him as an absolute idealist.

Curiously, moreover, Emerson's supposed absolutism has been described as taking two nearly contradictory forms. As the title of Stephen E. Whicher's influential study *Freedom and Fate* indicates, critics have charted in Emerson's thought a shift from a naive affirmation of individual power, in his early works, to a more sober focus, in his later works, on the forces that limit the power and autonomy of individual acts.[9] The "early" Emerson posited by this widely accepted narrative celebrates an autonomous self whose power lies in its ability to access—through the inner promptings of its own "genius," "soul," or "moral sentiment"—a divine unity in which we all participate. The "late" Emerson, in contrast, celebrates the material forces that determine our human identities and acts. In short, Emerson is depicted as moving from an absolutist notion of freedom to an absolutist determinism, from a naive optimism that affirms the individual's ability to transcend and transform the limitations of our material world to a fatalistic optimism that affirms the limitations of our world as necessary parts of a divinely beneficent whole. These absolutist interpretations also shape the most common criticisms of Emerson's politics: his early idealist emphasis on individual power is seen as renouncing collective politics, and as blaming suffering and inequality on people's failures to achieve individual regeneration; conversely, his late, fatalistic acquiescence is seen as discouraging political action by reinforcing a laissez-faire faith in the ability of large, impersonal forces to create a moral result.

One prominent trend in recent scholarship extends these long-standing patterns in Emerson criticism. Many critics continue to accept the traditional interpretation of Emerson's thought and focus their efforts on reassessing its political consequences within a given historical or ideological context. For example, Sacvan Bercovitch's argument that Emerson shifted from a "utopian" critique of capitalism to an "ideological" apology for capitalism updates the Whicherian opposition between Emerson's early idealism and late acquiescence. Myra Jehlen, in contrast, has asserted that Emerson's individualism always existed in a contradictory relationship with the fatalistic implications of his monism. Because Emerson views truth as absolute and wholly independent of human actions—so Jehlen's argument goes—he concludes that we have access to truth only through our preexisting harmony with or intuition of nature, and that our actions merely express or replicate this truth. This severe proscription of human creativity provides, according to Jehlen, a powerful metaphysical support for the amorality of capitalism: it simultaneously removes any responsibility for political action (since nature does not need human reforms or revolutions) and authorizes economic and nationalistic expansion (since nature comprehends all such activity). Similarly, Christopher Newfield contends that the theme of self-transcendence or abandonment that runs throughout Emerson's writings encourages submission to the "benevolent despotism" of American democracy, which substitutes oligarchy and consumerism in place of any meaningful collective control, while Dana Nelson has argued that Emerson's theory of "great men" supports an antidemocratic submission to the "representativity" of American presidential politics. All of these approaches exhibit what Richard Teichgraeber has astutely diagnosed as the "guiding cliché" of new historicist criticism: "namely, the proposition that what might look like dissent or subversion in literary discourse always turns out to be, on closer inspection, a set of attitudes or ideas that a dominant political and economic order can appropriate to justify and sustain itself."[10] Perhaps more important, for my purposes, is the fact that these writers' assessments of the political and ideological implications of Emerson's individualism remain trapped within an outdated interpretive paradigm that assumes his thought oscillates between the absolutist poles of an idealistic and a fatalistic optimism.

There exists, of course, an influential countertrend in Emerson criticism, one that, over the past thirty years, has reasserted Emerson's status as a central figure in American thought—and, indeed, as an underappreciated influence on Continental thought—not despite, but because of the ideas explored in his essays. Where so many critics have bemoaned a lack of philosophical logic or coherence, these critics have seen a deliberate emphasis on the complexity, contradiction, and antagonism that characterizes experience. Where others have proclaimed a lack of literary form, these critics have traced a rhetorical strategy that mirrors Emerson's interest in antagonism, action, and transition. And where others have seen an absolute idealist, these critics have found a thinker who explores the possibilities for power that exist within and against the limitations of the cultural and material environment—an Emerson whose vision of the limited yet sufficient opportunities for human agency and power prefigures the philosophy of American pragmatism.

To be sure, the idea that Emerson's thought has a significant pragmatic strain is not new, having been voiced by earlier critics such as Kenneth Burke and Frederic Carpenter,[11] not to mention by James and Dewey themselves. But the most influential figures in the recent rediscovery of a pragmatic Emerson have been Stanley Cavell, Richard Poirier, and Harold Bloom. Cavell perhaps has done the most to assert Emerson's importance as a philosopher. Identifying a series of related concerns in Emerson's thought—an embrace of ordinary language and experience, of "onward" or "aversive" thinking, and of moral perfectionism—Cavell has argued that Emerson is not a builder of philosophical systems, but rather a thinker who practices philosophy as "a mode of thought that undertakes to bring philosophy to an end," anticipating the projects of thinkers such as Nietzsche, Wittgenstein, and Heidegger. For Poirier, Emerson exemplifies a tradition in which literary performance—the reshaping of inherited language and literary conventions—dramatizes the self's fundamental desire to express itself by engaging and reinflecting the resistant cultural and material environment. Poirier has cogently detailed how this Emersonian stress on performance—with its emphasis on action and transition, and its rejection of the desire for metaphysical certainty—has deep affinities with the pragmatism of William James. Finally, Bloom has described Emerson as the founder of the American difference in Romanticism, a writer whose pragmatic emphasis on knowing as an act of power and will leads him to employ a rhetoric of discontinuity in which the self is a "voice" that "splinter[s] and destroy[s] its own texts," a rhetoric that Bloom reads as a quintessentially American, and proto-Nietzschean, rebellion against the continuities of historical time and tradition.[12]

While these writers have helped to reestablish the connections between Emerson and pragmatism, they do not resolve the question of how

far, and to what purpose, one can claim the "pragmatic" character of
Emerson's thought. Indeed, Cavell—in an essay whose titular question
asks, "What's the Use of Calling Emerson a Pragmatist?"—worries that
stressing the pragmatic aspects of Emerson's thought risks erasing the
distinctiveness of his philosophical achievement, or, worse, of replicat-
ing the all-too-familiar gesture of Emerson criticism, that of proclaiming
his historical importance and influence only to imply that his thought is
somehow inadequate or obsolete:

> To my mind, to understand Emerson as essentially the forerun-
> ner of pragmatism is perhaps to consider pragmatism as represent-
> ing more effectively or rationally what Emerson had undertaken to
> bring to these shores. This is the latest in the sequence of repres-
> sions of Emerson's thought by the culture he helped to found, of
> what is distinctive in that thought. Such a repression has punctu-
> ated Emerson's reputation from the first moment he could be said
> to have acquired one.[13]

In other words, in stressing the pragmatic elements of Emerson's vision,
there is a danger of perpetuating the idea that his thought is somehow
deficient if taken on its own, that his ideas are not really coherent until
they are incorporated in the more consistent pragmatic logic of a James or
Dewey. If Cavell and Poirier have taught us anything, it is the impudence
of condescending to a writer as capacious and complex as Emerson. As
Poirier asserts, we must not treat Emerson "as anything less than the great
and difficult writer he is, as a writer who has already anticipated any degree
of sophistication that might be brought to him."[14] The challenge for critics
who would place Emerson in a genealogy of American pragmatism, then,
is to avoid the pitfall of reducing Emerson to less than the still-relevant,
still-indispensable thinker that he is, the rare kind of writer who requires
us to return to him again and again, and always rewards us when we are
willing to assume the complexity of his thought and follow it where it leads.
    In response to Cavell's question, then, I would contend that there are
important benefits to be gained not by calling Emerson a pragmatist,
which would be anachronistic, but by reading Emerson pragmatically—by
applying the fundamental methods and attitudes of pragmatism in order
to highlight the ways in which similar attitudes are already present in,
and central to, Emerson's vision. There are political reasons for placing
Emerson at the head of a pragmatic tradition that runs through James
to twentieth-century writers like Dewey, Burke, and Ralph Ellison, for

this tradition highlights what are, in my estimation, the most politically valuable aspects of Emerson's individualism, while also revising and augmenting his ethics to meet urgent ethical challenges posed by our contemporary world. Demonstrating the political value of placing Emerson at the head of a specifically pragmatic tradition of individualist ethics is a task for this book as a whole. I can outline here, however, a second major benefit of reading Emerson pragmatically. Instead of depicting Emerson, as Cavell fears, as a merely incipient or incoherent pragmatist, reading Emerson pragmatically provides the clearest refutation to the central assumption that has been used to assert the incoherence of his thought: the charge, outlined above, that the potential pluralism of his individualist ethics is undermined by the absolutist optimism of his early idealism and his later fatalism. A pragmatic approach to Emerson helps reveal the anti-absolutist balance that lies at the heart of his vision—a vision of human power and agency as existing in an antagonistic relation within and against the limits of our material existence; a vision that is expressed with remarkable consistency in Emerson's early and late works alike. William James's pragmatic method for mediating between the absolutist oppositions of traditional philosophy points the way to such a pragmatic reading of Emerson, as is evidenced in the way that James himself approached Emerson's writings.

Emerson's influence on James is well established.[15] Emerson was a friend of Henry James Sr., and made occasional visits to the James household—during one of which he "blessed" the infant William. At a youthful age, James was exposed to Emerson's writings through his father's library, and through evenings in which his father read Emerson's essays aloud to the family. In his personal copies of Emerson's works (the first of which he obtained in 1871), James marked numerous passages, made marginal notes, and compiled indexed lists of quotes—in pencil, blue pencil, and black ink, suggesting that he read Emerson carefully several times over the course of his career.[16] Perhaps most importantly, James reread nearly all of Emerson's collected works—no small feat—in preparation for delivering an address during the 1903 centennial celebration of Emerson's birth. He wrote to his brother Henry that "reading of the divine Emerson, volume after volume, has done me a lot of good," and to another correspondent he remarked that "reading the whole of him over again continuously has made me feel his greatness as I never did before. He's really a critter to be thankful for."[17] Emerson was thus freshly in James's mind during the important years 1904 to 1907, when he published essays later collected as *Essays in Radical Empiricism* and wrote the lecture series later published as *Pragmatism.*

Moreover, as Frederic Carpenter first documented, the indexes of passages that James inscribed in the flyleaves of his copy of Emerson's *Miscellanies: Embracing Nature, Addresses, and Lectures* (the most heavily-indexed volume among his copies of Emerson) include one titled "against my philosophy," covering passages that seem to express a monistic belief in absolute unity, and a second titled "pragmatism," under which James lists passages conveying pragmatic attitudes toward language, action, and truth.[18] Though these headings do not reappear in his other copies of Emerson's works, passages representing one or the other of these tendencies constitute a large portion—if not the majority—of the passages that James marked throughout all the volumes of Emerson he owned. The pattern thus revealed in James's reading of Emerson is significant for two reasons: first, it proves that he identified a strong pragmatic strain in Emerson's thought, one at odds with the dominant image of Emerson as a naively optimistic, "transcendental" idealist. At the same time, however, it indicates that James, like other readers after him who have striven to construct a pragmatic Emerson, wrestled with the question of how to reconcile Emerson's pragmatic attitudes with the presence of passages that suggest a more abstract or monistic idealism.

Before turning in detail to James, it will be helpful to consider the various ways readers might respond to the presence of monistic passages in Emerson. Such passages are indeed frequent in his works, occurring even in those essays whose overall arguments offer pragmatic exhortations to seek value in the opportunities for action that exist within the limits of our world. For example, the essay "Self-Reliance," belying the absolute autonomy commonly associated with its titular subject, is primarily concerned (if not obsessed) with the constraints that limit individual originality and with the efforts individuals must make to achieve integrity within these constraints. Yet only a few lines after voicing the deeply pragmatic conclusion that "Power ceases in the instant of repose; it resides in the moment of transition from a past to a new state," Emerson indulges in the following flourish of monistic rhetoric: "This is the ultimate fact which we so quickly reach on this, as on every topic, the resolution of all into the ever-blessed ONE. Self-existence is the attribute of the Supreme Cause, and it constitutes the measure of good by the degree in which it enters into all lower forms."[19] This one example will suffice for my purposes; interested readers can find similar passages sprinkled throughout Emerson's works. The important question is, how does one deal with the apparent conflict such passages raise between a pragmatic and a monistic Emerson?

One might simply conclude that there is indeed an unresolved contradiction at the heart of Emerson's thought, of which he was perhaps unaware and which confirms his reputed incapacity for philosophical coherence. Yet such a conclusion would ignore the ways in which Emerson explicitly employs contrast and contradiction as a compositional and rhetorical strategy, playing with the tension between opposing tendencies or poles of human thought. As George Kateb notes,[20] Emerson describes precisely such a method in the opening of "Fate," where he suggests that our human concepts cannot logically comprehend the antagonistic realities of experience:

> This is true, and that other is true. But our geometry cannot span these extreme points, and reconcile them. What to do? By obeying each thought frankly, by harping, or, if you will, pounding on each string, we learn at last its power. By the same obedience to other thoughts, we learn theirs, and then comes some reasonable hope of harmonizing them.[21]

The Emerson who employs such a method is not striving for a logically consistent philosophy so much as experimenting with the power of different analytical perspectives; consequently, readers need to be wary of taking Emerson's voicing of any particular perspective as expressing his "true" philosophical opinion. Emerson undoubtedly does require such interpretive caution, for he was capable of claiming, in one of his more irascible and eccentric moments, "let me remind the reader that I am only an experimenter. Do not set the least value on what I do, or the least discredit on what I do not, as if I pretended to settle any thing as true or false."[22]

Yet any reader who would not dismiss Emerson as a merely relativistic provocateur must attempt to gauge the comparative value that Emerson finds in the different "strings" he "harps on," must attempt to judge how Emerson is able to "harmonize" seemingly opposed monistic and pluralistic insights. Emerson's renunciation of a constraining logical consistency thus justifies readers in emphasizing certain strands of his thought as essential to his philosophical vision, and dismissing others as inessential. Kateb, for example, values Emerson's pluralistic embrace of antagonism because it trains the self in a democratic receptiveness to and reverence for the particulars of the material world, but he finds this central aspect of Emerson's thought threatened by a contrasting "religiousness," by expressions of belief in a divine unity suffusing the particulars of our world. Kateb assumes that such monistic statements are sincere, answering a temperamental yearning in Emerson's sensibility, but ultimately concludes—somewhat uneasily—that readers are justified in viewing them as inessential.[23] Kateb's conclusion is worth quoting in full, for it succinctly outlines the main interpretive strategies for dealing with Emerson's monism:

> First, we can tolerate his religiousness because we judge it to be comparatively minor. It is more than a blemish—perhaps more than a flaw—but it is a good deal less than an insuperable obstacle. Second, we can elicit a secular meaning from his religious conceptions just as he extracted his own religiousness from church religions. We can translate him as he translated his tradition. We can push him in a more unreligious direction. In doing that, we would actually be far less coercive than he was: we would have much less to do than he did. And, last, we can simply work with the inexhaustible abundance of detachable utterance his writings contain by easing its way, unencumbered by religiousness, to us. Here, too we would follow Emerson's precept. He speaks of "a class of passages" in Shakespeare "which bear to be separated from their connexion as single gems do from a crown and choicely kept for their intrinsic worth." We can, by these and other proceedings, be self-reliant readers of the great teacher of self-reliance.[24]

Kateb is surely correct that Emerson himself offers a theory of historical change and reading that authorizes us as readers to appropriate those aspects of his thought that are relevant for our present uses. Starting with the opening paragraph of his first book, *Nature*, Emerson stressed that inherited traditions and ideas grow obsolete and threaten to obscure our perception of new possibilities unless they are treated not literally as absolute truths, but poetically (or pragmatically) as tools that can be translated or turned to meet the new needs of our present. Symbols, as he writes in "The Poet," "must be held lightly, and be very willingly translated into the equivalent terms which others use," or, as he counseled graduating theologians in his Divinity School address, "all attempts to contrive a system" are "cold" and "vain": "Rather let the breath of new life be breathed by you through the forms already existing."[25] This attitude helps explain the presence of religious or idealistic vocabularies in Emerson, for it suggests that Emerson deliberately retained terms such as "the Soul," "God," and "Providence" even as he translated them into a secular philosophy and ethics—as is indicated by the furor that erupted in the wake of his Divinity School address.[26] Extending this Emersonian practice, we are well justified in translating Emerson, in stressing the pragmatic applications of his ideas that remain alive for us today, and leaving behind the vestiges of a monistic idealism in his writing. (And, as Kateb suggests, such a translation is minimal compared with Emerson's attempt to translate traditional theology into a post-theological ethics.)

Similarly, the coexistence of monistic and pluralistic strands in Emerson's thought can be seen as symptomatic of his position within a historical moment characterized by fundamental changes in Western intellectual attitudes. Emerson's life straddled the transition from a theological to a post-theological worldview: the Unitarianism that shaped his education and early career as a minister was already a rejection of the absolutist theology of Calvinism in favor of a more ethical Christianity,[27] and Emerson in turn soon abandoned the elements of traditional Christian theology that Unitarianism retained. Emerson's career also coincided with the growing ascendancy of the secularism promoted by natural science, as well as with a concurrent transition in philosophy, one that Lopez describes as the shift from a Kantian to a post-Kantian idealism. Lopez suggests that Emerson's essays reveal the tension of these transitions, exemplifying "an unwieldy but singularly mid-nineteenth-century composite or synthesis—one that looks backward to . . . idealist, organicist, and theistic traditions, as it concurrently looks forward to the power philosophies characteristic of the later nineteenth century."[28] In this regard, too, Emerson instructs us how to read him, asserting in "The American Scholar" that no writer can "entirely exclude the conventional, the local, the perishable from his book," and concluding that "the discerning will read, in his Plato or Shakspeare, only the least part,—only the authentic utterances of the oracle;—all the rest he rejects."[29] In sum, if we see Emerson as a transitional figure in intellectual history, there is a clear Emersonian logic for emphasizing the emerging pragmatism of his thought rather than its residues of an obsolete idealism, for emphasizing the future Emerson was moving toward rather than the past he was leaving behind.[30]

Such arguments, it seems to me, form the basic contours of the rationale that any reader who wants to recover a pragmatic Emerson must
employ, and perhaps, for most readers, they are sufficient. For William
James, however, the opposition between monism and pluralism was, as
mentioned above, the most "pregnant" of all philosophical oppositions,
the one with the most far-reaching consequences for our moral lives.
Monistic absolutism—whether of the optimistic or pessimistic variety—
was anathema to James's entire ethical vision. Thus, in claiming Emerson as an intellectual ancestor, it is unlikely that he would easily dismiss
Emerson's monistic elements, picking only those "detachable utterances"
(in Kateb's terms) that fit his philosophy. Here I depart from the assessment of Charles Mitchell, who concludes that James "wanted to make
use of Emerson, not make sense of him, and his method was to mine
Emerson for the valuable insights he contained, take these along, and
leave the detritus behind."[31] No doubt James did make selective use of
Emerson, as all readers do, and, as I discuss below, James did conclude
that Emerson's voicing of monist and pluralist perspectives revealed a
lack of logical consistency. However, in an important sense James went
further than most readers have in attempting to "make sense" of the
conflict between Emerson's monism and his pluralism. After all, James's
pragmatic method was precisely designed to make sense of—to measure
the practical consequences of—conflicts between opposing philosophical positions. By applying his pragmatic method to the question of Emerson's monism or pluralism, James developed a more extensive rationale
than those sketched above for viewing Emerson's thought as essentially
pluralistic and melioristic—and thus as anticipating central strands of
his own pragmatism.

In order to explain why Emerson's possible monism was such a serious obstacle for James and how he dealt with this obstacle, it is necessary to outline in cursory fashion certain fundamental aspects of James's
pragmatism. James describes pragmatism as a method for resolving
philosophical disputes by gauging the practical consequences that competing beliefs have for human behavior and its results.[32] Faced with the
absolutist dichotomies of traditional philosophy—such as monism versus pluralism, idealism versus materialism, a belief in free-will versus
fatalism—Jamesian pragmatism evaluates the consequences or benefits
of each position, and when possible seeks a middle ground that combines benefits from each. It is the hope of such a synthesis—the desire

for a philosophy that combines empiricism's engagement of particular facts with idealism's faith in the power of ideas and belief—that provides the driving force behind James's philosophical project. This pragmatic method also implies an "attitude of orientation,"[33] a turn away from questions of origins and causes—such as, who made the world—and toward questions dealing with the present and with future consequences, such as: what kind of world is it,[34] and, crucially, what kind of behavior does it require from us—how shall we act in and toward our world?

Applying this pragmatic method to major philosophical disputes like the existence of free will and the debate between theism and materialism, James concludes that they boil down to the question of whether genuine novelty occurs or not—in short, to the question of monism versus pluralism. Our beliefs, choices and actions can have significance only, James argues, in a world in which our acts help realize one possibility instead of another, help realize a possibility that otherwise might not occur. Pluralism describes such a world: one not unified by any single purpose, one with genuine indeterminacy and novelty. In contrast, monism implies that the apparent changes of our world reflect no real novelty or indeterminacy, but merely express a preexistent absolute order—whether it be the omniscient purpose of a deity or the inexorable laws of matter.[35] Similarly, James argues that our moral judgments—such as regret that one result should have occurred instead of another—make sense only in a world where different results are indeed possible. In a truly monistic world, all evils and sufferings must be accepted as necessary parts of the transcendent unity—whether that unity is viewed optimistically as beneficent, or pessimistically as evil. Pragmatically weighing the consequences of these competing descriptions of the universe, James concludes that monism leads to a fatalism that intolerably frustrates two fundamental aspects of human nature: our need actively to engage our world, and the moral sentiments that motivate our acts by judging some results to be better than others. Our world can be a moral world only if it is a pluralistic world, James concludes, and we ought not to believe in a deterministic universe, so long as experience justifies us in believing otherwise.[36]

One last aspect of James's general approach needs to be stressed here. James insists that monism is by definition the absolutist position in the debate between monism and pluralism. To assert transcendent unity is logically to exclude the existence of *any* novelty or contingency. In contrast, pluralism is an anti-absolutist position. It does not assert absolute contingency; it does not deny the existence of diverse and pervasive kinds of unity in our universe, nor deny that there is a great deal of determinism in our world—that the possibilities for change are in many ways determined and hemmed-in. It only denies that there is absolute determinism; it only insists that there is some small—yet sufficient— degree of indeterminacy that allows our acts to help introduce novelty into our world.[37] With this distinction in mind, James analyzes what an assertion of "unity" might practically mean. Most importantly, he concludes, it could refer to the "generic unity" that obtains among similar things in our universe—a unity without which human thought would be impossible, since no inferences from past experiences to new experiences could be drawn. Or it might refer to the genuinely deterministic—and for James morally intolerable—assertion of an absolute unity suffusing the apparent diversity of our world. But short of this absolute position, James argues, assertions of unity are relatively empty statements, merely summarizing with a unifying name—such as "world" or "universe"— the "sum total of all the ascertainable particular conjunctions and concatenations" that exist in experience. Such vague assertions of wholeness do, James admits, have an emotional value in expressing a sheer wonder at the existence of the universe. "We all have some ear for this monistic music," he acknowledges.[38] But as long as one acknowledges a significant—indeed any—degree of indeterminacy in the world, one is in effect taking the pluralistic view that our world is both "one" *and* "many"—characterized by both union and disunion, determinism and indeterminacy. In such a world our actions and choices do matter, and our philosophical emphasis should shift away from a search for "the" truth that names a divine unity and toward the question of which of our finite truths will guide our actions so as to help us create a better future.

With this line of argument in mind, we can understand why James, when confronted with the seemingly contradictory expressions of monism and pluralism in Emerson's thought, would focus on the following key questions: First, what kind of a world does Emerson describe— what is his "view of the universe"? Is it one in which genuine diversity, novelty, and contingency exist? And, second, how is his essential view of the universe revealed or clarified in its practical consequences on human behavior; how does Emerson counsel us to act in and toward our world? As we trace James's answers to these questions, it becomes apparent why he would conclude that Emerson—his affirmations of unity notwithstanding—articulated an effectively pluralistic view of reality. It also becomes evident how Emerson's subsequent emphasis on action prefigures central aspects of James's own pragmatic ethics.

James's clearest and most detailed discussion of these issues appears in the 1903 address he delivered at the Concord celebration of the centennial of Emerson's birth.[39] Describing Emerson's essential "insight and creed," James writes: "Through the individual fact there ever shone for him the effulgence of the Universal Reason. The great Cosmic Intellect terminates and houses itself in mortal men and passing hours. Each of us is an angle of its eternal vision, and the only way to be true to our Maker is to be loyal to ourselves."[40] On first blush, this passage seems to depict a monistic assertion of the "Universal Reason" with its "eternal vision," but in fact the tension between the universal and the particular that James describes here neatly encapsulates why Emerson's "transcendentalism" emerges as an essentially pluralistic vision. If one asserts a universal divinity, but insists that this divinity is incarnated or immanent in the finite particulars of the material world—"housed" in "mortal men and passing hours" as James puts it—and, further, insists that this divinity can be accessed or engaged "only" by embracing one's partiality, by "being true" to the "angle" of reality that one's self embodies, then the notion of a supernatural divinity or ideality transcending the material world tends to drop away, and one is left, for all practical purposes, with a naturalistic, pluralistic vision. As Kenneth Burke asserts in *A Grammar of Motives*, a pantheistic equation of god and nature slides almost inevitably into a naturalistic vision. Applying a parallel logic to Emerson's 1836 *Nature*, Burke argues that Emerson's view of "the everyday world" as "a *diversity* of *means* for carrying out a *unitary purpose*" leads to a pragmatic focus on the world "as a set of instrumentalities," so that "Emerson's brand of transcendentalism was but a short step ahead of out-and-out pragmatism."[41] James, in *The Varieties of Religious Experience*, describes Emerson's thought in markedly similar terms: "Modern transcendental idealism, Emersonianism, for instance, also seems to let God evaporate into abstract Ideality. Not a deity *in concreto*, not a superhuman person, but the immanent divinity in things, the essentially spiritual structure of the universe, is the object of the transcendental cult." James saw that Emerson, by relinquishing the idea of a supernatural, anthropomorphic divinity, explicitly denounced the location of spirituality in any dimension beyond our material world: "Other world! there is no other world!" Emerson affirms in a passage that James quotes in his centenary address.[42]

Having identified as Emerson's primary creed the idea that divinity is to be found in all the facts of everyday life, James proceeds to the crucial question of whether this commits Emerson to a monistic optimism:

> Such a conviction that Divinity is everywhere may easily make of one an optimist of the sentimental type that refuses to speak ill of anything. Emerson's drastic perception of differences kept him at the opposite pole from this weakness. . . . Never was such a fastidious lover of significance and distinction, and never an eye so keen for their discovery. His optimism had nothing in common with that indiscriminate hurrahing for the Universe with which Walt Whitman has made us familiar. For Emerson, the individual fact and moment were indeed suffused with absolute radiance, but it was upon a condition that saved the situation—they must be worthy specimens,—sincere, authentic, archetypal; they must have made connection with what he calls the Moral Sentiment, they must in some way act as symbolic mouthpieces of the Universe's meaning. To know just which thing does act in this way, and which thing fails to make the true connection, is the secret (somewhat incommunicable, it must be confessed) of seership, and doubtless we must not expect of the seer too rigorous a consistency. Emerson himself was a real seer. He could perceive the full squalor of the individual fact, but he could also see the transfiguration. . . .
>
>   Be it how it may, then, this is Emerson's revelation:—The point of any pen can be an epitome of reality; the commonest person's act, if genuinely activated, can lay hold on eternity.[43]

One can see James in this passage addressing the pragmatic concerns outlined above: what kind of world does Emerson describe, and what consequences does this description have for human conduct? First, James argues that Emerson's pluralistic emphasis on difference, diversity, and particularity prevents him from being an absolute monist. Here James couches the issue in terms of optimism, but in the notebook that served as his draft for the address, James framed it in more technical terms as a tension between "monism" and a pluralistic "radical individualism." There, too, James concluded that Emerson's monistic tendency—his faith, reflecting an "inborn temperamental optimism" that "the best in us was one life with the universal best"—was effectively offset by his opposing pluralism: "But it was only at its best and in its ecstasies that Life was thus One; for Emerson never drew a consequence from the Oneness that made him any less willing to acknowledge the rank diversity of individual facts."[44] Second, James casts this distinction between monism and pluralism in terms of its consequences for our moral lives: a true monism would endorse an "indiscriminate" optimism, one that celebrates all facts as necessary parts of a perfect unity. In contrast, James stresses that Emerson's optimism is "saved" by his insistence that the spirituality or ideality immanent in everyday facts is not absolute but potential or conditional—dependent on our ability to see the moral possibilities latent in the actualities of our present, to see *which* facts do "act as symbolic mouthpieces of the Universe's meaning," and on our ability to help realize those possibilities through efforts that are "genuinely activated." In effect, James here is identifying a major line of Emerson's influence on pragmatism: this Emersonian optimism, one that locates the morality of our world in a potential that must be realized with the aid of human actions, prefigures the attitude of "meliorism" that is central to both James's and Dewey's pragmatism: the belief that in a pluralistic world with genuine contingency there exists the *possibility* that our actions may result in meaningful progress, in transformations of our environment (and our lives) that will render the goods of experience more secure, enduring, and extensive—and, further, that this fighting chance for progress is not only sufficient for, but well suited to, our active, agonistic human nature.[45]

This assessment of Emerson's optimism is closely tied to, and reinforced by, the other main focus of James's centenary address: Emerson's ethic of self-culture or individualized vocation. For in stressing the concept of vocation as central to Emerson's vision, James again emphasizes the connection between philosophy and ethics, employing the pragmatic method of clarifying the meaning of abstract principles or doctrines by gauging their consequences for human behavior. In other words, the essentially pluralistic nature of Emerson's optimism is evidenced by his ethical focus on the cultivation of individuality. Years earlier, in "The Sentiment of Rationality,"[46] James had already argued that the true content of Emerson's philosophy lay not in its mystic assertions of unity, but in the specificity of its calls to action. "However vaguely a philosopher may define the ultimate universal datum, he cannot be said to leave it unknown to us so long as he in the slightest degree pretends that our emotional or active attitude towards it should be of one sort rather than another," James asserts, and then proceeds to list Emerson's philosophy as among those that avoid a vague mysticism because they specify the type of action our world requires from us: "Emerson's creed that everything that ever was or will be is here in the enveloping now; that man has but to obey himself,—'He who will rest in what he *is*, is a part of Destiny,'—is in like manner nothing but an exorcism of all skepticism as to the pertinency of one's natural faculties."[47] In his centenary address, James similarly stresses Emerson's ethic of vocation as the defining characteristic of his worldview. While Emerson may affirm that individuals can participate in the universe's tendency toward benefit, he insists that they can do so only by working within the limits of their own peculiar and partial talents. To repeat James's description cited above, we each represent only an "angle" of the larger vision, and can be "true to our Maker" only by being "loyal to ourselves." Or, as James puts it a few paragraphs later: "Nothing can harm the man who rests in his appointed place and character. Such a man is invulnerable; he balances the universe, balances it as much by keeping small when he is small as by being great and spreading when he is great." The importance that James attributes to this concept of vocation indicates a second major line of influence running from Emerson to James, for James's own pluralism likewise results in an ethic of individualized vocation. This description of the Emersonian self who in his small way "balances the universe" prefigures James's own vision, in the closing pages of *Pragmatism*, of individuals whose actions "create" "moment[s] in the world's salvation" by helping to realize ideals at the universe's "growing places."[48]

Perhaps the greatest benefit of reading Emerson pragmatically— through the lens of James's or Burke's interpretation of him, for example—is the way in which these subsequent pragmatists alert one to the anti-absolutist, pluralistic attitudes that are already existent in Emerson's texts. Chapter 2 is devoted to exploring these aspects of Emerson's thought in detail, but it is worth exploring a few examples here to show how the conclusions that James reaches in his centenary address can help us better appreciate both the complexity and the coherence of Emerson's philosophic vision.

Consider, for instance, James's and Burke's observations on how the tension between Emerson's potential monism and his opposing pluralism results in a pantheistic or pragmatic focus on the particulars of the material world. This dynamic can be seen in "Self-Reliance," where Emerson, in the essay's opening paragraph, famously asserts: "To believe your own thought, to believe that what is true for you in your private heart is true for all men,—that is genius." Read in isolation—or in *Bartlett's Familiar Quotations*—this might indeed be taken as a monistic assertion that the individual's thoughts apprehend the absolute. The trouble with such a reading, of course, is that numerous other passages in "Self-Reliance" suggest that individuals have no such access to a unifying thought that is "true for all men." Quite the contrary, Emerson announces that "the only right is what is after my constitution, the only wrong what is against it," implying that truth and morality are relative, individualized matters of following the promptings of one's own "genius" or talents. Further, he insists that the "truth" one's genius reveals today may be different from what it reveals tomorrow, and he counsels us to brave the resulting risk of contradiction: "Speak what you think now in hard words, and to-morrow speak what to-morrow thinks in hard words again, though it contradict everything you said to-day."[49] The point is, if Emerson really were a monist who believed we have access to an absolute truth, then why would he prate about self-reliance or nonconformity at all, why advise us to follow the truths of our own constitutions? Why not instead enjoin readers (as his friend Thomas Carlyle did) to seek communal solidarity in a shared vision of the absolute?

Following this line of thought, it is crucial to note that the definition of genius in "Self-Reliance" does *not* say that geniuses apprehend absolute truth, only that they "believe" they do. As the essay's opening paragraph continues, it becomes clear that such a belief is necessary because it impels us to action. "Speak your latent conviction, and it shall be the universal sense," Emerson exhorts, implying that one cannot really have a conviction until it is spoken; an inward belief is merely "latent" until it is realized in action.[50] Moreover, the claim that one's conviction might become the "universal sense" is complicated by the rest of the paragraph, which describes the possibilities for self-expression in strange terms of assertion and domination:

> In every work of genius we recognize our own rejected thoughts: they come back to us with a certain alienated majesty. Great works of art have no more affecting lesson for us than this. They teach us to abide by our spontaneous impression with good-humored inflexibility then most when the whole cry of voices is on the other side. Else,

to-morrow a stranger will say with masterly good sense precisely
what we have thought and felt all the time, and we shall be forced to
take with shame our own opinion from another.[51]

Truth here appears less as "universal" knowledge to be shared than as
an occasion for action that *cannot* be shared. To have another give voice
to and confirm "precisely what we have thought and felt all the time"
does not create an encouraging solidarity; instead, it robs us of the self-
expression achieved by actively realizing our own "latent conviction."
We are "alienated" from truths that we have not translated into action,
and the "property" we have lost is the opportunity for self-cultivation.
"What a man does, that he has," Emerson avows in "Spiritual Laws," or,
as he expresses it in "Self-Reliance," "that which a man is does always by
necessity acquire, and what the man acquires is living property."[52]

Far from an unalienated access to universal truth, then, Emerson's
definition of genius—to "believe" that "your own thought" is "true for
all men"—describes a will to act in spite of the fragmentation and partiality that characterizes even our best human efforts. "Self-Reliance"
thus anticipates the argument that Emerson makes more explicitly in his
1844 essay "Nature," that "Exaggeration is in the course of things": "Nature sends no creature, no man into the world, without adding a small
excess of his proper quality." This "excess" proves to be absolutely necessary, for "a man can only speak, so long as he does not feel his speech
to be partial and inadequate. It is partial, but he does not see it to be so
whilst he utters it." Similarly, in "The Uses of Great Men," Emerson suggests that all individuals—as foolish as we are—share the monomaniacal confidence of geniuses: "Is it not a rare contrivance that lodged the
due inertia in every creature, the conserving, resisting energy, the anger
at being waked or changed? Altogether independent of the intellectual
force in each, is the pride of opinion, the security that we are right." Such
a foolish confidence (as opposed to a foolish consistency) is beneficial,
Emerson insists, for only by acting will an individual express his or her
individual character. This helps explain, to return to "Self-Reliance,"
why Emerson counsels us to disregard our paralyzing fears of partiality and inconsistency. When Emerson claims that his contradictory acts
"will be found symmetrical, though I mean it not," he is not asserting a
transcendent or unified self, but only a self that adequately expresses its
own power and limitation: "All the sallies of his will are rounded in by
the law of his being. . . . We pass for what we are. Character teaches above

our wills."[53] Contrary to any monistic overtones in Emerson's exhortations to individual power, what emerges instead is a frankly pluralistic vision that advises individuals to seek power through the exercise of their own finite talents.

A second example is afforded by Emerson's essay "Nominalist and Realist," which prefigures the pluralist argument of James's lecture "The One and the Many"—namely, that the world is both "one" and "many," characterized by both unity and diversity. Weighing, in a Jamesian fashion, the claims of opposing philosophical camps—one locating essential reality in material particulars, the other locating it in general ideas—Emerson concludes, much as James after him does, that generalization and particularity correspond to two fundamental operations of human thought: "We are amphibious creatures, weaponed for two elements," Emerson asserts, "having two sets of faculties, the particular and the catholic."[54] Accordingly, Emerson's essay explores both perspectives in turn, pragmatically voicing the value of each and declining to push this dialectic to a synthesis, instead portraying particularity and generalization as necessary antagonisms in human experience:

> We must reconcile the contradictions as we can, but their discord and their concord introduce wild absurdities into our thinking and speech. No sentence will hold the whole truth, and the only way in which we can be just, is by giving ourselves the lie; Speech is better than silence; silence is better than speech;—All things are in contact; every atom has a sphere of repulsion; Things are, and are not, at the same time;—and the like. All the universe over, there is but one thing, this old Two-Face, creator-creature, mind-matter, right-wrong, of which any proposition may be affirmed or denied. Very fitly, therefore, I assert, that every man is a partialist, that nature secures him as an instrument by self-conceit, preventing the tendencies to religion and science; . . . and now I add, that every man is a universalist also, and, as our earth, whilst it spins on its own axis, spins all the time around the sun through the celestial spaces, so the least of its rational children, the most dedicated to his private affair, works out, though as it were under a disguise, the universal problem.[55]

Here Emerson expresses precisely the dynamic that James stresses in his centenary address, that an individual can participate in the "universal" forces of nature only through the "self-conceit" of pursuing his or her "private affair," only by exploiting the opportunities for power afforded by his or her unique and partial talents.

Moreover, much as James claims that to acknowledge any degree of genuine diversity and disunion effectively makes one a pluralist, so Emerson's practical recommendations for human behavior—his exhortations to individualized activity—are firmly planted within the pluralism of the natural world:

> Nature will not be Buddhist: she resents generalizing, and insults the philosopher in every moment with a million of fresh particulars. It is all idle talking: as much as a man is a whole, so is he also a part; and it were partial not to see it. . . . You are one thing, but nature is *one thing and the other thing*, in the same moment. She will not remain orbed in a thought, but rushes into persons; and when each person, inflamed to a fury of personality, would conquer all things to his poor crotchet, she raises up against him another person, and by many persons incarnates again a sort of whole. She will have all. Nick Bottom cannot play all the parts, work it how he may: there will be somebody else, and the world will be round. Everything must have its flower or effort at the beautiful, coarser or finer according to its stuff. They relieve and recommend each other, and the sanity of society is the balance of a thousand insanities. . . . [Nature] would never get anything done, if she suffered admirable Crichtons, and universal geniuses. She loves better a wheelwright who dreams all night of wheels, and a groom who is part of his horse: for she is full of work, and these are her hands.[56]

Emerson once described his writings as repetitions on a central theme, "the infinitude of the private man,"[57] a type of statement that, unfortunately, readers too often have taken at face value, for as is indicated by this passage's description of "personality" as an "inflamed fury" or "insanity," Emerson just as frequently stresses the individual's pathetic finitude. This is not to suggest, however, that Emerson's ethic of individualized vocation—his respect for the "wheelwright who dreams all night of wheels" and the "groom who is part of his horse"—is simply an acceptance of limitation, a surrender or abandonment to the larger forces of nature that use individuals as "instruments" or "hands" (though such abandonment does indeed represent an important aspect of his vision), for there is perhaps no writer who more furiously resents and resists the constraints on individuality than does Emerson. Rather, his vision of individuality exists in the tension or antagonism between limitation and power. Adopting the attitude that Kenneth Burke identifies as typifying pragmatism,[58] Emerson accepts limitations only in order to struggle against them: his ethics are always concerned with achieving a maximal integrity and power within the constraints of personhood. For Emerson, moreover, to stress limitation is not to belittle individuals, but in fact to assert the intrinsic value of all individuals and the diversity of possible experiences they embody. In Emerson, as in James, a pluralist acceptance of limitation implies an egalitarian affirmation of difference. As Emerson asserts in a sentence from "Nominalist and Realist" that James approvingly quotes in his centenary address: "If John was perfect, why are you and I alive? As long as any man exists, there is some need of him; let him fight for his own."[59]

If James provides a clear pragmatic rationale for viewing Emerson's monism as incidental to the essentially pluralistic thrust of his thought, this is not to claim that James saw Emerson as a pragmatist, nor to deny that James continued to see significant differences between Emerson's writings and his own. Neither do I want to establish James as the ultimate authority on the pragmatic aspects of Emerson's thought; indeed, one result of reading Emerson pragmatically, of looking for lines of continuity between his and James's thought, is that it can point us toward conclusions that go beyond James's own willingness or ability to see the consistency of Emerson's anti-absolutist attitudes and methods.

Consider, for example, the following passage from a letter James wrote to W. C. Brownell in 1909, responding to an essay the latter had written on Emerson:

> I have read your splendid essay (on Emerson) and return it. . . . I agree also entirely in your light estimate of his monistic metaphysics, and his Platonic philosophy in general. He evidently had no capacity whatever for metaphysic argument, but he found that certain transcendentalist and Platonic phrases *named* beautifully that *side* of the universe which for his soul (with its golden singing sense that the vulgar immediate is at naught relatively to the high and noble, gleeful and consoling life behind it) was all-important. So he abounded in monistic metaphysical talk which the very next pages belied. I see no great harm in the literary inconsistency. The monistic formulas do express a genuine direction in things, though it be to a great extent only ideal. His dogmatic expression of them never led him to *suppress the facts they ignored*, so no harm was done. (See, *e.g.*, the last couple of pages of his essay on history.) Of course to me they seem simply

weak, those Platonic formulas, but there are readers whom they inspire, so let them pass![60]

Several aspects of James's stance toward Emerson here deserve emphasis. First, James reasserts the logic articulated in his centenary address,
that because Emerson did not insist on the logical consequences of a true
monism, did not "suppress" the pluralistic diversity of "facts," the monistic assertions in his writings are ultimately of little consequence. Second is the way in which James draws distinctions between his own and
Emerson's visions. James reads Emerson's juxtaposition of monistic and
pluralistic passages as a symptom of Emerson's own temperament. In the
opening lecture of *Pragmatism*, James famously describes philosophy
as being largely and legitimately determined by people's temperamental needs—needs that are often in conflict, as he summarizes in his list
of "tender-minded" and "tough-minded" leanings. Most people, James
acknowledges, "have a hankering for the good things on both sides,"
with the result that the "philosophic layman ... never straighten[s]
out his system, but liv[es] vaguely in one plausible compartment of it
or another to suit the temptations of successive hours." Philosophers,
however, cannot brook such logical inconsistency, James argues: "We
cannot preserve a good intellectual conscience so long as we keep mixing incompatibles"—such as monism and pluralism—"from opposite
sides of the line.[61] James's "radical empiricism" was designed, in part,
to achieve a logical consistency while still combining the "good things"
from opposing philosophical camps: to maintain a consistent logic of
"tough-minded" empiricism while also acknowledging the empirical
reality and force of the ideas and beliefs craved by our "tender-minded"
side. In short, James describes Emerson's mixing of opposing philosophical positions as a common human practice, though one that disqualifies
Emerson as a philosopher—at least in James's sense of that term.

Third, and perhaps most importantly, while James is certainly correct
that Emerson never attempted to develop a consistent doctrine such as
radical empiricism,[62] one can nonetheless feel that James is being unduly
condescending in concluding that Emerson's lack of logical consistency
proves that he "had no capacity whatever for metaphysic argument." Following the suggestion of critics such as Cavell, Poirier, and Kateb, we are
much more likely today than James was to see Emerson's inconsistencies
as a deliberate strategy, one with philosophical significance and power.
Indeed, James's condescension to Emerson here exemplifies the potential

that Cavell fears—that judging Emerson by the standard of pragmatism will obscure the distinctiveness of Emerson's own philosophical complexity. That James, one of the most important bearers of the Emersonian legacy, can still voice the commonplace view that Emerson lacks philosophical rigor only goes to prove Cavell's point that Emerson's achievement as a philosopher largely has been repressed by the "culture he helped to found."[63] Indeed, taking as an example the conclusion of the essay "History" that James recommends to Brownell, one can extend James's insight beyond and against James's own conclusions, and argue that Emerson's voicing of conflicting perspectives is not evidence of his failure as a philosopher, but rather a writerly practice that anticipates central aspects of James's own philosophy.

The conclusion of "History" no doubt appealed to James because it so dramatically renounced the potential monistic implications of statements earlier in the essay: for instance, in its opening paragraph that asserts, "There is one mind common to all individual men," and that, "Who hath access to this universal mind is a party to all that is or can be done, for this is the only and sovereign agent."[64] Emerson's overall argument in "History" does not reflect the monistic connotations of these statements, for the possibility of communing with the common mind is demystified and treated, as "Self-Reliance" treats it, in terms of the self's relation to the media of culture—to language, artifacts, the surviving products and records of other people's actions. Indeed, Emerson's theory of the self's relation to texts from the past prefigures the pragmatic view that the truth of inherited ideas lies in their ability to meet the needs of our present experience.[65] Even where Emerson's arguments follow such a pragmatic tack, however, there are moments of monistic rhetoric of the type that attracted James's ire: in his copy of "History," for instance, James underlined the phrase "that the mind is One, and that nature is correlative," and, by a similar passage in "The American Scholar" that discusses "the philosophical doctrine of the identity of all minds," James questioned in the margin: "Why not 'commerce'—instead of identity."[66] Given his concern over such moments, it is not surprising that James was attracted to the conclusion of "History," in which Emerson voices an abrupt and dramatic shift in his argument, renouncing any claim to unified knowledge:

Is there somewhat overweening in this claim? Then I reject all I have written, for what is the use of pretending to know what we know not?

> But it is the fault of our rhetoric that we cannot strongly state one fact
> without seeming to belie some other. I hold our actual knowledge
> very cheap. Hear the rats in the wall, see the lizard on the fence, the
> fungus under foot, the lichen on the log. What do I know sympathet-
> ically, morally, of either of these worlds of life? As old as the Cauca-
> sian man,—perhaps older,—these creatures have kept their counsel
> beside him, and there is no record of any word or sign that has passed
> from one to the other. . . . I am ashamed to see what a shallow village
> tale our so-called History is. How many times must we say Rome,
> and Paris, and Constantinople! What does Rome know of rat and liz-
> ard? What are Olympiads and Consulates to these neighbouring sys-
> tems of being? Nay, what food or experience or succour have they for
> the Esquimaux seal-hunter, for the Kanaka in his canoe, for the fish-
> erman, the stevedore, the porter?[67]

After spending much of his essay affirming that history—as embodied
in inherited culture—provides people with a wealth of tools for engaging nature and bringing it under human dominion, Emerson ends by
insisting that our concepts and truths inevitably alienate us from reality
and blind us to crucial aspects of the world around us. Instead of rhap-
sodizing on the "universal mind," Emerson here focuses insistently on
brute particulars of nature whose alien otherness resists our conceptual
systems—rats in our walls, lizards on our fences. The implications of
this argument reveal important lines of influence between Emerson and
James. It was James, after all, who argued that "language works against
our perception of the truth," blinding us to the more evanescent, transitional aspects of experience, and who argued that "reality 'independent'
of human thinking," which had not already been "cooked," "peptonized"
or "*faked*" by the impositions of our concepts, was almost impossible to
perceive.[68] Moreover, Emerson's query—"What do I know sympathetically, morally" of "these neighbouring systems of being"—anticipates the
ethical imperative that James articulates in "On a Certain Blindness in
Human Beings" and "What Makes a Life Significant": the need to strive
to recognize and value other experiences and other beings potentially
obscured by the limits of our own individual and cultural perceptions.

Yet while these affinities clearly explain James's admiration for the
conclusion of "History," James in his letter to Brownell fails to consider
that the contradictions in Emerson's prose might reflect a conscious
strategy with a similarly pragmatic significance and force. As Richard
Poirier has eloquently argued, James's pragmatic axiom that a truth or

idea appears "less as a solution, then, than as a program for more work" extends an Emersonian emphasis on action and transition—an emphasis that Emerson enacts in his essays by revealing and moving beyond the constraints of his own utterances.[69] Indeed, the closing paragraphs of "History" are a prime example of such Emersonian performance: they are important not only for the ideas they express, but as a gesture of Emerson's willingness to abandon or renounce previously held conclusions, truths, and certainties. Further, such a habit of abandoning or renouncing the certainties of any single perspective helps instill precisely that antidogmatic openness to other beings and experiences that James deems to be so ethically important. Merely to stress, as James does in the above-quoted letter, that Emerson's voicing of contradictory views saves him from his potential monism (while true) is clearly insufficient, and to conclude that the contradictions in Emerson's prose reveal his incapacity for philosophical argument misses the boat altogether. In assessing the conclusion of "History" and other essays where Emerson deploys contradictions and reversals in his arguments, we can see, even if James did not, a more pragmatic method behind Emerson's madness.

As I hope these examples demonstrate, to read Emerson pragmatically can help us appreciate the anti-absolutist attitudes expressed in his writings—so long as the perspectives afforded by his pragmatic successors are used to approach Emerson without condescension, with the eye for complexity that his writings demand of readers, and almost unfailingly reward. But to assert that Emerson's writings are far more coherent than critics normally have granted—to claim, for instance, that his early and late works do not shift in emphasis from freedom to fate but express a remarkably consistent vision of human agency as existing in tension with limitation—is not to minimize the complexities and even contradictions in his philosophical vision. For, to hazard what I hope is not too clichéd or facile a paradox, the consistency of Emerson's vision lies precisely in its contradictions, in his characteristic habit of confronting, articulating, and exploiting the antagonistic facets of human experience. Thus, when we turn in chapter 2 to Emerson's individualist ethics, we will encounter a self that is simultaneously empowered and enfeebled by culture; a self that exists only in its relations to its social and material environments, and whose acts thus are always socially implicated, yet also a self that retains an integral power to control the value of its own experience; a self that finds sustenance and meaning in its interactions with others, yet accepts stern limits on just how far individuals can help each other; and a self whose power alternately lies in its ability to focus and narrow its activity, and a contrasting willingness to abandon the security of familiar tasks for new ones. Similarly, while Emerson's ethic of self-culture constitutes a tragic embrace of limitation, it also implies a pluralistic, egalitarian regard for the sufficient power and significance of each person's talents, and while it affirms the power of ideas radically to reform our institutions and conduct, it also locates reform in more strategic efforts to redirect existing ideas, institutions, and practices to new purposes. Such complexities at the heart of his vision explain Emerson's enduring influence, and explain why Dewey could conclude 1903—in an extravagant prediction we have yet to fulfill—that "when democracy has articulated itself, it will have no difficulty in finding itself already proposed in Emerson."[70]

TWO

"LET US HAVE WORSE COTTON AND BETTER MEN"

Emerson's Ethics of Self-Culture

P ragmatism, as noted in my introduction, rejects absolutism in favor of an experimental and melioristic approach to inquiry and conduct. Relinquishing the notion of truth as providing any absolute certainty, and rejecting simplistic notions that truth provides an objective account of an unchanging reality, pragmatism views ideas as limited human constructs—hypotheses or tools whose truth resides in their ability to guide our actions to beneficial results. By extension, all such results must in turn be treated as only provisional ends, and most importantly as means to further action. It is worthwhile here to cite again William James's claim that an idea or concept "appears less as a solution, then, than as a program for more work, and more particularly as an indication of the ways in which existing realities may be *changed*"[1]—for it encapsulates the pragmatic view that ideas are tools for fulfilling human purposes and transforming our environments. This statement points, as well, toward the extensive affinities between James's pragmatism and the thought of his most important American precursor, Ralph Waldo Emerson. Emerson, too, asserts that human actions, inspired and facilitated by ideas, have an immense practical power to transform reality. Yet it is not in the results of our acts, Emerson insists, that life's most precious value lies, but in the possibilities for continued activity—specifically, in the expression and cultivation of self that individuals achieve through action.

These anti-absolutist emphases on process, change, and growth that link Emerson and James help explain why individualism plays such a central role in both writers' ethics. James insists that a universe that changes and grows is a pluralistic universe, characterized by contingency, limitation, and diversity, and the possibility for change that James views as the saving grace of our world is tied to the existence and encouragement of individuality: the possibilities immanent in a specific situation often require the purposes, perceptions, and energies of individual actors to bring them to fruition. Similarly, Emerson's emphasis on action and change leads him to view the cultivation of individuality both as a primary moral end—a fundamental measure of any just society—and as a necessary means, an essential source of the novelty and change that revitalize society and expand the possibilities for human experience. In articulating these twin rationales for individualism, Emerson prefigures not only James's ethics, but also Dewey's embrace of individuality as essential to democratic community.

While Emerson's "transcendentalism" is often dismissed as an abstract, monistic idealism that ignores tragic limitations, and his individualism correspondingly criticized for a naive optimism, his writings in fact depict a pluralistic world governed by limitation, antagonism, and change, and his individualist ethics are explicitly offered as a healthy, and necessary, response to the tragic limits of our world. In both his early and later writings, Emerson argues that life depends on the interplay between "power"—the vital energies of expression, growth, and change—and limitation or "fate"—the necessity of energy to take a specific form. "Though Fate is immense," he writes, "so is power, which is the other fact in the dual world, immense. If Fate follows and limits power, power attends and antagonizes Fate." This concept of antagonism is central to Emerson's thought: it describes a beneficial, creative struggle out of which new strengths and values are born; a goading, an instigation, and an inspiration. Emerson, after all, is the writer who intriguingly describes the friend as a "beautiful enemy." This agonistic view of life shapes Emerson's ethic of self-culture, which locates value in the strength, knowledge, and facility we gain in struggling against the resistances of our world. From this perspective, limitation is not regrettable, but the necessary condition of our lives, the indispensable resistance against which we develop our identities and talents: "We must have an antagonism in the tough world for all the variety of our spiritual faculties," Emerson insists, "or they will not be born."[2]

The moral and political implications of Emerson's individualism reflect his attempt to articulate an ethics commensurate with a world of limitation and power. Far from valorizing an atomistic, autonomous self, Emerson describes the self as inherently relational—as existing only through its interactions with its natural and cultural environments. Indeed, I know of no writer so profoundly conscious as Emerson is of our dependence on inherited traditions, tools, and ideas. His ethic of self-culture reflects a profound sense that individual acts are always socially indebted and implicated: he is deeply concerned that the social resources that empower individual acts also threaten to hinder us from discovering and cultivating our most vital talents, and he defines such self-cultivation as our primary moral responsibility. Yet he also insists that the social indebtedness of individual acts entails an obligation to others. Emerson's ethics attempt to synthesize these demands: he envisions community as a collection of mutually inspiring and antagonizing individuals who, in their diversity of vocations, serve as catalysts for the creative change that reinvigorates society. Self-reliance thus is not opposed to community (as is often assumed), but a means to more vital community. While Emerson's ideal of nonconformist integrity extends, in one vein, to a Nietzschean questioning of traditional morality and obligation, it also prefigures Dewey's ideal of democracy-as-community.[3]

These pragmatic aspects of Emerson's thought also reveal his views on politics and reform to be far more complex than is often granted. Emerson's statements on the socioeconomic division of labor indicate how his emphasis on the quality of active selfhood departs from and critiques a capitalist logic of individualism; similarly, his stance on the central political struggle of his era—the sectional crisis over slavery—demonstrates that his skepticism toward institutional vehicles of reform is not an individualistic renunciation of politics, but instead balances an affirmation of the possibility of reform with an insistence that real reform must be rooted in the changed behavior of citizens.

"There Is No Other World": A Tragic Ethics of Limitation and Power

In town I also talked with Sampson Reed, of Swedenborg & the rest. "It is not so in your experience, but is so in the other world."—"Other world?" I reply, "there is no other world; here or nowhere is the whole fact; all the Universe over, there is but one thing,—this old double, Creator-creature, mind-matter, right-wrong."

—Ralph Waldo Emerson

Emersonian transcendentalism often has been equated with a desire to transcend wholly the material world and its tragic limits, to access or participate in an infinite power by intuiting the divine unity pervading nature.[4] Yet throughout his essays, Emerson describes human power as emerging only within and against the material limitations of experience. Contrary to the prevalent view that he celebrates an autonomous self, Emerson is acutely aware of our dependence on "society," a term that in his writings refers not only the influences of other people and the benefits derived from a social organization of labor, but more broadly comprehends cultural traditions, institutions, tools, ideas and technologies, the most pervasive of which—language—structures our very thoughts. This cultural basis of human intelligence quite literally means that we can hardly act or even think without using social resources. "So deep is the foundation of the existing social system, that it leaves no one out of it," Emerson writes in "The Conservative": "All men have their root in it. You who quarrel with the arrangements of society . . . are under the necessity of using the Actual order of things, in order to disuse it; to live by it, whilst you wish to take away its life. The past has baked your loaf, and in the strength of its bread you would break up the oven."[5] We must always build the future out of the cultural materials we inherit from the past.

Yet if they inescapably limit our perceptions and actions, the myriad ideas that we inherit from the past also constitute powerful tools for creative change. Ideas, Emerson would remind us, are distorting lenses that shape and focus our perception of reality. The limitation of every idea or concept is, somewhat paradoxically, the source of its power: ideas are summarized lessons derived from past, experiences that a "former age has epitomized into a formula or rule," as Emerson puts it;[6] they provide shortcuts in experience, or focus selectively on generalized patterns, relationships, or laws. Through such concentration, ideas have a tremendous power to shape our perception and behavior, as Emerson argues in the essay "Circles":

> Much more obviously is history and the state of the world at any one time directly dependent on the intellectual classification then existing in the minds of men. The things which are dear to men at this hour are so on the account of the ideas which have emerged on their mental horizon, and which cause the present order of things as a tree bears its apples. A new degree of culture would instantly revolutionize the entire system of human pursuits.[7]

"Idealism," Emerson asserts, is not some moonshiny abstractionism, but "shows itself ethical and practical." In a logic that clearly anticipates James's defense of the practical consequences of will and belief, Emerson argues that to move beyond the confines of our present ruling ideas—to shift from an old mental perspective to a new one—not only has a radical power to reform "the minds of men" (our values, desires, and our subsequent actions), but that when ideas are then applied through those actions, they have a tremendous practical power to transform material reality itself. "New arts destroy the old. See the investment of capital in aqueducts made useless by hydraulics; fortifications, by gunpowder; roads and canals, by railways; sails, by steam; steam by electricity." "By the aggregate of these aids," Emerson marvels in *Nature*, "how is the face of the world changed, from the era of Noah to that of Napoleon!" As such passages suggest, a tough-minded, empiricist focus on technology and physical forces reveals at bottom an idealist faith in the plasticity of reality: "Everything looks permanent until its secret is known," Emerson affirms in "Circles": "Permanence is but a word of degrees."[8]

Emerson's view that inherited culture both limits and enables new creative acts anticipates the attitude of practical activism that is so central to the thought of James and Dewey: the acknowledgement, on the one hand, that the possibilities for the future are limited by the actualities of our present, and, on the other, the insistence that each present does embody sufficient possibilities for change. This pragmatic side of Emerson's idealism is evident from the opening paragraph of his first book:

> Our age is retrospective. It builds the sepulchres of the fathers. It writes biographies, histories, and criticism. The foregoing generations beheld God and nature face to face; we through their eyes. Why should not we also enjoy an original relation to the universe? Why should not we have a poetry and philosophy of insight and not

of tradition, and a religion by revelation to us, and not the history of theirs? Embosomed for a season in nature, whose floods of life stream around and through us, and invite us by the powers they supply, to action proportioned to nature, why should we grope among the dry bones of the past, or put the living generation into masquerade out of its faded wardrobe? The sun shines to-day also. There is more wool and flax in the fields. There are new lands, new men, new thoughts. Let us demand our own works and laws and worship.[9]

While this passage opens in a tone of complaint against the burden of the past, its overall stance is not anxious but confident. History, Emerson suggests, should not be viewed as a static body of inherited traditions, but rather as a process of growth and change. If history is inherited culture that inhibits new creative acts, it is also temporal change that demands and enables new creation. This is evident in Emerson's metaphors: though they seem to establish a dichotomy between culture and nature, they in fact depict natural and cultural change as contiguous processes. The same historical change that makes old forms outdated and constricting allows us to create new forms: the same natural change that kills the fathers brings us life today; the same sun that dries their bones and fades their wardrobes creates new flax and wool for us to weave our own garments. This trope of clothing, with natural fibers woven on human looms, blurs any clear line between natural and cultural creation.[10] Emerson is not rejecting the past, but affirming our right to its legacy—a legacy of action, not of particular forms or stable meanings. The impulses that drove our ancestors to weave their own wardrobe did not die with them, but now exist in us, and we best use the past when we extend their activity by creating forms of our own. As Emerson puts it in "Self-Reliance": "There is at this moment for you an utterance as brave and grand as that of the colossal chisel of Phidias, or trowel of the Egyptians, or the pen of Moses, or Dante, but different from all these." Nature here is not posited as a means to escape history and culture; Emerson's call for "action proportioned to nature" is rather an insistence that the human acts that spur historical change are driven by the same energies that animate nature. For Emerson, then, creative action is not a matter of transcending the natural world, but of emulating nature's own energies of growth and power: "Nature is transcendental," Emerson claims in "The Transcendentalist," for it "exists primarily, necessarily, ever works and advances."[11]

Yet while Emerson is confident that each historical moment offers sufficient possibilities for new creative acts, he also insists that creative acts are constrained both by the cultural media with which they must be articulated and the environment they strive to reshape. For Emerson, creative change is a process of *limited* transcendence, in which people turn inherited cultural tools to new uses, exceeding their previous reality only by facilitating the emergence of another, also limited reality. Thus he approvingly notes in his journal one woman's definition of transcendentalism as "a *little* beyond."[12] By acting with and against the ideas and tools we inherit, we can help create results that transcend the reality previously defined by those tools: we can, to use the central trope of the essay "Circles," "draw a new circle" beyond the limits of our previous circle. Yet as this trope indicates, the creative power of each transformative act becomes part of a new circle, a new environment that in turn resists further transformations:

> For it is the inert effort of each thought, having formed itself into a circular wave of circumstance,—as, for instance, an empire, rules of an art, a local usage, a religious rite,—to heap itself on that ridge, and to solidify and hem in the life. But if the soul is quick and strong, it bursts over that boundary on all sides, and expands another orbit on the great deep, which also runs up into a high wave, with attempt to again stop and to bind. But the heart refuses to be imprisoned; in its first and narrowest pulses, it already tends outward with a vast force, and to immense and innumerable expansions.[13]

This passage, perhaps as well as any in Emerson, embodies the major pragmatic elements of his thought. First, there is his assertion that the reality defined by any human action or idea—even one as grand as "an empire"—will be limited and constraining. Emerson announces the far-reaching consequences of this fact in "The Poet," where he writes, "Every thought is also a prison; every heaven is also a prison." The essay "Circles" is peppered with similar assertions, such as "every action admits of being outdone," "around every circle another can be drawn," "every ultimate fact is only the first of a new series," and "there is not a piece of science, but its flank may be turned to-morrow." Second, since no truth or act provides any ultimate security, Emerson concludes that we can seek a more stable value or integrity only by embracing action and change: "a man cannot have his flank turned," he argues, only by virtue of his "preferring truth to his past apprehension of truth; and his alert

acceptance of it, from whatever quarter." Or, as he puts it more dramatically in "Self-Reliance": "Power ceases in the instant of repose; it resides
in the moment of transition from a past to a new state, in the shooting of
the gulf, in the darting to an aim."[14] Third, Emerson views this inevitable
limitation of every act not as a misfortune, but as imposing the salutary
necessity of continual re-creation. "The heart refuses to be imprisoned,"
he affirms in the passage quoted above: desire cannot be satisfied by any
achieved status, but ever urges us to new acts. It is in the repeated drama
of limitation, struggle, and change—of ever working to draw a new
circle—that Emerson tells us we must seek value.

This value that we gain through action is designated in Emerson's
writings by a variety of names—such as "power," "character," "virtue"
(including its original meaning of "strength"), "self-reliance," and
"culture"—all of which describe a cultivation of personal power, of the
knowledge and facility of performance that is gained only through action. In this sense, self-reliance is indeed an ethics of independence, but
far from denying the forces that limit the individual, it is explicitly a
response to limitation. The products of our acts, Emerson insists, are
subject to failures and losses beyond our control; the one thing we can
control, however, is our effort in response to these limits, the strength we
develop even when our actions are deflected or defeated, or when their
material fruits are unjustly wrested from us:

> What a man does, that he has. What has he to do with hope or fear? In
> himself is his might. Let him regard no good as solid, but that which
> is in his nature, and which must grow out of himself as long as he ex-
> ists. The goods of fortune may come and go like summer leaves; let
> him scatter them on every wind as the momentary signs of his infi-
> nite productiveness.[15]

Emerson's essays are full of similar claims, as in "The American Scholar,"
where he provocatively asserts that "the one thing in the world, of value,
is the active soul." The familiar ring of Emerson's hortatory rhetoric in
such passages too often has been conflated with a hackneyed rugged
individualism, making it difficult, perhaps, to recognize that he is calling for a fundamental shift in our location of value, away from material
products and toward the cultivation of people's intellectual, creative, and
spiritual potential. Emerson not only suggests that people *can* afford to
"scatter" the "goods of fortune," to abandon the achieved fruits of their
efforts, he insists they can't afford *not* to do so, for the promised security

of accumulated products or achieved status threatens to become a stifling obstacle to further vitality and growth. People "can and must detach themselves" and "new powers shall appear," he argues in "Self-Reliance"; or, as he puts it in "Circles," "People wish to be settled; only as far as they are unsettled is there any hope for them." Yet if Emerson insists on an ethics of abandonment, it is only because he views it as the means to a more stable kind of value: "that which a man is does always by necessity acquire, and what the man acquires is living property." This "living property" is precisely the cultivation of one's own facilities for performance, the "force of character" that Emerson insists is "cumulative," for "your own gift you can present every moment with the cumulative force of a whole life's cultivation." While this ethics of self-reliance is a response to, and not a denial of, limitation, Emerson does indeed suggest that such a fundamental shift in our location of value gives us a certain control over and even freedom from fate: "In the Will work and acquire, and thou hast chained the wheel of Chance, and shalt sit hereafter out of fear from her rotations."[16]

It is in light of this ethics of self-culture that one must understand Emerson's claim—repeated throughout his writings—that the universe is moral or benevolent. As discussed in chapter 1, Emerson often has been dismissed as an absolute optimist whose abstract assertion of the world's morality ignores, subsumes, or co-opts the reality of material limits and suffering. Consider, for instance, Myra Jehlen's interpretation of the "Discipline" chapter of *Nature*, which, like the later essay "Compensation," asserts that "All things are moral."[17] Jehlen argues that Emerson, by claiming that the sufferings of our world, such as poverty and death, are, "benevolent guides to intellectual truths," in effect "has co-opted the material reality of limits and powerlessness" in order to "assert the possibility of transcendence—of freedom and omnipotence": "The facts that some are indebted to others and that all owe the final debt of mortality have been made to testify to the primacy and infinite power of the individual in an infinitely benevolent universe."[18] In Jehlen's description, Emerson's philosophy appears like a Panglossian optimism or a secularized version of Calvinist providence, an assertion that people deserve the sufferings they endure, that the apparent injustices of our world in fact reflect an absolute, total justice that precludes any real losses or limitation. Jehlen's terms—"omnipotence," "infinite" individual power in an "infinitely benevolent universe"—all stress the absolutism of Emerson's moral vision.

Yet Emerson's essay "Compensation," which aside perhaps from "Fate" offers his clearest and most detailed description of the moral character of our world, does not ignore suffering or injustice. Exactly the opposite is true: Emerson articulates the tragic view that morality consists not in a total transcendence of limitation, but in an acceptance of the limits of our world and in an affirmation of the sufficient value we obtain in struggling against and, yes, overcoming, specific limitations. Accordingly, he opens "Compensation" by satirizing traditional religion's absolutist concept of justice, as expressed in a sermon on the last judgment:

> Yet what was the import of this teaching? What did the preacher mean by saying that the good are miserable in the present life? Was it that houses and lands, offices, wine, horses, dress, luxury, are had by unprincipled men, whilst the saints are poor and despised; and that a compensation is to be made to these last hereafter, by giving them the like gratifications another day,—bank-stock and doubloons, venison and champagne? This must be the compensation intended; for, what else? Is it that they are to have leave to pray and praise? to love and serve men? Why, that they can do now. The legitimate inference the disciple would draw was,—"We are to have *such* a good time as the sinners have now;"—or, to push it to its extreme import,—"You sin now; we shall sin by and by; we would sin now, if we could; not being successful, we expect our revenge tomorrow."[19]

The "fallacy" of this sermon's logic, Emerson concludes, lies "in the immense concession that justice is not done now." This is hardly an assertion that the material world perfectly rewards individual merit, or that transcendence to "infinite individual power," as Jehlen puts it, is possible. Rather, in rejecting the concept of a justice that restores all losses, a justice beyond our world, Emerson rejects the notion that our material world *should* perfectly reward us, for the latter idea is implicit in the former: the very concept of a heavenly compensation implies the need to overcome the imperfections of worldly rewards and sufferings. Emerson's satire on heaven suggests that banishing justice to an ideal realm does not transcend the moral limits of our world; it implicitly reproduces them in a vengeful reversal (an argument that anticipates Nietzsche's critiques of "slave morality" and "ressentiment").

The moral character that Emerson ascribes to our world in "Compensation" is a morality based in the generative, antagonistic interplay between power and limitation: "If the good is there, so is the evil; if the affinity, so the repulsion; if the force, so the limitation," he claims, and it is this dynamic tension that leads him to conclude in the next breath, "Thus is the universe alive. All things are moral."[20] Our world is moral because the primary value of our life—knowledge and the capacity for ongoing growth and performance—must be earned; it cannot be stolen:

> But because of the dual constitution of things, in labor as in life, there can be no cheating. The thief steals from himself. The swindler swindles himself. For the real price of labor is knowledge and virtue, whereof wealth and credit are signs. These signs, like paper money, may be counterfeited or stolen, but that which they represent, namely, knowledge and virtue, cannot be counterfeited or stolen. These ends of labor cannot be answered but by real exertions of the mind, and in obedience to pure motives. The cheat, the defaulter, the gambler, cannot extort the knowledge of material and moral nature which his honest care and pains yield to the operative. The law of nature is, Do the thing, and you shall have the power: but they who do not the thing have not the power.[21]

It is important to note the limits of Emerson's claim here. People, he acknowledges, can be unjustly deprived of the material products of their labor, but the person who so deprives others achieves a merely material gain at the cost of a much higher good, the development and exercise of his or her own self: "he has resisted his life, and fled from himself, and the retribution is so much death." To exploit the labor of others, or to use resources provided by others for any purpose other than to engage in a meaningful work of one's own, is in Emerson's view ethical suicide. That the material world is, from the perspective of the human will, alien and resistant, a fact often viewed as the sign of the world's injustice, actually guarantees a certain immutable justice. It is because power and value can only be gained in a struggle against the resistances of our world that Emerson posits a "league between virtue and nature" that "engages all things to assume a hostile front to vice."[22]

That Emerson is pointedly turning necessity into a virtue only underscores the way in which his optimism is frequently misread. Indeed, the exhortation to make virtue out of necessity is a fair summary of Emerson's ethics, for he insists that our failures, as well as our successes, can yield the benefit of increased power and knowledge.

> Our strength grows out of our weakness. . . . When [a great man] is pushed, tormented, defeated, he has a chance to learn something; he

has been put on his wits, on his manhood; he has gained facts; learns his ignorance; is cured of the insanity of conceit; has got moderation and real skill. The wise man throws himself on the side of his assailants.[23]

"In general," he concludes, "every evil to which we do not succumb is a benefactor," a stance that is echoed in Nietzsche's famous maxim that "What does not kill me makes me stronger."[24] Limitation, from this Emersonian perspective, is not to be bemoaned, for the limits of our world give us our individual identities; it is only against the resistance and limitation of our material environments that we know, express, and develop our creative powers. The circumstances of the world that restrict, thwart, and eventually kill us are also what prompt Emerson's expressions of gratitude, most notably in "Experience" and "Fate." Emerson values limitations, presenting them as occasions for the circumscribed acts and performances that define us as human.

This attitude toward limitation suggests another way of reading Emerson's claim that "All things are moral," for it asserts the significance of all the facts and forces that determine our existence—not just those that fit our human concepts of merit and desert. Whether just or not, the circumstances of our environment, both by responding to and resisting our efforts to control and reshape them, accurately reflect our limited position within nature. Thus, Emerson argues, an individual "comes at last to be faithfully represented by every view you take of his circumstances": our character and strength is reflected in our struggles and defeats as well as our accomplishments. As we have already seen in the essay "Circles," even when our acts successfully change our environment, they then become part of a new environment or "circle" that re-acts upon us. Already implicit in *Nature*'s claim that, "Every spirit builds itself a house; and beyond its house a world; and beyond its world a heaven," is the corollary Emerson voices in "Fate": "Every spirit makes itself a house; but afterwards the house confines the spirit."[25] As Kenneth Burke suggests, tragedy expresses precisely this kind of relation between self and environment:

> The act, in being an assertion, has called forth a counter-assertion in the elements that compose its context. And when the agent is enabled to see in terms of the counter-assertion, he has transcended the state that characterized him at the start. In this final state of tragic vision, intrinsic and extrinsic motivations are merged. That is, although

purely circumstantial factors participate in his tragic destiny, these are not felt as exclusively external, or scenic; for they bring about a *representative* kind of accident, the kind of accident that belongs with the agent's particular kind of character.[26]

Using Burke's definition, then, we can describe Emerson's ethics as "tragic" because they accept the imperfect results of our actions as accurate representations of our human power and our limitation.[27]

It is important to stress that, if Emerson offers a tragic vision, this does not mean that he urges us to a fatalistic acquiescence. "The doctrine of Compensation is not the doctrine of indifferency,"[28] Emerson insists, for to view limitations as occasions for struggle, power, and overcoming encourages us to take an activist attitude toward the resistant realities of our world. As Burke explains in *Attitudes toward History*, Emerson's doctrine of compensation—the idea that "in all evil, there is inevitably some compensatory good"—does not subsume or co-opt evil, but articulates a pragmatic response to it, a "*meliorist . . .* project for living" that views our losses and defeats as enabling and requiring action. As Burke paraphrases, "Calamities arise, and by compensation, they force us to turn them into benefits, lest we perish."[29] As will be noted in chapter 6, Burke judges this refusal to accept limits without also affirming our ability to act in response to them, as perhaps Emerson's most important legacy to the pragmatic tradition he helped inspire.

"The Most Indebted Man": The Social Self and the Ethics of Vocation

Probably more than any other American thinker, Emerson is viewed as a champion of individual originality and independence, yet the enduring value of his thought, in no small part, lies precisely in the ways that his essays belie this popular image. Emerson remains America's most profound and complex theorist of individuality, one who indeed urges readers to seek an independent, original, or authentic existence, but who portrays such an existence as a tenuous status achievable only through strenuous and skillful effort. Emerson depicts the self as existing only in its relations with its environment: "The world,—this shadow of the soul or *other me*, lies wide around," he writes in "The American Scholar," "Its attractions are the keys which unlock my thoughts and make me acquainted with myself." "A man is a bundle of relations" whose "faculties refer to natures out of him, and predict the world he is to inhabit," he notes in "History," but the self's potential is realized, "unlocked" or unfolded, only through the interactions of experience: "He cannot live without a world. . . . No man can antedate his experience, or guess what faculty or feeling a new object shall unlock, any more than he can draw today the face of a person whom he shall see to-morrow for the first time."[30] As this simile suggests, the Emersonian self exists in process; your future self, called forth by tomorrow's or next year's experiences, may greet you like a stranger.

It is not only the natural environment, but perhaps more significantly the cultural environment that shapes and unlocks the Emersonian self. The individual is both "the correlative of nature" and "the compend of time," having access to "the civil and metaphysical history of man." "What Plato has thought, he may think; what a saint has felt, he may feel; what at any time has befallen any man, he can understand. Who hath access to this universal mind is a party to all that is or can be done." Inherited culture or history, which "is the record" of "the works of this mind," provides us with examples of the diverse possibilities of human activity, as well as with products, conclusions, and tools derived from others' actions, thereby expanding tremendously the individual's range of experience and power. "We wish for a thousand heads, a thousand bodies," Emerson writes in "The Uses of Great Men." "Is this fancy? Well, in good faith, we are multiplied by our proxies. How easily we adopt their labors! Every ship that comes to America got its chart from Columbus. Every novel is a debtor to Homer. Every carpenter who shaves with a foreplane borrows the genius of a forgotten inventor."[31]

It would wrong, of course, to suggest that Emerson portrays the self as wholly dependent on or determined by its environment. Individuality, as he portrays it, is instead a complex interaction between self and environment. For all the ways in which Emerson describes the self as socially constituted and constrained, there clearly does exist in his vision a self on which to rely, resources each individual possesses for engaging his or her environment. Each person embodies a unique set of possibilities and aptitudes: "The power which resides in him is new in nature," Emerson affirms in "Self-Reliance," "and none but he knows what that is which he can do, nor does he know until he has tried." For Emerson, as for James and Dewey after him, individuality—the diversity of people's different interests, impulses, and capacities—introduces a crucial element of novelty into the world. Yet Emerson also insists that the self's inherent potential for individuality or originality can only be realized through interaction with its environment. For instance, when he exhorts readers, "Trust thyself: every heart vibrates to that iron string," the gloss he provides in the subsequent sentence may surprise some: "Accept the place the divine providence has found for you, the society of your contemporaries, the connection of events. Great men have always done so, and confided themselves childlike to the genius of their age."[32] To "trust yourself" does not mean to turn inward to an autonomous mind (or to transcend material particulars to commune with an "over-soul"); to find your self, you must immerse yourself in the possibilities of action provided by your historical moment.

Yet if Emerson contends that individuality can only be realized in a social context, he also asserts—in a logic that again indicates his influence on Dewey—that the interaction between individual and society must allow for the nourishment and growth of individuals' most vital talents. This dynamic comes together in his concept of "vocation," which, in Emerson as in the Protestant traditions from which it emerges, refers to the specific work to which one is "called"—the work that both employs one's god-given talents *and* performs some necessary work in the world. In judging the proper relation of self to environment, Emerson clearly gives priority to the self; viewing the cultivation of human potential as our highest aim, he insists that one's vocation should be determined primarily by the promptings of one's creative impulses: "the action which I in all my years tend to do, is the work for my faculties," he claims. "Each man has his own vocation. The talent is the call."[33] Thus, though we must seek our vocations amidst the people and events of our day, we must not allow society's conventional definitions of work and success to prevent us from pursuing the work that will realize our most vital selves:

> The common experience is, that the man fits himself as well as he can to the customary details of the work or trade he falls into, and tends it as a dog turns a spit. Then is he a part of the machine he moves; the man is lost. Until he can manage to communicate himself to others in his full stature and proportion, he does not yet find his vocation.[34]

Though Emerson admits that people too often merely "fall into" the employments that society prescribes to them, he argues that, if they have the courage to pursue the "call" of their talents, those gifts will find both recognition and employment in society: "By doing his work, he makes the need felt which he can supply, and creates the taste by which he is enjoyed."[35]

Such expressions of confidence in our ability to achieve a self-reliant mode of living are never naive on Emerson's part; indeed, he continually exhorts readers to self-reliance, I would argue, precisely because he is so keenly aware of the obstacles to authentic action. Paramount among these obstacles is our profound dependence, as symbol-using animals, on the resources of culture. First, if culture is the source of human beings' tremendous power, it is also, by reason of the very powers it makes available, a threat to the individual's capacity to discover and cultivate his or her own unique energies:

> Every mind must know the whole lesson for itself,—must go over the whole ground. What it does not see, what it does not live, it will not know. What the former age has epitomized into a formula or rule for manipular convenience, it will lose all the good of verifying for itself, by means of the wall of that rule. Somewhere, sometime, it will demand and find compensation for that loss by doing the work itself.[36]

This passage explains why Emerson in "Self-Reliance" claims, "Society everywhere is in conspiracy against the manhood of every one of its members": society is a threat precisely because it offers to do so much for us. The ready-made tools, products, and occupations that culture supplies often keep us from actively cultivating the powers of performance that Emerson views as our primary good in life. Second, because the ideals, values, and models of behavior that culture offers us are derived from the past, they easily can prevent us from truly living in our present. "The Greek sculpture is all melted away," Emerson notes in "Circles," because "the genius that created it creates now somewhat else." If we rely too much on the ideas of the past, they will prevent us from perceiving and participating in the energies of creative change that are moving our present toward a different future. As he writes in "The Uses of Great Men," "When nature removes a great man, people explore the horizon for a successor; but none comes, and none will. In some other and quite different field the next man will appear; not Jefferson, not Franklin, but now a great salesman; then a road-contractor; then a student of fishes; then a buffalo-hunting explorer, or some semi-savage Western general."[37]

How to act in society without losing one's individual integrity, how to use the resources for action that culture provides without becoming enervated by them, is arguably the central problem that Emerson attempts to resolve in his ethics. As inherently cultural beings, we cannot avoid using the resources of culture; the crucial question is, how and to what purpose do we use them? "Books are the best of things, well used; abused, among the worst," Emerson contends in "The American Scholar": "What is right use?" he continues, "They are for nothing but to inspire." This statement summarizes his view not only on books, but on all the tools, institutions, and ideas of culture. Properly used, culture provides powerful aids to help individuals pursue their own vocation. Emerson's first caveat is that we must not merely accept the results, products, or benefits that culture makes available to us: "We are too passive in the reception of these material or semi-material aids. We must not be sacks or stomachs," he argues in "The Uses of Great Men." Instead, we must seek value in our own continued activity and growth, and treat culture as a means for inspiring and facilitating them. Culture is more than just a collection of tools; by preserving the works of other people, culture records inspiring examples of human action, and, as Emerson insists, "Activity is contagious": "I cannot even hear of personal vigor of any kind, great power or performance, without fresh resolution. We are emulous of all that men can do." Thus Emerson likens culture to a "gymnasium" that allows us to witness "summersaults, spells, and resurrections, wrought by the imagination," and thereby "inspires an audacious mental habit." Just as he says books are for "nothing but to inspire," so he argues that culture is of value to us only as it inspires us to acts of our own: "Other help," he concludes, "I find a false appearance."[38]

If approached in this spirit, as examples of the diverse range of human activities for us to emulate in our own actions, culture provides powerful resources for helping us to find our own vocations. An inspiring otherness, which Emerson claims we feel in both our friends and in works of genius, characterizes our basic relation to culture:

> Other men are lenses through which we read our own minds. Each man seeks those of different quality from his own, and such as are good of their kind; that is, he seeks other men, and the *otherest*. The stronger the nature, the more it is reactive. Let us have the quality pure. A little genius let us leave alone. A main difference betwixt men is, whether they attend their own affair or not. . . . His own affair, though impossible to others, he can open with celerity and in sport. . . . And every one can do his best thing easiest.[39]

The diversity of culture is an otherness that helps us define our selves. The vocations offered by culture are necessarily "other"—no individual can perform them all. By seeking out the "otherest," we receive a double benefit. First, we learn the general lesson that individual limitation is the path to individual power. The most powerful individuals are the "otherest"—those who concentrate most exclusively on their specialized talents, who "attend their own affair." Second, the "otherest" or most specialized actors represent the greatest diversity of activities, among which we can experiment in efforts to find that vocation which best suits our talents. In both of these senses, other people are the "lenses through which we read our own minds."

As an example of an individual who pursues his own vocation by experimenting with the varied opportunities for action that society offers, consider the portrait of a "sturdy lad" from "New Hampshire or Vermont" in "Self-Reliance":

> If our young men miscarry in their first enterprises, they lose all heart. If the young merchant fails, men say he is *ruined*. If the finest genius studies at one of our colleges, and is not installed in an office within one year afterwards in the cities or suburbs of Boston or New York, it seems to his friends and to himself that he is right in being disheartened, and in complaining the rest of his life. A sturdy lad from New Hampshire or Vermont, who in turn tries all the professions, who *teams it, farms it, peddles*, keeps a school, preaches, edits a newspaper, goes to Congress, buys a township, and so forth, in successive years, and always, like a cat, falls on his feet, is worth a hundred of these city dolls. He walks abreast with his days, and feels no shame in not "studying a profession," for he does not postpone his life, but lives already. He has not one chance, but a hundred chances.[40]

In his examples of healthy or powerful actors, Emerson suggests that the pursuit of one's true vocation, of a true cultivation of self, requires two distinct modes of activity, which I will designate, borrowing some of Emerson's own terms, as an ethic of "abandonment" and a contrasting ethic of "concentration." Both modes are evidenced in the above portrait. From one perspective, this sturdy lad's power consists in his willingness to abandon or relinquish the achieved security of his accomplishments, of each activity he masters, in order to attempt new tasks. Exemplifying Emerson's claim in "Self-Reliance" that "life only avails, not the having lived," that "power ceases in the instant of repose," but "resides in the moment of transition from a past to a new state," he finds success in *succession*, in the experience of exploring different activities "in turn" over "successive years." Yet this abandonment is also simultaneously a cultivation or concentration of higher type of value: if he rejects society's location of value in accumulated products or the secured status of an institutionalized profession, it is because he finds value in the cultivation of self—the catlike facility of performance that allows him to always land on his feet—that is gained only through a continual willingness to tackle new challenges.

These contrasting modes of abandonment and concentration merit more detailed attention, for they are recurrent themes in Emerson's writings and are integral to his vision of the self as existing in a process of growth and change. Abandonment, for Emerson, not only describes the revitalizing transition to new acts, but also refers to a surrender of intention that is a necessary aspect of any creative act. "The way of life is wonderful: it is by abandonment," Emerson affirms at the end of "Circles," for "the one thing we seek with insatiable desire is to forget ourselves, to be surprised out of our propriety, to lose our sempiternal memory, and to do something without knowing how or why; in short, to draw a new circle."[41] This rather rhapsodic assertion can be clarified if we consider that drawing a new circle means to facilitate, through one's actions, the emergence of a new reality beyond our existing reality. An actor or inventor can indeed have intentions guiding his or her efforts to create a new tool or idea, but to the extent that an act is truly creative, to the extent that it helps create a truly novel result, that result by definition is different from previous utilities or perceptions, and thus beyond merely individual intention. Emerson describes this suprapersonal aspect of invention in an 1826 journal entry:

> I pursue my speculations with confidence & tho' I can discern no remoter conclusion I doubt not the train I commence extends farther than I see as the first artificer of glass did not know he was instructing men in astronomy & restoring sight to those from whom nature had taken it. There is no thought which is not seed as well as fruit. It spawns like fish.[42]

Creation here consists in making something the full use of which you cannot know, in exceeding or transcending a current horizon of utility. This nonintentional aspect of invention literally helps to reshape reality: the first "artificer" in glass could not *foresee* how the telescope would change how *we see* the universe, any more than the inventor of the steam engine could intend all the changes in the "realities" of space and time brought by the railroad.[43] The unforeseeable, alien power of novel

creation is depicted even more strikingly in the following passage from
"Self-Reliance":

> When good is near you, when you have life in yourself, it is not by
> any known or accustomed way; you shall not discern the foot-prints
> of any other; you shall not see the face of man; you shall not hear any
> name,—the way, the thought, the good, shall be wholly strange and
> new. It shall exclude example and experience. You take the way from
> man, not to man.[44]

Creative change, this passage suggests, always entails a move away from
the known, away from the already conceptualized and humanized; indeed, Emerson's trope of leaving behind all traces of human identity suggests that each time we encounter a new reality, it forces us to reconceive
ourselves, our concept of the human, as well.

Recalling, however, Emerson's argument in "The Conservative" that
there is no simple way to escape the limits of one's cultural moment—
that one must use "the Actual order of things, in order to disuse it"—it is
clear that Emersonian abandonment must be a process of transcendence
that emerges from within, and augments, the energies of cultural change
already nascent in a historical moment. In other words, "abandonment"
describes the fact that an individual's creative power comes from combining his or her own acts and intentions with larger forces of cultural
change that we can influence, but never totally control. "Do your work,
and I shall know you," Emerson writes in "Self-Reliance," but he frequently celebrates those individuals who let society work for them, who
are best able to recognize, harness and direct the energies and desires of
other individuals composing society. Thus, in his underappreciated essay
on Shakespeare, Emerson describes "the greatest genius" as "the most
indebted man":[45]

> He finds himself in the river of the thoughts and events, forced on-
> ward by the ideas and necessities of his contemporaries. He stands
> where all the eyes of men look one way, and their hands all point
> in the direction which he should go. . . . The world has brought him
> thus far on his way. The human race has gone out before him, sunk
> the hills, filled the hollows, and bridged the rivers. Men, nations, po-
> ets, artisans, women, all have worked for him, and he enters into their
> labors. Choose any other thing, out of the line of tendency, out of the
> national feeling and history, and he would have to do all for himself:
> his powers would be expended in the first preparations. Great genial
> power, one would almost say, consists in not being original at all; in

being altogether receptive; in letting the world do all, and suffering the spirit of the hour to pass unobstructed through the mind.[46]

Elaborating on his suggestion from "Self-Reliance," that trusting yourself requires "accept[ing] the place the divine providence has found for you, the society of your contemporaries, the connection of events," Emerson here portrays individual vocation or power as a process of merging one's unique talents with the opportunities for action embodied in one's social environment. Culture, as is typical in Emerson, is here described as both a constraining limitation and a source of tremendous power. In one sense, society severely limits and determines the form and direction of an individual's efforts: if one acted "out of the line of tendency" of the historical moment, "he would have to do all for himself." These constraints of culture, however, also bring a potent compensation: Emerson's "greatest genius," by bringing his own talents to bear on the needs of the moment, by allowing his own efforts to be enlisted in the "spirit of the hour," not only finds exercise and fulfillment for his personal faculties, but participates in, and is augmented by, a power far beyond his merely individual force.

Clearly, "abandonment" so conceived, as an enlistment of one's own energies in larger currents of cultural change, is not incompatible with an ethics of cultivating individual power, but rather is a means to it. As such, it is not incompatible with the second mode encompassed by Emerson's model of vocation—namely, an ethics of "concentration" that suggests that society's resources for facilitating a diversity of human activities are valuable because they allow individuals to focus and train their efforts in some specialized area of activity, thereby maximizing their performative powers. In the opening paragraph of his essay "Power," for instance, Emerson proclaims that "A cultivated man, wise to know and bold to perform, is the end to which nature works." As the essay progresses, Emerson insists that self-cultivation is of necessity largely a matter of so focusing one's efforts as to achieve this requisite knowledge and boldness of performance: "The friction in nature is so enormous that we cannot spare any power. It is not a question to express our thought, to elect our way, but to overcome resistances of the medium and material in everything we do. Hence the use of drill, and the worthlessness of amateurs to cope with practitioners." If pursuing a vocation can be considered a matter of "drill," of developing the facility needed to overcome the resistances of one's medium, Emerson also indicates, in an argument that strikingly anticipates Nietzsche's philosophy, that such drill facilitates a process of sublimation, of "stopping off decisively our miscellaneous activity, and concentrating our force on one or a few points; as the gardener, by severe pruning, forces the sap of the tree into one or two vigorous limbs, instead of suffering it to spindle into a sheaf of twigs."[47]

Like Nietzsche, Emerson suggests that such a truncation of one's pursuits is not a limitation of self, but a path to an increased and higher form of power, as is clear in the logic of sublimation that concludes his essay "Wealth":

> The true thrift is always to spend on the higher plane; to invest and invest, with keener avarice, that he may spend in spiritual creation, and not in augmenting animal existence. Nor is the man enriched, in repeating the old experiments of animal sensation, nor unless through new powers and ascending pleasures, he knows himself by the actual experience of higher good, to be already on the way to the highest.[48]

An ethics of concentration, of "drill" and "routine,"[49] Emerson insists, need not be static or constraining, but can be a means to the progression, growth and melioration of self—to a "self-overcoming," in Nietzsche's terms. And yet, one can easily feel that this ethic of concentration exists in some tension with the ethic of abandonment as it is expressed in Emerson's example of the "sturdy lad from New Hampshire or Vermont" discussed above: that is, as a willingness to pursue, experimentally, a range of pursuits, one after the other. Emerson himself clearly is concerned with the possibility that vocational concentration may become a fragmenting and stultifying cage. In "The American Scholar," he argues that individuals "in the *divided* or social state" of specialized labor "strut about so many walking monsters,—a good finger, a neck, a stomach, an elbow, but never a man," and concludes that "the individual, to possess himself, must sometimes return from his own labor to embrace all other laborers."[50]

As I note below in my discussion of his views on the division of labor, Emerson believes it would be "pedantic" to suggest that each individual should renounce the tremendous power of specialized activity in order to perform, for him or herself, the full range of society's occupations. He does, however, argue that the same resources of culture that allow individuals to focus on specific vocations can and should be used to mitigate the more pernicious effects of such specialization. In his essay "Culture," Emerson suggests that "culture" construed as the cultivation of self requires a broad familiarity with "culture" construed as society's transmitted body of knowledge, practices, and artifacts: "Culture is the suggestion, from certain best thoughts, that a man has a range of affinities, through which he can modulate the violence of any master-tones that have a droning preponderance in his scale, and succor himself against himself." By providing examples of creative acts from the full spectrum of human endeavor, culture invites the individual to develop a variety of talents that will help discipline his or her "dominant talent."[51] Crucially, Emerson insists, the goal of culture is not to subdue the energy of that dominant talent, but to refine and harness it:

> The student we speak to must have a motherwit invincible by his culture, which uses all books, arts, facilities, and elegancies of intercourse, but is never subdued and lost in them. He only is a well-made man who has a good determination. And the end of culture is not to destroy this, God forbid! but to train away all impediment and mixture, and leave nothing but pure power.[52]

This passage neatly expresses Emerson's belief that a diversity and a concentration of activity should be complementary. Not only can the experience of engaging a variety of pursuits save one from the monomaniacal cramp of one's primary task, but a broader culture, far from diluting that primary talent, can develop a greater facility in deploying it.

I want to approach this dynamic between abandonment and concentration from one last perspective, by considering briefly the relation between action and thought in Emerson's ethics. George Kateb, in a study that offers an eloquent case for Emerson's importance as a theorist of "democratic individuality," argues that a hierarchy exists in Emerson's thought between what Kateb terms "mental" and "active" self-reliance. According to Kateb, Emerson values most those forms of individuality that transcend any narrow egotism in order to cultivate a "receptivity" or openness to the world around us.[53] Applying this standard, Kateb posits several crucial distinctions within Emersonian self-reliance. First, under the rubric of "active" self-reliance, Kateb identifies two competing modes of identity: on the one hand, a fluid self whose "movement through life" is "a restless, unfixed," and "unceasing creation and abandonment of channels and positions," and, on the other, a self defined by its primary vocation or work, by its "perfect adherence to one commitment." Kateb argues that such vocational commitment is the "highest form of active self-reliance," because it involves a surrendering of one's ego, an

abandonment to one's work. Thus far, Kateb's approach is wholly consonant with the dynamic between abandonment and concentration I have
sketched above. But Kateb further argues that such an active, vocational
self-reliance—though it is "the project of practical democracy" that "can
never and should never be completely or continuously abandoned"—is
too beset by an inescapable partiality to attain the receptivity of true
self-reliance, which only can be attained in thought: "the contempla-
tive mind can be more truly self-reliant than a person striving for self-
reliance in the world," Kateb concludes, and active self-reliance "seems
incomplete or inadequate unless one makes the effort to disclose it and
make it signify, and such an effort of contemplation and interpretation is
of course a mental one." "Mental" self-reliance, as Kateb defines it, is the
ability sympathetically and imaginatively to entertain the various and
often antagonistic ideas and aspects that compose our world, an ability exemplified in the "perspectivist" method of Emerson's essays, which
give voice to or "impersonate" one perspective after another.[54]

Kateb's formulation is of great value, both in the philosophical complexity it grants to Emerson's vision of the self, and in the ethical significance it locates in Emerson's embrace of nonegotistical receptivity,
which constitutes a democratic and pluralistic mandate to recognize
the particulars of our world as innately valuable. Yet Kateb's dichotomy
between active and mental self-reliance, I believe, is misleading: action
and thought are better construed as another manifestation of the tension between concentration and abandonment that I have discussed in
this section. Kateb relegates this tension mainly to the realm of "active"
self-reliance, and implies that thought constitutes a realm of greater detachment and liberation. I would stress that any such differences are a
matter of degree, not kind. We should recall, after all, Emerson's claim
that "Every thought is also a prison," or that when an individual has
"once acted or spoken with eclat, he is a committed person": that is, expressing or even "impersonating" a thought is, for Emerson, potentially
as narrowing or confining as an action, indeed, is *itself* a kind of action.[55] While Kateb is surely correct that, for Emerson, action by itself,
without translation into thought or consummation as knowledge, is
incomplete, yet the converse is also true: thought is barren and stultifying if it is not in turn translated into new action. If thought provides
a liberating detachment from the constraints of particular acts, action also revitalizes the self by providing a liberating abandonment of

the limits of each consummating thought, as Emerson insists in "The American Scholar":

> The mind now thinks; now acts; and each fit reproduces the other. When the artist has exhausted his materials, when the fancy no longer paints, when thoughts are no longer apprehended, and books are a weariness,—he has always the resource, *to live.* Character is higher than intellect. Thinking is the function. Living is the functionary. The stream retreats to its source. A great soul will be strong to live, as well as strong to think. Does he lack organ or medium to impart his truths? He can still fall back on this elemental force of living them. This is a total act. Thinking is a partial act.[56]

This passage describes action and thought as inseparable: they are "fits" that "reproduce" each other, alternate seizures or spasms in our driving impulse to power, expression, and knowledge. Far from valorizing thought over action, as Kateb argues, Emerson here expresses the pragmatic view that thought and action are best conceived as complementary forms or phases of experience: if thinking derives conclusions and generalizations from experience, the value of such thoughts lies in their ability to redirect us to engage the particulars of experience, in our ability to put them into practice in our lives. As Dewey puts it, our ideas are both consummatory *and* instrumental.

As I hope to show later in this chapter, this question of how Emerson depicts the relation between action and thought has a significant impact on how one estimates the political and ethical consequences of his individualism. For to assert, as Kateb does, that the highest form of individuality lies in a mental cultivation of receptivity that is compromised by the commitments of action, is to perpetuate (albeit in a much more sophisticated form) the commonplace view that Emerson resists political or reformist action because it entails an unacceptable loss of self-reliance—because to commit one's self to active efforts at reforming our world is necessarily to sacrifice one's highest self to others. Similarly, since he conceives of it as detached from efforts to engage and reshape the world, Kateb ultimately suggests that the highest, "mental" form of self-reliance—even though it instills a reverence for otherness—is ethically untenable, that individualism is a luxury that must be sacrificed to more prosaic efforts to create just conditions for others.[57] By contrast, if one sees in Emerson a more pragmatic attitude toward action, his ethics appear as an attempt to articulate a synthesis in which one's efforts to engage and reform the world are indispensable to the highest self-cultivation, in which responsibility to one's self can be reconciled with one's responsibilities to others. Although his efforts to articulate such an ethics lead Emerson to critique, in a Nietzschean fashion, the equation of morality with sacrificing one's self for others, they also lead him to presage, in important ways, Dewey's synthesis of individuality and community.

"I Do Not Wish to Expiate, but to Live": Emerson's Nietzschean Critique of Morality

The most fraught issue with which any individualist ethics must contend is how to justify the morality of individualized activity—especially given the almost unquestioned equation, within the Judeo-Christian religious tradition, of moral action with a renunciation of self for the benefit of others. Unquestionably the most famous and trenchant critic of this renunciatory morality is Friedrich Nietzsche, who argues that morality must be reconceived not in absolutist terms of good and evil, but in terms commensurate with the "will to power," the impulse to expression, growth, and overcoming that, according to Nietzsche, drives all life. Yet before Nietzsche there was Emerson, who, as scholars have only in recent years more widely documented, profoundly influenced the German philosopher.[58] Indeed, the ethics of self-culture and vocation that I have explored in this chapter led Emerson to question, in terms quite similar to Nietzsche's, many of Western culture's basic assumptions about what constitutes the morality or goodness of one's actions. In rejecting an absolutist concept of justice, and locating value instead in the cultivation of self that individuals can achieve within the tragic limits of our world; in asserting that finding one's true vocation requires resisting and moving beyond the conformities of inherited culture—including definitions of goodness; and in concluding that we can truly help others only by inspiring them to cultivate powers of their own, Emerson pointed the way toward redefining morality not as renunciation, but in affirmative, generative terms of power and growth, and, subsequently, pointed the way toward rethinking the ethical relations between self and others.

Both Emerson and Nietzsche argue that the security promised by an absolutist concept of morality, though craved by human weakness, is actually hostile to life: it defines morality in negative, renunciatory

terms, turning people against their own natural impulses and imposing a rigid concept of "good" on the diversity of their unique creative
possibilities. In a sequence from *The Genealogy of Morals* that recalls—
and perhaps was inspired by—the opening of "Compensation" discussed
above, Nietzsche offers a parallel critique of those who live in expectation of the Last Judgment: "In faith in what? In love of what? In hope of
what?—These weak people—some day or other they too intend to be the
strong, there is no doubt of that" (48). To answer this question—"*what* is
it that constitutes the bliss of this Paradise?"—Nietzsche quotes a long,
grisly description by Thomas Aquinas of the torments of the damned,
presented as a spectacle to the saved, "*in order that their bliss be more
delightful for them.*"[59] For Nietzsche, this example exposes the perverse
psychology involved in the traditional conception of "goodness"—which
he labels as a morality of "ressentiment."[60] By defining the natural world
and human instincts as evil, and thus equating goodness with expiatory
suffering and a renunciation of strength, "the weak" are able to gain not
only a sense of meaning for their suffering, but also a sense of superiority and power over those who are strong enough to thrive in the world.
Traditional morality fulfills "the will of the weak to represent *some*
form of superiority": "They monopolize virtue, these weak, hopelessly
sick people, there is no doubt of it: 'we alone are the good and just,' they
say. . . . [H]ow ready they themselves are at bottom to *make* one pay; how
they crave to be *hangmen*."[61]

Beyond his evident disgust at the pettiness of such a morality, at the
will to domination hiding behind a pretense of piety, Nietzsche is even
more aghast at the tremendous suffering that "sick" humanity has in-
flicted upon itself to secure this concept of goodness. In his analysis of
the "ascetic ideal," Nietzsche acknowledges that it does serve life, but
only in a perverse and costly fashion. The ascetic ideal gives meaning to
humanity's earthly sufferings by interpreting the fallen world as a punishment for human sinfulness, and may thus offer people the strength to
disdain the limitations and sorrows of our world (as in the extreme case
of the martyred saint). However, Nietzsche insists a morality founded on
renunciation is intolerably hostile to life: according to the ascetic ideal,
life "opposes and excludes" goodness, "*unless* it turn against itself, *deny
itself:* in that case, the case of the ascetic life, life counts as a bridge to
that other mode of existence." So "monstrous a mode of valuation" forces
men to view their own natures, and the natural world, as corrupt and

evil, with the result that "the animal 'man' finally learns to be ashamed of all his instincts."[62] Moreover, an absolute concept of good leads to constraining, conformist definitions of moral behavior. A healthier morality, one not hostile to the impulsive springs of human life, would need to encourage each individual to forge a good life out of his or her unique talents and drives. A nonabsolutist morality, fully realized, would imply a wholly individualized standard of value. Thus Nietzsche revises the classic dictum, "virtue is the health of the soul," as "'*your* virtue is the health of *your* soul.' For there is no health as such, and all attempts to define a thing that way have been wretched failures. Even the determination of what is healthy for your *body* depends on your goal, your horizon, your energies, your impulses, your errors, and above all the ideals and phantasms of your soul."[63]

When one turns from such arguments to "Self-Reliance," familiar passages take on a decidedly Nietzschean tone, as Emerson prefigures many aspects of Nietzsche's critique of renunciatory morality:

> Virtues are, in the popular estimate, rather the exception than the rule. There is the man *and* his virtues. Men do what is called a good action, as some piece of courage or charity, much as they would pay a fine in expiation of daily non-appearance on parade. Their works are done as an apology or extenuation of their living in the world,—as invalids and the insane pay a high board. Their virtues are penances. I do not wish to expiate, but to live. My life is for itself and not for a spectacle. I much prefer that it should be of a lower strain, so it be genuine and equal, than that it should be glittering and unsteady. I wish it to be sound and sweet, and not to need diet and bleeding.[64]

Traditional morality—which associates "good" with the absolute (as in God, or the perfect justice of a heavenly reward) and thus opposes it to our material existence—too often translates into a backwards attitude toward moral behavior. It cordons off morality into a small sector of our lives, conceding the immorality of the majority of our actions. Morality becomes "the exception" rather than the "rule," divorced from the main activities of our life: "there is the man, *and* his virtues." Morality is then essentially renunciatory: "virtues" become "penances," an "apology" for "living in the world." Such a morality does not effectively help us live more morally, for it only reinforces the expectation that our material existence is corrupt—that it will require expiation. Emerson instead insists that we should strive to make our whole lives healthy and moral, "genuine and equal," "sound and sweet," so as "not to need diet and bleeding."

When Emerson asserts that he does "not want to expiate, but to live," he is concerned, like Nietzsche, that our absolute concepts of morality stifle life by preventing us from seeing and developing our own unique creative possibilities:

> Whoso would be a man must be a nonconformist. He who would gather immortal palms must not be hindered by the name of goodness, but must explore if it be goodness. Nothing is at last sacred but the integrity of your own mind. Absolve you to yourself, and you shall have the suffrage of the world. I remember an answer which when quite young I was prompted to make to a valued adviser, who was wont to importune me with the dear old doctrines of the church. On my saying, What have I to do with the sacredness of traditions, if I live wholly from within? my friend suggested,—"But these impulses may be from below, not from above." I replied, "They do not seem to be to be such; but if I am the Devil's child, I will live then from the Devil." No law can be sacred to me but that of my nature. Good and bad are but names very readily transferable to that or this; the only right is what is after my constitution, the only wrong what is against it. A man is to carry himself in the presence of all opposition, as if every thing were titular and ephemeral but he. I am ashamed to think how easily we capitulate to badges and names, to large societies and dead institutions.[65]

Emerson here argues for a standard of value that is consonant with, that encourages, each individual's active and creative impulses: in asserting that "nothing is at last sacred but the integrity of your own mind" and that "the only right is what is after my constitution," he is insisting that value must be located in our active lives, in the development of our human capacities. Traditional morality, trapped in absolutist notions of good and evil, reduces the variety of human powers and possibilities into an artificial dichotomy: according to Emerson's "valued adviser," human impulses come from "above" or "below," they are pure or corrupt, pious or sensualist. Such a morality is destructive, because the development of value in life simply does not follow such rigid categories: "Power is in nature the essential measure of right," Emerson writes later in the essay, and a healthy morality must work with, and not against, this natural tendency to growth and power. Each individual embodies new possibilities for life: "The power which resides in him is new in nature," Emerson affirms;

yet, he complains, "We but half express ourselves, and are ashamed of that divine idea which each of us represents. It may be safely trusted as proportionate and of good issues, so it be faithfully imparted, but God will not have his work made manifest by cowards."[66] As is evident from Emerson's reported dialogue with his valued adviser, we are "ashamed" to seek morality in the expression of our talents in large part because of society's rigid concepts of morality: we are "hindered by the name of goodness," and "capitulate to badges and names, to large societies and dead institutions."

It is crucial to stress that an ethics that attempts to acknowledge and exploit the instinct of power that pervades all life need not be a lawless or indiscriminate celebration of impulse. Neither Nietzsche nor Emerson renounces all moral valuation—or suggests that all human instincts ought to be indiscriminately indulged. Emerson is at pains to stress this point in "Self-Reliance":

> The populace think that your rejection of popular standards is a rejection of all standard, and mere antinomianism; and the bold sensualist will use the name of philosophy to gild his crimes. But the law of consciousness abides. There are two confessionals, in one or the other of which we must be shriven. You may fulfil your round of duties by clearing yourself in the *direct*, or, in the *reflex* way. Consider whether you have satisfied your relations to father, mother, cousin, neighbour, town, cat, and dog; whether any of these can upbraid you. But I may also neglect this reflex standard and absolve me to myself. I have my own stern claims and perfect circle. It denies the name of duty to many offices that are called duties. But if I can discharge its debts, it enables me to dispense with the popular code. If any one imagines that this law is lax, let him keep its commandment one day.[67]

This passage does not reject moral responsibility; it insists we "must be shriven" in one of two fashions. There is the conventional method of measuring yourself against the expectations that society imposes on you. The problem with such a "reflex" standard, as Emerson argues in his critique of conventional "virtue" discussed above, is that it threatens to define morality as something divorced from your own most essential work, as "expiation" instead of "life." At the least, a strictly conventional sense of morality will distract you, as Emerson suggests by comically, yet affectionately, running his list of domestic duties to "cousin, neighbour, cat, and dog." He does not reject such responsibilities, but insists, "these relations I must fill after a new and unprecedented way." Instead, he asserts the viability of a healthier moral standard that sees a creative and active human life as a sufficient moral end. To demand of yourself that your life's work justify your existence—to "absolve me to myself" as he puts it—imposes a strict responsibility to cultivate your powers to their fullest: "I have my own stern claims and perfect circle," he insists. Rejecting conventional morality is no simple liberation, but requires the courage to define a moral life without the security of society's definitions: "truly it demands something godlike in him who has cast off the common motives of humanity, and has ventured to trust himself for a task-master" Emerson concludes, voicing a sentiment that could have come straight from Nietzsche.[68]

Indeed, one of the major threads connecting Emerson and Nietzsche is their shared insight, and obsession, that the conventionalized, codified values that culture offers individuals provide a security that is comforting but ultimately harmful, for it allows people to avoid the activity that is the only means for developing their talents and strength. "I know," Nietzsche writes,

> there are a hundred decent and praiseworthy ways of losing *my own way*, and they are all truly highly "moral"! Indeed, those who now preach the morality of pity even take the view that precisely this and only this is moral—to lose one's *own* way in order to come to the assistance of a neighbor. I know just as certainly that I only need to expose myself to the sight of some genuine distress and I am lost. . . . All such arousing of pity and calling for help is secretly seductive, for our "own way" is too hard and demanding and too remote from the love and gratitude of others, and we do not really mind escaping from it— and from our very own conscience—to flee into the conscience of others and into the lovely temple of the "religion of pity."[69]

Much like Emerson's critique of the "reflex" standard of morality (and reminiscent of passages in which Emerson critiques pity[70]),Nietzsche here argues that traditional (Christian) morality, which equates goodness exclusively with sacrificing one's own work and strength for the sake of others, provides a respectable and secure escape from the strenuous task of finding sufficient value in ourselves, in our own activity. Nietzsche, again like Emerson,[71] understands the human emotion behind pity; he knows he is "lost" if confronted by "genuine distress," and he does not deny that an ethics of pity makes people "good" in a certain way: "If one intends it to convey that such a system of treatment"—that offered by ascetic morality—"has *improved* men, I shall not argue: only I should have to add what 'improved' signifies to me—the same thing as 'tamed,' 'weakened,' discouraged . . . when such a system is chiefly applied to the sick, distressed, and depressed, it invariably makes them *sicker*, even if it does 'improve' them."[72] Nietzsche impels us to recognize that a morality of self-sacrifice is neither absolute nor inevitable, and, judged on its relative merits, is in many ways harmful for both the bestower and recipient of pity.

But how, specifically, are we to conceive an individualized ethics of power that is *not* a mere lawlessness, the "stern claims and perfect circle" that Emerson describes? For both Emerson and Nietzsche, the answer lies in an ethics of sublimation or, as Nietzsche puts it, "self-overcoming," in which our energies are trained and redirected, so that they find expression while being harnessed for a "higher" activity.[73] First, it must be repeated that, for Emerson and Nietzsche, a morality that simply renounces our impulses to power cannot effectively create new human values or facilitate healthy human life. "Goodness," Nietzsche would teach us, is not some absolute beyond our world, but rather resides in benefits and powers created within our world, within the processes of growth and change that drive life. History, he argues, provides numerous examples of new values emerging from the conflicts between, and transformation of, older impulses. Here, again, Nietzsche finds an important precursor in Emerson, who writes in his essay "Considerations by the Way" that "the good of evil" is "the first lesson of history": "most of the great results of history are brought about by discreditable means," driven at least in part by base human impulses such as "selfishness, fraud, and conspiracy":[74]

> The right partisan is a heady narrow man, who, because he does not see many things, sees some one thing with heat and exaggeration, . . . [and thus] seems inspired, and a godsend to those who wish to magnify the matter, and carry a point. Better, certainly, if we could secure the strength and fire which rude, passionate men bring into society, quite clear of their vices. But who dares draw out the linchpin from the wagon-wheel?[75]

Nature, including humankind, simply cannot do without the unruly energies that impel life and change: "Passion, though a bad regulator, is a powerful spring." Thus we must seek morality not in the suppression of our impulses to power, but rather in the modulation, discipline and transformation of them: "there is no man who is not at some time indebted to his vices. . . . We only insist that the man meliorate, and that the plant grow upward, and convert the base into the better nature."[76]

Much as Emerson rejects a renunciatory ethics of "expiation" for an ethics of "living"—an ethics governed by the "stern claims and perfect circle" of one's own vocation—so Nietzsche makes it clear that he does not reject all morality, but instead demands that morality must serve the affirmative, creative goal of expanding our human capacities:

> At bottom I abhor all those moralities which say: "Do not do this! Renounce! Overcome yourself!" But I am well disposed toward those moralities which goad me to do something and do it again, from morning till evening, and then to dream of it at night, and to think of nothing except doing this *well*, as *I* alone can do it. When one lives like that, one thing after another that simply does not belong to such a life drops off. . . . What we do should determine what we forego; by doing we forego—that is how I like it, that is my *placitum*. But I do not wish to strive with open eyes for my own impoverishment; I do not like negative virtues—virtues whose very essence is to negate and deny oneself something.[77]

The crucial distinction, then, is between a morality that is essentially negative—that views the repression of "bad" human instincts as a moral end in itself—and an affirmative morality that exploits the active impulses of human life, that encourages us to train and discipline our human faculties in order to refine and strengthen them. Taking the chaste life of the true philosopher as his example, Nietzsche insists that an affirmative morality will indeed require a willful modulation and even renunciation of certain human impulses: crucially, however, the philosopher's chastity does not reflect "any kind of ascetic scruple or hatred of the senses"— "he does not deny 'existence,' he rather affirms *his* existence and *only* his existence." There is nothing moral per se in renunciation: it is only valuable in the context of an individual's life, if it enhances his or her active existence: "Every animal—therefore *la bete philosophe*, too—instinctively strives for an optimum of favorable conditions under which it can expend all its strength and achieve its maximal feeling of power. . . . Thus the philosopher abhors *marriage*, together with that which might persuade to it—marriage being a hindrance and calamity on his path to the optimum."[78] The ethic Nietzsche describes here has striking affinities to that which Emerson depicts in the passage from "Culture" discussed earlier.

In each case, virtue is not found by renouncing human impulses; rather, value emerges out of a struggle between the variety of human impulses— whether, as Nietzsche describes, one lets nonessential energies "drop off" as one focuses more intensely on one's dominant talent,[79] or, as Emerson describes, one cultivates a broader range of human affinities in order to temper and refine that dominant talent. Moreover, both writers insist that the increased vitality of human activity is itself a sufficient moral end. Emerson's claim that culture should aim to "train away all impediment and mixture, and leave nothing but pure power," is echoed by Nietzsche's view that the primary good we seek in life is to "expend" our "strength" and attain our "maximal feeling of power."

"There Are No Common Men": Community, Individuality, Pluralism

If Emerson suggests that morality must be reconceived in terms of an ethics of power and self-cultivation, and if this ethics leads him to be skeptical of the moralities of pity, giving, and self-sacrifice, this does not mean that he rejects the idea of community or the crucial influence that other people have upon the individual. Yet Emerson's location of value in self-cultivation undoubtedly problematizes many traditional conceptions of community that stress shared, codified group values and duties. Instead, Emerson envisions a community comprising individuals who encourage and antagonize each other by pursuing their varied vocations. While this vision of community is in many ways unsettling and strange, it expresses attitudes that are important to any possible democratic notions of community: namely, an egalitarian faith in the sufficient value of each individual's life and talents, and a pluralistic rationale for the necessity of celebrating and encouraging diversity.

The familiar image of Emerson as the champion of self-reliance too often has obscured the fact that he views the influence of other people as absolutely essential to the self: in our friends, in the diverse energies of our society or "the times," in works of genius, and in language itself, the individual is continually stimulated by others. Like many Romantic thinkers, Emerson subscribes to an incredibly lofty and demanding ideal of friendship,[80] a faith in the ability of another to help reveal and draw out one's own ideal potential:

> There is a power in love to divine another's destiny better than that other can, and, by heroic encouragements, hold him to his task. What

has friendship so signal as its sublime attraction to whatever virtue is in us? We will never more think cheaply of ourselves, or of life. We are piqued to some purpose, and the industry of the diggers on the railroad will not again shame us.[81]

That the friend's love "piques" one to a purpose indicates how inseparably, for Emerson, true affection is intermixed with antagonism. "Better be a nettle in the side of your friend than his echo,"[82] he writes. True friends are those who goad us from some superior height, whose power and virtue apprise us of our shortcomings and inspire us to acts of self-overcoming or transcendence:

> The continual effort to raise himself above himself, to work a pitch above his last height, betrays itself in man's relations. We thirst for approbation, yet cannot forgive the approver. The sweet of nature is love; yet, if I have a friend I am tormented by my imperfections. The love of me accuses the other party. If he were high enough to slight me, then could I love him, and rise by my affection to new heights. A man's growth is seen in the successive choirs of his friends. For every friend whom he loses for truth, he gains a better.[83]

These psychological dynamics that Emerson locates in friendship can seem either perverse or simply honest. Emerson frankly acknowledges that affection is intermixed with our desire for power: one admires those whom one feels to be superior, and strives to merit their affection by living up to their example, and, subsequently, one's growth as an individual causes old affections to loosen as new ones are formed.

This model of human attraction, it is true, has a cold edge from which Emerson does not shrink:

> Men cease to interest us when we find their limitations. The only sin is limitation. As soon as you once come up with a man's limitations, it is all over with him. Has he talents? has he enterprise? has he knowledge? it boots not. Infinitely alluring and attractive was he to you yesterday, a great hope, a sea to swim in; now, you have found his shores, found it a pond, and you care not if you never see it again.[84]

Yet Emerson would persuade us that such dynamics of human interaction are not finally exploitative, but rather exemplify the healthy model of society: if we leave others behind, we do so to form new, more true and vital relationships, and we encourage those from whom we part to grow into new, more vital relationships of their own. Characteristically,

Emerson's acknowledgment of the limitation we discover in all people is tempered by a balancing affirmation of growth and possibility. Emerson has faith that all individuals are capable of responding to the antagonism of true friendship by awakening to their own unrealized potential: "every man has at intervals the grace to scorn his performances," so that he "puts himself on the side of his enemies, listening gladly to what they say of him, and accusing himself of the same things."[85] This passage explains why Emerson describes the friend as a "beautiful enemy," and it is such antagonistic fellowship, Emerson insists, that all people at bottom crave from society: "Men are in all ways better than they seem. . . . What is it we heartily wish of each other? Is it to be pleased and flattered? No, but to be convicted and exposed, to be shamed out of our nonsense of all kinds, and made men of, instead of ghosts and phantoms."[86]

This model of friendship serves as Emerson's paradigm for all healthy social relations. The attraction that works of genius have for us, for instance, is that they supply the highest office of friendship. There is "no compliment," Emerson writes, "like the addressing to a human being thoughts out of a certain height, and presupposing his intelligence. This honor, which is possible in personal intercourse scarcely twice in a lifetime, genius perpetually pays."[87] Yet if works of genius provide a compensation for the difficulty of finding true friendship in society, even geniuses betray the limitation that marks all humanity: "Every hero becomes a bore at last," Emerson notes with humor—and with more relief than disappointment. The true benefits of society, then, must be sought in diversity, in the inspiration and vitalization we receive from the variety of individuals who compose our society: "Ah! yonder in the horizon is our help:—other great men, new qualities, counterweights and checks on each other. We cloy of the honey of each peculiar greatness."[88] This pattern can be seen in Emerson's description of "conversation," which serves as another model for Emersonian community:

> Conversation is a game of circles. . . . The parties are not to be judged by the spirit they partake and even express under this Pentecost. To-morrow they will have receded from this high-water mark. To-morrow you shall find them stooping under the old pack-saddles. Yet let us enjoy the cloven flame whilst it glows on our walls. When each new speaker strikes a new light, emancipates us from the oppression of the last speaker, to oppress us with the greatness and exclusiveness of his own thought, then yields us to another redeemer, we seem to recover our rights, to become men.[89]

The influence of each powerful actor we encounter if liberating is also limiting; yet each powerful act inspires new acts that replace, counter, and complement it. Society so conceived as a "game of circles"—as a process of following upon, furthering, and bettering acts of others with acts of one's own—energizes and augments the powers of its individual members. Such diversity of activity is, in Emerson's vision, necessary to the life of a community and to the lives of individuals within that community.

Needless to say, Emerson is keenly aware of the obstacles to realizing this ideal. For if society is a source of creative antagonism that can inspire individuals to the vocations that will cultivate their unique talents, society is also, Emerson continually reminds us, a source of repressive conformity, of prescribed customs, occupations, duties, and moralities that threaten to divert individuals from finding their own authentic modes of living. To be a vital member of a community requires, for Emerson, that one exist in healthy tension or conflict with that community: "Whoso would be a man"—or, to translate Emerson's sexist language, who would be an authentic, vital individual—"must be a nonconformist." Thus the constraints of community are the target of some of Emerson's most blistering and fascinating rhetorical performances, as he strives to find literary strategies for expressing such nonconformist resistance.

As an example, consider the paragraph from "Self-Reliance" that opens with the above-quoted assertion that manhood requires nonconformism. The possibilities and limits of being a nonconforming member of society are explored in this paragraph through a remarkable series of reported—or imagined—spoken encounters. The first is the exchange with the religious advisor already discussed in the section on Emerson and Nietzsche above. What I now want to call attention to is the *tone* of this exchange: Emerson expresses a bemused fondness toward the venerable "valued adviser" who was "wont to importune me with the dear old doctrines of the church." The conventional moralities of society can seem so reasonable: to reject them would be like arguing with your grandfather. So what to do? Again, the tone of Emerson's response suggests an answer: "'They do not seem to be to be such; but if I am the Devil's child, then I will live then from the Devil.' . . . Good and bad are but names very transferable to that or this." In literal terms, this is blasphemous, but it is delivered in a strangely placid tone, almost with a shrug of the shoulders, as if to say, "If you want to call it immoral, no problem, it doesn't faze me." Tonally, Emerson is trying to adopt a cool detachment, the kind of "nonchalance" and "good humored inflexibility" he speaks of earlier in the essay.[90]

This experiment, however, doesn't last long. Emerson next questions how far one can maintain such good-humored detachment, precisely because conventional morality always seems so reasonable: "Every decent and well-spoken individual affects and sways me more than is right," he complains. It is so easy to fall in line and do all the things that society associates with a proper life, Emerson seems to be saying, and it is the good people, with good causes, who can really suck you in. So Emerson abruptly shifts his tone mid paragraph, and adopts another voice, another strategy. "I ought to go upright and vital, and speak the rude truth in all ways," he proclaims, and then delivers another series of imagined dialogues, in which he practices this ethic of "speaking the rude truth":

> If malice and vanity wear the coat of philanthropy shall that pass? If an angry bigot assumes this bountiful cause of Abolition, and comes to me with his last news from Barbadoes, why should I not say to him, "Go love thy infant; love thy wood-chopper: be good-natured and modest: have that grace; and never varnish your hard, uncharitable ambition with this incredible tenderness for black folk a thousand miles off. Thy love afar is spite at home." Rough and graceless would be such greeting, but truth is handsomer than the affectation of love. Your goodness must have some edge to it,—else it is none. The doctrine of hatred must be preached as the counteraction of the doctrine of love when that pules and whines. I shun father and mother and wife and brother, when my genius calls me. I would write on the lintels of the door-post *Whim.* I hope it is somewhat better than whim at last, but we cannot spend the day in explanation. Expect me not to show cause why I seek or why I exclude company. Then again, do not tell me, as a good man did to-day, of my obligation to put all poor men in good situations. Are they *my* poor? I tell thee, thou foolish philanthropist, that I grudge the dollar, the dime, the cent, I give to such men as do not belong to me and to whom I do not belong. There is a class of persons to whom by all spiritual affinity I am bought and sold; for them I will go to prison, if need be; but your miscellaneous popular charities; the education at college of fools; the building of meeting houses to the vain end to which many now stand; alms to sots; and the thousandfold Relief Societies;—though I confess with shame I sometimes succumb and give the dollar, it is a wicked dollar which by and by I shall have the manhood to withhold.[91]

Clearly, this is an experiment in "preaching the doctrine of hatred," and it devolves into a rant. Emerson is using the essay genre as a place to indulge in hypothetical voices, as is evidenced by his conditional qualifiers: "*why should I not say* to him," he asks, or "Rough and graceless *would be* such a greeting," he admits, in a rather comic understatement. Emerson is not suggesting that we go about "speaking the rude truth" in such a brusque manner, that we launch into a tirade if the Sierra Club or Jehovah's Witnesses come knocking at our door. The untenability of such a stance is precisely the point: Emerson knows such a strident rejection of conventional morality is impractical in actual social exchanges. Indeed, he admits that he usually gives some money and sends them away. Yet he is interested in pushing this kind of pose to its extreme; he is deliberately trying to sound as obnoxious as he can: in his ugly retort, "Are they *my* poor?" or his use of slavery, a real and unambiguous evil in 1841, as a metaphor for his alternative individual standard of morality ("There is a class of persons to whom by all spiritual affinity I am bought and sold"), he is adopting a deliberately offensive rhetoric. Earlier in the essay, he claims that a person who has "once spoken or acted with éclat" becomes a "committed person"—with, as Richard Poirier notes, a carceral pun on being "committed":[92] when Emerson blurts out, "Are they *my* poor," he has become a very committed person indeed, trapping himself in an extreme, uncomfortable position.

While such passages acknowledge that it is difficult to maintain a nonconformist integrity within a community, Emerson nonetheless affirms it is a workable goal. If the shrill rhetoric of his imagined response to the "foolish philanthropist" is untenable, he offers later in "Self-Reliance" another prescription for "speaking the truth"—not rudely—in our social relations:

> Check this lying hospitality and lying affection. Live no longer to the expectation of these deceived and deceiving people with whom we converse. Say to them, O father, O mother, O wife, O brother, O friend, I have lived with you after appearances hitherto. Henceforward I am the truth's. . . . I shall endeavour to nourish my parents, to support my family, to be the chaste husband of one wife,—but these relations I must fill after a new and unprecedented way. I appeal from your customs. I must be myself. I cannot break myself any longer for you, or you. If you can love me for what I am, we shall be the happier. If you cannot, I will still seek to deserve that you should. . . . If you

are true, but not in the same truth with me, cleave to your compan-
ions; I will seek my own. . . . Does this sound harsh to-day? You will
soon love what is dictated by your nature as well as mine, and, if we
follow the truth, it will bring us out safe at last.—But so you may give
these friends pain. Yes, but I cannot sell my liberty and my power, to
save their sensibility.[93]

The tone here, in so markedly different a register from the earlier passage, is at pains to combine an affection and responsibility for others
with an assertion that one's first responsibility must ever be to one's own
principles or genius. Emerson explicitly notes that he is not rejecting social relations or duties; rather, he is asserting that such relationships can
only be healthy if they encourage and reflect the liberty of the individuals
involved. The best way to form or reform our social relations is through
an uncompromising insistence on our individual integrity: this is not,
Emerson suggests, an anticommunitarian stance, but the path to truer
community.

If Emerson's location of value in self-culture leads him to endorse a
nonconformity within community, it also leads him, on occasion, to express a Nietzschean scorn of pity that seems to belittle the needs and in-
firmities of others, as in the following passage from "Experience" where
he acknowledges "our constitutional necessity of seeing things under
private aspects," but argues that this "need makes in morals the capital
virtue of self-trust":

The life of truth is cold, and so far mournful; but it is not the slave
of tears, contritions, and perturbations. It does not attempt another's work, nor adopt another's facts. It is a main lesson of wisdom to
know your own from another's. I have learned that I cannot dispose
of other people's facts; but I possess such a key to my own, as per-
suades me against all their denials, that they also have a key to theirs.
A sympathetic person is placed in the dilemma of a swimmer among
drowning men, who all catch at him, and if he give so much as a leg or
finger, they will drown him. They wish to be saved from the mischiefs
of their vices, but not from their vices. Charity would be wasted on
this poor waiting on the symptoms. A wise and hardy physician will
say, *Come out of that*, as the first condition of advice.[94]

Such passages understandably worry those readers who fear that Emersonian self-reliance can too easily justify the capitalist ideology of individualism that blames the victim by attributing success and failure to

individual merit rather than structural or environmental inequalities. Again, however, I believe it is necessary to recognize how Emerson is articulating an alternative "economy" of individualism: in this passage, he honestly assesses the costs and benefits of locating value in the cultivation of human talents. He in effect is revisiting the central message of "Compensation": if true value—the knowledge, virtue, and power that individuals earn only through action—cannot be stolen, but accrues to them even in their defeats and misfortunes, Emerson here acknowledges the corollary fact that such value cannot be given to others. We can ultimately help others only by convincing them of their capacity to forge an authentic existence of their own. Far from being disdainful, the underlying logic is one of empowerment. To insist that others *must* help themselves is also to insist that they *can*, that each individual has his or her own life and work, different from ours, yet equally valuable.

In asserting that individuals can best aid each other only indirectly, Emerson is not articulating an atomistic vision of autonomous individuals. Instead, his individualism implies a vision of society that is pluralistic, that affirms individuality both as a primary moral end and as the necessary means to the greater health of society. Emerson—in contrast to Nietzsche[95]—repeatedly expresses an egalitarian faith in the capacity of each individual to lead a morally significant life. The cultivation of knowledge, virtue, and power gained through action ennobles even the most prosaic of human vocations:

> I cannot doubt that the high laws which each man sees implicated in those processes with which he is conversant, the stern ethics which sparkle on his chisel-edge, which are measured out by his plumb and foot-rule, which stand as manifest in the footing of the shop-bill as in the history of a state,—do recommend to him his trade, and though seldom named, exalt his business to his imagination.[96]

Emerson asserts that each person's life is intrinsically valuable because it embodies or expresses a particular possibility of human experience: "The eye was placed where one ray should fall," he claims in "Self-Reliance," "that it might testify of that particular ray."[97]

Moreover, by arguing that individuals attain power only through embracing limitation, through accepting and exploiting the possibilities of a limited vocation defined both by one's innate talents and by the opportunities afforded by one's social environment, Emerson also affirms that individuality introduces a novelty into the world that facilitates the creative change that constitutes society's vitality and health. Recall, if you will, Emerson's description of the "greatest genius" as "the most indebted man," which argues that individuals help realize possibilities of change already nascent in society. Yet if they work with a borrowed cultural power, individuals still supply an essential element in this process of change: creative change occurs when some individual or individuals have the skill to recognize the nascent possibilities in a given context, and when they, or some other individuals, also possess the skill and energy to realize those possibilities. While geniuses are those who best achieve this merging of individual and social power, the model of vocation that geniuses embody is in fact proper to all individuals: geniuses are only "relatively great," Emerson argues: they are of a "faster growth," or are "such in whom, at the moment of success, a quality is ripe which is then in request." "Other days will demand other qualities," Emerson concludes: the dynamic relation between self and environment has the egalitarian result that different talents will be demanded at different times: "Rotation is the law of nature," he asserts: "When nature removes a great man, people explore the horizon for a successor; but none comes and none will. . . . In some other quite different field, the next man will appear."[98]

If Emerson cites "great men" as egalitarian symbols of the fact that all individuals must play a limited social role, he is not positing an equality of fortune. Indeed, the fact that individual power depends on harnessing cultural energies of change guarantees unequal success, for in each historical moment some talents will be valued more than others: "Certain men affect us as rich possibilities, but helpless to themselves and to the times,—the sport, perhaps, of some instinct that rules in the air;—they do not speak to our want." Nature's "law of rotation" means that many, indeed most, people are doomed to obscurity: "Why are the masses, from the dawn of history down, food for knives and powder?" Emerson asks: "The cheapness of man is every day's tragedy."[99] Yet this tragic fact of human limitation, waste, and failure does not lessen the necessity and value of all individuals' diverse talents:

> Is it a reply to these suggestions, to say, society is a Pestalozzian school: all are teachers and pupils in turn. . . . And if any appear never to assume the chair, but always to stand and serve, it is because we do not see the company in a sufficiently long period for the whole

rotation of parts to come about. As to what we call the masses, and common men;—there are no common men. All men are at last of a size; and true art is only possible, on the conviction that every talent has its apotheosis somewhere. Fair play, and an open field, and freshest laurels to all who have won them! But heaven reserves an equal scope for every creature.[100]

Society's "law of rotation" does not guarantee equality. If historical change places different talents in demand, the pace of such change does not correspond with people's lifetimes. Thus many people, even assuming they have the opportunities to develop their talents, will not find those talents in demand, will be destined "always to stand and serve." At best, Emerson seems to envision an egalitarian society with equal opportunity but unequal success. Yet he still insists that individualism is a necessary democratic ideal or belief: "true art is only possible on the conviction that every talent has its apotheosis somewhere." It is necessary to cultivate within society the broadest diversity of individual talents to ensure the existence of actors with the skills needed to capitalize on the creative possibilities of each new present. Ultimately, however, individuality is not merely a means, but an end. Even if many talents don't find their "apotheosis" in the work of the world, still "heaven reserves an equal scope for every creature." The talents of each person must be viewed as inherently valuable: "there are no common men." Hence, Emerson's individualism creates an ethical mandate to create a society that affords to all individuals the opportunities to develop their native talents.

As this line of argument makes clear, Emerson's individualism implies not just a tolerance, but a celebration of human diversity. Although in his journals Emerson sometimes gave voice to the type of racist prejudices that often afflicted even those who, like himself, supported the abolition of slavery and just treatment of Native Americans, these are best viewed as unfortunate but ultimately inessential aberrations from the central tenets of his thought, which clearly have antiracist implications.[101] Take, for instance, the following 1845 journal entry on the anti-Catholic and anti-immigrant principles of the Native American Party ("Native American" here referring not to our current usage of that term, but to an Anglocentric nativism):

I hate the narrowness of the Native American party. It is the dog in the manger. It is precisely opposite to all the dictates of love & magnanimity: & therefore, of course, opposite to true wisdom. It is the result of

science that the highest simplicity of structure is produced, not by few
elements, but by the highest complexity. Man is the most composite of
all creatures, the wheel-insect, the *volvox globator*, is at the beginning.
Well, as in the old burning of the Temple at Corinth, by the melting &
intermixture of silver & gold & other metals, a new compound more
precious than any, called the Corinthian Brass, was formed so in this
Continent—asylum of all nations, the energy of the Irish, Germans,
Swedes, Poles, & Cossacks, & all the European tribes,—of the Afri-
cans, & of the Polynesians, will construct a new race, a new religion, a
new State, a new literature, which will be as vigorous as the new Europe
which came out of the smelting pot of the Dark Ages, or that which earlier emerged from the Pelasgic & Etruscan barbarism.[102]

This conviction that human identity is essentially composite, that the
healthiest society is that which most embraces pluralism, helps explain
why an African-American writer like Ralph Ellison could place his own
work, and his own pluralist vision of America, within the tradition of
Emersonian individualism.

As a final example that Emerson's individualism does not reject community so much as demand that we reconceive it, consider his commentary from "New England Reformers" on the wave of socialist experiments
in voluntary association that swept across Emerson's New England in the
1830s and 1840s:

> I do not wonder at the interest these projects inspire. The world is
> awakening to the idea of union, and these experiments show what it
> is thinking of. It is and will be magic. Men will live and communi-
> cate, and plough, and reap, and govern, as by added ethereal power,
> when once they are united; . . . But this union must be inward, and
> not one of covenants, and is to be reached by a reverse of the methods
> they use. The union is only perfect, when all the uniters are isolated.
> It is the union of friends who live in different streets or towns. Each
> man, if he attempts to join himself to others, is on all sides cramped
> and diminished of his proportion; and the stricter the union, the
> smaller and the more pitiful he is. But leave him alone, to recognize
> in every hour and place the secret soul, he will go up and down do-
> ing the works of a true member, and, to the astonishment of all, the
> work will be done with concert, though no man spoke. Government
> will be adamantine without any governor. The union must be ideal
> in actual individualism.[103]

A passage such as this is usually read as evidence that Emerson's individualism precludes any meaningful commitment to community or to collective

efforts at reform.[104] Yet Emerson actually embraces "union" as a "magic" and necessary ideal that must and will be realized. He is mainly urging that true community can be achieved only by encouraging a true liberty and diversity of individual activity. His attempt to imagine community and individuality wholly reconciled—describing the union as "only perfect, when all the uniters are isolated"—does suggest a utopian synthesis that may never be attained. Yet in this regard it is worth noting Dewey's argument that although the ideal of democracy as community has never, and may never, be fully realized, such ideals still have practical value as aims to guide our efforts.[105] Emerson, in insisting that the true community must not sacrifice the integrity of its individual members, looks forward to Dewey's claims that the highest aim of a community must be cultivating the human potential of its individual members, and that a community should embrace the broadest diversity of individual activity as the best means for creating vibrant and progressive social relations.

"Stand in Primary Relations with the Work of the World": Emerson on the Social Division of Labor

Because it argues for the morality of individualized activity, individualism is often conflated with, or seen as too easily co-opted by, capitalist ideology. Yet there is a fundamental difference between the tradition of individualist ethics running from Emerson to later thinkers such as James, Dewey, and Ellison and the classic capitalist logic of comparative advantage. The latter is based on a standard that measures value in accumulated products or profit: by allowing individuals or nations to specialize in the areas of production each can perform more efficiently than others, specialization and trade (in theory) create increased wealth for all in the form of cheaper, more plentiful consumer goods. In the logic of this theory, the pursuit of individual wealth is morally justified because market forces purportedly transform even blatantly self-interested behavior into a force for the common benefit. In contrast, Emerson supports individualized activity, and the social division of labor that is its corollary, not because it maximizes products or profits, but because, properly utilized, it can serve to maximize the cultivation of human talents. This reassertion that value resides not in the quantity of consumer goods a society produces but in the active quality of human experience it fosters in its individual members constitutes in our day, as it did in Emerson's, a powerful perspective from which to criticize the alienations and materialist excesses of American culture—a fact that helps explain why Emerson has inspired writers ranging from Thoreau to Dewey to Ellison. Furthermore, Emerson's reflections on the division of labor are essential to any reevaluation of his ethics, for they show him to be wrestling with the ways that our individualized activities may implicate us in social inequalities and injustices, and striving to explain why, even in the face of these dilemmas, individualism remains a viable and perhaps necessary mode of living.

Like his near-contemporary Karl Marx,[106] Emerson is obsessed with the alienation of value. In his famous analysis from *Capital*, Marx describes how, under capitalism, the value of commodities becomes alienated from "use value," their utility as tools to enrich human life, and located instead in "exchange value," their ability to generate profit for reinvestment. The proper relation between means and ends is inverted, as instead of capital serving human needs, human efforts increasingly serve the overriding imperative to accumulate more capital. People become, in Marx's view, slaves to the very methods of efficiency that were supposed to liberate them—most notably wage laborers, who become mere cogs in a production machine designed to accumulate wealth for the owners of capital. Emerson barely read Marx;[107] like most of his American and European contemporaries, Emerson's concept of "socialism" was shaped by the various experiments in "voluntary association" or communal living that emerged in the first half of the nineteenth century. Yet his thought is permeated by a similar conviction that the means have become tyrannizing ends-in-themselves: that instead of products being used to enrich and facilitate human activity, human activity has been reduced to a mere search after products. He voices this complaint perhaps most dramatically in his "Ode, Inscribed to W. H. Channing":

> The horseman serves the horse,
> The neatherd serves the neat,
> The merchant serves the purse,
> The eater serves his meat;
> 'Tis the day of the chattel,
> Web to weave, and corn to grind;
> Things are in the saddle,
> And ride mankind.[108]

Or, as he protests in "Self-Reliance": "Men have looked away from themselves and at things so long," that "they measure their esteem of each other by what each has, and not by what each is."[109]

As this last quote suggests, Emerson describes the alienation of value from the self to things as entailing a corresponding alienation between people. Marx addresses a similar concern in his analysis of "commodity fetishism" in *Capital*. Any division of labor, Marx insists, is a social division that establishes social relations and creates a social product. Under a system of private property, however, such social interdependence is expressed only in the alienated form of commodity exchange: a human relation between members of a society becomes merely a market relation between products. Market value becomes viewed as inherent in the product itself, not as an expression of the social labor costs of different products; socially created value is falsely attributed to the individual producer, and social obligation is limited to payment of this false standard of individual desert.[110] In "New England Reformers," Emerson expresses an analogous sense that economic trade distorts or obscures the true relations between individuals in a society:

> Who gave me the money with which I bought my coat? Why should professional labor and that of the counting-house be paid so disproportionately to the labor of the porter, and woodsawyer? This whole business of Trade gives me to pause and think, as it constitutes false relations between men; inasmuch as I am prone to count myself relieved of any responsibility to behave well and nobly to that person whom I pay with money, whereas if I had not that commodity, I should be put on my good behavior in all companies, and man would be a benefactor to man, as being himself his only certificate that he had a right to those aids and services which each asked of the other. Am I not too protected a person? is there not a wide disparity between the lot of me and the lot of thee, my poor brother, my poor sister? Am I not defrauded of my best culture in the loss of those gymnastics which manual labor and the emergencies of poverty constitute?[111]

Emerson here expresses his two main concerns about how a division of labor may become distorting and unhealthy. First, by allowing others to perform necessary tasks for us so that we may specialize in one activity, we threaten to "defraud" ourselves of the self-cultivation we would achieve in doing those tasks for ourselves. This danger is exacerbated by a system of trade that translates our social interdependence into a monetary exchange, reducing to a mere price the value of a person's talents and contributions. Those who can easily purchase the fruits of others' labor because their talents are highly paid, Emerson fears, are "too protected" persons. But he is equally concerned about the corollary danger that in so defrauding ourselves we defraud others as well; we fail to discharge our true duty to them. Applying the logic that I have traced throughout this chapter, Emerson here suggests that one's responsibilities to one's self and to others should converge in the pursuit of one's vocation. A person's "only certificate" to use the "aids and services" supplied by others, he argues, lies not in money but in "himself": one is justified in benefiting from others only if one becomes a "benefactor" to others through the cultivation of one's own best self.

In claiming that the pursuit of a specialized vocation can fulfill one's social responsibilities, Emerson does not minimize the dilemmas posed by the social division of labor. He acknowledges that the social interdependence facilitated by trade implicates the individual in a welter of unequal and often unjust social relations. Noting, in 1841, that "the ways of trade are grown selfish to the borders of theft," he concludes:

> We are all implicated, of course, in this charge; it is only necessary to ask a few questions as to the progress of the articles of commerce from the fields from where they grew, to our houses, to become aware that we eat and drink and wear perjury and fraud in a hundred commodities. How many articles of daily consumption are furnished us from the West Indies. . . . The abolitionist has shown us our dreadful debt to the southern negro. In the island of Cuba, in addition to the ordinary abominations of slavery, it appears, only men are bought for the plantations, and one dies in ten every year, of these miserable bachelors, to yield us sugar.[112]

Moreover, Emerson argues that the injustices woven throughout our system of economic and social independence can too easily lead to a feeling of individual impotence and an abdication of ethical responsibility for society's inequities:

> One plucks, one distributes, one eats. Every body partakes, every body confesses, . . . yet none feels himself accountable. He did not create the abuse; he cannot alter it. What is he? an obscure private person who must get his bread. That is the vice,—that no one feels himself called to act for man, but only as a fraction of man.[113]

Here, in "Man the Reformer," a lecture that articulates the main principles that Thoreau would later express in the "Economy" chapter of *Walden*, Emerson suggests that individuals might avoid participating in these inequities by providing their wants with their own manual labor: "what help for these evils? How can the man who has learned but one art, procure all the conveniences of life honestly? Shall we say what we think?—Perhaps with his own hands." Like Thoreau, Emerson suggests that the true goal of economy should be to free one's self from dependence on products produced dishonestly or unjustly, and to free oneself from labor wasted in the pursuit of unnecessary luxuries, so that one can devote one's energies in clear conscience to the higher task of self-cultivation. "Economy is a high, humane office, a sacrament when its aim is grand," he asserts: "Parched corn eaten to-day that I may have roast fowl to my dinner on Sunday, is a baseness; but parched corn and a house with one apartment, that I may be free of all perturbations, that I may be serene and docile to what the mind shall speak, . . . is frugality for gods and heroes."[114]

Yet if he can at times voice such a Thoreauvian call for economic self-sufficiency, Emerson ultimately rejects any attempt to find ethical integrity in a withdrawal from the interdependencies of society. It is quite simply inconceivable that Emerson would have himself embarked on an experiment such as Thoreau made in the cabin he built (on Emerson's property) at Walden Pond, for Emerson's acute sense of the cultural basis of human intelligence leads him to view social interdependence not as the result of a particular economic order, but as the inescapable condition of all human action and thought. Recall his assertion from "The Conservative" that the "existing social system" is "so deep" that "it leaves no one out of it," or his wonderment, in "The Uses of Great Men," at the indebtedness of all our individual acts, be it the novelist's debt to Homer or the carpenter's indebtedness to the "forgotten inventor" of the foreplane. As inherently cultural beings, our individual acts are so dependent on the social resources for specialized activity that it would be too costly, if not impossible, to seek ethical integrity in a complete self-sufficiency. "I do not wish to be absurd and pedantic in reform," Emerson declares in "Man the Reformer": "If we suddenly plant our foot, and say,—I will neither eat nor drink nor wear nor touch any food or fabric which I do not know to be innocent, or deal with any person whose whole manner of life is not clear and rational, we shall stand still."[115]

In arguing that it would be "pedantic" to renounce the benefits of a so-cial division of labor, Emerson is not absolving individuals from the re-sponsibility to acknowledge and fulfill their ethical commitments to oth-ers. Just the opposite is true: he suggests that our inescapable dependence on social resources implicates all of our individual acts in social relations and responsibilities. We are justified in utilizing the resources supplied by others, Emerson insists, *only* if we use them for the ethical purpose of engaging in our own true vocation—an activity that both employs our best talents and performs some necessary work in the world: "No, it is not the part & merit of a man to make his stove with his own hands, or cook & bake his own dinner: Another can do it better & cheaper; but it is his essential virtue to carry out into action his own dearest ends, to dare to do what he believes & loves."[116] By utilizing cultural resources provided by specialized labor, you can "multiply your presence," but "in labor as in life there can be no cheating";[117] a specialized vocation must be a vehicle for engaging the work of humanity, not avoiding it:

> I do not wish to overstate this doctrine of labor, or insist that every man should be a farmer, any more than that every man should be a lexicographer. . . . But the doctrine of the Farm is merely this, that every man ought to stand in primary relations with the work of the world, ought to do it himself, and not to suffer the accident of his having a purse in his pocket, or his having been bred to some dishon-orable and injurious craft, to sever him from those duties; and for this reason, that labor is God's education.[118]

For Emerson, the choices of vocation that society offers are inescapably moral choices: the division of labor inherent in culture must be used not to exploit and live off others,[119] but to enable each of us to work more vi-tally. The efficiencies of social interdependence should be used, Emerson argues, to maximize individuals' opportunities for developing their own active powers; accordingly, he expresses a willingness to reform capitalist institutions whenever these purchase a merely material gain at the cost of suppressing human potential: "I would not have the laborer sacrificed to the result,—I would not have the laborer sacrificed to my convenience and pride, nor to that of a great class of such as me. Let there be worse cotton and better men."[120]

These views on the division of labor reflect Emerson's general belief that the most effective way to live ethically within society—and to reform it—is by focusing on the ends or purposes to which we use the institutions and resources of society. In this regard, it is worth considering again Emerson's claim from "Self-Reliance" that "I may . . . absolve me to myself":

> There are two confessionals, in one or the other of which we must be shriven. You may fulfil your round of duties by clearing yourself in the *direct*, or, in the *reflex* way. Consider whether you have satisfied your relations to father, mother, cousin, neighbour, town, cat, and dog; whether any of these can upbraid you. But I may also neglect this reflex standard and absolve me to myself. I have my own stern claims and perfect circle. It denies the name of duty to many offices that are called duties. But if I can discharge its debts, it enables me to dispense with the popular code. If any one imagines that this law is lax, let him keep its commandment one day.[121]

This strident assertion of the morality of individualized acts, even those that seem to disregard social obligations, reflects economic calculations of both efficient means and valuable ends. The sheer variety of social relatedness that makes every act socially indebted also, somewhat paradoxically, frees individuals to appropriate the resources provided by cultural specialization: it would be far too inefficient, if not impossible, to consider all the responsibilities incurred in the most basic human acts. Consider the social debts you might incur in the first fifteen minutes of a waking day: to the laborers who built your alarm clock, sewed your bathrobe, harvested your coffee beans, and produced the newspaper on your doorstep—a web of indebtedness that goes well beyond Emerson's list of "cousin, neighbor, town, cat and dog." However, if it is impossible to measure all the moral responsibilities implied in the social *sources* of our acts, Emerson's logic suggests that we can and must measure the *use* to which those resources are put, the aim of our individual pursuits. To claim that one can absolve one to one's self is not a rejection of moral accountability, but rather an assertion that people must pay their social debt in this "direct" way by obeying the "stern claims and perfect circle" of a meaningful vocation.

Clearly, however, Emerson defends individualized activity not merely as a means to fulfilling our social duties, but as a moral end. When he advises readers to "Absolve you to yourself,"[122] he is expressing the radical shift in the location of value that is implied in his ethics of self-culture. As in the essay "Compensation," he is urging us to seek "salvation" neither in heaven nor in the alienable products of our labor but in the cultivation of self we achieve through action. Though he asserts our duty to direct our individual energies into moral pursuits, this definition of value as the active expression and development of self means that "moral" activity comprehends a potentially unlimited spectrum of human endeavors. Emerson's economics thus are based on a logic of maximizing vital experience: he asserts the value of people exercising diverse talents, enjoying different aspects of life, keeping different possibilities of consciousness alive. His writings are full of exhortations to expand human consciousness by exploring through our actions new relations to the world. He asserts the morality of affording people the freedom to follow the call of their own creative impulses, even in seemingly extravagant, luxurious ways. Man "is by constitution expensive," he claims in the essay "Wealth": "He is born to be rich. He is thoroughly related."[123] For some readers, such an expanded view of moral activity may seem amoral, but it is important to note that it is based on a moral and economic calculation—the decision that, since life is never safe or secure, moral activity cannot mean merely preserving life, but living it, as expressed in Emerson's declaration, "I do not wish to expiate, but to live. My life is for itself and not for a spectacle." While this view, as discussed above, has strong affinities to Nietzsche, it also looks forward to Dewey's vision of the ideal relation between individual and community. Like Emerson, Dewey asserts that the wealth of society lies in the quality of human experiences and capacities it nurtures; that, instead of defining value by a narrowly utilitarian standard, a democratic society must view the "true meaning of social efficiency" as "identical" with the "complete development of personality," of "what is unique in an individual," for such individuality brings "greater promise for a social service which goes beyond the [mere] supply in quantity of material commodities."[124]

One last point needs to be made about Emerson's stance on the social division of labor: namely, while he suggests that we can best strive to live ethically within society by ensuring that we use its efficiencies and resources for moral purposes, this does not mean that he renounces efforts to reform the institutions of society. For example, after rejecting any "absurd and pedantic" criticism of the social division of labor that would compel us to live in "absolute isolation from the advantages of civil society," he immediately qualifies his position: "But I think we must clear ourselves each one by the interrogation, whether we have earned our bread to-day by the hearty contribution of our energies to the common benefit? and we must not cease to *tend* to the correction of these flagrant wrongs, by laying one stone aright every day."[125] If it is impossible to wash one's hands (to borrow Thoreau's terminology)[126] of all the inequities in the myriad social relationships in which we are implicated, that does not mean that we should not reform as many as we can. Thus, along with our primary responsibility of ensuring that we devote our energies to a valuable vocation, Emerson also enjoins us to the continual effort of reforming unjust social relations. Indeed, he sees these two responsibilities as connected, envisioning a synthesis in which our individual efforts to live ethically within society will help foster reform:

> But it is said, "What! will you give up the immense advantages reaped from the division of labor, and set every man to make his own shoes, bureau, knife, wagon, sails, and needle? This would be to put men back into barbarism by their own act." I see no instant prospect of a virtuous revolution; yet I confess, I should not be pained at a change which threatened a loss of some of the luxuries or conveniences of society, if it proceeded from a preference of the agricultural life out of the belief, that our primary duties as men could be better discharged in that calling. Who could regret to see a high conscience and a purer taste exercising a sensible effect on young men in their choice of occupation, and thinning the ranks of competition in the labors of commerce, of law, and of state? It is easy to see that any inconvenience would last but a short time. This would be great action, which always opens the eyes of men. When many persons shall have done this, when the majority shall admit the necessity of reform in all these institutions, their abuses will be redressed, and the way will be open again to the advantages which arise from the division of labor, and a man may select the fittest employment for his peculiar talent again, without compromise.[127]

Emerson here expresses his characteristic view that the first step in social reform must be to reform our individual motives and purposes, to reassert control over our tools—over our social organizations, institutions, and technologies—by reconfirming that our primary goal should be the cultivation of human potential. If more people sought to be "rich" in the higher values of life, and were willing to be "poor" in merely materialistic terms, it would have a transformative effect on our social division of labor. If more individuals were to choose occupations based on a desire to express and develop their own dearest talents, and less pursued the occupations of "commerce," "law," and "state" that bring conventional status and wealth, our society might be poorer in monetary wealth, but far richer in the more important wealth of human culture. Again like Thoreau, Emerson affirms that individual actions taken within a system can help impel the reform of that system: the principled pursuit of a true vocation is a "great action, which always opens the eyes of men," inspiring them to more principled paths of their own; moreover, he is confident that, if enough people pursued higher ends, social institutions such as the division of labor, which at present may serve largely materialistic and exploitative ends, could be turned to a higher ethical purpose.

This emphasis on human attitudes and motives as a primary force for social change will, no doubt, be viewed by some as naive, as neglecting the power that social structures and institutions have to restrict the possibilities of reform. Yet I would suggest that Emerson's views are specifically pragmatic, in two regards. First, one can see in Emerson's stance an eminently practical insistence, borne out only too well by history, that attempts to reform social institutions without also reforming people's motives, values, and behaviors, are doomed to failure. In *Woman in the Nineteenth Century*, Margaret Fuller cogently asserts the necessity of individual reform, even as she argues that it must proceed in "parallel movement" with efforts at institutional reform, a dynamic that she dramatizes as a dialogue between Goethe's Romanticism and Charles Fourier's socialism: "Fourier says, As the institutions, so the men! . . . Goethe thinks, As the man, so the institutions!" To which Fuller responds, "Ay! But Goethe, bad institutions are prison walls and impure air that make him stupid. . . . And thou, Fourier, do not expect to change mankind at once. . . . If these attempts are made by unready men, they will fail."[128] Secondly, Emerson's prescription for reforming the social division of labor is an example of the practical activism that typifies a pragmatic approach to social reform. Asserting that ideals can be realized only out of the actualities of our present, and subsequently viewing present realities not merely as circumstances that limit change but also as materials and means that can be turned to new purposes, pragmatism concludes that the most efficient way to facilitate social reform is to preserve those aspects of our existing institutions that can be enlisted toward the new ends we desire to achieve. Richard Teichgraeber has described Emerson's writings on economic issues as a mode of "connected criticism" that employs just such a strategy, appropriating the vocabulary of the marketplace in order to convince his readers that the economic practices and principles with which they are already conversant could be used for a higher ethical purpose than the mere pursuit of material wealth.[129] As I explore in chapters 4 and 5, John Dewey struck a similar balance in approaching a society increasingly dominated by the corporate-industrial institutions of modern capitalism: combining, on the one hand, a sober insistence that those economic conditions exerted an enormous determining influence on the prospects for reform—defining both the major problems to be remedied, and the resources available for remedying them—with, on the other hand, a melioristic faith that existing conditions could be redirected and reharnessed to more humane ends, were we to forge the political will to reassert control over the tools we have created.

The Necessary Foundations of Reform: Self-Reliance and Politics

Probably the most common criticism of Emersonian individualism is that it precludes the commitment to meaningful political efforts at social reform. Cornel West, for instance, argues that Emerson's commitment to the "moral transgression" of individual nonconformity, his mystical celebration of "individual intuition over against collective action," and his fatalistic or "organic conception of history" doom him to the politically impotent position of a "petit bourgeois libertarian, with at times anarchist tendencies and limited yet genuine democratic sentiments."[130] In Sacvan Bercovitch's formulation, Emerson exemplifies the way in which liberal individualist "dissent" occupies a fundamentally "ambiguous" status between subversion and co-optation. Liberal democracy socializes individuals, Bercovitch contends, "not by repressing radical energies but by redirecting them, in all their radical potential, into a constant conflict between self and society." As a theory of this conflict, Emerson's individualism is "not . . . a form of co-optation [but] a form of utopia developed within the premises of liberal culture and therefore especially susceptible to co-optation by liberal strategies of socialization." Emerson failed to challenge the premises of liberal culture because his inability to endorse the collective methods of socialism forced him to halt his early utopian social critique at "the *edge* of class analysis," with the result, Bercovitch concludes, that Emerson increasingly employed his individualism as an "ideological apology" for the inequities of American society.[131]

Emerson's thought clearly does remain within the broad tradition of liberalism, yet does this doom his ethics, as West and Bercovitch suggest, to political impotence? In assessing the political consequences of Emerson's individualism, we must avoid the tendency, all too frequent in Emerson scholarship, to reduce his thought to absolutist positions. West's argument, for instance, repeats the familiar idea that an individualism valuing nonconformist originality must be opposed to social engagement, yet, as I have maintained in this chapter, Emerson rejects the notion that individuality can be achieved in isolation from the compromises of society, arguing instead that individuals can achieve integrity and fulfillment only by engaging the opportunities for action in their social circumstances. Similarly, one recognizes in Bercovitch's claim that Emerson's individualism shifted from utopian critique to ideological apology an updated version of the familiar Whicherian dichotomy between an early Emerson's naive, idealistic assertion of freedom and a late Emerson's more sober fatalism.

Interestingly enough, even those critics who have offered more positive assessments of Emerson's politics often have reconfirmed such dichotomies. In his landmark study *Virtue's Hero*, Len Gougeon documents in detail that Emerson was much more involved in the abolitionist movement than usually has been acknowledged, thereby dispelling the vision of Emerson as an idealist aloof from the muddy struggles of reformist politics.[132] Yet even as he sets the historical record straight, Gougeon's reading of Emerson's philosophy perpetuates a Whicherian opposition between an early Emerson who professed an idealistic, optimistic faith in an "inevitable ameliorative fate"[133] impelling our world toward progress, and a late Emerson who, sobered by the experience of the Fugitive Slave Law and its aftermath, increasingly viewed progress as contingent upon individual and collective efforts for reform. According to Gougeon, Emerson's antislavery speeches of the 1840s reflect "his basic optimism that all things tend naturally to goodness, and that even an abomination like slavery would finally yield to this 'beautiful necessity,'" an optimism that relieved individuals of responsibility for direct political action: "the obligation of individuals was primarily to cooperate with the fatalistic evolution of goodness and to contribute their energies in ways appropriate to themselves."[134] By the 1850s, Gougeon argues, Emerson replaced this optimistic faith with the view "that the reform of society would be wrought through the persistent and cooperative efforts of heroic individuals working with, and through, the fatalistic forces at hand."[135]

To posit such a shift in Emerson's thought has broad implications for the way one assesses his individualism, for it implies that an ethics of vocation that affirms the value of individualized activity is ethically naive or irresponsible, precluding the kind of political action necessitated by the realities of our world. George Kateb has voiced just such a concern about Emersonian individualism. Even though he recognizes the Nietzschean anti-absolutism of Emerson's thought and judges Emerson's vision of individuality as among America's most important contributions to the idea of democracy, Kateb argues that Emerson's decision actively to support the abolition movement constituted a "profound" "deviation" from his earlier individualism, a deviation that reveals a fundamental conflict or limitation in Emersonian self-reliance:

> What is remarkable is not that Emerson frequently makes public speeches against slavery and even campaigns in 1851 for a particular anti-slavery candidate, John Gorham Palfrey. . . . The aberration is that he urges solidarity—indeed mobilization—on others, and, when the occasion arises, does not shrink from advocating violence in the effort to destroy slavery. That profound change is a deviation from his theory of self-reliance, not its transformation. Or, we can say that Emerson accepts the sacrifices of every sort—including the abandonment of the aspirations of free persons to self-reliance— which are needed to give all Americans, not just some, the chance for self-reliance.[136]

In short, Kateb suggests that self-reliance is in some important respect incompatible with political engagement, that the pursuit of one's own individualized activities and experiences—including the highest or "mental" self-reliance that Kateb views as essential to the cultivation of a democratic sensitivity to the otherness of our world—is a luxury that, as Emerson tacitly acknowledged through his increasing support of the abolition movement, must be sacrificed to the collective efforts necessary to eradicate the injustices that oppress others.[137]

Kateb's argument raises far-reaching questions concerning the ethical viability of individualism, questions to which I will return at the end of this chapter. In the discussion that follows, I hope to show why assessments of Emerson's attitudes toward politics must move beyond the dichotomies of naive optimism versus resigned fatalism and detached

individual freedom versus constricting political engagement, dichotomies that, in one form or another, underlie the critical views summarized above. As I have argued throughout this chapter, Emerson describes
cultural change as occurring within the dynamic, antagonistic interplay
of power and limitation, freedom and fate; moreover, he describes individual actions—actions that are inevitably socially indebted and implicated—as playing an essential role in facilitating such change. When
seen as extensions of these anti-absolutist attitudes, Emerson's views on
reform and politics appear more complex than is generally granted. Emerson's stance on reform cannot be reduced merely to an individualist
distrust of collective action; instead, he combines a pragmatic affirmation of the possibility and even inevitability of reform with an equally
pragmatic skepticism toward reforms that are not enacted in changed
behavior. Emerson's commitment to individualism does not preclude
collective action per se: he envisions the demands of individuality as existing in a productive, vitalizing tension with the demands for collective
action. These attitudes can be traced in Emerson's antislavery speeches,
revealing his evolving stance on abolition to be not some fall from a naive
optimism, but rather a maturation of his consistently tragic, melioiristic
view of the possibility for progress.

Certain central aspects of Emerson's individualism—his profound sense
that all the media and institutions of culture are constricting and limiting, and his concurrent belief that human value lies in the ability of
people to express their individuality with and against these media—
undoubtedly imply a healthy distrust of collective political institutions.
Yet Emerson's critique of political institutions must be seen in the larger
context of his pragmatic attitude toward culture: just as he locates value
in active experience—in the cultivation of power, knowledge, and virtue
that is achieved through action—rather than in the results or products
of our acts, so he locates morality in behavior and not in codes, laws,
or institutions. If this view extends to a utopian, anarchist critique of
political institutions, it also translates into a practical political mandate
to examine human behavior critically and reform it.

Beginning with the opening paragraph of his first book, *Nature*, Emerson portrays culture as both limiting our capacity for original action
and as allowing for change that is sufficient to our human needs. This

view of culture shapes the related tension that lies at the core of Emerson's attitude toward politics, government, and reform. On the one hand, he insists that political change is desirable and inevitable; on the other, he shows an indifference to and even cynicism about the reform of legal codes and institutions. In "New England Reformers," for instance, he voices the view that, since our actions inescapably depend on imperfect and distorting institutions, morality must lie in the uses to which we turn the traditions we inherit:

> It is handsomer to remain in the establishment better than the establishment, and conduct that in the best manner, than to make a sally against evil by some single improvement, without supporting it by a total regeneration. Do not be so vain of your one objection. Do you think there is only one? Alas! my good friend, there is no part of society or of life better than any other part. All our things are right and wrong together. The wave of evil washes all our institutions alike. Do you complain of our Marriage? Our marriage is no worse than our education, our diet, our trade, our social customs. Do you complain of the laws of Property? It is a pedantry to give such importance to them. Can we not play the game of life with these counters, as well as with those; in the institution of property, as well as out of it.[138]

It would be pedantic, Emerson suggests, to assume that culture could ever *not* be a resistant and potentially corrupting medium. By the same token, however, he views culture as not only requiring but enabling performance: though cultural media are constricting, they can be turned to our purposes. Culture neither guarantees morality nor prevents it. This duality is expressed in his question, "Can we not play the game of life with these counters, as well as with those"? Culture allows for moral action, but morality is achieved only through our acts, through the *way* we "play the game of life" with the imperfect cultural tools we inherit. This pragmatic skepticism toward reform is not, however, a rejection of it; quite the contrary, even as he argues that institutional reform is insufficient to guarantee morality, Emerson portrays it as both necessary and inevitable. In turning our inherited traditions to new uses, we inescapably re-create both our world and our selves. Recall, again, *Nature*'s affirmation that, by weaving the new "wool and flax in the fields" into garments of our own, we can indeed enjoy "an original relation to the universe" shaped by "our own works and laws and worship." For Emerson, such revitalizing change is a fundamental goal of human activity, a belief that, as he makes clear in a passage from "Man the Reformer" that echoes the opening lines of *Nature*, commits him to social and political reform: "The world not only fitted the former men, but fits us. . . . What is a man born for but to be a Reformer, a Re-maker of what man has made"?[139]

In his 1844 essay "Politics," Emerson's attitude toward reform exhibits precisely this complex dynamic:

> The old statesman knows that society is fluid; there are no such roots and centres; but any particle may suddenly become the centre of the movement, and compel the system to gyrate round it, as every man of strong will, like Pisistratus, or Cromwell, does for a time, and every man of truth, like Plato, or Paul, does forever. But politics rests on necessary foundations, and cannot be treated with levity. Republics abound in young civilians, who believe that the laws make the city, that grave modifications of the policy and modes of living, and employments of the population, that commerce, education, and religion, may be voted in or out; and that any measure, though it were absurd, may be imposed on a people, if only you can get sufficient voices to make it a law. But the wise know that foolish legislation is a rope of sand, which perishes in the twisting; that the State must follow, and not lead the character and progress of the citizen; the strongest usurper is quickly got rid of; and they only who build in Ideas, build for eternity; and that the form of government which prevails, is the expression of what cultivation exists in the population which permits it. The law is only a memorandum. We are superstitious, and esteem the statute somewhat: so much life as it has in the character of living men, is its force. The statute stands there to say, yesterday we agreed so and so, but how feel ye this article today? Our statute is a currency, which we stamp with our own portrait: it soon becomes unrecognizable, and in process of time will return to the mint. Nature is not democratic, nor limited-monarchical, but despotic, and will not be fooled or abated of any jot of her authority, by the pertest of her sons: and as fast as the public mind is opened to more intelligence, the code is seen to be brute and stammering. It speaks not articulately, and must be made to. Meantime the education of the general mind never stops.[140]

From one perspective, political change is inevitable because people are constantly reforming society by changing the quality and focus of their pursuits: laws, like coins, are "stamped" "with our own portrait"; they reflect "man" as defined by the range of human activities in the period from which they emerge. As human pursuits continually change, laws grow obsolete; the coin grows "unrecognizable" and must "return to the mint." However, the corollary of Emerson's belief that activity *guarantees* political change is his assertion that it also *limits* change: real political change must be based in the behavior of a society's citizens. Emerson thus combines an affirmation of the inevitability of institutional reform with a skepticism toward it.

Crucially, this insistence that institutional reform must be accompanied by behavioral change does not translate into a renunciation of political action. The idea that individuals can facilitate and even impel broad forces of creative change, which is fundamental to Emerson's thought, obtains in the realm of politics as well: persons who understand the tendencies of an era can articulate those tendencies and galvanize others behind new moral purposes. Indeed, a new idea can "revolutionize the entire system of human pursuits"; poets utter ideas that "become the songs of the nations," and each institution appears as "the lengthened shadow of one man."[141] Again, however, this assertion that people can change society through the power of ideas carries a reverse assertion: in order to compel meaningful political change, ideas must effect a real change in people's habits. Thus, in the passage from "Politics," the "old statesman," the actor whose creative medium is government, "knows that society is fluid," and that a new idea may "compel the system to gyrate round it." Yet he also knows that "politics rest on necessary foundations": policies must be based in the "modes of living, and employments of the population," and thus reform must "follow, and not lead the character and progress of the citizen."

This tension at the center of Emerson's attitude toward politics undoubtedly has a utopian element. As the unabashedly utopian flight in the closing pages of "Politics" shows, Emerson's insistence that morality is based not in laws but in the behavior of citizens, if carried to its logical conclusion, results in anarchism. However, if his theory of reform admits of anarchist extensions, it also has practical political applications. He found only too much confirmation of his political theories in the central political event of his lifetime: the sectional struggle over slavery that came to a head for Emerson in the Compromise of 1850. In the willingness of Massachusetts legislators and judges to enforce the Fugitive Slave Law, he found embittering evidence that morality cannot be codified or legislated, but must exist in the actions of citizens:

> I wish that Webster & Everett & also the young political aspirants of
> Massachusetts should hear Wendell Phillips speak, were it only for

the capital lesson in eloquence they might learn of him. This, namely, that the first & the second & the third part of the art is to keep your feet always firm on a fact. They talk about the Whig party. There is no such thing in nature. They talk about the Constitution. It is a scorned piece of paper. He feels after a fact & finds it in the money-making, in the commerce of New England, and in the devotion of the Slave states to their interest, which enforces them to the crimes which they avow or disavow, but do & will do.

 Cotten thread holds the union together, unites John C. Calhoun & Abbott Lawrence. Patriotism for holidays & summer evenings with music & rockets, but cotten thread is the union.[142]

The sectional crisis forced Emerson to apply his political theories to American democracy. The level of human liberty in America could not be guaranteed merely by the rights asserted in the Constitution or the form of government established there. Political freedom was determined by the actions of Americans—by the willingness of legislators and judges to preserve the liberty promised in the law, and by the willingness of citizens to pay the price of true reform. The crisis of 1850 showed that this political will did not exist in Massachusetts: the primary political reality was revealed as the "cotten thread" uniting the manufacturing and commercial economy of New England to Southern planters. Emerson was compelled to abandon the notion that one could combine a principled opposition to slavery with support for union with the slave states. The Fugitive Slave Law made dramatically clear that membership in the Union implicated Northerners in the continuance of slavery: "Here is a measure of pacification & union. What is its effect? that it has made one subject, one only subject for conversation, & painful thought, throughout the Union, Slavery. We eat it, we drink it, we breathe it, we trade, we study, we wear it."[143]

 Indeed, Emerson acknowledged that the question of ethical responsibility did not end with the kind of political and legal ties constituted in the federal union, but implied the need for radical reform in people's daily behavior:

> Do not then, I pray you, talk of the work & the fight, as if it were any thing more than a pleasant oxygenation of your lungs. . . . This is not work. It needs to be done but it does not consume heart & brain, does not shut out culture, does not imprison you as the farm & the shoe-shop & the forge. . . . Let the diet be low, & a daily feast of commemoration of their brother in bonds. Let them eat his corn cake dry, as he

does. Let them wear negro-cloths. Let them leave long discourses to the defender of slavery, and show the power of true words which are always few. Let them do their own work. He who does his own work frees a slave. He who does not his own work, is a slave-holder. Whilst we sit here talking & smiling, some person is out there in field & shop & kitchen doing what we need, without talk or smiles. Therefore, let us, if we assume the dangerous pretension of being abolitionists, & make that our calling in the world, let us do it symmetrically. The world asks, do the abolitionists eat sugar? do they wear cotton? do they smoke tobacco?[144]

This passage implies a much more radical logic of reform than merely insisting that men renounce the most direct economic links to slavery, for the complicity of the Union with slavery is only an extreme case of the ethical responsibility implied in all social organization and specialization. Emerson's suggestion that all must "do their own work" requires more than the renunciation of sugar, cotton, and tobacco. Even those who do necessary, vital intellectual or political work that "needs to be done" must be aware that this "is not work"—that it is enabled by the drudgery of others, by the tasks of the "farm & the shoeshop & the forge" that "consume heart & brain" and "shut out culture." Emerson was aware that the social interdependence that implicates individuals in the inequities of society is so pervasive, that one could escape ethical complicity only through a subsistence lifestyle in which each person literally "did his own work." However, as I argued in the previous section of this chapter, he believed that social specialization and interdependence are so fundamental to human intelligence that to renounce them in the name of reform would entail unacceptable losses in power and in the variety of human experience—would cause us to "stand still." Here I simply want to emphasize that Emerson's skepticism about reform reflects the fact that he takes reform with deadly seriousness, insisting that it must be effected in our daily behavior, and considering the radical consequences of true reform: "Every reform is only a mask under cover of which a more terrible reform, which dares not yet name itself, advances. Slavery & Anti-slavery is the question of property & no property, rent & anti-rent; and Anti-slavery dare not yet say that every man must do his own work, or, at least, receive no interest for money. Yet that is at last the upshot."[145]

It is in the context of these attitudes toward political reform that the basis for and extent of Emerson's distrust of collective politics must be gauged. Emerson does not oppose collective interests or action as such;

rather, he distrusts the institutional vehicles of collective will. This distrust stems from a central tenet of his thought—that inherited culture threatens to obstruct the creative change that is crucial to the vitality of our individual and social lives:

> Parties are also founded on instincts, and have better guides to their own humble aims than the sagacity of their leaders. They have nothing perverse in their origin, but rudely mark some real and lasting relation. We might as wisely reprove the east wind, or the frost, as a political party, whose members, for the most part, could give no account of their position, but stand for the defence of those interests in which they find themselves. Our quarrel with them begins, when they quit this deep natural ground at the bidding of some leader, and, obeying personal considerations, throw themselves into the maintenance and defence of points, nowise belonging to their system. A party is perpetually corrupted by personality. Whilst we absolve the association from dishonesty, we cannot extend the same charity to their leaders. They reap the rewards of the docility and zeal of the masses which they direct. Ordinarily, our parties are parties of circumstance, not of principle; as, the planting interest in conflict with the commercial; the party of capitalists, and that of operatives; parties which are identical in their moral character, and which can easily change ground with each other, in the support of many of their measures. Parties of principle, as, religious sects, or the party of free-trade, of universal suffrage, of abolition of slavery, of abolition of capital punishment, degenerate into personalities, or would inspire enthusiasm. The vice of our leading parties in this country (which may be cited as a fair specimen of the societies of opinion) is, that they do not plant themselves on the deep and necessary grounds to which they are respectively entitled, but lash themselves to fury in the carrying of some local and momentary measure, nowise useful to the commonwealth.[146]

It is crucial to note that Emerson affirms the principle of political association, not only for parties of "principle," but even for those based on the frankly material grounds of "the defence of interests in which [people] find themselves," for such association reflects "some real and lasting relation." Indeed, somewhat surprisingly, he argues that collective interests form the valid basis for parties, and that the threat of political corruption comes from mere individualism or "personality." Yet if Emerson asserts the fundamental legitimacy of collective interests, he fears that collective political institutions (like all cultural institutions) threaten to become distorting and stifling. Parties, he declares, are too susceptible to the ambitions and interests of their leaders; they become focused on goals that have more to do with the perpetuation of their institutional power than with the thoughtful application of principle.

This skepticism toward political parties and movements did not lead Emerson to renounce collective politics. Like James and Dewey after him, Emerson believed that the vitality of cultural change is maximized when individuals, exercising their own particular talents, utilize and facilitate cultural resources and processes. When political events of the 1850s led him to endorse collective efforts to abolish slavery—first in the political agitations of abolitionist organizations, and later in the national mobilization for the war—he envisioned individual energies and collective organizations as existing in a relationship of productive or complementary tension: "whilst I insist on the doctrine of the independence and the inspiration of the individual," he professed in his 1855 "Lecture on Slavery," "I do not cripple but exalt the social action. . . . A wise man delights in the powers of many people."[147] Emerson here implies not only that the wise individual will embrace the strength of collective action, but that collective actions gain strength from the wisdom of individuals. Individual conscience, though it undoubtedly complicates collective action, is also necessary to it, for individuals of strong conscience embody the commitment to principle that energizes their compatriots and helps prevent organizations from betraying their professed ideals. Emerson expressed this Thoreauvian logic in his 1844 speech commemorating the tenth anniversary of emancipation in the British West Indies:

> Virtuous men will not again rely on political agents. They have found out the deleterious effect of political association. Up to this day, we have allowed to statesmen a paramount social standing, and we bow low to them as to the great. We cannot extend this deference to them any longer. The secret cannot be kept, that the seats of power are filled by underlings, ignorant, timid, and selfish. . . . What happened notoriously to an American ambassador in England, that he found himself compelled to palter, and to disguise the fact that he was a slave-breeder, happens to men of state. Their vocation is a presumption against them, among well-meaning people. The superstition respecting power and office, is going to the ground. The stream of human affairs flows its own way, and is very little affected by the activity of legislators. What great masses of men wish done, will be done; and they do not wish it for a freak, but because it is their state and natural

> end. There are now other energies than force, other than political, which no man in future can allow himself to disregard. There is direct conversation and influence. A man is to make himself felt, by his proper force.[148]

Some, no doubt, would read this passage as evidence of a transcendentalist call to individual reformation and "moral suasion" that precludes commitment to meaningful political action.[149] Yet Emerson's insistence on the force wielded by "virtuous men" is not a rejection of politics so much as a call for an alternative, truly democratic politics. "Politics" construed as the legal status quo is indeed condemned by Emerson as inescapably complicit with slavery: "men of state," officials of the political union between Massachusetts and the slave states, are, like the unhappy ambassador of Emerson's anecdote, compelled to disguise their participation in slavery.[150] In counseling people to cease their reliance on "political agents," Emerson is calling for political power to be returned to its source in the will of the people. Individual conscience here is envisioned as the driving force behind a collective politics, as is clear in Emerson's assertion that "What great masses of men wish done, will be done." Similarly, his claim that the "stream of human affairs" is "very little affected by the activity of legislators" is not a renunciation of politics, but rather an extension of the pragmatic view sketched above—that morality resides not in institutions or legal forms so much as in the political will of the people that justice should be done.

The question remains whether this embrace of a synthesis between individual and collective action represents, as Kateb argues, a deviation from Emerson's ideal of self-reliant individualism. It will be helpful to explore first the related question of whether Emerson's increasing support for the abolition movement constituted a departure from an optimistic belief in the inevitability of progress that had previously led him to downplay the need for political action. It is undeniable that the political events of the 1850s pushed Emerson, as they did many who favored abolition, to adopt a wider view of the problem of slavery and to endorse ever more radical means for its eradication. Emerson came to believe that the South would never voluntarily emancipate its slaves (as Great Britain had done in 1834), that the Union was not worth preserving if it meant condoning the continued existence of slavery, that Northern complicity with slavery was a major obstacle to abolition, that civil disobedience was the only morally viable response to an unjust law such as the Fugitive Slave

Act, and that the war was not only necessary, but must have as its goal emancipation and the reconstruction of Southern society.[151] Yet I would challenge the assertion, expressed in Gougeon's account, that Emerson's evolving views on abolition represent a major shift in his views on the morality of our world and how goodness is to be realized in it. One of the main themes I have pursued in this chapter is that Emerson, in both his early and later essays, consistently portrays "freedom" and "fate" as existing in a productive, antagonistic tension. His affirmation of the benevolent or progressive tendency of our world is a tragic, melioristic vision, one in which good emerges out of the struggle between power and limitation, a struggle in which our human actions are necessary, both because of the ethical character we cultivate in our efforts to reform our world, and because of the beneficial, though limited, results our acts may help realize. Instead of evidencing, as Gougeon suggests, his fall from an optimistic belief in "inevitable amelioriative fate,"[152] Emerson's antislavery addresses of both the 1840s and 1850s express this tragic and activist vision of progress.

To illustrate this point, I would like to consider key passages from two speeches, Emerson's 1844 address on emancipation in the British West Indies and an address he delivered ten years later, on the fourth anniversary of Daniel Webster's speech supporting the Fugitive Slave Law. Richard Teichgraeber has offered a detailed reading of these speeches, stressing that they show the continuity and development of Emerson's approach as a "connected critic" who criticized Northern society's complicity with slavery while simultaneously appealing to those values of Northern society that could be enlisted in the abolitionist cause.[153] Teichgraeber concludes that, while the 1854 speech shows an increased awareness of the obstacle posed by Northern complicity with slavery, Emerson never fully relinquished his hope that the Northern states would "somehow regain their true moral and political bearings and act to end slavery."[154]

For my purposes, Teichgraeber's analysis of Emerson's "connected criticism" is valuable because it highlights that even in the 1844 address, Emerson does not offer a naive vision of progress as inevitable. Rather, he criticizes both British and American society as embodying the mere "shopkeeping civility" of a "trading nation": "we are shopkeepers, and have acquired the vices and virtues that belong to trade."[155] The cause of emancipation in Britain, he suggests, was furthered in no small part by the baser motives of this "shopkeeping" mentality:

Slavery is no scholar, no improver; it does not love the whistle of the railroad; it does not love the newspaper, the mailbag, a college. . . . For these reasons, the islands proved bad customers to England. It was very easy for manufacturers less shrewd than those of Birmingham and Manchester to see, that if the state of things was altered, if the slaves had wages, the slaves would be clothed, would build houses, would fill them with tools, with pottery, with crockery, with hardware; and negro women love fine clothes as well as white women. In every naked negro of those thousands, they saw a future customer.[156]

"It was inevitable that men should feel these motives," Emerson concludes, but he does not imply that progress can be safely left to the operations of such economic interest. First, contrary to the notion that he optimistically ignored evil, Emerson acknowledges that human beings are driven by motives more sinister than merely economic ones: "We sometimes say, the planter does not want slaves, he only wants the immunities and the luxuries which the slaves yield him. . . . [G]ive him a machine that will yield him as much money as the slaves, and he will thankfully let them go. . . . But I think experience does not warrant this favorable distinction, but shows the existence, beside the covetousness, of a bitterer element, the love of power, the voluptuousness of holding a human being in his absolute control." Secondly, Emerson asserts that emancipation required the political efforts of individuals and organizations acting in the name of higher principles of justice: while it was "inevitable" that people should be moved by economic motives, Emerson concludes: "they do not appear to have had an excessive or unreasonable weight. On reviewing this history, I think the whole transaction reflects infinite honor on the people and parliament of England. It was a stately spectacle, to see the cause of human rights argued with so much patience and generosity," effecting a revolution "achieved by plain means of plain men, working not under a leader, but under a sentiment."[157] This praise of the efforts of British abolitionists is clearly meant as a call to action—one that is endorsed both by Emerson's own gesture in adding his voice to the abolitionist cause, and in his exhortation, already discussed above, for Americans to cease their reliance on "political agents" and to ensure that "what great masses of men wish done, will be done." If Emerson here retains his characteristic faith in the power of ideals, the speech does not paint a naive picture of inevitable progress: rather, it depicts progress as emerging out of the very mixed moral fabric of our world, out of the tension between our "shopkeeping" virtues *and* vices—a vision consistent with the Nietzschean view of historical progress or "melioration" expressed in such works as "Considerations by the Way" and "Fate."

In *Essays, First Series*, published three years before his 1844 speech on British emancipation, Emerson had already defined the morality of our world in such essentially tragic terms: in the essay "Compensation," which locates the moral character of our world in the power and knowledge we cultivate by struggling against the limitations and injustices of experience, or in "Circles," which insists that any effort to reform our circumstances, to "draw a new circle," will at best find a limited success. In his 1854 address on the Fugitive Slave Law, Emerson explicitly applies this tragic view of progress to the struggle over slavery. To show how this ethical vision informs Emerson's call to action in 1854, I will quote at length from the final third of this address:

> These things show that no forms, neither Constitutions nor laws nor covenants nor churches nor bibles, are of any use in themselves; the devil nestles comfortably into them all. There is no help but in the head and heart and hamstrings of a man. Covenants are of no use without honest men to keep them. Laws are of no use, but with loyal citizens to obey them. . . .
>
> I conceive that thus to detach a man, and make him feel that he is to owe all to himself, is the way to make him strong and rich. And here the optimist must find if anywhere the benefit of slavery. We have many teachers. We are in this world for nothing else than Culture: to be instructed in nature, in realities; in the laws of moral and intelligent nature; and surely our education is not conducted by toys and luxuries,—but by austere and rugged masters,—by poverty, solitude, passions, war, slavery,—to know that paradise is under the shadow of swords; that divine sentiments, which are always soliciting us, are breathed into us from on high and are a counterbalance to an universe of suffering and crime,—that self-reliance, the height and perfection of man, is reliance on God. . . .
>
> It is of no use to vote down gravitation or morals. What is useful will last; whilst that which is hurtful to the world will sink beneath all the opposing forces which it must exasperate. . . .
>
> I know that when seen near, and in detail, slavery is disheartening. But nature is not so helpless but it can rid itself at last of every wrong. . . . But the spasms of nature are centuries and ages and will tax the faith of short-lived men. . . .

Whilst the inconsistency of slavery with the principles on which
the world is built guarantees its downfall, I own that the patience
it requires is almost too sublime for mortals and seems to demand
of us more than mere hoping. And when one sees how fast the rot
spreads,—it is growing serious,—I think we demand of superior
men that they shall be superior in this, that the mind and the virtue give their verdict in their day and accelerate so far the progress of
civilization. . . .

I hope we have come to an end of our unbelief, have come to a belief that there is a Divine Providence in the world which will not save
us but through our own co-operation.[158]

The ethics Emerson advocates in this speech are based on the assumption
that human action finds a tragic mixture of success and resistance in the
material world. As in "Compensation," which asserts that the nature of
things resists crime, that the primary value of power and knowledge cannot be stolen, and the criminal obtains a merely material benefit at the
cost of impoverishing his own self, Emerson here asserts that slavery is
inconsistent "with the principles on which the world is built." Yet if he implies that the abolition of slavery is inevitable, this optimism is essentially
tragic (indeed, following James's definition, it is not properly optimistic,
but melioiristic), for it is clear that such moral progress must be achieved
against a resistant world: we are "instructed in realities" by "austere and
rugged masters" such as "poverty," "war," and "slavery." If, again following the logic of compensation, the "optimist" can find a "benefit" even in
the stern opportunities for action and "education" afforded by the need
to combat such evils, this moral benefit is only "a counterbalance to an
universe of suffering and crime." Perhaps most importantly for my argument, Emerson insists that nature's bias toward justice does not preclude
human action; instead, the inevitable discrepancy between nature's tragic
justice and our human desires requires action: the slow "spasms of nature" must "tax the faith of short-lived men," "demand[ing] of us more
than mere hoping." Thus Emerson exhorts his audience to act to "accelerate" the "progress of civilization" and give the inevitable "verdict" on
slavery "in their day." Whatever "providence" exists in Emerson's world,
it clearly "will not save us but through our own co-operation."[159] While,
in comparison to his 1844 address, this 1854 speech offers a more explicit
articulation of Emerson's tragic view of progress, it does not signal a major
shift in his view of the moral potential of our world, nor of how human
action participates in realizing that potential.

If Emerson's support for the abolition movement is consistent with the reformist and activist tendencies that always characterized his thought, what of Kateb's argument that the collective mobilization necessary to combat a large-scale social problem is in some fundamental sense incompatible with Emersonian self-reliance, with the pursuit of an individual vocation that expresses and fulfills ones own unique potential? Undoubtedly, there arise in the lives of individuals and societies crises that require individuals to enlist their energies into efforts to resolve those crises, to divert their energies from the pursuits into which they otherwise, by personal inclination, devote them. The national struggle over slavery pushed Emerson much further than was his temperamental wont into the realm of collective politics, and forced him to abandon the more scholarly role he felt was his true vocation for a stance as political orator in which he felt uncomfortable. He often opened his antislavery speeches with professions of his unfitness and disinclination for political activism. Indeed, in a journal entry reflecting on the public letter he wrote to Martin Van Buren protesting the government's plan to forcibly remove the Cherokee Nation from their ancestral lands, Emerson described the task of having to adopt a stance of righteous indignation—even for a cause he heartily believed in—as almost unbearably onerous: "It is like dead cats around one's neck. It is like School Committees & Sunday School classes & Teachers' meetings & the Warren street chapel and all the other holy hurrahs." He feared his letter was a shrill and ineffective response—"merely a Scream"—but admitted this uncomfortable action was the only tenable one: "sometimes a scream is better than a thesis."[160]

The vehemence of this response should not be taken as proof, however, that individualism and collective action are fundamentally opposed, and that the need for collective action creates an ethical mandate to abandon individualism as an untenable luxury. Such a conclusion assumes, reductively, that conflict is a sign of incompatibility, rather than a source of healthy antagonism. To assert, as Emerson surely does, that individual fulfillment and social responsibility exist in a relation of compromise and negotiation, is not to posit individualism and collective action as mutually exclusive. Indeed, the essay "Self-Reliance" repeatedly insists that individual integrity cannot be achieved in a "mechanical" isolation from the compromises of society, and Emerson's concept of vocation implies a pursuit that not only fulfills the self, but also performs necessary work in the world. How to balance the ethical mandate to value and promote individualized activity with the mandate to support cooperative efforts at reform is a central tension not only in Emerson's writings, but in the work of the pragmatic thinkers he influenced, as evidenced in James's vision of national service that would provide a "moral equivalent" for the collective effort exemplified by war, and in Dewey's assertion that, in a fully democratic way of life, the demands of community should harmonize with the full and free cultivation of individuality.

Although, as Dewey admitted, such an ideal might be a utopian aim that can never be fully realized, yet the tradition of pragmatic individualism asserts the necessity of striving to reconcile, or at least maintain in a productive tension, the demands of individuality and community. Emerson's vision, like those of James, Dewey, and Ellison, is essentially pluralistic, depicting human power and revitalizing change as maximized when individuals can utilize and cultivate their diverse interests, skills, and energies by engaging the problems, tendencies, and opportunities embodied in their social contexts. Instead of seeing individualism as a luxury that must be sacrificed to collective action, writers in the Emersonian tradition view individualism as a necessary means and end. They remind us that, if the challenges facing society often require collective mobilization, the creativity, integrity and efficiency of such collective efforts are maximized by utilizing the diverse talents of society's individual members. In this sense, Emerson's involvement in the abolition movement was not, as Kateb suggests, a profound deviation from his ethics of individualism, for if Emerson did divert his energies from their normal scholarly paths, he contributed to the cause in a fashion that utilized his vocational talents as a writer and orator. More broadly, the cultivation of individuality remains a viable and enduring end. If individuals are obligated to enlist their energies in collective struggles to eradicate suffering and injustice, the goal of such collective action is surely to establish a society in which justice is widespread enough, and suffering low enough, that individuals may in good conscience pursue the diverse possibilities for self-realization, and have the opportunities and liberty to do so. It is in this commitment to individuality, both as a mode of personal fulfillment and as a key to the health of society, that the abiding value of the Emersonian legacy lies.

PART TWO

PRAGMATISM

James and Dewey

MOMENTS IN THE WORLD'S SALVATION

James's Pragmatic Individualism

This then is the individualistic view. . . .
It means many good things: e.g.
Genuine novelty
order being *won*, paid for.
the smaller systems the truer
man [is greater than] home [is greater than] state or church.
anti-slavery in all ways
toleration—respect of others
democracy—good systems can always be described in individualistic terms
hero-worship and leadership.
the vital and the growing as against the fossilized and fixed in science, art,
religion, government and custom.
faith and help
in morals, obligation respondent to demand.
Finally, it avoids the *smugness* which Swift found a reproach.

—William James

They don't make intellectuals like William James anymore.[1] James forged a career whose remarkable breadth seems unimaginable in the academic and popular cultures of today. He traversed and blended several disciplines, writing pioneering works in psychology and religion in addition to the work for which he is most famous—providing one of the founding articulations of pragmatism, the most distinctive and influential school in American philosophy. Moreover, James was a true public intellectual[2]: he was an expert contributing to his discipline at the highest level, writing texts that continue to challenge and inspire professional philosophers, but he also translated his work—in essays of "popular philosophy"[3] and in widely attended public lectures that were collected in books like *The Will to Believe* and *Pragmatism*—into forms that effectively communicated to popular audiences how ideas debated by philosophers might actually have significance in their own lives. While this penchant for popularizing has led academic philosophers at times to chide James for a lack of precision or rigor, such criticisms have never cast into doubt the significance of his contributions, and the accessibility of James's works, written in a style that communicates the enormous vitality, charm, and passion of his personality, probably ensures that James's version of pragmatism will continue to eclipse those of Dewey or Charles Sanders Peirce among general readers—and even most academics.

Yet if—or perhaps because—James remains an influential spokesman for pragmatism, his individualism is often lamented as detracting from the power or relevance of this thought. Critics who stress pragmatism's progressive, even radical, political potential tend to view James's individualism as an unfortunate encumbrance (perhaps, as Dewey at times suggested, a vestige of the "pioneer" era in American history, sadly outmoded for more modern times[4]), one that separates James from the more thoroughly "social" thought of pragmatists like Dewey and Mead.[5] It would be better, such critics imply, if pragmatism could be divested of its individualistic aspects. A central aim of the present study is to challenge the assumptions behind such assessments.

The first such assumption is that pragmatism *can* be divested of its individualism. The outline quoted above—from a lecture series that Robert D. Richardson reports can be viewed as a "first draft for *Pragmatism*"[6]— identifies individualism with benefits that readers familiar with James will recognize as key elements of his own pragmatism and pluralism: "the vital and the growing as against the fossilized and fixed"; "Genuine novelty"; "order being *won*, paid for"; and "toleration—respect of others." If individualism indeed means such things, it becomes hard to see not only *if* Jamesian pragmatism could have its individualism removed, but *why* such radical surgery, if possible, would be desirable. Much of the challenge here is to distinguish between classic liberal individualism and a pragmatically reconstructed individualism, and to envision what the latter might look like: to understand why pragmatists would view the cultivation of individuality as an essential social concern; why individuality is both an essential means to the ongoing experimental reconstruction of experience and a primary end for any truly humane society—especially any society that aspires to democracy, since, as James asserts above, good democratic systems "can always be described in individualistic terms."

A second, related assumption involves the relation of James's "individ-ualistic" and Dewey's "social" ethics. While it would be hard to deny that the focus and tenor of James's ethical writings are more individualistic than Dewey's, any stark opposition between James's and Dewey's ethics perpetuates a dualism of individual versus collective approaches to re-form that Dewey explicitly rejects. It overlooks how a reconstructed indi-vidualism remains central to Dewey's ideal of democracy-as-community and, not least, risks dismissing James in a reductive and condescending manner. Accordingly, in part 2 of this study, I hope to show how indi-vidualism remains central to the pragmatisms of both James and Dewey, and while attempting to do justice to the particularity of each thinker, to stress the considerable continuity between their visions.

Part 1 explored central strains in Emerson's thought that mark him as an intellectual precursor to pragmatism: a tragic, melioristic belief that power and value are created within and against the material limits of our world; an affirmation that our most vital and secure value resides not in the necessarily limited product of any act, but in transition and growth, in the capacities for continued activity we cultivate through our successive acts; and, in accord with these views, a model of the self as relational—as existing only through its interactions with its environment—and as a process; all of which make "self-culture" a central locus of ethics, the cultivation of individuality being, for Emerson, both the highest end of human association and a necessary means for creating vital communi-ties. The question now is how James (and Dewey) extend these Emerso-nian themes with a pragmatic difference: that is, what difference does it make to reconceive individualism through an explicitly pragmatic lens?

As John E. Smith notes, the pluralism of James's thought is reflected in the texture of his writings: while it has "a *main drift* that cannot be missed," "his thought does not have the unity of a single system."[7] The main strands that compose the fabric of James's thought are his prag-matic method and theory of truth; his doctrine of radical empiricism; his pluralistic metaphysics; and his advocacy of a melioristic attitude to-ward moral possibility and loss. Perhaps the clearest way to relate these various strands—and to explain how they support a reconceived indi-vidualism—is to focus on how James (like Dewey after him) articulated a radically reconstructed concept of "experience"[8] as a mutually trans-forming interaction between a living creature and its environment. The consequences of the pragmatic model of experience are far-reaching and momentous: by placing consciousness, knowing, and truth wholly within the interactions of human beings and their environments, explaining them as functions, phases, or results of those interactions, pragmatism affirms that human interests, purposes, and actions play an inevitable and legitimate role in the discovery and creation of truth. A *sufficient* role, as well: the interactions (or in Dewey's terms the "transactions") of experience—and the habits, ideas and truths we gain in interacting with our environment—are sufficient, without recourse to any transcendental power or order, to generate the means for the ongoing task of intelligently directing and remaking experience. This points to what is arguably pragmatism's central gesture. Rejecting the dualistic metaphysics that has dominated the Western philosophical tradition in favor of a pluralism that stresses interconnection and process, pragmatism places entities often thought of as transcendent—Truth, Reason, the Soul or Subject, Reality—within the processes and changes of experience; and in so doing does not diminish them as merely material, finite, or changing, but affirms their sufficiency for our human needs. Indeed, pragmatism is at its heart an affirmation of the creative power of human intellect and imagination. To embrace a pragmatic model of experience is to affirm the open-ended plasticity of both the self and the environment. And hence, as both James and Dewey stress, to be a pragmatist is to reject absolutism and dogmatism for a thoroughgoing experimentalism: to reject views that see either human nature or reality as fixed (or undergoing changes determined by fixed ends), and to treat truths not as names for some unchanging reality, but as tools to employ in our ongoing efforts to remake both our world and ourselves.

This model of experience as a mutually transforming transaction between self and environment points, as well, to pragmatism's central revisions of classic liberal individualism. For to see both self and environment as plastic is to reject Lockean liberalism's view of "the individual" as "naturally" endowed with liberty and equality, and its view that the only legitimate state is one limited (as far as possible) to protecting the individual's preexisting liberty (and property) from "artificial" social constraints. In contrast, pragmatism views the self as existing only through habits forged in interaction with the environment—which is always, for humans, social as well as natural. This does not, however, posit a self rigidly determined by its environment, but rather a self that is plastic and, hence, educable. Similarly, though pragmatism sees even the highest human capacities—including reason, imagination, conscience, and free will[9]—as products or results of experience, those capacities, once formed, introduce an indispensable subjective contribution to the intelligent reconstruction of experience—through the imaginative projection of ideals or ends, and the deliberation on anticipated and achieved consequences. Moreover, if pragmatism rejects the notion of a transcendent subject or self, pragmatism also reaffirms individual selves, grounded in individual bodies and brains, as the most vital loci in experience, as the seats of all human energies, desires, ideals, and satisfactions. Experience always exists as the experiences of individuals, life experienced *by* specific individuals, and, as James's doctrine of radical empiricism implies, the reality of concepts like goodness, reason, freedom, justice, or God (in any sense that we as humans can know or enjoy them) must reside in their experienceable effects in the lives of individual sentient beings.[10]

Accordingly, pragmatism turns away from classic liberalism's negative project of protecting individuals' natural liberty from the constrictions of society, and toward the constructive project of experimentally remaking social institutions with a primary eye to their ability to *create* individuality—to educate and liberate individuals' varied capacities. Pragmatism views individuality as both a necessary means and essential end in this ongoing process of reform. Individuals' diverse energies, initiatives and imaginations introduce an indispensable element of novelty into the experimental processes of social reconstruction, and the character of selfhood that individuals cultivate through participation in cooperative efforts—a character that always resides in the growing quality of present experience individuals enjoy as they pursue meaningful goals—constitutes a primary good we enjoy as humans and a primary standard of the morality of our social relations and our world.

It is Dewey, not James, who explicitly articulates this pragmatic critique of classic liberalism and offers the most systematic argument as to why a pragmatically reconstructed individualism remains essential to the ideal and practice of democracy.[11] Yet, as Dewey himself asserted, it was James's landmark *Principles of Psychology* that laid the crucial groundwork for the experimentalism that undergirds a pragmatic reconception of individualism. Moreover, in celebrated essays like "The Moral Philosopher and The Moral Life" and "On a Certain Blindness in Human Beings," James offers some of the most eloquent and cogent defenses of the individualistic ethics necessitated by a pluralistic vision of our world. Viewed in the broader context of his thought, James's individualism, no less than Dewey's, can be seen as an integral and necessary expression of his pragmatism.

Pragmatic Truth and Pluralistic Meliorism: Fighting Out Our Thinking Lives in a Universe Still in the Making

In the lecture series later published as *Pragmatism*, James eschews the stance of philosopher-as-disinterested-seeker-after-the-truth, frankly acknowledging his hortatory intent of persuading his audience to embrace pragmatism. James's stance here is not simply that of an intellectual attempting to connect with a general audience. Nor is it the stance of a philosopher attempting to persuade his audience of some truth that remains true whether they recognize it or not. In a far more radical sense James's appeal—and the impetus behind his efforts as a public intellectual—is a logical extension of his pragmatic insistence that philosophies, like all human truths, are subject to the verdict of human needs in the trials of experience. In a real sense, a philosophy can become true only if we make it true: if people adopt it as a hypothesis or belief, act upon it, and subsequently find it verified in the fruit it bears in their lives. "The whole function of philosophy," he asserts, "ought to be to find out what definite difference it will make to you and me, at definite instants of our life, if this world-formula or that world-formula be the true one," and "the finally victorious way of looking at things will be the most completely *impressive* way to the normal run of minds."[12] That philosophy will be most widely adopted—and, James insists, legitimately so—that proves most rational by best satisfying the intellectual, practical, and moral demands of our nature.[13] James urges his audience to adopt pragmatism precisely on such practical grounds, specifically citing its unique ability to "combine" two fundamental human needs, a "scientific loyalty to facts" with "the old confidence in human values and the resultant spontaneity, whether of the religious or of the romantic type."[14]

James's pragmatism, and the way it supports a reconceived notion of individualism, can only be understood in relation to these broader moral goals. Pragmatism, in James's formulation, has two main components. First, it embraces a "method" and "attitude of orientation" that measures truth in terms of concrete consequences in human experience, that seeks to

> interpret each notion by tracing its respective practical consequences. What difference would it practically make to any one if this notion rather than that notion were true? If no practical difference whatever can be traced, then the alternatives mean practically the same thing, and all dispute is idle. . . . There can *be* no difference anywhere that doesn't *make* a difference elsewhere—no difference in abstract truth that doesn't express itself in a difference in concrete fact and in conduct consequent upon that fact, imposed on somebody, somehow, somewhere, and somewhen.[15]

Implied in this method is an empiricist "attitude of orientation" that "turns away from abstraction and insufficiency, from verbal solutions, from bad *a priori* reasons, from fixed principles, closed systems, and pretended absolutes and origins," and "towards concreteness and adequacy, towards facts, towards action and towards power." Second, pragmatism encompasses a "genetic theory" of truth that views ideas and theories as "instruments" whose function is to "marr[y] old opinion to new fact," instruments that *"become true just in so far as they help us get into satisfactory relation with other parts of our experience."*[16] For James, these pragmatic stances have momentous practical implications. Pragmatism's empirical method affirms that our beliefs, through the actions they inspire, have powerful concrete consequences; similarly, a definition of truth as a leading-function within experience, of beliefs "becoming" true or verified based on the consequences we encounter as we act upon those beliefs, implies a universe whose reality and truth are *"still in the making,"* a universe in which we have the right to believe that our moral desires and actions matter, so long as we find that belief verified by practical fruits in our experience.[17] Pragmatism ultimately means that pluralism—the metaphysical hypothesis James argues is most rational to our intellectual and moral needs—is at least a viable hypothesis, one that requires us to forego the certainties of absolute Truth but that inspires a melioristic attitude toward the successes and losses of our existence that best meets the practical needs of our human nature.

These two themes—the definition of mind as essentially active or teleological in nature, and the subsequent right to believe that our beliefs and actions may help create the morality of our world—form the consistent core of James's thought from his very earliest to his latest works. All the main strands of James's thought—his radical empiricism, his pragmatism, and his pluralist meliorism—can be understood as enabling these central arguments. In an 1878 piece critiquing Spencer's "correspondence" theory of mind, James already offers a pragmatic assertion that knowing is not a "mere passive mirroring of outward nature," but a process shaped by the purposes and needs of the knower in his interaction with his environment, and a process that transforms the environment:

> The knower is not simply a mirror floating with no foot-hold anywhere, and passively reflecting an order that he comes upon and finds simply existing. The knower is an actor, . . . he registers the truth which he helps to create. Mental interests, hypotheses, postulates, so far as they are bases for human action—action which to a great extent transforms the world—help *make* the truth which they declare. In other words, there belongs to mind, from its birth upward, a spontaneity, a vote. It is in the game, and not a mere looker-on; and its judgments of the *should-be*, its ideals, cannot be peeled off from the body of the *cogitandum*, as if they were excrescences, or meant, at most, survival.[18]

By 1904, in essays like "Does 'Consciousness' Exist?" and "A World of Pure Experience" that rejected the subject-object dualism professed in *Principles of Psychology*, James had carried this model of mind to its logical conclusion, describing experience as essentially a matter of activity: more specifically, as a mutually transforming interaction between a creature and its environment.

Consider the definition of pluralism he offers in his conclusion to the 1909 *A Pluralistic Universe*:

> Pragmatically interpreted, pluralism or the doctrine that [the universe] is many means only that the sundry parts of reality *may be externally related*. Everything you can think of, however vast or inclusive, has on the pluralistic view a genuinely "external" environment of some sort or amount. Things are "with" one another in many ways, but nothing includes everything, or dominates over everything. . . . For pluralism, all that we are required to admit as the constitution of reality is what we ourselves find empirically realized in every minimum of finite life. Briefly it is this, that nothing real is absolutely simple, that every smallest bit of experience is a *multum in parvo* plurally related, that each relation is one aspect, character, or function, way of its being taken, or way of its taking something else; and that a bit of reality when actively engaged in one of

these relations is not *by that very fact* engaged in all the other relations simultaneously. . . . [A] thing may be connected by intermediary things, with a thing with which it has no immediate or essential connexion. It is thus at all times in many possible connexions which are not necessarily actualized at the moment.[19]

James's vision of experience here anticipates key elements of Dewey's mature metaphysics: a universe that is wholly transactional, in which all things are processes or "events" that exist only through their interactions with other things.[20] Such a universe, with genuine possibilities that *might* be actualized immanent in the myriad relations between things, is characterized by tragic limitation, since possibilities always exceed actualities and the realization of one necessarily excludes others; but is also a universe in which novelty emerges when things interact with each other so as to realize such latent connections—and, crucially, a universe in which the actions and purposes of thinking beings can help realize new interactions and create novel realities. This reveals the ethical import of James's radical empiricism—specifically, his insistence that "the parts of experience hold together from next to next by relations that are themselves parts of experience," so that "the universe needs . . . no extraneous trans-empirical connective support" in order to make knowing possible:[21] namely, to place knowing wholly within experience, while it requires us to accept truth and reality as existing within a pluralistic dynamic of genuine indeterminacy and loss, also affirms our ability to help re-create reality. As James puts it in *Pragmatism*, "truth grows up inside of all the finite experiences. They lean on each other, but the whole of them, if such a whole there be, leans on nothing. All 'homes' are in finite experience; finite experience as such is homeless. Nothing outside of the flux secures the issue of it. It can hope for salvation only from its own intrinsic promises and potencies." While the vision of reality as a "flux" whose outcome is unsecured may seem terrifying to our "tender-minded" desire for security, James trusts that the consequent vision of a universe "unfinished, growing in all sorts of places, especially in the places where thinking beings are at work," a "universe with such as *us* contributing to create its truth," will so satisfy our moral desire for significance and responsibility, as to make us more than willing to accept the open challenge of a pluralistic world.[22]

James's pragmatic theory of truth, by placing truth or knowing as a function within the knower's interaction with his environment, similarly affirms that our interests, desires, and actions play a legitimate and inescapable creative role. "Human motives sharpen all our questions, human satisfactions lurk in all our answers, all our formulas have a human twist," he contends: "We plunge forward into the field of fresh experience with the beliefs our ancestors and we have made already; these determine what we notice; what we notice determines what we do; what we do again determines what we experience."[23] Within this mutually transforming dynamic of experience, our desires, habits and beliefs determine how we act on the environment, and the resultant reaction of the environment upon us reshapes our habits and beliefs:

> In the realm of truth-processes facts come independently and determine our beliefs provisionally. But these beliefs make us act, and as fast as they do so, they bring into sight or into existence new facts which re-determine the beliefs accordingly. So the whole coil and ball of truth, as it rolls up, is the product of a double influence. Truths emerge from facts; but they dip forward into facts again and add to them; which facts again create or reveal new truth (the word is indifferent) and so on indefinitely. The "facts" themselves meanwhile are not *true*. They simply *are*. Truth is the function of the beliefs that start and terminate among them.[24]

To measure meaning in terms of practical consequences and truth in terms of satisfactory leading into future experiences, is thus to affirm a twofold manner in which human purposes help create truth: our interests and desires inspire actions that have real consequences, that help create new facts; they also embody the demands by which the value of future results—and hence the truth of the ideas that help lead to those results—are judged.

James stresses that these dynamics particularly obtain in regard to moral truths, which go beyond questions of fact ("what sensibly exists") to judgments of what "would be good if it did exist." The largest metaphysical and moral truths—competing beliefs about the nature of reality (the "ultimate universal datum") and the "radical question of life, . . . [of] whether this be at bottom a moral or an unmoral universe"—are like any human truths: their alternate meanings reside in the differences they make "in concrete fact and in conduct consequent upon that fact," and the truth of any belief resides in our experience of whether the consequences of acting upon it prove satisfactory.[25] Applying this pragmatic method to metaphysical disputes over design, free will, and materialism-versus-theism, James concludes they are meaningless when considered

retrospectively. For example, the question of whether our world was created by a divine creator or purely mechanical physical forces is moot with
regards to the past, whose facts are determined: the resulting world being the same, we should be equally grateful in either case. Prospectively,
however—with regards to the question "What is this world going to be?
What is life eventually to make of itself?"—James argues that beliefs such
as theism and free-will have momentous practical significance, which he
locates in a "melioristic" promise or hope that "the future may be other
and better than the past has been."[26] Such moral questions are, for James,
subsumed under what he calls "the most central" and "pregnant" "of all
philosophical problems," that of monism versus pluralism, whether our
universe is controlled by an underlying unity that precludes any genuine contingency, or contains enough disunion and free play to allow for
genuine possibilities.[27] Monism must view all the details of our world as
the inevitable results of an omnipotent law—be it the will of a theistic
providence or the operations of amoral physical forces. Thus monism
tends toward the absolutist extremes of optimism, which claims that the
world—including its evils—is already perfectly good, and pessimism,
which claims that the world will never be good, and that our moral desires are futile or irrelevant.[28] Only pluralism, James argues, describes a
universe that is rational to the mental and moral demands of our human
nature. Our actions are meaningful—and the moral beliefs and judgments that inspire them make sense—only if they have the potential to
help realize some possibilities while precluding others: "I cannot understand the willingness to act, no matter how we feel, without the belief that
acts are really good and bad. I cannot understand the belief that an act is
bad, without regret at its happening. I cannot understand regret without
the admission of real, genuine possibilities in the world." Because this
contingency that makes our choices and actions meaningful also implies
the possibility of failure and the inevitability of tragic choices, James's
pluralism steers a middle course that is "neither optimistic nor pessimistic, but melioristic, rather. The world, it thinks, may be saved, on condition that its parts shall do their best. But shipwreck, in detail, or even on
the whole, is among the open possibilities."[29]

James acknowledges that this vision of a universe with real pluralism
and contingency, with no guarantee of a safe final outcome, is "repugnant
and irrational in a certain way," yet contends that "every alternative . . . is
irrational in a deeper way." If we deny the existence of chance and see the

results of our world as determined—as fulfilling, for example, the will of an omnipotent and providential deity—then we can judge our world as moral only by asserting that even the most horrific evil is a necessary part of a perfect whole. Our moral impulses, James affirms, rightly rebel against such absolutist optimism: "the scale of evil actually in sight defies all human tolerance," and thus "whoever claims *absolute* teleological unity . . . brings us no farther than the book of Job did—God's ways are not our ways, so let us put our hands upon our mouth. A God who can relish such superfluities of horror is no God for human beings to appeal to." By encouraging the melioristic stance that the morality of our world lies in the *possibility* of moral progress, pluralism rejects this "theoretical" problem of evil, focusing instead on "the practical problem of how to get rid of it." A universe with real contingency is sufficient to the moral needs of our nature, James argues, for we can accept tragic, unrecoverable losses as an acceptable price to pay for a world whose possibilities imbue our moral lives with significance. Indeed, he goes further, arguing that a world with real chances, and hence real defeats, is not a regrettable condition we reluctantly find sufficient, but one that fills the deepest needs of our active nature. People require not only the hope of success, but also resistances and evils to overcome—things "that we can act *with*," and things "that we must react *against*." Indeed, he insists that the strenuous character of human nature requires resistance *more* than success: a "worse defect in a philosophy than that of contradicting our active propensities is to give them no object whatever to press against." It is the "strange paradox of our moral nature," he notes, that "though the pursuit of outward good is the breath of its nostrils, the attainment of outward good," the vision of goodness as a certain and completed fact, "would seem to be its final suffocation and death."[30]

The hortatory tenor of James's approach to such questions—as Dewey remarked, James was foremost a moralist[31]—reflects his contention that experience always includes an ineradicable element of risk and faith. Our most certain truths—including our "belief in truth itself"—are hypotheses, subject to failure and revision, and in engaging the world we always incur the uncertain consequences of acting on our chosen beliefs: "on this line" he says, "we agree to fight out our thinking lives." James urges us to approach the moral truth of our universe as an open question, a work in progress, a *process* of acting on our beliefs about the world and verifying (or revising) them in the course of our experience. James here applies the logic articulated in "The Will to Believe": that there are cases when "faith . . . creates its own verification,"[32] where belief in a future fact is necessary to inspire the actions required to realize the fact. The truth of a pluralistic meliorism depends on our acting on the belief that our actions may (and often do) help decide outcomes in our world, and on our faith that the results of acting on this belief—the meaning, character, and power we gain in our successful and failed struggles against the evils of our world—will prove sufficient to our moral needs:

> Every human being must sometime decide for himself whether life is worth living. Suppose that in looking at the world and seeing how full it is of misery, of old age, of wickedness and pain, and how unsafe his own future, he yields to the pessimistic conclusion, cultivates disgust and dread, ceases striving, and finally commits suicide. He thus adds to the mass M of mundane phenomena, independent of his subjectivity, the subjective complement x, which makes of the whole an utterly black picture illumined by no gleam of good. Pessimism completed, verified by his moral reaction and the deed in which this ends, is true beyond a doubt. $M + x$ expresses a state of things totally bad. The man's belief supplied all that was lacking to make it so, and now that it is made so the belief was right.
>
> But now suppose that with the same evil facts M, the man's reaction x is reversed; suppose that instead of giving way to the evil he braves it, and finds a sterner, more wonderful joy than any passive pleasure can yield in triumphing over pain and defying fear; suppose he does this successfully, and however thickly evils crowd upon him proves his dauntless subjectivity to be more than their match— will not everyone confess that the bad character of the M is here the *conditio sine qua non* of the good character of the x? Will not everyone instantly declare a world fitted only for fair-weather human beings . . . to be from a moral point of view incommensurably inferior to a world framed to elicit from the man every form of triumphant endurance and conquering moral energy? . . . [T[he highest good can be achieved only by our getting our proper life; and that can come about only by help of a moral energy born of the faith that in some way or other we shall succeed in getting it if we try pertinaciously enough. The world *is* good, we must say, since it is what we make it— and we shall make it good.[33]

The position James articulates here—echoed in other key moments of his writings—represents the ethical culmination of his pragmatism. A pragmatic definition of truth as a function within the transactions of experience requires us to renounce the security of pretended absolutes for a world of contingency and flux, but affirms the role that our beliefs and actions play in creating the morality of our world. The facts of our world depend, at least in part, on our actions and the beliefs that motivate them, and true beliefs about the moral nature of our world are simply beliefs that allow us to engage that world in a manner satisfying to our mental and moral needs. This constitutes a radical departure from the dominant tradition that views the morality of the world as guaranteed by its ontological cause, fixed teleology, or eternal order: the notion of a "universe with such as *us* contributing to create its truth," James asserts, constitutes "an alteration in the 'seat of authority' that reminds one almost of the protestant reformation."[34]

The real significance of this last analogy, which might be dismissed as a hubristic miscalculation of pragmatism's epochal significance, lies in stressing how pragmatism's metaphysics include an inescapably individualistic element.[35] In the passage above, James describes the morality of our world as an ongoing struggle that has an ineradicably subjective component, a struggle that—despite our fundamentally social nature—gets fought out on an individualized basis. The human purposes that help create facts and truth exist as the beliefs, choices, and judgments of individuals. In a pluralistic universe—where, as described above, things exist in myriad actual and potential relations to other things, so that "nothing includes or dominates over everything," and a thing that is "actively engaged in one of these relations is not *by that very fact* engaged in all the other relations simultaneously"— both the knowing of the world and the interactions between things that result in novel realities occur in a radically diffuse manner. The conceiving of things and their various relations; subsequent acts to realize or utilize these relations in ways that help create novel results; and the experiencing of these consequences, upon which the truth of those conceptions are judged—these *all* occur in the experience of individuals who exist in particular and different parts of the universe. Though we are cultural, symbol-using animals whose perceptions and purposes are thoroughly shot through with ideas derived from other humans' thinking, truth still has, as James describes it, an ineradicably individual locus, always emerges in the experiences of individuals—in the "x" that each individual adds to the facts of the world through his beliefs and acts, and in the subsequent experiencing of the "M+x" that constitutes the "verification" of those beliefs.

Pluralism also means, of course, that the transformations effected and verifications experienced by any individual can never cover the whole of truth: the verification of a truth like the morality of our universe cannot "occur in the life of a single philosopher" but requires the "co-operation of generations ... to educe it": "all the evidence will not be 'in' till the final integration of things, when the last man has had his say and contributed his share to the still unfinished x." Thus, for James, the task of "making" the truth of our world is simultaneously individualized *and* collective. "Let it not be said," he asserts, "that x is too infinitesimal a component to change the character of the immense whole in which it lies imbedded."[36] For if to believe in a pluralistic universe—where "truth grows up inside of all the finite experiences," where reality grows "in all sorts of places, especially in the places where thinking beings are at work"—implies that no individual's experience can ever cover the whole of truth, it also implies that the whole of truth can never be made or verified except in and through individuals' experiences.

The individualistic focus and tenor of James's arguments surely mark a difference between him and John Dewey: it is not Dewey's style to rhapsodize, as James does, on the "dauntless subjectivity" of the individual choosing to brave a melioristic stance toward the risks of a pluralistic world. Yet such differences ought not obscure the fact that the individualism James articulates is a logical extension of the pluralistic metaphysics and melioristic ethics he shares with Dewey—the fact that Dewey too describes individuality as ineradicable and precious, as a means of introducing a crucial element of novelty and imagination into our attempts to remake our world, and as a central end or aim of any democratic community. James's choice to employ a rhetoric designed to inspire in his readers (and himself) an energetic faith in the efficacy and significance of their individual choices and actions can be explained in any numbers of ways: as reflecting James's own temperamental and psychological need to overcome depression; as a response to the philosophical landscape of his day, especially the biological determinism of Herbert Spencer; or, as Deborah Coon has argued, as an "anarchistic" response to the corporate and imperialistic forms of "bigness" that he saw as increasing dominating turn-of-the-century American democracy.[37]

What is clear, is that James saw the individualism implicit in a pluralistic meliorism as one of pragmatism's main strengths as a philosophy. Pragmatism offered the most rational and healthy philosophy, he argued, not only because it affirmed "the old confidence in human values" and "spontaneity"—but specifically because it asserted the power and necessity of individuals' deploying of those values. No philosophy can succeed, he argues, unless it ascribes to the universe "a character for which our emotions and active propensities shall be a match. Small as we are, minute as is the point by which the cosmos impinges upon each one of us, each one desires to feel that his reaction at that point is congruous with the demands of the vast whole—that he balances the latter, so to speak, and is able to do what it expects of him"[38] (a claim that explains *half* of what James means in the lecture outline above, when he says individualism means "obligation respondent to demand"[39]). "Any mode of conceiving the universe which makes an appeal to this generous power," he continues, which "makes the man seem as if he were individually helping to create the actuality of the truth whose metaphysical reality he is willing to assume, will be sure to be responded to by large numbers." As this passage clarifies, James views individualism—like pluralism and meliorism—as a hypothesis or faith: a belief to be tested by its ability to lead us into satisfying relations in experience, and a belief, he argues, whose truth will reside, in part, in its ability to unleash the diverse energies of human mind interacting with the creative changes of our pluralistic world. "All great periods of revival, of expansion of the human mind, display in common, we shall find, . . . simply this: that each and all of them have said to the human being, 'The inmost nature of the reality is congenial to *powers* which you possess.'"[40] James promoted pragmatism as heralding such a revival, as the philosophical and ethical culmination of democratizing tendencies in modern history, while Dewey after him hoped that a pragmatic experimentalism could help usher in a broader ideal and practice of democracy as a way of life. A pragmatic reconception of individualism was for James—and for Dewey after him—a central part of these hopes.

The individualist ethics that emerge from James's pluralistic meliorism are, as I discuss below, most clearly outlined in the "Pragmatism and Religion" lecture that concludes *Pragmatism*. But to understand fully how individualism figures in James's ethics, we must first turn from these broader contours of his pragmatism, to the more specific analyses of mind and the self articulated in his seminal *Principles of Psychology*.

The Jamesian Self: Habit, Character, and Destiny

Sow an action, and you reap a habit; sow a habit and you reap a character; sow a character and reap a destiny.

—William James

The occasional lectures and essays that most clearly articulate James's individualist ethics can be fully understood only in relation to his *Principles of Psychology*, which not only contains his most sustained analysis of selfhood,[41] but more broadly outlines the analyses of mind that shape his model of self and individuality.[42] John Dewey called *Principles* "the greatest among the great works of James," and repeatedly cited it as the work that most influenced his own instrumentalism.[43] Although *Principles* officially maintains a subject-object dualism, its landmark achievement, Dewey argues, lies in the way it prefigures James's eventual rejection of such dualism for a wholly transactional model of experience, by describing mind as a set of processes within the mutually transforming interactions of an organism and its environment.[44] This "biological behavioristic" approach does not produce a reductively materialistic view of experience as "merely biological," Dewey insists, for James's fundamentally active, teleological model of mind—as directing the efforts of a creature to transform the environment to meet its needs—constitutes a pragmatic theory of truth "in embryo," and implies the central pragmatic faith that human "interest and purpose are capable of directing knowing and the fruits of knowing" so as to "render experience in all its aspects richer and freer." Most importantly, Dewey argues, by stressing the "interactivity of organism and environment," James paved the way for a wholly experimental approach to human conduct, for a scientific approach to understanding, and hence controlling, the "organic conditions" and the "environing conditions" that cooperate in bringing "experienced situations . . . into existence."[45]

Extending Dewey's insights, I want to stress how the model of moral selfhood elaborated in *Principles* reflects this vision of experience as a mutually transforming interaction in which self and environment are both plastic. James's analyses of the various aspects and properties of mind stress, in general, the creative power of human purposes to remake experience, and outline, more specifically, different ways that individuality introduces a crucial element into this process: a "sagacity" for intuiting conceptions that may either stem from the physiological idiosyncrasy of individual brains *or* be cultivated in the habits of vocational expertise that focus attention; the "fringes" of individual consciousness that intimate new directions and connections beyond one's attentive focus; and the strength of will needed to attend and consent to an ideal in a moral situation of difficult or tragic choice. At the same time however, James insists that the creative potential of individuality is realized only through an interaction of individual and environment: offering a Darwinian analysis of the dynamic between "great men" and their environment, he insists that individuality effectively catalyzes change only when the novel element it offers is "selected" by the needs and opportunities immanent in the environment. James, in Emersonian fashion, democratizes this model of individuality, insisting that we all can, and should, strive to cultivate the habits of moral and even "heroic" selfhood that will prepare us to recognize and struggle for the ideal possibilities embodied in those parts of the pluralistic universe we inhabit.

This model of moral selfhood depends upon the plasticity or educability of the self that is implied in a transactional model of experience, a plasticity that James locates in the centrality of habit in human conduct. Prefiguring fundamental strains of Dewey's social psychology, James describes character as a complex composite of habits, and argues that even our higher intellectual and moral faculties—such as association, reasoning, and choice or volition—depend on habits. Character is thus to a large extent plastic: selfhood is a process of education, of remaking character by choosing new actions (and ends) and thereby cultivating new habits. While James stresses the power of individual choice in self-culture, he also stresses how environmental conditions encourage the experiences that create and reinforce good habits. These aspects of James's psychology—along with his insistence that even our strongest base instincts are modifiable—prefigure Dewey's ideal of democracy-as-education, and help illuminate how James's "Moral Equivalent of War" offers a distinctly pragmatic model of social reform.

James opens *Principles* by situating the processes of mind firmly within the interactions of an organism and its environment: "minds inhabit environments which act on them and on which they in turn react," so that "mental life seems to intervene between impressions made from without upon the body, and the reactions of the body upon the outer world again," and the criterion of "mentality" is "*the pursuance of future ends and the choice of means for their attainment.*"[46] The function of knowing thus is explicitly active or teleological: not to copy reality, but to focus selectively on specific aspects of reality and thereby allow a creature to transform the environment in ways that serve its needs. "Consciousness," James asserts, is a *"fighter for ends,"* a *"selecting agency."* The various aspects of mental activity James analyzes—such as sensation, perception, conception, attention, and habit—all reveal this dynamic of "selective attention" motivated by human interest and purpose: "few of us are aware," he notes, "how incessantly" this "choosing activity" is "at work in operations not ordinarily called by these names." "To begin at the bottom, what are our very senses themselves but organs of selection?" he asks, whose selectivity is then compounded by attention, which "out of all the sensations yielded, picks out certain ones as worthy of its notice and suppresses all the rest." What we define as "things" are really only "special groups of sensible qualities, which happen practically or aesthetically to interest us, to which we therefore give substantive names," and when we proceed to conceptualize a thing, in order to reason about how it may behave or be manipulated, "the mind selects again," and "chooses certain of the sensations to represent the thing most *truly*": "all Reasoning depends on the ability of the mind to break up the totality of the phenomenon reasoned about, into parts, and to pick out from among these the particular one which, in our given emergency, may lead to the proper conclusion." Hence, *"the only meaning of essence is teleological,"* James concludes: "The essence of a thing is that one of its properties which is so *important for my interests* that in comparison with it I may neglect the rest." James here not only anticipates the pragmatic view that the truth of a belief about an object depends on whether the consequences of acting on that belief prove satisfactory to our purposes, but affirms as well the corollary assertion that our purposes and actions contribute to the creation of novel fact and truth: that our habits and beliefs determine what we notice and what we do, which actions in turn help shape future outcomes. Our purposes and interests order experience by carving it out and adding to it: "Consciousness, from our natal day, is of a teeming multiplicity of objects and relations," James writes, later explicating that "millions of items of the outward order are present to my senses which never properly enter into my experience. Why? Because they have no *interest* for me. *My experience is what I agree to attend to.* Only those items which I *notice* shape my mind—without selective interest, experience is an utter chaos."[47]

Crucially, if James stresses that experience is malleable to the creative power of human purpose and intellect, he also insists that experience is thereby imbued with an inherently ethical or tragic quality:

> We see that the mind is at every stage a theatre of simultaneous possibilities. Consciousness consists in the comparison of these with each other, the selection of some, and the suppression of the rest by the reinforcing and inhibiting agency of attention. . . . The mind, in short, works on the data it receives very much as a sculptor works on his block of stone. In a sense the statue stood there from eternity. But there were a thousand different ones beside it, and the sculptor alone is to thank for having extricated this one from the rest. . . . Other sculptors, other statues from the same stone! Other minds, other worlds from the same monotonous and inexpressive chaos! My world is but one in a million alike embedded, alike real to those who abstract them. How different must be the worlds in the consciousness of ant, cuttle-fish, or crab![48]

Moving, as he typically does, from a pragmatic analysis of truth as an active process in experience, to the metaphysical and ethical concerns that follow from this analysis, James here anticipates the pluralistic concerns voiced in "The Moral Philosopher and the Moral Life" and "On a Certain Blindness in Human Beings": that, in a pluralistic world, the realization of one possibility necessarily excludes others, and that, as practical creatures carving out the world to meet our own needs, we are inevitably ignorant to the ideals and purposes with which other beings create their own order in the universe.[49]

James's analyses of mental processes in *Principles* also specify ways in which individuality manifests itself as a creative force within the interactions of experience. In an oft-quoted remark, James cites the wisdom of an "unlearned carpenter of my acquaintance," that "There is very little difference between one man and another; but what little there is, *is very important*."[50] By way of unpacking this axiom, it is first worth stressing that, though we are separate individual beings, there is much about our behavior that is uniform, not individual. James explains this in evolutionary and cultural terms: as members of the human species, animals with human brains and bodies, our habits and purposes—and thus the things we attend to in experience—will in many ways be remarkably similar,[51] and this physiological similarity will compounded by what James, in *Pragmatism*, calls "common sense," the cultural constructs of human intelligence that have become so conventional that they almost inescapably shape our reality: "the world *we* feel and live in will be that which our ancestors and we, by slowly cumulative strokes of choice, have extricated out of this, like sculptors, by simply rejecting certain portions of the given stuff."[52]

Yet there are also crucial ways in which our experience is individualized. One capacity James particularly stresses is "sagacity"—the ability to perceive or intuit the essence of a thing as pragmatically defined; namely, that aspect of a thing that will allow us to manipulate it best for our purposes, to predict and control how it will interact with other things—which ability is, James argues, essential to reasoning.[53] Sagacity is closely allied to "association by similarity," the capacity to determine how two things that in many ways may seem quite unlike are in one crucial regard—crucial, that is, for the purpose we have at hand—alike. James argues that this capacity, on which the unique power of human reasoning depends, varies significantly in individuals—both in terms of one's general facility for association by similarity, and in terms of the specific subjects or topics in which one has such facility. In part, he describes sagacity as an intuitive affair that cannot be taught, "Even when his interest is distinctly defined in his own mind, the discrimination of the quality in the object which has the closest connection with it is a thing which no rules can teach." When considering *"why does it require the advent of a genius in many cases before the fitting character is brought to light,"*[54] James attributes such sagacity to a physiological idiosyncrasy of individual brains:

> The conceiving of the law is a spontaneous variation in the strictest sense of the term. It flashes out of one brain, and no other, because the instability of that brain is such as to tip and upset itself in just that particular direction. But the important thing to notice is that the good flashes and bad flashes, the triumphant hypotheses and the absurd conceits, are on an exact equality in respect of their origin. . . . And the personal tone of each mind, which makes it more alive to certain classes of experience than others, more attentive to certain impressions, more open to certain reasons, is equally the result of that invisible and unimaginable play of the forces of growth within the nervous system, which, irresponsibly to the environment, makes the brain peculiarly apt to function in a certain way.[55]

Yet if James views the highest form of sagacity exhibited by geniuses as physiological, he also affirms that sagacity can be learned through experience, through cultivating the habits of vocational expertise that serve to focus a professional's attention on the salient details and possibilities of a situation:

> A library, a museum, a machine-shop, are mere confused wholes to the uninstructed, but the machinist, the antiquary, and the bookworm perhaps hardly notice the whole at all, so eager are they to pounce upon the details. . . . A layman present at a shipwreck, a battle, or a fire is helpless. . . . But the sailor, the fireman, and the general know directly at what corner to take up the business. They "see into the situation"—that is, they analyze it—with their first glance. It is full of delicately differenced ingredients which their education has little by little brought to their consciousness.[56]

Such accumulated experience, James asserts, allows experts to perform the extrapolation to novel circumstances that is akin to more intuitive leaps of sagacity: "Saturated with experience of a particular class of materials, an expert intuitively feels whether a newly-reported fact is probable or not, . . . instinctively knows that, in a novel case, this and not that will be the promising course of action."[57]

In this latter case, individuality is not simply an innate physiological trait, but rather emerges from the dynamic interaction of organism and environment. Individuality here describes the particularity of a person's self considered as a history or career—the unique set of habits and capacities one person has cultivated by deploying his innate talents in his particular circumstances. In some regards, all carpenters may be more alike than different, may experience some situations in ways that set them apart from lay persons, and yet the particular experiences of each carpenter will also afford differences of insight that might make a great deal of difference in a specialized situation.[58] The main point is that individual sagacity—whether innate or cultivated—plays a crucial role in realizing possibilities in a pluralistic universe. In a universe where all things "at all times exist in many possible connexions which are not necessarily actualized at the moment" and "a thing may be connected by intermediary things, with a thing with which it has no immediate or essential connexion," there will be possibilities immanent in a situation that will not come to fruition unless an individual with the sagacity to intuit those possibilities acts upon them.

This individual, James elsewhere insists, must also in some significant fashion love the circumstances he is engaged with:

Every Jack sees in his own particular Jill charms and perfections to the enchantment of which we stolid onlookers are stone-cold. And which has the superior view of the absolute truth, he or we? Which has the more vital insight into the nature of Jill's existence, as a fact? Is he in excess, being in this matter a maniac? or are we in defect, being victims of a pathological anaesthesia as regards Jill's magical importance? Surely the latter; surely to Jack are the profounder truths revealed. . . . We ought, all of us, to realize each other in this intense, pathetic and important way.

If you say that this is absurd, and that we cannot be in love with everyone at once, I merely point out to you that, as a matter of fact, certain persons do exist with an enormous capacity for friendship and for taking delight in other people's lives; and that such persons know more of truth than if their hearts were not so big.[59]

The argument James here applies to our ability to imagine the significance of others' lives can be applied more broadly to our relations with the world. James's frequent assertions that reason cannot be artificially divorced from the sentiments, passions, and beliefs that shape human conduct, suggest that the truth or reality of a situation—its possibilities and its ills—will be most adequately known by an observer whose attention, imagination, and willingness to pledge himself in action are heightened by a meaningful intimacy and caring. Such caring, further, seems necessarily an individual or localized affair: a matter of emotional attachments forged through the intimacy a person develops in the course of living with, and working on, the materials of a specific environment.

In the above cases, the creative force of individuality depends upon a *focusing* of attention and energy. And yet James is profoundly aware that our habits and concepts—while productively and necessarily focusing our attention—inevitably limit our perception as well, ignore and suppress as much as they reveal. As he famously argues in the "Stream of Thought" chapter of *Principles*, the "transitive parts" of consciousness tend—in part because of the structure and syntax of our language—to be suppressed or ignored in our practical focus on the "substantive" conclusions and "resting places." Yet for pragmatism, a concept's function is to lead us satisfactorily into new experiences; it must appear "less as a solution . . . than as a program for more work, and more particularly as an indication of the ways in which existing realities may be *changed*." Further, given a world where experience "grow[s] by its edges," and "one moment of it proliferates into the next by transitions which, whether conjunctive or disjunctive, continue the experiential tissue," James affirms that "Life is in the transitions as much as in the terms connected; often, indeed seems to be there more emphatically."[60] This deeply Emersonian side of James's thought—which Richard Poirier has eloquently explored[61]—leads him to valorize the creative aspect of individual experience that lies not in a focusing of attention, but rather in the vague "fringe" or "halo of felt relations" that surround and exceed every mental or verbal image in the stream of thought, intimating possible connections and transitions:

> One may admit that a good third of our psychic life consists in these rapid premonitory perspective views of schemes of thought not yet articulate. . . . "[T]endencies" are not only descriptions from with-out, but . . . are among the *objects* of the stream, which is aware of them from within, and must be described as in a very large measure constituted of *feelings of tendency,* often so vague that we are unable to name them at all. It is, in short, the re-instatement of the vague to its proper place in our mental life which I am so anxious to press on the attention. . . . Every definite image in the mind is steeped and dyed in the free water that flows around it. With it goes the sense of its relations, near and remote, the dying echo of whence it came to us, the dawning sense of whither it is to lead. The significance, the value, of the image is all in this halo or penumbra that surrounds and escorts it. . . . Great thinkers have vast premonitory glimpses of schemes of relations between terms, which hardly even as verbal im-ages enter the mind, so rapid is the whole process. We all of us have this permanent consciousness of whither our thought is going.[62]

For James, the diversity of individual experience exists most vitally not in the conceptions and connections we have already forged, but in the feeling of diverse relations that extend from one part of experience in many directions. If moral selfhood entails the ability to recognize the ideal possibilities of a given situation, this requires cultivating a salutary openness to the vague aspects of experience that point beyond the practi-cal focus of any given moment.[63] This mandate has crucial ethical con-sequences for our relations to others, as well; as James famously argues in "On a Certain Blindness in Human Beings," an awareness of the other possibilities beyond our own purpose enjoins us to respect the other be-ings who might cherish them.

Lastly—but for James most importantly—because our ability to help realize nascent possibilities in the world requires not just the sagacity to recognize them, but the willingness to act energetically enough to help bring them into being, moral selfhood requires the strength of will requisite to so commit ourselves, especially in moral situations of a difficult or tragic choice. James locates will in the feeling of effort we experience in effecting certain voluntary actions: its "*essential achievement*" being to "*ATTEND to a difficult object and hold it fast before the mind*" until that idea successfully dominates "the disposition of the man's consciousness" so as to effect the desired action (or inhibition of an action). This effort of attention, James adds, becomes an affirmative "fiat" of "*consent to the reality of what is attended to*": "When an idea *stings* us a certain way," he notes, we adopt an "imperative" stance toward it, "we say *let it be* a reality." The consent of will ultimately "means *our* adoption of things, *our* caring for them, *our* standing by them." The existence and necessity of this individual energy is most evident, he notes, in moral choices, ones in which we are aware that choosing to pursue one good comes at the painful cost of losing other goods, where a "dead heave of the will" indicates that "the chooser realizes," "in the very act" of choosing the "triumphant alternative" and "murdering the vanquished possibility," just "how much in that instant he is making himself lose."[64]

The amount of effort a person can put forth in such situations, James argues, is the most profound standard by which we judge ourselves as moral beings; the "dumb responses" of our volitional consents "seem our deepest organs of communication with the nature of things":[65]

> When a dreadful object is presented, or when life as a whole turns up its dark abysses to our view, then the worthless ones among us lose our hold on the situation altogether. . . . But the heroic mind does differently. To it, too, the objects are sinister and dreadful, unwelcome, incompatible with wished-for things. But it can face them if necessary, without for that losing its hold upon the rest of life. The world thus finds in the heroic man its worthy match and mate; and the effort which he is able to put forth to hold himself erect and keep his heart unshaken is the direct measure of his worth and function in the game of human life. He can *stand* this Universe. . . . He can still find a zest in it, not by "ostrich-like forgetfulness," but by pure inward willingness to face the world with those deterrent objects there. And hereby he becomes one of the masters and the lords of life. He must be counted with henceforth; he forms a part of human destiny.[66]

The valorization of "heroic" selfhood (and manhood) here should not obscure the fact that James's meliorism seeks to democratize radically such heroism: the constant hortatory theme of his writings is that we all can and should aspire to find in the risks and hardships of a pluralistic universe an inspiring sense of moral challenge and meaning. James's emphasis on the necessity of individual will is—like his broader meliorism—a moral postulate or belief. Whether to believe that our actions as individuals, as small as they may be, are effective causes, is, he insists, a practical question of analysis, and the truth of any choice we make in attributing causality (whether, for instance, we locate it in an individual's acts or in large-scale environmental factors) can only be determined in relation to our purposes and how satisfactorily the belief serves them.[67] It is on this basis that James urges us (as Emerson does) to treat heroic individuals as models for emulation: by "imagining as strongly as possible what differences their individualities brought about in this world, whilst its surface was still plastic in their hands, . . . each one of us may best fortify and inspire what creative energy may lie in his own soul." A belief in the moral efficacy of our wills will be verified in the only way, for a pragmatist, it could ever be: if that belief inspires our will to act, and the experience of action (successful and thwarted) yields us a sense of possibility and meaning that we find sufficient to the moral needs of our nature. The effort to attend to a difficult idea, James acknowledges, might do no more than "deepen and prolong [its] stay in consciousness" for a mere second: "but that second might be *critical*" when faced with competing moral demands, in allowing one idea to "develop itself" in consciousness and "exclude the other": "When developed it may make us act; and that act may seal our doom." The conditional mood here is crucial: possibility is all James insists upon. "The whole feeling of reality, the whole sting and excitement of our voluntary life, depends on our sense that in it things are *really being decided* from one moment to another."[68] So long as we find our belief in the significance of our individual will and actions verified in our experience, James argues we would be foolish not to adopt a melioristic and individualistic faith.

Although the "Stream of Thought" and "Consciousness of Self" chapters in *Principles* constitute a sustained analysis of selfhood, James does not here—or anywhere in his corpus—attempt as systematic an analysis of moral selfhood as Dewey does in his 1938 *Ethics*. In the broadest terms, James notes, moral selfhood encompasses all that education teaches us about reasonable choice—"the whole of one's training to moral and prudential conduct, and of one's learning to adapt means to ends."[69] But the aspects of individuality outlined above—a sagacity for recognizing new conceptions and ideals, a salutary openness to the vaguer tendencies and possibilities of experience, and the love and will to commit one's self in the struggle to realize ideals—are the elements of moral selfhood that are most distinctive to James's philosophical vision. These ethical aspects of the analyses of mind offered in *Principles* form the central themes of the more explicitly ethical essays discussed in this chapter's concluding section below.

While James affirms these contributions that individuality makes to the creative remakings of the world, he also asserts that individuality—whether based in a physiological difference or cultivated habits—can be realized and exercise its creative power *only* within the possibilities defined by environing conditions. Adapting a Darwinian logic of individuals as "spontaneous variations" that are "selected" by their environment, James describes individuals and their environing communities as existing in a dynamic of mutual transformation.[70] Both individual selves and communities, he argues, are best thought of as careers or histories; they have real contingencies and turning points where some possibilities are excluded as one is pursued and realized. The ability of an individual, at a specific moment in his life, to pursue (and even imagine) possibilities of future selfhood is limited by his environment (by both the habits it has encouraged leading up to that moment and the opportunities for action it now presents); conversely, the direction of change at a specific moment in a community's career depends upon the contingent presence or absence of individuals with the abilities—and power—to further opportunities embodied in that moment:

> The mutations of societies, then, from generation to generation, are in the main due directly or indirectly to the acts or the example of individuals whose genius was so adapted to the receptivities of the moment, or whose accidental position of authority was so critical that they became ferments, initiators of movement, setters of precedent or fashion, centres of corruption, or destroyers of other persons, whose gifts, had they free play, would have led society in another direction. . . . [Nations] may be committed by kings and ministers to peace or war, by generals to victory or defeat, by prophets to this religion or to that, by various geniuses to fame in art, science, or industry. . . . Communities obey their ideals; and an accidental success fixes an ideal, as an accidental failure blights it. . . . The fermentative influence of geniuses must be admitted as, at any rate, one factor in the changes that constitute social evolution. The community

may evolve in many ways. The accidental presence of this or that fer-
ment decides in which way it *shall* evolve. . . . If shown a certain way,
a community may take it; if not, it will never find it. And the ways are
to a large extent indeterminate in advance. A nation may obey either
of many alternative impulses given by different men of genius, and
still live and be prosperous, just as a man may enter either of many
businesses. Only the prosperities may differ in their type.

But the indeterminism is not absolute. Not every "man" fits every "hour." . . . A given genius may come either too early or too
late. . . . [W]hat makes a certain genius now incompatible with his
surroundings is usually the fact that some previous genius of a different strain has warped the community away from the sphere of his
possible effectiveness. . . . Each bifurcation cuts of certain sides of
the field altogether, and limits the future possible angles of deflec-
tion. . . . [T]he social surroundings of the past and present hour exclude the possibility of accepting certain contributions from individuals; but they do not positively define what contributions shall be
accepted, for in themselves they are powerless to fix what the nature
of the individual offerings shall be.[71]

The most important aspects of James's analysis here all follow from his
assertion that genuine, plural contingencies exist in—and due to—the
mutually transforming interactions of individuals and their environments. First, it is not an optimistic teleological account: at any moment
a community may pursue various possible paths, and the path a society
takes, while it may prove prosperous, may also prove disastrous, and any
achieved form of prosperity will always come at the exclusion of other possible prosperities. There is also no guarantee that the direction taken at any
moment will be determined either by the most urgent or important needs
of the community (there is no "invisible hand" here directing results to
a beneficial, rational outcome), nor that individuals with the skills most
needed by the moment will exist, or if they exist, will prevail as the crucial actors directing social change. Change may be determined by a person
whose "genius" best fits "the receptivities of the moment" (which in itself
need not imply beneficial changes), but may also be determined by persons
whose "accidental position of authority" allows them to become "centres
of corruption" and "destroyers of other persons" and other possibilities.

Which is all to say that James here is offering the radically contingent view of history that pluralism requires—one that acknowledges
real risk and tragic exclusions. But the corollary of such genuine risk,
as James always stresses, is the genuine possibility of success and the

consequent affirmation that our individual choices have meaning. James asserts that individuality plays an ineradicable creative role. Although he admits individuality is not merely physiological, but is significantly shaped by environmental "infra social" forces,[72] it would be absurd, he argues, to think that individuality does not introduce an independent element of contingency into social change—to think, for instance, that the individuality of those persons who serve as the critical "ferments" in a given social situation can be accounted for as wholly determined by the environment. It would be absurd, he notes, to suggest that the advent of a Shakespeare was somehow necessitated or explained by the environment, so that had he "died of cholera infantum, another mother at Stratford-upon-Avon would needs have engendered a duplicate copy of him, to restore the sociologic equilibrium."[73] Taking seriously the creative potential of individuality leads James, as it does Emerson, to an ethics of vocation that is both egalitarian and tragic. Egalitarian, for to posit a pluralistic universe, in which creative change is fostered when the diverse insights, passions and skills of individuals interact with the myriad nascent possibilities that obtain between things, is to affirm that each person has a potentially significant role to play in realizing the possibilities of experience. While most of us do not have the unique sagacity of geniuses, we should all strive to cultivate the habits of sagacity, openness, and will that can prepare us to recognize and realize the possibilities immanent in our environment. Tragic, because possibilities in such a universe always exceed actualities, and the gifts of many persons will fail to find meaningful fruition in the circumstances of the moment. For James, social progress and a meaningful individual life require that one not dwell on the risk of failure and loss, but instead pursue the possibility of finding an adequate opportunity to develop and use our talents. As Emerson puts it in "The Uses of Great Men," though "the cheapness of man is every day's tragedy," yet "true art is only possible, on the conviction that every talent has its apotheosis somewhere."[74]

In broader terms, James's affirmation of the importance of individuality provides the mandate for a democratic and experimentalist approach to managing social change: a mandate to cultivate individuality among all the members of society, to help all persons to develop their potentials, so that they might in turn help realize the most inclusive range of ideals in experience; to adopt meritocratic institutions that increase the likelihood that individuals with the most needed talents will be in positions to use them on behalf of the public good; and to adopt experimental and democratic and processes for establishing the goals, and judging the results, of cooperative efforts. James most clearly articulates this vision—which aligns him with thinkers like Emerson, John Stuart Mill, and John Dewey—in the ethics of experimental process and melioristic vocation advocated in "The Moral Philosopher and the Moral Life" and "Pragmatism and Religion." Before turning to those texts, however, we must first explore how James's sense of the educability of human nature—based on the pervasive role of habit—undergirds his ethics of remaking our selves and world.

The ability to cultivate traits of moral selfhood depends upon the plastic nature of the self. If a transactional model of experience allows pragmatists like James and Dewey to assert the power of individuality to help remake the environment, it also allows them emphasize the remarkable extent to which selfhood is plastic. To insist that individuality emerges only within the interactions of a self and environment is to view selfhood as a history or career, one in which the environing circumstances that limit the self also elicit the self's creative possibilities. As Dewey argues in "Time and Individuality," to assert that transaction, temporality, and individuality are central to the fabric of our pluralistic reality is to reject the Aristotelian view that change unfolds a potential already fixed by an organism's nature or "kind," and see instead real contingency at the heart of selfhood.

> First, and negatively, the idea . . . is excluded that development is a process of unfolding what was previously implicit or latent. Positively it is implied that potentiality is a category of existence, for development cannot occur unless an individual has powers or capacities that are not actualized at a given time. But it also means that these powers are not unfolded from within, but are called out through interaction with other things. . . . When the idea that development is due to some indwelling end which tends to control the series of changes passed through is abandoned, potentialities must be thought of in terms of consequences of interactions with other things. Hence potentialities cannot be *known* till *after* the interactions have occurred. There are at a given time unactualized potentialities in an individual because and in so far as there are in existence other things with which it has not yet interacted.[75]

Dewey's ideal of democracy—which makes education a fundamental goal of all forms of human association—is based on this plastic potential of human nature, which Dewey locates in the pervasive role of habit.[76] Habit, the ability of an organism to incorporate into its dispositional makeup modes of interaction with its environment, describes the nexus of the mutually transforming interaction between a living creature and its environment; it describes the mechanism by which the environment shapes the individual creature, and by which in turn the creature reacts upon the environment. While habit is often associated with routine or calcified aspects of conduct, pragmatism insists that habit in fact enables us to remake ourselves. If individuality exists only through interactions with environing conditions, it is not therefore fatally determined by them, for—as Dewey insists in the passage above—objective conditions provide the opportunities for new interactions through which the self grows and changes. To the extent that selfhood is composed of habits formed in interactions with objective conditions, it can be remade through the process of pursuing new ends, recreating environing conditions, and thereby cultivating new habits. The essentials of this pragmatic view of habit, which underpins the whole of Dewey's social thought, are established in James's *Principles of Psychology*. Indeed, James's most significant contribution to a pragmatic reconception of individualism probably lies in the way his analysis of habit affirms that we both can and must remake human personality by reconstructing the conditions of human association.

"When we look at living creatures from an outward point of view," James notes, "one of the first things that strikes us is that they are bundles of habits." Some of James's greatest insights were, as a psychologist, to recognize the remarkable extent to which we are, as the old cliché runs, creatures of habit and, as a moralist, to assert the consequences of this fact. James's definition of habit is rooted in his biological approach to mind as an intermediating function coordinating stimuli from environing conditions and effecting motor responses to those conditions. Far from yielding a deterministic account of conduct, this biological approach stresses the adaptability and dynamism of living creatures, a dynamism that James locates in the "*plasticity of the organic materials of which their bodies are composed*"—especially the ability of the brain to form pathways of neural discharge that are persistent yet modifiable, which allows living creatures to translate their interactions with the environment into patterns of adaptive response. Habit, considered as a fundamental law of organic behavior, is not constricting but enabling: without such organized patterns of response, living creatures could not pursue their practical interests in the world. In human behavior, James notes, habit *"simplifies the movements required to achieve a given result, makes them more accurate and diminishes fatigue,"* and *"diminishes the conscious attention with which our acts are performed"*; without this focusing and economizing of effort, he concludes, we "would be in a sorry plight." The role of habit is especially pronounced in human conduct, James argues, because we differ from other animals in the superior plasticity of our brains, in the fact that so few of our instincts are fixed, but instead require experience to train them into habits. Indeed, he concludes, the basic function of human instincts is to *"giv[e] rise to habits"*—and even then remain plastic to further modifications: "in man the negation of all fixed modes is the essential characteristic. He owes his whole pre-eminence as a reasoner, his whole human quality of intellect, we may say, to the facility with which a given mode of thought in him may recombine anew. Only at the price of inheriting no settled instinctive tendencies is he able to settle every novel case by his reason of novel principles. He is, *par excellence,* the *educable* animal."[77]

Viewed from this perspective, it "appears that habit covers a very large part of life"; indeed, it becomes hard to see what aspects of human behavior are *not* conditioned and enabled by habit. If selfhood is a process or history, then "character"—the capacities and dispositions that constitute a self at any given moment in its history—can be described as a composite of habits: "character," James notes, "is an aggregate of tendencies to act in a firm and prompt and definite way upon all the principal emergencies of life." Anticipating Dewey's definition of character as "the interpenetration of habits," James argues that our highest moral faculties, such as reasonable deliberation and choice—depend on the ability of habits to mutually inhibit and modify each other. Even "the most complex habits" are, from a physiological point of view, "nothing but *concatenated* discharges in the nerve-centres, due to the presence there of systems of reflex paths, so organized as to wake each other up successively," and any habit or instinct, as such a reflex path, is liable to be "'inhibited' by other processes going on at the same time, . . . must take its chances with all the other arcs, and sometimes succeed, and sometimes fail, in drafting off the currents through itself."[78] Extending this analysis, James, like Dewey after him, rejects any dualistic opposition of reason to instincts, impulses, or habits, instead describing reason as a process of deliberation enabled by the diversity of human habits:

> Nature implants contrary impulses to act on many classes of things, and leaves it to slight alterations in the conditions of the individual case to decide which impulse shall carry the day. . . . They are all impulses, congenital, blind at first, and productive of motor reactions of a rigorously determinate sort. *Each one of them, then, is an instinct*, as instincts are commonly defined. *But they contradict each other*— "experience" in each particular opportunity of application usually deciding the issue. *The animal that exhibits them loses the "instinctive" demeanor* and appears to lead a life of hesitation and choice, an intellectual life; *not, however, because he has no instincts—rather because he has so many that they block each other's path*. . . . In other words, there is no material antagonism between instinct and reason. Reason, *per se*, can inhibit no impulses; the only thing that can neutralize an impulse is an impulse the other way. Reason may, however, make an *inference which will excite the imagination so as to set loose* the impulse in the other way.[79]

James here anticipates Dewey's analysis of deliberation as a process that is wholly dependent upon habit: a process of imaginative rehearsal of possible courses of action—which are themselves projections of existing habits—in which a "reasonable" course of action is that which best (or most inclusively) harmonizes the competing habits that compose one's character.[80] As James notes in the passage quoted previously, this ability of habits mutually to modify each other in choosing what end to pursue—this "facility with which a given mode of thought may in him may recombine anew"—is what makes humankind "*par excellence, the educable* animal." For the interaction of our diverse habits not only allows us to exercise those habits in novel combinations befitting novel situations, but in so doing we strengthen and reinforce one combination of habits and weaken other habits, thereby literally remaking the dispositional composition of our selves.

The "*ethical implications of the law of habit*," James asserts, are "numerous and momentous." Indeed, James's entire approach to ethics— from his most specific pedagogical suggestions to his broadest vision of individual vocation in a pluralistic universe—reflect this dynamic by which our actions in and on the world around us recast our habits and so remake our characters. On the one hand, James acknowledges the enormous conservative force of habit: our dependence, as practical beings, upon habits of attention and action (and the fact that our brains are most plastic when we are young) means that "in most of us, by the age of thirty, the character has set like plaster, and will never soften again," and "dooms us all to fight out the battle of life upon the lines of our nurture or our early choice, and to make the best of a pursuit that disagrees, because there is no other for which we are fitted, and it is too late to begin again." James thus claims that habit is "the enormous fly-wheel of society, its most precious conservative agent" that "alone . . . keeps us all within the bounds of ordinance, . . . saves the children of fortune from the envious uprisings of the poor," and "prevents the hardest and most repulsive walks of life from being deserted by those brought up to tread therein."[81]

Yet the curiously conservative note James strikes here—concluding "on the whole, it is best . . . for the world" that we "should not escape" the constricting force of habit—is an anomaly in his writings. In accord with his pluralistic celebration of openness and possibility, James typically emphasizes how the operations of habit allow and even empower an ethics of self-refashioning. The dynamic of habit implies that every interaction we have with our environment reshapes our brain, either strengthening existing neural pathways and combinations or forging new ones: "*an unmodified brain*" is, "strictly speaking," a "physiological impossibility." Thus a "physiological" approach to mind is "the most powerful ally of hortatory ethics," for it stresses that we are inevitably remaking our character in the acts we pursue every day—a fact that "has its good side as well as its bad one": "As we become permanent drunkards by so many separate drinks, so we become saints in the moral, and authorities and experts in the practical and scientific spheres, by so many separate acts and hours of work." Over the course of time, our accumulated actions literally remake ourselves: "the daily drill and the years of discipline end by fashioning a man completely over again, as to most of the possibilities of his conduct." Thus choices about which ends to pursue, and what kind of future to help create, are fundamentally choices about character. In "critical ethical moments," where a person must "choose which *interest* out of several, equally coercive, shall become supreme," the "choice really lies between one of several equally possible future Characters. What he shall *become* is fixed by the conduct of this moment." Moreover, though character is a cumulative product, James also insists that such choices have a more immediate impact: prefiguring Dewey's argument that the function of a projected end-in-view is to provide order and meaning to *present* activity, James suggests that in choosing ends to pursue, an individual not only chooses what future self he or she will strive to become, but thereby changes the present quality or tendency of his or her character. What is at stake is "less what act he shall now choose to do, than what being he shall now resolve to become."[82]

James specific prescriptions for education and self-culture likewise stem from this central dynamic of activity, habit, and choice. To see experience as wholly transactional, and to see mind as structured by habits that we gain only through interactions with our environment, implies that our ability to imagine or choose an action (and thus also our ability to deliberately cultivate a habit) depends on our first having undergone an experience of that activity:

> Since a willed movement is a movement preceded by an idea of itself, the problem of the will's education is the problem of a how the idea of a movement can arouse the movement itself. . . . [F]ramed as we are, we can have no *a priori* idea of a movement, no idea of a movement which we have not already performed. Before the idea can be generated, the movement must have occurred in a blind, unexpected way, and left its idea behind. . . . [I]n physiological terms, . . . the problem is that of the formation of *new paths*.[83]

This observation has far-reaching consequences, ones crucial to both James's and Dewey's views of education, for it implies that our highest intellectual and moral capacities—James is here talking about will and choice—depend on, and can be cultivated through, action. Not only can we imagine or choose an action only if we have undergone it, and so formed a new path in our nervous system, but we can hope for reliable success in choosing and performing an action *only* if that experience undergone has been strengthened into a habit.

Hence, James describes education as hinging on activity: on leading students (or one's self) through the repeated actions that will successfully form instincts into beneficial habits. "The great thing . . . in all education," he asserts, "is to *make our nervous system our ally instead of our enemy*":[84]

> *Seize the very first possible opportunity to act on every resolution you make, and on every emotional prompting you may experience in the*

direction of the habits you aspire to gain. It is not in the moment of
their forming, but in the moment of their producing *motor effects*,
that resolves and aspirations communicate the new "set" to the
brain. . . . No matter how full a reservoir of *maxims* one may possess, and no matter how good one's *sentiments* may be, if one have not
taken advantage of every concrete opportunity to *act*, one's character
may remain entirely unaffected for the better.[85]

Two consequences of this general view, as James elaborates them, merit
special note. First, an individual can deliberately remake his character—
literally give a new "set" to his brain—by willfully and persistently performing acts that will cultivate beneficial habits and weaken harmful
ones. "There is no more valuable precept in moral education," he asserts,
"than this": "if we wish to conquer undesirable emotional tendencies in
ourselves, we must assiduously, and in the first instance cold-bloodedly,
go through the *outward movements* of those contrary dispositions which
we prefer to cultivate. The reward of persistence will infallibly come,
in the fading out of the sullenness or depression, and the advent of real
cheerfulness and kindliness in their stead." Second, James also insists
that the effective cultivation of new habits requires not only individual
will and persistence, but the salutary support of conditions: one must
"accumulate all the possible circumstances which shall re-enforce the
right motives; put yourself assiduously in conditions that encourage the
new way." James thus contends that "in all pedagogy the great thing is to
strike while the iron is hot, and to seize the wave of the pupil's interest
in each subject," so that impulses may be effectively trained into habits.
This can occur only if the diverse range of our instincts finds proper exercise in the interests and activities afforded by the social environment:
"In a perfectly-rounded development, every one of these instincts would
start a habit toward certain objects and inhibit a habit toward certain
others. Usually this is the case; but, in the one-sided development of civi-
lized life, it happens that the timely age goes by in a sort of starvation
of objects, and the individual then grows up with gaps in his psychic
constitution which future experiences can never fill."[86]

The view of education that James outlines here anticipates, in important ways, the Deweyan ideal of democracy-as-education explored
in chapters 4 and 5. Dewey, like James, stresses that our highest moral
faculties must be cultivated through actions that create habits. If, for instance, we want people to find satisfaction in acting with others toward

ends that serve the common good (a key component of Dewey's model of moral selfhood), we must give them enough opportunities for acting in that fashion, and for experiencing the satisfactions of doing so, till it becomes a habitual impulse, a part of their dispositional makeup whose demand to be satisfied will exert a steady and effective force on choice. Further, providing the opportunities for such activity requires attending to the social conditions that shape our habits: in this sense, "education" happens not only, or even primarily, in schools, but in all the forms of associated activity that help form our habits. And, lastly, Dewey, like James, stresses that, if our habits *must* be deliberately remade, they also *can* be. In marked contrast to the Freudian psychology that has dominated much contemporary thinking about the self, which posits certain primal impulses (sexual and violent) as essential drivers of human conduct, impulses that can be repressed or sublimated only in an incomplete manner that renders a divided human psyche, James and Dewey's pragmatic emphasis on the plasticity of human habits insists that even our most primal and recalcitrant impulses can be successfully reshaped and redirected by experience. Regarding sexual instincts, James notes that "here, if ever, . . . we ought to find those characters of fatality, infallibility, and uniformity" that characterize our most instinctive impulses, but the "facts are just the reverse": "the sexual instinct is particularly liable to be checked and modified by slight differences in the individual stimulus, by the inward condition of the agent himself, by habits once acquired, and by the antagonism of contrary impulses operating on the mind."[87] These aspects of James's thought that look ahead to Dewey are most clearly evidenced, as I discuss at the end of this chapter, in the vision of reform articulated in "The Moral Equivalent of War."

In "The Vanishing Subject in the Psychology of James," Dewey argued that perhaps the most striking aspect of *Principles of Psychology* was the manner in which James, while officially professing a dualism of subject and object, mental and material, in fact described almost all aspects of selfhood (whether they be "material," "social" or even "spiritual") as *objective*—as existing in those parts of an individual's environing conditions (including his body) in which he takes the most intense interest.[88] Thus, though James is at great pains to identify a "nucleus" or inner core of the self that constitutes some wholly subjective, spontaneous contribution the self adds to experience—which, as discussed above, he ultimately locates in the phenomenon of will, the energy of effort an individual can

put forth in consenting to a difficult but necessary idea—he then, having
asserted this spontaneous contribution, suggests that such energy is not
a sheer act of will, the spontaneous effort of a "heroic mind," but rather
the result of habits cultivated through interactions with environment.
James stresses, for instance, that will can only choose among actions
and ideas that are themselves products of habit—its "power is limited
to *selecting* amongst those which the associative machinery has already
introduced"—and, further, implies that the effort of will is itself a faculty, like a habit, that can be cultivated, exercised, and strengthened: "the
problem of the will's education" in "physiological terms" is like the challenge of creating any other habit that will enable voluntary action—"the
problem . . . of the formation of *new paths*." Accordingly, James advises
readers to "*Keep the faculty of effort alive in you by a gratuitous exercise
every day*. That is, be systematically ascetic or heroic in little unnecessary
points, do every day or two something for no other reason than that you
would rather not do it." A person "who has daily inured himself to habits
of concentrated attention, energetic volition, and self-denial," will "stand
like a tower" when "the hour of dire need draws nigh,"[89] which provides
further gloss on the claim, already noted, that "we become saints" just
as we become drunkards, "by so many separate acts and hours of work."

The crucial point, for the purposes of this study, is how thoroughly
the moral self James advocates is a product and process of education.
When James examines the phenomenon of "self-love," he concludes that
selfhood exists most meaningfully not in the mere fact of our individual
existence, the sheer fact of subjectivity, but in those aspects of the environing world in which an individual has cultivated a habitual interest:
"To have a self that I can *care* for, nature must first present me with some
object interesting enough to make me instinctively wish to appropriate
it for its *own* sake, and out of it to manufacture one of those material,
social, or spiritual selves, which we have already passed in review." Thus,
speaking of the "social self," he asserts that the recognition and identity
we crave from others is "not as being a bare I," but as an I who "belongs
to a certain family and 'set,' who has certain powers, possessions, and
public functions, sensibilities, duties, and purposes, and merits and des-
erts."[90] To clarify what is at stake here, let me refer to a salient example
of moral courage from Dewey's *Democracy and Education*, discussed at
some length in chapter 4: the case of a doctor who, in a time of plague,
continues to tend to sick patients, although he does so at risk to his life.

This is clearly an example of the kind that James's makes paramount to the moral self: the ability to consent to and act upon a difficult, but morally necessary, ideal when doing so risks sacrificing other interests or ideals we value highly. What James and Dewey make clear is that this capacity comes not from some sheer effort of will, from the ability to renounce aspects of one's self in pursuit of a nobler, higher good. Rather, it stems from cultivated habits that constitute selfhood. Dewey's doctor has, through years of professional training, practice, and service, cultivated habits of a professional and vocational selfhood strong enough to demand satisfaction even in such a difficult situation; a self that exists so profoundly in the interests defined by these professional duties and functions could not renounce them except by incurring a loss of self or identity that would be more profound than the mere loss of subjectivity brought by death.

"Sow an action, and you reap a habit; sow a habit and you reap a character; sow a character and reap a destiny." This handwritten motto James inscribed in his copy of *Psychology, Briefer Course*, encapsulates the way in which, for James, questions of human conduct that begin in the physiological bases of habit, extend to the largest questions of moral selfhood and metaphysics. Our acts are the building blocks through which a self that exists in the objective transactions of experience can remake its character and become a self equipped to play a moral role in a pluralistic universe—James's "heroic" self in which the world "finds its worthy match and mate," who has the sagacity, love and openness to recognize the ideals at stake in instances of moral possibility and risk, and the strength of will to pledge his or her efforts (and self) in striving to realize those ideals, and who thereby "forms a part of human destiny." In James's pluralistic, melioristic vision, remaking our selves and remaking the world are inextricably linked and interdependent processes. James's pragmatic individualism, as articulated in his most explicit statements on ethics, elaborates various aspects of this central moral vision.

Individuality and Community in James's Ethics: Pluralism, Experimentalism, Democracy

In concluding my consideration of James, I want to explore how his most explicit articulations of an individualist ethics extend the major elements of his pragmatism that I have mapped above: his pragmatic theory of truth, his pluralistic meliorism, and his transactional model of self-hood. James's most explicit statements on ethics are articulated in a series of occasional lectures—"The Moral Philosopher and the Moral Life," "On a Certain Blindness in Human Beings," and "What Makes a Life Significant"—that are both well known and clearly evince his individu-alistic commitments. Yet perhaps because James never wrote a more sys-tematic treatment of ethics—likely since his entire philosophical project is so thoroughly moralistic—the individualistic aspects of the ethics laid out in these lectures are too seldom recognized as logical extensions of his pragmatism. For James, a pragmatic theory of truth, with its assertion that our beliefs and the actions they inspire enter legitimately into the creation and verification of truths, reminds us that we have the right—indeed the obligation—to choose the moral hypotheses on which we will base our ef-forts to lead meaningful and moral lives. Specifically, pragmatism allowed James to argue for the moral hypotheses he believed were most rational to our intellectual and moral needs: a pluralistic meliorism that describes a universe still in the making, whose ultimate outcome and moral truth can be shaped by our actions and the beliefs that inspire them, and a belief in a God whose qualities—and limitations—are consistent with such a plu-ralistic universe of real contingency and loss. James's work is motivated by this consistent hortatory aim: to convince us that we can energetically rise to the challenges and rewards of life in a pluralistic universe of real possibility and loss, and to urge us to cultivate and exercise the qualities of moral selfhood required by such a universe. Thus the melioristic vision of individualized vocation that concludes *Pragmatism* represented for James the most rational consequences of the philosophy articulated in the pre-ceding lectures. Moreover, though James's ethics have important collec-tive or communal aspects (as discussed below), his message is pointedly addressed to us *as individuals*. To believe in pluralism, James insists, is to see individuality—individual purposes, insights, desires, actions, and en-ergies of will—as an indispensable means and end in the process through which possibilities become "realized" in the dual sense of that term: both actualized or brought into being, and judged or experienced as moral goods. These dynamics mandate, on the one hand, an individualistic as-sertiveness, since many goods in experience will be realized only if certain individuals pursue their varied purposes and ideals with sufficient energy. On the other hand, because such insistent focus inevitably blinds us to other ideals we might pursue—and, crucially, to ideals cherished by other beings—pluralism requires an individualistic openness to new possibilities and tolerance for the aims others pursue.

These twin individualistic strains of James's ethics are consistent with the familiar image of the "anarchistic" James who declared himself an enemy of "bigness" in all forms.[91] While most readers acknowledge the democratic value of James's impassioned plea for tolerance and openness toward others' desires, some critics conclude such individualism seriously limits James's political vision: the "hands-off" credo James voices implies too negative a model of liberty, while his fear of institutional "bigness" renders him incapable of endorsing the collective efforts at reforming social conditions that would constitute a more positive effort to provide individuals with concrete, liberating opportunities. In order to complicate this familiar line of argument—and the too-facile opposition it draws between an individualistic James and a more socially engaged Dewey—I close by examining James's late lecture "The Moral Equivalent of War." Though not normally read in relation to his individualism, this lecture provides crucial evidence that James's pluralistic model of a self whose habits are formed in the transactions of experience led him to embrace a more collective project of reforming social institutions in order to educate individuals in the habits of moral selfhood. The attitudes toward reform that underlie James's argument embody some of pragmatism's most appealing political features—features that look ahead to Dewey's ideal of democracy as education.

It is in "The Moral Philosopher and the Moral Life" that James offers his most comprehensive discussion of ethics. Though brief, this piece lays out in bold strokes an approach to morals that is radically pluralistic, empiricist, experimental, and democratic—providing the broad ethical framework in which the individualist strains of James's ethics must be understood. James focuses mainly on two related questions: the "metaphysical" question of the nature or meaning of "good," "ill," or "obligation," and the "casuistic" problem of how to rank or measure various goods. In Pragmatism James famously argues that truth is not some quality or essence inhering in objective reality, but involves judgments about the usefulness of the ideas we use to engage our world: facts simply "are," James affirms, while truth involves "what we say about them," which means true in relation to particular purposes.[92] This general theory of truth applies more obviously in the case of moral truths, which involve questions not of what is, but what ought to be, or which result would be better than another. Things in our world have moral meaning or quality, James insists, only within the experience of a particular sentient being who feels or judges them to be good or bad, better or worse:

> Nothing can be good or right except so far as some consciousness feels it to be good or thinks it to be right.... [T]he real superiority and authority which are postulated by the philosopher to reside in some of the opinions, and the really inferior character which he supposes must belong to others, cannot be explained by any abstract moral "nature of things" existing antecedently to the concrete thinkers themselves with their ideals. Like the positive attributes good and bad, the comparative ones better and worse must be *realized* in order to be real. If one ideal judgment be objectively better than another, that betterness must be made flesh by being lodged concretely in someone's actual perception.[93]

James then notes that this location of moral value in the desires and judgments of particular beings also explains the nature and source of "obligation":

> Take any demand, however, slight, which any creature, however weak, may make. Ought it not, for its own sole sake, to be satisfied? If not, prove why not. The only possible kind of proof you could adduce would be the exhibition of another creature who should make a demand that ran the other way.... Any desire is imperative to the extent of its amount; it *makes* itself valid by the fact that it exists at all.[94]

As James acknowledges, this empiricist approach to morals constitutes a radical departure from traditional theological and philosophical schemes that "imagine an abstract moral order in which the objective truth resides."[95] In contrast, James describes a universe in which moral truth and meaning exist in a radically dispersed and particularized form: a moral meaning can *only* exist in the quality of satisfaction a particular being experiences upon the advent of a result in a particular situation, or in the perceived lack of satisfaction from a situation when a desired ideal is not actualized.

This empiricist location of morality within the experiences of concrete beings leads James to conclude that only a pluralistic theory of morals is possible. If one posits a "divine thinker with all-enveloping demands," then "his ideal universe" would indeed provide an ultimate moral standard, but since "exactly what the thought of the infinite thinker may be is hidden from us even were we sure of his existence," James notes that the plurality of goods and obligations felt by concrete beings admits of no theoretical or ideal unification, beyond the "*most* universal" or generic principle "that *the essence of good is simply to satisfy demand*":

> The demand may be for anything under the sun. There is really no more ground for supposing that all our demands can be accounted for by one universal underlying kind of motive than there is ground for supposing that all physical phenomena are cases of a single law. The elementary forces in ethics are probably as plural as those of physics are. The various ideals have no common character apart from the fact that they are ideals. No single abstract principle can be so used as to yield to the philosopher anything like a genuinely useful casuistic scale.[96]

Similarly, if the essence of "the good" is simply to satisfy demand, and any desire creates by virtue of its existence a legitimate claim, there is no "guiding principle" that can unify ethical philosophy beyond the injunction "simply to satisfy at all times *as many demands as we can*[.] That act must be the best act, accordingly, which makes for the *best whole*, in the sense of awakening the least sum of dissatisfactions. . . . [T]hose ideals must be written highest which *prevail at the least cost*, or by whose realization the least possible number of other ideals are destroyed."[97]

James here enacts one of the defining moves of pragmatism, arguing that moral philosophy must turn away from the search for theoretical solutions and toward an experimental search for practical solutions to specific problems—toward, as James's title suggests, the moral life. Truths, pragmatists assert, cannot provide us with any theoretical certainty; they do, however, provide indispensable tools for analyzing the ills of a particular situation, projecting ideas for remaking that situation, and judging the subsequent results of our efforts. Crucially, this pluralistic approach to morals also emphasizes that the practical task of judging ideals and outcomes is acutely urgent and fraught with inevitable failure, for an irreducible plurality of possible goods necessarily implies tragic limitation. A world in which each part of experience exists in plural relation to myriad other parts is one with genuine possibilities that *might* be actualized immanent in the varied relations between things, but also an inherently tragic world where each ideal realized excludes other possibilities:

the casuistic question . . . is most tragically practical. The actually
possible in this world is vastly narrower than all that is demanded;
and there is always a *pinch* between the ideal and the actual which
can only be got through by leaving part of the ideal behind. There
is hardly a good which we can imagine except as competing for the
possession of the same bit of space and time with some other imagined good. Every end of desire that presents itself appears exclusive
of some other end of desire. . . . So that the ethical philosopher's demand for the right scale of subordination in ideals is the fruit of an
altogether practical need. Some part of the ideal must be butchered,
and he needs to know which part.[98]

James's striking image of "butchering" the ideal insists upon the concrete nature of the gains and losses at stake in our moral lives. It stresses
the material basis of ideals, for to say an ideal is "possible," as he argues in "Pragmatism and Religion," is to argue that it is "concretely
grounded"—with various elements necessary to its actualization currently in existence.[99] Any such ideal *not* brought to fruition implies the
dying (or killing) off of that particular physical combination. More importantly, James's verb stresses the flesh-and-blood reality of the sentient beings whose desires project these ideals and invest the concretely
grounded possibilities of our world with moral meaning. And, third,
the violence of the phrase clearly signals to us that our efforts to realize our own ideals—in one sense the most constructive, life-affirming
thing we do as human beings—carries this inevitable threat of violence
to others.

Armed with these conceptions of the moral life—a pluralistic sense
that the goods and obligations of our world are as varied as the possible
demands sentient beings may feel in their interactions with the world, a
heightened awareness of the tragic competition between ideals and the
beings who hold them dear, and a consequent sense that the guiding
principle of morals must be to create conditions that allow for the most
inclusive satisfaction of demands—James argues that the task of morals
can be adequately fulfilled *only* through an experimental and democratic
process:

Everywhere the ethical philosopher must wait on facts. The thinkers who create the ideals come he knows not whence, their sensibilities are evolved he knows not how; and the question as to which of
two conflicting ideals will give the best universe then and there, can

be answered by him only through the aid of the experience of other men. . . . In point of fact, there are no absolute evils, and there are no non-moral goods; and the *highest* ethical life—however few may be called to bear its burdens—consists at all times in the breaking of rules which have grown too narrow for the actual case. There is but one unconditional commandment, which is that we should seek incessantly, with fear and trembling, so to vote and to act as to bring about the very largest total universe of good which we can see. Abstract rules indeed can help; but they help less in proportion as our intuitions are more piercing, and our vocation is the stronger for the moral life. For every dilemma is in literal strictness a unique situation; and the exact combination of ideals realized and ideals disappointed which each decision creates is always a universe without a precedent, and for which no adequate previous rule exists. . . . He knows that he must vote always for the richer universe, for the good which seems . . . most apt to be a member of a more inclusive whole. But which particular universe this is he cannot know for certain in advance; he only knows that if he makes a bad mistake the cries of the wounded will soon inform him of the fact. In all this the philosopher is just like the rest of us non-philosophers, so far as we are just and sympathetic instinctively, and so far as we are open to the voice of complaint.[100]

This passage—one of the most eloquent overviews of a pragmatic approach to ethics—is striking, first, for its pluralistic rationale for experimentalism: to affirm that novelties emerge from the myriad interactions of plurally interrelated parts of experience, is to insist that "every dilemma is in literal strictness a unique situation," and that the future results emerging out of any situation can never be fully predicted. Accordingly, we must "vote" and "act" to realize "the good which seems most apt to be a member of a more inclusive whole," but the collective results of our actions are "always a universe without precedent" that cannot be judged "in advance," so that our ideal aims must *always* be provisional and experimental, open to revision based on evaluation of actual results. Moreover, our existing, conventionally recognized truths and ideals, derived from past and different situations, will inevitably prove inadequate to cover different and novel situations: they cannot provide certainty, but only helpful principles to guide us in analyzing the specific ills, benefits, and promises of any given problem or attempted solution.

Second, it is critical to note the complementary interplay of individual and communal elements that compose the democratic aspect of James's experimental process. Individuality is for James an ineradicable factor in ethics, for individuals "realize" moral outcomes in the dual sense noted above: they are both the necessary agents of acts that help possibilities become real, and they are the seats of the moral feelings and judgments in which the morality of those outcomes exists. The "thinkers who create the ideals" and the "sensibilities" that motivate their efforts and judgments come we "know not whence"; and the "cries of the wounded" that any new result may elicit come from countless individuals whose perspectives we can never adequately "know for certain in advance." If particular human actors are central to morals, it is important to stress that particular humans are both individual and social: our perceptions, habits, acts, and ideals are all thoroughly shot through with inherited social ideals and truths that render our experience, in some ways, remarkably homogenized; conversely, each person also has a unique history, social position, temperament, and set of habits that shape his particular desires, purposes, and perceptions. To recall the folksy wisdom of James's "unlearned carpenter": "There is very little difference between one man and another; but what little there is, *is very important.*" The individual and communal aspects of experience each carry their own insights and limitations, and must balance and correct each other. As practical beings intent on our own purposes, our individual perceptions inevitably ignore values and possibilities perceived by others: "The very best of men must not only be insensible, but ludicrously and peculiarly insensible, to many goods."[101] Furthermore, James is acutely aware that locating moral value within the experience of individual beings carries the risk of subjectivism:[102] absent the verdict of some divine knower, the *only way* to ensure any objectivity for our moral judgments—any assurance that one's own cherished ideals would in some objective sense increase the moral value of the universe—is to listen to the testimony and judgments of other sentient beings. Individuals must depend on a communal response: the question as to "which of two conflicting ideals will give the best universe then and there" can be answered "only through the aid of the experience of other men." We must intently and actively listen to the judgments of others, especially the "cries of the wounded," when a new ideal is proposed or a new outcome achieved, and we must rely on the cumulative voice of the human community, as embodied in the truths and judgments derived from past experiences: the "philosopher must be a conservative," James asserts, in accepting that "the presumption in cases of conflict must always be in favor of the conventionally recognized good."[103]

Yet communal standards and judgments clearly impose their own dangerous constrictions. If our individual perspectives and purposes blind us, so too do the conventional or social ideals we have internalized. We are "blinded to the real difficulty of the philosopher's task by the fact that we are born into a society whose ideals are largely ordered already. If we follow the ideal which is conventionally highest, the others which we butcher either die and do not return to haunt us; or if they come back and accuse us of murder, everyone applauds us for turning a deaf ear." If James fears subjectivism, he has a more visceral fear of this opposing communal threat, for conventionally accepted values all too easily become dogmatically asserted as absolute and enforced by the dominant power structures. "Pent in under every system of moral rules," he notes, "are innumerable persons whom it weighs upon, goods which it represses." In relation to "that exuberant mass of goods with which all human nature is in travail, and groaning to bring to the light of day," the prospect of "individual moralists" serving as "pontiffs armed with the temporal power . . . to order which ideal shall be butchered and which shall be suffered to survive," rouses "all one's slumbering revolutionary instincts": "better chaos forever," James affirms, "than an order based on any closet-philosopher's rule, even though he were the most enlightened possible member of his tribe."[104]

The remedy to these communal excesses, James insists, lies in the salutary effects of individuality. It is the diversity of individual perceptions and purposes deployed throughout the various circumstances of our world that gives birth to that "exuberant mass of goods" James extols. Moreover, given that conventionally accepted truths, as noted above, inevitably become obsolete, James's injunction that the "presumption must always be in favor of the conventionally recognized good" is countered by the assertion that "the *highest* ethical life—however few may be called to bear its burdens—consists at all times in the breaking of rules which have grown too narrow for the actual case."[105] Individuals, with their particularized positions, purposes, and passions, are an indispensable source of insight into the novel problems and possibilities in experience and—as American thinkers from Emerson and Thoreau, to

James, Dewey, and Ellison all stress—individuals' willingness to challenge existing orthodoxy provides an indispensable democratic leaven to community.

For James, the experimental process of morals must be "democratic" in a specific sense that synthesizes the communal with the individual. We each have subjective biases that must be remedied by appeal to a community of moral inquirers and judges, and we share communal blindnesses that must be remedied by the insights of individuals. To achieve such a synthesis, the experimental process of remaking our world must be guided by a principle of inclusivity—the assertion that the better outcome will always be that which satisfies the richest total of demands, a principle based on the fundamental legitimacy of each sentient being's demands to be included, as far as possible, in the resulting whole. Further, putting this principle into practice requires not just a tolerance of others' values and pursuits, but an active attempt to remain imaginatively and sympathetically "open to the voice of complaint."

James's vision of an experimental process that synthesizes individual and communal elements suggests important links between his pragmatism and that of John Dewey, and highlights how pragmatism constitutes an alternative to classic liberal individualism. As I discuss in chapter 5, Dewey criticized classic liberalism for a narrow view of democracy as merely political and for promoting an absolutist vision of the individual and state: in the classic liberal view, democracy is a social contract among individuals for the minimal and negative purpose of protecting the individual liberty and equality that each individual inherently possesses. By contrast, Dewey insists democracy must be an ideal or way of life that shapes all aspects of human endeavor, and that supports our ongoing experimental efforts to remake the (social and natural) environments we inhabit, and, in the process, to remake our selves. Further, while Lockean liberalism portrays society as a regrettable necessity that individuals reluctantly accept, Dewey stresses that association is the fundamental fact of human life, not merely a safeguard for individual liberties but the medium of shared meaning that provides the highest enrichment of human experience. James's vision in "The Moral Philosopher and the Moral Life" has clear affinities to Dewey's project. The "moral life" he describes is really nothing less than *human* life, for *all* our efforts to achieve new goals involve moral choices and judgments. "In point of fact," James notes, "there are no non-moral goods."[106] For James, like Dewey, democracy is ultimately a subset of—or inseparable aspect of—the larger human project of experimentally remaking experience in order to maximize its meaning and value. And for James, as for Dewey, our efforts to realize our individual ideals gain their highest meaning only when they are validated by others as contributing to a richer and more meaningful universe.

The two main strains of James's individualist ethics supply the complementary aspects of moral selfhood required to support this democratic, experimentalist process. The first strain, most clearly expressed in the melioristic ethics of vocation articulated in "Pragmatism and Religion," affirms that our individual ideals, beliefs, and acts are necessary factors in realizing the moral possibilities of our world. This argument pulls together several major strands of James's pragmatism discussed in the first two sections in this chapter: first, the pluralistic view that things exist in multiple relations to other things (realized and latent) and that novelties emerge when parts of our world interact so as to actualize certain latent connections and combinations, and second, the accompanying assertion that many such possible results will emerge only when the right human actor intervenes—one equipped with the habits of moral selfhood James outlines in *Principles of Psychology*. In "Pragmatism and Religion," James describes such situations in terms of "concretely grounded" possibilities—what "possibility" always means: that "some of the conditions of production of the possible thing actually are here"—and stresses those occasions when our actions can supply the final elements needed to realize a possibility. James then applies this pragmatic definition to the "salvation of the world," arguing that pragmatism must "incline towards" the melioristic view that "treats salvation as neither inevitable nor impossible," but "as a possibility, which becomes more and more of a probability the more numerous actual conditions of salvation become."[107] James's larger aim, as always, is to persuade his audience that the idea of a pluralistic universe is most rational to our human needs, as it offers us the melioristic hope that our beliefs and actions may help create a better universe, and that a world that so imbues our actions with meaning—though it implies the inevitably of tragic exclusions and losses—is not merely sufficient to our human needs, but is best suited to our agonistic need for meaningful striving:

Take, for example, any one of us in this room with the ideals he cherishes and is willing to live and work for. Every such ideal realized will be one moment in the world's salvation. But these particular ideals are not bare abstract possibilities. They are grounded, they are *live* possibilities, for we are their live champions and pledges, and if the complementary conditions come and add themselves, our ideals will become actual things. What now are the complementary conditions? They are first such a mixture of things as will in the fulness of time give us a chance, a gap that we can spring into, and, finally, *our* act.

Does our act, then, *create* the world's salvation so far as it makes room for itself, so far as it leaps into the gap? Does it create, not the whole world's salvation of course, but just so much of this as itself covers of the world's extent?

Here I take the bull by the horns, and in spite of the whole crew of rationalists and monists, of whatever brand they be, I ask *why not?* Our acts, our turning-places, where we seem to ourselves to make ourselves and grow, are the parts of the world to which we are closest, the parts of which our knowledge is the most intimate and complete. Why should we not take them at their face-value? Why may they not be the actual turning-places and growing-places which they seem to be, of the world—why not the workshop of being, where we catch fact in the making, so that nowhere may the world grow in other kind of way than this?[108]

The elements of James's vision I want to stress are, first, the radically pluralistic, experimentalist, and melioristic model of moral meaning he presents, and, second, the crucial role that individuality plays in the creation of moral value. James reimagines "salvation" as having no ontological or teleological necessity: not as the foreordained outcome of a providential or omnipotent deity, but as the possibilities for moral meaning immanent *within* the material and temporal limitations of our pluralistic world. James's claim that "every such ideal realized will be one moment in the world's salvation"—again with the dual meaning of the word "realized"—recalls the pluralistic definition of "the good" from "The Moral Philosopher and the Moral Life": the idea that the moral value of our world is thoroughly diffused and "disseminated," existing in the diversity of particular ideals that individuals are able to translate into realized outcomes, *and* in the increased moral meaning individuals experience in those outcomes. This location of moral goods in particular empirical outcomes turns away from evil as a theoretic problem (as it appears in traditional theologies that posit a unifying deity), and toward the practical problem of experimentally seeking remedies to particular ills: "the way of escape from evil on this system is *not*," James asserts, "by getting it 'aufgehoben,' or preserved in the whole as an element essential but 'overcome'": rather, "*It is by dropping it out altogether, throwing it overboard and getting beyond it, helping to make a universe that shall forget its very place and name.*"[109]

James's vision is radically temporal, too, in that each unfolding "moment" of salvation must be succeeded and extended (and perhaps ultimately fulfilled) by subsequent moments. James's melioristic ideal of "salvation" here exhibits the fundamental temporality implied in the pragmatic theory of truth as an ongoing process of "verification" in which ideas are "made" true or "become" true. To the extent that a melioristic belief that our efforts may create a more moral universe leads us to consequences that verify that belief—so long as it inspires us to form ideals, and we experience a sufficient success in our efforts to realize them—in so far is that belief *made* true in our experience, verified in each present moment. Salvation becomes an ideal whose ultimate or complete fulfillment is endlessly deferred—as James insists, the moral truth of our universe cannot be determined until the last human has "had his say," added his efforts and judgments—and yet whose truth is "realized" or actualized in the growth of meaning we experience in each present moment of striving toward this ideal. As James puts it in "The Sentiment of Rationality," "the world *is* good, we say, since it is what we make it—and we shall make it good."[110] In these regards, James's vision of ideals, meaning, and progress is wholly consonant with Dewey's claim that the most vital function of an ideal or "end-in-view"—including our highest ideals like democracy, community, or liberty—is not as goals we will ever wholly actualize, but as aims that provide direction for our ongoing efforts at reconstructing experience, ideals that, in our efforts to better approach them, imbue our present activity with an enriched quality of meaning.

Second, it is crucial to note how this melioristic vision of moral progress affirms a necessary role for individuality, while also stressing the collective context individuality requires to achieve its fullest meaning. In his description of individuals striving to realize ideals in "the parts of the world to which we are closest, the parts of which our knowledge is the most intimate and complete," individuals watching for the "complementary conditions" that "concretely ground" the possibility of an ideal, providing a "mixture of things as will in the fullness of time give us a chance, a gap that we can spring into," James deploys all the aspects of moral selfhood outlined in *Principles of Psychology*: the sagacity, whether inborn or the cultivated insights of vocational expertise, to recognize the ills and possibilities in a given situation; the love necessary to generate the most profound insights into a situation—a love generated by the intimacy we develop with those parts of the world with which we are most closely engaged; and the strength of will to attend and consent to an ideal in a moral situation of difficult or tragic choice. James asserts that individuals, through these qualities, exert a creative force and help produce novel outcomes in the world: our acts are "the actual turning-places and growing-places . . . of the world," so that each successful act that realizes an ideal *does* "create the world's salvation so far as it makes room for itself," creating an improved moral quality in that extent of the world its influence "covers." Moreover, expressing the model of selfhood he shares with Dewey—and applying again the pragmatic view that pursuit of an ideal imbues present activity with quality and meaning—James insists that in remaking our circumstances we remake ourselves, that we redirect and strengthen the quality of our character as we devote our activity toward realizing an ideal: our "acts" are "turning-places" where we not only help the world grow, but "seem to ourselves to make ourselves and grow." Individualism here, like meliorism and pluralism, is a belief, a moral postulate to be verified pragmatically: if one believes one's acts may supply the missing condition necessary to realize an ideal, and that belief inspires one to rise to the occasion and act, and if that belief in turn meets sufficient success to verify it, then, as James asks, "*why not*" accept this pragmatic faith in the power and meaning of our individual acts? James's individualism, like the meliorism of which it is an essential component, is at heart a belief which he asserts is inspiring and rational to our human needs, and which we have the right—and responsibility—to test in the trials of experience.

This affirmation of individuality, however, must be understood within the tragic and collective frameworks in which James places it. The possibilities immanent in the fabric of a pluralistic universe, which enable the creative power of individuality, also make failure, exclusion, and loss inevitable. Hence, an energetic willingness to act upon the possibility that our efforts *may* successfully realize ideals must be achieved in the face of the knowledge that our acts may fail, that our own lives may be snuffed out unfulfilled, our most cherished plans and energies come to nothing, excluded by other elements and energies in the universe. James urges us that we can indeed embrace a "drastic kind of universe," one in which "there should be real losses and real losers, and no preservation of all that is": that the "disseminated and strung-along successes" achieved in a pluralistic universe are "sufficient" for our "rational needs" despite the fact of "unatoned" loss—"even though the lost element be one's self." Indeed, James characteristically argues such a universe is not just satisfactory, but well suited to our needs, that a universe without real loss would lack the elements of seriousness, risk, and challenge humans need and crave in order to make life meaningful. "May not the notion of a world already saved *in toto* anyhow, be too saccharine to stand? May not religious optimism be too idyllic? Must *all* be saved? . . . Doesn't the very 'seriousness' that we attribute to life mean that ineluctable noes and losses form a part of it, and that there are genuine sacrifices somewhere, and that something permanently drastic and bitter always remains at the bottom of its cup?"[111]

We see here again why James's pragmatism endorses a vision of heroic individuality. For if, as James proposes, to be "a genuine pragmatist" means to "accept sincerely" such a "drastic" universe, to be "willing to live on a scheme of uncertified possibilities which he trusts; willing to pay with his own person, if need be, for the realization of the ideals which he frames"—then a pragmatic meliorism clearly requires the strength of will James identifies with moral selfhood: the ability to consent to an ideal, and commit one's energies to it, even in those cases where the tragic costs of such choice are painfully evident. As noted above, this heroic individualism is democratized in James, in that he insists *all* people can aspire to such moral fortitude and be prepared to risk the energies of their lives for the ideals they cherish. As he brought matters home to his audience for the *Pragmatism* lectures, the ideals held by "any one of us in this room" are not "bare abstract possibilities," for "we are their live champions and pledges."[112]

It is important to note that the Jamesian self is not some autonomous, self-sufficient, or exceptional actor: the heroic possibilities of individual action are further democratized in that they require a collective context to provide moral meaning and psychological inspiration. James's terminology of a "moment" in the world's salvation stresses the ways in which individualized, local efforts to remake the world necessarily contribute to a collective result. My efforts to realize ideals in my corner of the world will combine with all the efforts of other beings living and acting in my historical moment to create the new world of next week or next year, while in the long term the melioristic task of verifying the moral value of our universe "requires the co-operation of generations": "all the evidence will not be 'in' until the final integration of things, when the last man has had his say and contributed his share."[113]

It is an empty truism, perhaps, to state that individual acts by definition compose a collective result, but the stance we take toward this fact, and the meaning we draw from it, is far from empty. For James, only a collective context can supply our individual acts with the meaning needed to guard us from a debilitating moral subjectivism. As he argues in "The Moral Philosopher and the Moral Life," it is only by subjecting our efforts to realize our ideals to the moral judgments of the community that we gain any objective assurance that our efforts to have indeed made the universe better. A central theme in lectures such as "What Makes a Life Significant" and "The Moral Equivalent of War" is that our individual lives achieve full significance only when enlisted in the service of ideals that contribute to some larger, collective effort. An individual's effort to achieve one moment in the world's salvation gains needed meaning and dignity for being part of the collective effort of human history—the attempt to build a more moral world. Moreover, this collective meaning is critical to the energy of will required by James's model of moral selfhood: without the belief that our own ideals promise to contribute to some larger moral good, most of us, James fears, would not be willing to pay "with our own persons" to realize our ideals. We could not attain what he famously termed "the strenuous mood" in morals, in which we are "indifferent to the present ill, if only the greater ideal be attained."[114] James concluded that a wholly naturalistic ethics—a "merely human world without a God"—could not offer the moral meaning needed to elicit this "maximal stimulating power." The hope that we are creating a more moral world for our human descendents is insufficient to motivate our strongest individual energies, for "we do not love these men of the future keenly enough." James accordingly argued that only the postulate of a divinity who values the outcomes of our struggles depicted a universe maximally rational to our human needs.[115]

To overlook these collective aspects of James's ethics—which extend, in the largest sense, beyond a merely a communal scope to a cosmic sense of cooperation with the divine—is to seriously distort the ethical thrust of his individualism. In marked contrast to classic liberal individualism—which posits an individual primarily motivated by rational calculations of self-interest, describes society as a social contract or contrivance designed to safeguard individual rights and property, and only secondarily argues that the market efficiencies generated by individuals' self-interested pursuits benefit the common good—James's individualism describes a self engaged in the collective moral project of experimentally remaking our world, a self whose ideals and actions must always be tested for their ability to harmonize, coexist, and participate with the ideals of the other sentient beings striving to shape their own meaningful experiences.

The collective and tragic contexts of James's individualism explain the second main strand of his individualist ethics. For if a pluralistic world requires an assertive self—whose purposes focus his attention in a fashion that helps him form ideals, see possibilities, and pursue them with the energy needed to realize them—this insistent practical nature of our intelligence also threatens to blind us to other possibilities we might pursue, and the possibilities held dear by other beings. This concern is most famously articulated in the companion essays, "On a Certain Blindness in Human Beings," and "What Makes a Life Significant":[116]

> We are practical beings, each of us with limited functions and duties to perform. Each is bound to feel intensely the importance of his own duties and the significance of the situations that call these forth. But this feeling is in each of us a vital secret, for sympathy with which we vainly look to others—the others are too much absorbed in their own vital secrets to take an interest in ours. Hence the stupidity and injustice of our opinions, so far as they deal with the significance of alien lives. Hence the falsity of our judgments, so far as they presume to decide in an absolute way on the value of other persons' conditions or ideals.[117]

This "certain"—as in inevitable—blindness we suffer as practical beings entails a clear ethical mandate:

> It absolutely forbids us to be forward in pronouncing on the meaninglessness of forms of existence other than our own; and it commands us to tolerate, respect, and indulge those whom we see harmlessly interested and happy in their own ways, however unintelligible these may be to us. Hands off: neither the whole of truth, nor the whole of good, is revealed to any single observer.[118]

Beyond this negative injunction to tolerate, indulge, and suspend criticism on other beings' values, James also advocates a positive effort to overcome our blindness by cultivating a sympathetic, loving appreciation for other beings and their ideals.[119] This aspect of moral selfhood harmonizes with James's injunction, in "The Stream of Thought" chapter of *Principles*, that we should "reinstate the vague" in our "mental life," remaining open to the "fringe" of possibilities that exist beyond our own attentive focus. Taken together, such loving receptivity can, on remarkable occasions, leave us open to a "gleam of insight" into the "the vast world of inner life beyond us," occasions when "our self is riven," the "whole scheme of our customary values gets confounded," and "a new centre and a new perspective must be found." Yet since our insistently practical makeup makes it unlikely we should "gain much positive insight into one another," we must "at least," James insists, "use our sense of our own blindness to make us more cautious in going over the dark places."[120]

Ultimately, these ethical concerns are best addressed by insisting on democratic procedures in the experimental processes of human experience. Democratic procedures provide a mechanism to keep us "open to the voice of complaint," making us more likely to hear the "cries of the wounded" whenever a new project is proposed or implemented. But democratic procedures are more than a mere safeguard; they are also a means of education, a mode of participating with others through which we can best cultivate the habits of conscientious and sympathetic openness to others that James demands. This broad view of democracy as education, explicitly championed by Dewey, represents a fulfillment of James's ethical commitments and concerns. James's healthy skepticism of our ability to overcome the blindnesses imposed by our practical nature is counterbalanced by his faith—expressed in *Principles of Psychology*—that our ability to cultivate new habits makes humans "*par excellence*, the *educable* animal." Critics have justly argued that James, in "What Makes a Life Significant" and "The Moral Equivalent of War," rather clumsily betrays his own class biases—even as he attempts to tackle the issue of blindnesses across class lines. Yet James's proposal for a universal conscription into an "army" engaged in public works is more important, I would suggest, as demonstrating James's commitment, in embryo perhaps, to the ideal of communal education I have just outlined: an effort to promote the shared experiences that would encourage members of modern industrial society to cultivate a more sympathetic sense of openness to, and solidarity with, others.

These complementary strains in James's individualist ethics—synthesized in his vision of a moral self that energetically pursues its own dearest insights and ideals while remaining conscientiously open to the threat of suppressing or excluding the ideals of others—reflect a specifically pragmatic conviction that individuality is both a necessary means and a primary end. Our collective effort to make a more moral world—one with a more inclusive realization of human values and richer possibilities for continued growth—will be maximized if we allow, encourage, and cultivate an individualized diversity of creative endeavors. This focus on individuality as means has a decidedly utilitarian component, for the goods that result from the insights and efforts of creative individuals provide tools and benefits that enrich the common good. Yet because it locates moral value (both "good" and "obligation") in the concrete experiences of striving, sentient beings, James's pragmatism insists that the judgments and feelings of individuals demand a foundational respect within morals—not for their utility, but simply due to the sheer fact of their existence. This dual argument for the need to respect individuality in all human endeavors, and the implied view that democracy is not just a political system but an ideal for organizing all human activity, provide the best elaboration for the claim James offers in the lecture outline quoted at the head of this chapter: that individualism "means" democracy—because "good systems can always be described in individualistic terms."

In an 1899 letter, James expressed his visceral distrust of the forces of institutional "bigness," a statement that has become rightly regarded as a statement of his individualistic and even "anarchistic" sympathies:

> As for me, my bed is made: I am against bigness and greatness in all their forms, and with the invisible molecular moral forces that work from individual to individual, stealing in through the crannies of the world like so many soft rootlets, or like the capillary oozing of water, and yet rending the hardest monuments of man's pride, if you give them time. The bigger the unit you deal with, the hollower, the more brutal, the more mendacious is the life displayed. So I am against all big organizations as such, national ones first and foremost; against all big successes and big results; and in favor of the eternal forces of truth which always work in the individual and immediately

unsuccessful way, under-dogs always, till history comes, after they
are long dead, and puts them on the top.[121]

James's political sympathies here reflect the full range of ethical concerns
explored above: a faith that the creative energies of experience emerge
most vitally when individuals use their diverse insights and aims to uncover the possibilities of local situations; the obligation to be tolerant
of and open to others' ideals and pursuits; a fear that institutionalized
ideals and authorities dogmatically suppress such creativity and openness; and an assertion that the "highest ethical life" is engaged by those
individuals with the insight and courage to open avenues for liberated
and renewed activity by "the breaking of rules which have grown too
narrow for the actual case."

My aim in this chapter has been to argue that such individualistic
commitments are not only integral aspects of James's pragmatic philosophy, but constitute an important element in the enduring political value
of pragmatism. Critics often reach an opposite conclusion, pointing to
James's individualism as precisely the element that fatally limits his political vision and separates him from the more politically valuable—because
more socially engaged—vision of John Dewey. An early and instructive
version of this argument was voiced by M. C. Otto, who criticized James
as "all but oblivious to the character-forming significance of the economic conditions under which men live and work," underestimating the
"degrading effects" of poverty, and hence ignoring the need to reform
the institutionalized structures of class inequality. In noting that James's
assumptions about those living under economic hardship (specifically
their capacity to find adequate meaning in their struggles) betray the biases and blindnesses of his own upper-class background, Otto's critique
seems right on the mark; he is probably also correct that these biases
hindered James from imagining or endorsing significant reforms of the
socioeconomic structure.[122] But Otto diagnoses these particular blindnesses in James as symptoms of a larger "tendency to slight" the shaping
power of "environmental circumstances," and, further, places the blame
for this alleged failing squarely upon James's individualism—arguing
that his individualistic aversion to "bigness" rendered him incapable of
endorsing any meaningful efforts of social reform:

> Like Emerson, he was captivated by the ideal of absolutely unentan-
> gled and unfettered individuality. . . . Social institutions endangered

the purity of individuality. Even organizations formed to combat economic injustice and to win for deprived men and women a better chance at the basic requisites of a satisfying life were likely, by encroaching upon the "sacredness of private integrity," to be a greater evil than they evil they were intended to remedy.[123]

Crucially, in Otto's scheme, the political failure that aligns James with Emerson also separates him from Dewey: James failed to "recognize the vital interdependence of the individual and the environmental objects and procedures of which he lives and achieves. This truth was still to be elucidated by John Dewey."[124] Though Otto voices a particularly trenchant version of this critique of James, the opposition he establishes between James's individualism and Dewey's embrace of social reform has been perpetuated by other critics—even as they place James and Dewey in a common pragmatic tradition.[125]

As I have attempted to show in this chapter, such conclusions are simply inaccurate regarding the pragmatic assumptions James and Dewey shared, and hence badly oversimplify—if not outright misrepresent— the relations between their respective politics. Specifically, the "vital interdependence of the individual and the environmental," which Otto claims *separates* James and Dewey, in fact describes the model of experience as a mutually modifying transaction between individual and environment that constitutes a central link between James and Dewey— indeed, the strand of James's thought to which Dewey acknowledged himself most indebted. This model of experience implies *both* that individuality provides an element of novelty that is indispensable in the reform of environmental circumstances, *and* that individuality flourishes only when environmental conditions supply the necessary opportunities. The consequences of this dynamic are evident in James's politics as well as Dewey's. If James is a critic of institutional bigness, he is also a thinker deeply committed to education—to the centrality of habit in human personality and the dependence of habit upon social environment. For James, no less than for Dewey, reforming social conditions and remaking human personalities are necessarily interconnected processes. Pragmatism's most enduring political strength may lie in the way this model of experience encourages a balanced view of reform that avoids either a naive optimism or a debilitating pessimism: on the one hand asserting the plasticity of both self and environment, that our most stubborn, native impulses can be redirected into new habits, and our most entrenched institutions remain capable of being remade; on the other hand insisting that reform is maximized only when the fullest range of human capacities are liberated in ongoing processes of experimental inquiry, and that such capacities are adequately educated only when social conditions are reformed with any eye to their pervasive influence on character.

James most clearly expresses these pragmatic attitudes toward reform in his late lecture, "The Moral Equivalent of War." James's proposal is well known: to establish a mandatory national service enlisting youths in a variety of work serving the public good, for only by providing some such activity that fulfills the positive ideals of military service and struggle can the social energies currently satisfied by war be redirected into a peaceful social regime. My interest is not to assess the merits of James's proposal per se, so much as to highlight how his strategy reflects several quintessentially pragmatic stances toward the task of reform: first that the future must be created out of the materials in our present, that an ideal is possible—not mere fantasy—only if its possibilities are "concretely grounded" in existing conditions; second, as James argues in *Pragmatism*, that "older truths" exert an immense conservative force that must be overcome in any effort of reform. Because the influence of existing truths is in most cases "absolutely controlling," the function of new truths is to "marr[y] old opinion to new fact": opportunities for change arise in problematic situations, when our "stock of old opinions" is confronted by a "new experience that puts them to a strain," but the new idea adopted will be that which "preserves the older stock of truths with a minimum of modification." The unthinkable destruction of modern warfare constitutes such a problematic opportunity, James argues, for despite the entrenched power of the martial ideal, the "science of destruction" has made war "absurd and impossible from its own monstrosity."[126] Yet without incorporating what remains valuable in the martial ideal, James concludes, no pacifist ideal can hope to supplant it.

This analysis implies that the most powerful way to enact social reform is recognize and co-opt those elements of competing ideals or truths that *can* be redirected and enlisted in the service of the desired new ideal: "Pacifists ought to enter more deeply into the esthetical and ethical point of view of their opponents. Do that first in any controversy . . . *then move the point,* and your opponent will follow."[127] The rhetorical and political strategy here is also—deeply relevant, given James's pacifist topic—a democratic means to avoid conflict, build consensus, and fulfill the moral obligation for experimental openness to the ideals of others that James calls for in his other moral essays.[128] James observes his own injunction that we must beware how our new ideals might be "butchering" others' ideals, that we must listen for the "cries of the wounded" in each new project we propose, and applies it to the ideals of the "militarist" camp. Acknowledging the "moral" and "aesthetic" "unwillingnesses" militarists feel at the prospect of having "the supreme theatre of human strenuousness closed," he asserts that such "insistent unwillingnesses, no less than other esthetic and ethical unwillingnesses, have, it seems to me, to be listened to and respected."[129] Such attitudes toward the inclusion and redirection of competing ideals and habits has led critics of pragmatism to accuse it of a renouncing ideals in favor of means, of compromising or capitulating to the status quo. The pragmatic rebuttal to this claim was most eloquently voiced by Dewey, in his public response to Lewis Mumford's charge of pragmatism's "acquiescence." An idealism without attention to available means, Dewey insisted, is an empty and sterile radicalism: "Not all who say Ideals, Ideals, shall enter the kingdom of the ideal, but those who know and who respect the roads that conduct to the kingdom."[130] For pragmatists, a truly activist stance toward social reform requires a tough-minded attention to the existing truths, ideals, and habits that must be redirected in order to achieve change.

Most importantly, for my purposes, James's "Moral Equivalent" exhibits a similarly balanced argument that our most primal instincts and entrenched habits can be redirected to new purposes, but that such reeducation requires reform of the social conditions that provide the means for cultivating new habits. Not unlike Freud, James accepts that an impulse to violence is one of the more primal human instincts, which James attributes (in an evolutionary sense) to the way the "gory nurse" of human history has "selected" the "more martial tribes": "We inherit the warlike type; and for most of the capacities of heroism that the human race is full of we have to thank this cruel history. Dead men tell no tales, and if there were any tribes of other type than this they have left no survivors. Our ancestors have bred pugnacity into our bone and marrow, and thousands of years of peace won't breed it out of us." Yet, applying the model of habit articulated in *Principles*—specifically, the claim that even our most primal instincts must be shaped through interactions with the environment into specific habits—James asserts that even such innate pugnacity remains plastic to our attempts to reeducate it, reform it into new habits. The experiences of military struggle, James argues, have shaped our belligerent instincts into specific habits—the "martial virtues" of "intrepidity, contempt of softness, surrender of private interest, obedience to command." While such virtues, James concludes, "must still remain the rock upon which states are built," it "would be simply preposterous if the only force that could work ideals of honour and standards of efficiency into English or American natures should be the fear of being killed by the Germans or the Japanese." "Patriotic pride and ambition in their military form" are manifestations of "a more general competitive passion" that could be cultivated through different experiences and directed to other ends: "But who can be sure that *other aspects of one's country* may not, with time and education and suggestion enough, come to be regarded with similarly effective feelings of pride and shame?" James asks, envisioning a future in which "on the ruins of the old morals of military honour, a stable system of morals of civic honour builds itself up. What the whole community comes to believe in grasps the individual as in a vise."[131]

It is easy enough to point out problematic or weak elements of James's argument: its intense investment in masculine notions of virtue that are themselves deeply implicated in the perpetuation of violence, its class biases and blindnesses, the environmentally antiquated notion of a war "against nature," and, not least, the obvious insufficiency of James's proposed means—a mandatory civic service—for creating a new pacific system of civic morals.[132] In some sense, such criticisms are unfair to James, who presents his argument as his "own utopia"—a bold sketch intended to lay out in one representative proposal a vision of how the seemingly intractable problem of war could be ameliorated. Despite such weaknesses, James's argument provides important evidence about the political consequences of his pragmatic individualism. James, the self-proclaimed enemy of "bigness," is proposing an extensive social reform—universal male conscription for several years of public service—and his explicit purpose is to educate individuals in the new habits of moral selfhood required for a more democratic (in this case, pacifist) society, viewing such education as a means to bind individuals more tightly ("as in a vise," he puts it) in a common sense of communal, civic duty. In direct contradiction to Otto's conclusions, James's individualism neither prevents him from endorsing institutional reform, nor blinds him to the pervasive role that social conditions play in educating individuality.

Instead, "The Moral Equivalent of War" shows how the politics that extend from James's pragmatic view of the self—with its dual insistence on the plasticity of human instincts, and on the necessity of reforming social conditions to reeducate those instincts—anticipate Dewey's broad commitment to social reconstruction as an ongoing process of democratic education. Dewey shared Otto's sense of the class blindnesses betrayed in James's argument: "only . . . a man who was brought up an aristocrat and who had lived a sheltered existence" Dewey noted, could imagine "that most people need any substitute for the fighting life . . . in order to keep up their battling nerve."[133] But Dewey's broader assessment of James's politics directly refutes Otto's conclusions; Dewey praises "The Moral Equivalent of War" for providing a psychology of habit and custom that directs our political efforts *toward* social reform. By rejecting the notion of "an ineradicable belligerent instinct that makes war forever inevitable," Dewey notes, James stresses that "social conditions rather than an old and unchangeable Adam have generated wars," and that "the ineradicable impulses that are utilized in [wars] are capable of being drafted into many other channels." Writing in the bitter aftermath of World War One, Dewey's main critique of James was that he underestimated how broad a project of social reconstruction was required to cultivate a system of pacific habits that would effectively supplant war: "It is now naïve to attribute war to specific isolable human impulses for which separate channels of expression may be found. . . . History does not prove the inevitability of war, but it does prove that customs and institutions which organize native powers into certain patterns in politics and economics will also generate the war pattern. The problem of war is difficult because it is serious. It is none other than the wider problem of the effective moralizing or humanizing of native impulses in times of peace."[134]

Dewey's assessment highlights the broad continuities between his and James's approaches to reform. It would be foolish to deny that there are real differences between the two thinkers, but these are best viewed, I would contend, as complementary emphases within a broadly shared philosophical and political vision. For instance, James's individualistic fear of "bigness" does reflect his more acute anxiety about the tragic conflicts within experience, about the blindnesses of our individual perspectives and the resultant threat of butchering or suppressing others' ideals. If these concerns are more "individualistic" or "anarchistic" than Dewey's, they do not—as the example of James's "Moral Equivalent" shows—result in an individualistic rejection of social reform: instead, they form a salutary check on Dewey's more placid confidence in shared experience and the ability to harmonize individual desires in communal goals. Similarly, it is undoubtedly true that Dewey articulates a much broader commitment to social reform than James does; indeed, Dewey's entire philosophical project can be described as urging the ongoing, experimental reconstruction of all aspects of human association to make them more humane and democratic. But Dewey's broad vision extends the pragmatic model of the intelligent remaking of experience that he shares with James—which, for James as well as Dewey, requires the harnessing of individuality within an explicitly communal experimental process.

Indeed, as we shall see, Dewey's ideal of democracy-as-community includes profound a commitment to the ongoing reconstruction of individualism. It is Dewey who argues that an experimental process of social reform requires rejecting any rigid opposition between "individualistic" and "collective" solutions. It is Dewey who insists that democracy must in a fundamental sense be local, existing most vitally in the interactions of particular individuals within the face-to-face communities they inhabit. And it is Dewey who insists that human conduct always consists of specific persons utilizing the resources and addressing the problems of particular situations—that "harmony with conditions is . . . a diversified affair requiring individual attack," and that individuality is "inexpugnable because it is a manner of distinctive sensitivity, selection, choice, response, and utilization of conditions."[135]

For all these reasons, the movement from James's pragmatism to Dewey's cannot be reduced to the progression from an "individualistic" to a "social" vision. To understand how these two central figures in American pragmatism share a pluralistic, experimentalist, and democratic commitment to individuality is to illuminate both how a reconstructed individualism remains an integral part of pragmatism, and why pragmatism offers a powerful alternative to classic liberal models of individual liberty.

FOUR

CHARACTER AND COMMUNITY

Dewey's Model of Moral Selfhood

Regarded as an idea, democracy is not an alternative to other principles of associated life. It is the idea of community life itself.

—John Dewey

Even if Emerson has no system, none the less he is the prophet and herald of any system which democracy may henceforth construct and hold by, and . . . when democracy has articulated itself, it will have no difficulty in finding itself already proposed in Emerson.

—John Dewey

The writings of John Dewey occupy a pivotal position in the genealogy of pragmatic individualism charted in this study.[1] Spanning the era from the Civil War to the Cold War (1859–1952), Dewey's life is remarkable for the sheer scope of social changes he witnessed and participated in, and the breadth of these changes is reflected in his prodigious range and output as a philosopher. When *Democracy and Education* was published in 1916, Dewey, at age fifty-seven, had already achieved a notable career as a philosopher of pragmatism and a pioneer of progressive educational reform.[2] In the subsequent decades, well into his eighties, Dewey's productivity was staggering, as he wrote a series of major works constituting his mature philosophy—ranging from the social psychology of *Human Nature and Conduct* (1922) and the naturalistic metaphysics of *Experience and Nature* (1925) to the aesthetics of *Art as Experience* (1934) and political reflections such as *The Public and Its Problems* (1927), *Liberalism and Social Action* (1937), and *Freedom and Culture* (1939). In these works of his later phase one can see Dewey deploying and adapting pragmatism, a philosophy that emerged in the final decades of the nineteenth century, to meet the demands of a twentieth-century world beset by the Great Depression, two world wars, and the threat of totalitarianism—that is to say, a world that in the scope and complexity of its dangers is more recognizably akin to our own present than to the context in which Peirce and James wrote. In this broad sense, Dewey remains indispensable to any attempt to gauge pragmatism's continuing relevance.

More specifically, Dewey is also crucial for understanding how pragmatism allows—and indeed requires—us to reconceive individualism. Of all the writers considered in the current study, Dewey articulates the most comprehensive critique of classic liberal individualism, as well as the most systematic argument as to why a reconstructed individualism is not merely compatible with, but essential to, a democratic ideal of community. Since any claim for the moral viability of individualism must justify its consonance with the common good, the scope and clarity of Dewey's arguments are important enough in their own right. His arguments gain added significance, however, when considered in relation to their Emersonian roots, for Dewey illustrates how a genealogy of American ethics that begins with Emerson—that poster-child for the alleged excesses of self-reliant individualism—can result in a rationale for community. The twin epigraphs above encapsulate the matter: if, as Dewey claims, the democratic ideal *is* the ideal of community, and if any form that democracy might take will find itself prefigured in Emerson, the inference is that Dewey sees in Emerson a democratic vision that supports and requires community.

While Dewey's philosophy covers an extensive range of topics, his approach is unified by one overarching theme: rejecting the tendency to treat the metaphysical dualisms of the Western philosophical tradition as rigidly exclusive—a tendency that in turn fosters false and distorting dualisms in our moral and political thought, Dewey champions a thoroughly experimental method of inquiry applied to all social and moral questions. Such a method treats ideas as having no absolute or supernatural authority, but as products of experience whose validity derives from having been "shaped and tested as tools of inquiry" and from being "treated as working hypotheses . . . subject to ready and flexible revision in the light of observed consequences."[3] This experimentalism provides the key to understanding Dewey's sweeping claim that whatever form democracy might take, "it will have no difficulty finding itself already proposed in Emerson." For Dewey (as for Emerson), social customs, ideas, and institutions emerge from one set of social conditions and inevitably become obsolete as conditions change, so it is impossible that Dewey would locate in Emerson some static model of democracy as a social "system." Dewey, however, closely associated the experimental method with "the method of democracy,"[4] and asserted that the democratic ideal was not some fixed form of society that could be fully realized, but rather a standard to direct the ongoing experimental process of remaking social relations. It is in this process—specifically, in the growing quality of shared meaning that invests experience as groups adopt more democratic means of pursuing common ends, and in the liberation of capacity that individuals achieve by more fully participating in the pursuit of these ends—that democracy is realized. Thus, if Dewey saw in Emerson certain fundamental characteristics of an experimental attitude toward intelligence and meaning, he could confidently affirm the enduring relevance of Emerson's vision to any directions or forms this democratic process might assume.

Considered in this light, Dewey's brief address on Emerson, delivered on the occasion of Emerson's hundredth birthday in 1903, is significant not merely because he defends Emerson's status as a philosopher (in contrast to the condescension that William James could exhibit toward Emerson),[5] but for the fact that he identifies in Emerson key elements of a pragmatic experimentalism. Dewey locates the essence of Emerson's thought in his commitment to evaluating inherited ideas by the test of experience: "in the fact that he takes the distinctions and classifications which to most philosophers are true in and of themselves and because of their systems, and makes them true of life, of the common experience of the everyday man. . . . [E]ven the prophets like Plato and Proclus whom Emerson holds most dear, [are reduced] to the test of trial by the service rendered the present and immediate experience." Emerson's faith in the efficacy and sufficiency of this method makes it possible to "regard [his] whole work as a hymn to intelligence, a paean to the all-creating, all-disturbing power of thought." Lastly, Dewey asserts that Emerson's thought is decidedly *anti*transcendental, if transcendentalism means the positing of a supernatural "Reality that is beyond or behind or in any way apart," finding instead in Emerson an affirmation that "spiritual democracy" is "the possession of the unquestionable Present." It is "for such reasons," Dewey concludes—by virtue of Emerson's faith that the intelligent appeal to trial by experience is itself sufficient to generate the means by which experience is to be ordered, its values enhanced and secured—that Emerson is "not only a philosopher, but . . . the philosopher of democracy."[6] For those familiar with Dewey, it is clear that he is identifying in Emerson central elements of his own thought:[7] his thoroughgoing naturalism that rejects any transcendental ideals outside the processes of experience; his commitment to an experimental method that views all truths, ideals, and principles as tools for solving specific problems; and his assertion that the primary values of our human existence—such as liberty, happiness, and progress—emerge in and through the process of reconstructing experience, and that they reside in the *quality* of present activity as it is enhanced by the direction of intelligent choice.

The fact that Dewey saw in Emerson attitudes prefiguring his own experimentalism sets the broad context for understanding how Emerson's vision of the self might harmonize with Dewey's stress on community; to explain this link, however, requires considering how Dewey's experimentalism supports a vision of democracy-as-community in which individuality plays a necessary role. Dewey insists that democracy, considered not merely as a form of government, but as a social ideal to be realized in *all* forms of human association, is the "way of life"[8] best suited to promoting an experimental approach to human problems. A democratic or "progressive" society finds its interests best served by empowering its individual members to revise its ideals, customs, and institutions; similarly, it seeks to achieve social cohesion and control not through coercion but through individuals voluntarily identifying their personal interests with the common good.[9] These dynamics also constitute the main traits of a community as Dewey defines it. Community exists to the extent that a social group allows its individual members opportunities to cultivate and liberate their talents by taking "a responsible share according to capacity in forming and directing the activities" of the group—and does so because it finds this liberation of individuals' capacities both an important good in its own right and the means by which a necessary element of individual imagination and initiative may be infused into the pursuit of common ends. Conversely, community requires that individuals should cultivate their capacities "in harmony with the interests and goods which are common."[10] The processes of selfhood that are necessary to achieving these dynamics of democratic or communal association are encapsulated in Dewey's concept of "character."

In this chapter, I explore the pragmatic model of selfhood and community that lies at the heart of Dewey's reconception of individualism. First, I trace how Dewey's pluralistic model of experience describes the self as existing in a dynamic of mutually transforming interaction with its environing conditions—a dynamic that Dewey, like James, locates in the central concept of habit. Next, I discuss how Dewey's vision of moral selfhood—one that builds on his definition of character as the "interpenetration of habits"—supports his assertion that the cultivation of individuality is not merely compatible with, but essential to democratic community. Character serves as the locus for, and the practical solution to, what Dewey identifies as the two main tasks of morals: the need to harmonize individuals' personal interests with the common good of the groups to which they belong, and the need to make morality reflective rather than customary—to ensure that the determination of common goods is based on evaluation of consequences, not mere obedience to conventional standards. The chapter concludes by considering some broad political implications of this conception of character. Dewey's transactional model of selfhood leads him to reject the tired dualism of "individual" versus "institutional" approaches to reform, insisting instead that reform requires both the remaking of social conditions so as to instill new habits of individuality and the necessary role that individual imagination and choice play in so remaking social conditions. Much of Dewey's enduring value as a political thinker can be traced to this dynamic model of reform: it allows him to acknowledge the shaping power of environment while still asserting individual freedom and responsibility, and to affirm the possibility of meaningful reform while acknowledging its difficulty. The centrality of character as both a means and end of this process of reform underlies Dewey's most fundamental political stance: a commitment to the ongoing reconstruction of all forms of association in order to make them educative of the habits of moral selfhood and liberating of individuals' capacities—which commitment to educating individuality Dewey identifies as the core of democracy as a moral ideal. These general contours of Dewey's politics provide the context for understanding his approach in *The Public and Its Problems* and *Individualism Old and New,* which, as chapter 5 explores, offer his most detailed reflections on the obstacles to and possibilities for reconstructing a new individualism consonant with democratic community.

The continuities between Dewey's and James's individualisms should be apparent—rooted, as they are, in their shared pluralism, experimentalism, and emphasis on the central importance of habit and education. But when one traces the prominence of character in Dewey's thought, affinities to the Emersonian ethics explored in chapter 2 become evident as well. These affinities are clearest in Dewey's insistence on the moral necessity of a dynamic selfhood—the necessity of cultivating the habit of testing and revising the conventional moral standards of one's own communities, and of being willing, in the process, to test and remake the habits that define one's current self. It is this vital link between moral character and the experimental method of trying inherited ideas against the changing demands of experience that best explains why Dewey dubs Emerson "the philosopher of democracy."

Deweyan Character: Habit, Deliberation, and the Good of Present Activity

Dewey's model of the self, like James's, must be understood in terms of the pluralistic metaphysics of experience he offers as an alternative to the dualisms of classic Western philosophy. In Dewey's naturalistic account, mutually transforming interaction or "transaction" is a primary fact of our world. Things exist only in and through interactions with other things. "Every existence is an event" with only relative stability;[11] that is, every entity exists as a temporal history or process of change—an "event"—that emerges from and is sustained by its interaction with other processes of change or events. A mountain, for example, exists by virtue of the interaction of processes such as shifting tectonic plates, volcanic flows, glacial advances and retreats, and the eroding effects of weather and vegetation. This transactional nature of existences has radical and far-reaching implications, for it implies a pluralistic world characterized by real contingency and potentially limitless change. Because existences in our world emerge *only* in and through the interactions of experience, and in their interaction mutually transform each other, there is an irreducible pluralism of ends—that is, there is no limit to the results that might eventually emerge within experience.[12] There are no "fixed ends" outside the interactive processes of experience that predetermine their conclusion: no antecedent entities such as liberalism's individual in the state of nature or Kantian categorical imperatives, for instance, that specify once and for all what form society must take or what a person's duty is. There are also no "final causes," such as Aristotle's pre-Darwinian model of fixed forms that prescribe the only path of development an individual organism can take (an acorn can only become an oak),[13] nor absolute ideals of the state toward which the development of history is inexorably moving, as in Hegelian idealism or Marxist materialism. Thus to "know" a thing is not, as classic "spectator" or "correspondence" theories of knowledge suggest, to comprehend or behold its unchanging essence, but to know *how* it will interact with other events in processes of change,[14] and a central goal[15] of knowing is to be able to control those processes of change so as to secure the recurrence of desirable ends and the emergence or creation of new ends.

This fundamental fact of interaction is expressed in Dewey's reconstruction of the concept of "experience," which he describes (borrowing a phrase from William James) as a "double-barreled" term comprehending both the objective environing conditions an organism experiences and the organism's process of experiencing them. It is characterized by a "primary integrity" that "recognizes ... no division between act and material, subject and object, but contains them both in an unanalyzed totality":[16]

> Life denotes a function, a comprehensive activity, in which organism and environment are included. Only upon reflective analysis does it break up into external conditions—air breathed, food taken, ground walked upon—and internal structures—lungs respiring, stomach digesting, legs walking.[17]

There can be no breathing apart from an atmosphere breathed, no eating apart from material eaten, no walking apart from a surface walked upon, no thinking in isolation from specific things thought about: "there is simply an activity which includes both." Where traditional Western philosophy posits dualism, entities reflecting "separate and independent realms," Dewey sees a continuity of interaction and temporal process. The dualisms of classic Western philosophy—subject versus object, mind versus body, material versus method, doing versus knowing, means versus ends, etc.—are in fact, he argues, distinctions drawn by human reflection, breaking down the "unanalyzed totality" of experience into its constituent aspects or phases. Such distinctions are necessary tools in the intellectual "control and enrichment of the subject-matters of crude but total experience," but to treat them as rigid or exclusive dualisms mires thinking in false dilemmas and imposes an absolutism that precludes the full use of experimental intelligence. For instance, assuming subjective mind or consciousness to be a separate realm from objective reality creates the specious problem of how the mind manages to know anything, and necessitates the positing of transcendental faculties or categories of knowledge to bridge the gap. Or, what *Experience and Nature* labels "*the philosophic fallacy*," the translating of "eventual functions" in experience into "antecedent existence,"[18] hinders intelligent efforts to control the emergence of such results: for instance, treating acquired traits such as reasonableness, conscientiousness, or individuality as endowments of human individuals prior to and separate from society precludes full attention to the ways specific social conditions cultivate and shape such character traits.

Dewey's critique of several prominent dualisms—subject versus object, means versus ends, and the individual versus the social—are crucial for understanding his vision of character, democracy and community. It is best to begin with the most basic, the relation of subject and object, as it is described in Dewey's central concepts of experience and habit. Experience, in Dewey's definition, is an inclusive term that comprehends the mutually transforming interaction between an organism and its environment:

> Wherever there is life, there is behavior, activity. In order that life may persist, this activity has to be both continuous and adapted to the environment. This adaptive adjustment, moreover, is not wholly passive; it is not a mere matter of the moulding of the organism by the environment. Even a clam acts upon the environment and modifies it to some extent. . . . Experience becomes an affair primarily of doing. . . . The organism acts in accordance with its own structure, simple or complex, upon its surroundings. As a consequence the changes produced in the environment react upon the organism and its activities. The living creature undergoes, suffers, the consequences of its own behavior. This close connection between doing and suffering or undergoing forms what we call experience.[19]

While all physical events exist by virtue of interaction with other events, experience names a more "vital" and "significant" "interaction of organism and environment, resulting in some adaptation which secures utilization of the latter."[20] The linguistic ability to share the results of

experience makes human intelligence uniquely powerful when compared to that of other animals, but the basic source of human intelligence remains this primary "connection between doing and suffering or
undergoing": it is because we are transformed by our interactions with
the environment that we are able to apply the lessons of past experiences
to help us navigate future ones.

Dewey's master term for this mutually transforming relation between
organism and environment is "habit." Habit names "that kind of human
activity which is influenced by prior activity and in that sense acquired."
Habit comprehends both the subjective and objective aspects of experience: habits are "ways of using and incorporating the environment,"
"working adaptations of personal capacities with environing forces." In
the processes of doing and undergoing, aspects of environing conditions
become literally *incorporated* in the self: "a predisposition formed by a
number of specific acts" becomes an "intimate and fundamental part of
ourselves." Contrary to the commonplace notion that habit designates
only routine or "external mode[s] of action," Dewey asserts that habits
"constitute the self. . . . They form our effective desires and they furnish
us with our working capacities." Habits compose the "self or character as
the abiding unity in which different acts leave their lasting traces" and
provide "the very make-up of desire, intent, choice, disposition which
gives an act its voluntary quality."[21]

Indeed, belying the familiar equation of habit with routine and rigidity, Dewey points out that the unique diversity of human intelligence, and
the plasticity of human nature that it enables, derive from the pervasive
extent to which humans depend upon habit—upon learned, acquired
behavior—and not on instinct. As compared to other animals that are
born with much more developed instincts for sustaining themselves in
their environment, the "native impulses" of a human infant are "inchoate
and scattered," "merely starting points for assimilation of the knowledge
and skill of the more mature beings upon whom he depends." Yet this
extreme dependence of human nature on collective habits or customs
is best seen, Dewey argues, as an "interdependence" that represents our
greatest intellectual strength. Habit is not in any simple sense *opposed*
to plasticity: indeed, plasticity resides in our ability to form new habits.
The "tremendous diversity of institutions" evidenced by various cultures
"springs from practically the same capital-stock of native instincts," and
hence can only be "accounted for" in terms of "acquired habits" and

"customs," the "social conditions which have educated original activities into definite and significant dispositions."[22] However, the corollary
of Dewey's claim that habit—as the ability to form new dispositions—
constitutes the plasticity of human nature is his acknowledgment that
the inherently assertive nature of existing habits and customs exerts a
powerful conservative force that must be overcome in any effort at reform.[23] Dewey here reverses the assumptions of both staunch conservatives who cite the "practical unalterability of human nature" and naive
reformers who imply that because social practices are merely customary
they are easily transformed; instead, he claims that it is our native impulses which are most plastic, capable of being shaped into a seemingly
unlimited variety of habits, and that, while social practices are indeed
customary and hence ultimately plastic as well, "it is precisely custom
which has the greatest inertia," introducing "a force of lag in human life"
that is "enormous."[24] Significantly, this duality in Dewey's view of habit
harkens back to Emerson, who similarly stresses that the thorough dependence of individual behavior upon cultural traditions threatens, on
the one hand, to impose a stifling conformity, while, on the other hand,
provides tremendous resources for extending and remaking an individual's capacities—recall how, in "The Uses of Great Men," he marvels at the
receptivity of human nature that appropriates the culturally transmitted
results of other actors' efforts: "we wish for a thousand heads," and "in
good faith, we are multiplied by our proxies. How easily we adopt their
labors!"[25]

"At first sight," Dewey admits, the relation between impulse and habit
seems to trap the potential for reconstructive change within "a vicious
circle," for if the plasticity of human nature that might modify established
habits resides in native impulses, "the direction of native activity" in turn
"depends upon acquired habits." "How then," Dewey wonders, "can we
get leverage for changing institutions?" Dewey's assertion that all human
intelligence depends on the habits formed in the doings and undergoings
of experience does indeed imply that any efforts to remake and redirect
existing habits can only be envisioned and carried out by the means of
those same habits. Elaborating the consequences of Emerson's claim that
action is "the preamble of thought," Dewey insists that the "formation
of ideas as well as their execution depends upon habit": "Only when a
man can already perform an act of standing straight does he know what
it is like to have a right posture and only then can he summon the idea

required for proper execution. The act must come before the thought, and a habit before an ability to evoke the thought at will." Yet to assert that ideas emerge from experience, that they are projections of habits, does not deny their subsequent creative function in inspiring and redirecting activity: "Every ideal is preceded by an actuality," as "desire for flowers comes after actual enjoyment of flowers," "but it comes before the work that makes the desert bloom, it comes before the *cultivation* of plants."[26]

To understand how character serves as both the means and end of reconstructive action—that is, how habits provide the means for projecting the ends that serve to reorganize our habits—it must be recalled that for Dewey selfhood is an event, and as such exhibits the pluralism characteristic of all events.[27] To say that the self is composed wholly of habits is not to imply that it is rigid or unchanging, for habits reflect or incorporate the diversity of the changing and varied environments in which an individual acts, changes, and learns: "No adult environment is all of one piece. The more complex a culture is, the more certain it is to include habits formed on differing, even conflicting patterns." Hence, "any self is capable of including within itself a number of inconsistent selves, of unharmonized dispositions"; "there is no one ready-made self behind activities," but only "complex, unstable, opposing attitudes, habits, impulses which gradually come to terms with one another, and assume a certain consistency of configuration." In "a changing world" no habit will fit all situations, and even the best habits will encounter novel conditions that require their "modification, no matter how good they have been."[28] This pluralism guarantees conflict among the habits that constitute the self, which conflict may take the form of an unhealthy lack of harmony or integration in the self, but which also, in Dewey's melioristic view, provides the saving opportunities for growth in which the ultimate health of the self resides, spurring the process of deliberation and choice of a new end that will redirect activity, thereby reorganizing and perhaps reharmonizing the habits that compose the self.

The role that habit plays in deliberation is crucial to understanding the centrality of character in Dewey's ethics. But before considering that process of deliberation, two aspects of Dewey's model of character need to be clarified. First, Dewey insists that character is defined by the essential continuity of self and act, of motive and consequences. In contrast to traditional theories that either, like Kantian ethics, locate morality exclusively in motive (a virtuous will that follows the absolute dictates of duty and reason regardless of consequences) and hence consider character as an end in itself, or, like classic Utilitarianism, locate morality exclusively in consequences and hence view character as a mere means to good results, Dewey insists that motive and consequences are really "two poles of the same thing," and that character functions as both a means and an end. There is an intimate connection between "character" and "outcome." "Consequences fix the moral quality of an act" and hence the character or disposition of the actor; conversely, character, or the "nature of desire and disposition," determines—"in the long run but not unqualifiedly"—the consequences of a person's acts. Dewey's qualifier here is crucial, for it acknowledges that contingency exists between the likely consequences of a habit and its actual consequences in any one circumstance. Dewey's term for this moral import of character is "tendency," which locates morality in "the probable effect of a habit in the long run."[29] Viewed in this light, to stress the importance of motive or disposition is *not* to transcend the consideration of consequences (as Kantian ethics purport to do), but to insist upon viewing consequences broadly by taking into consideration the "habitual, persistent" tendency of dispositions to determine consequences. For instance, an "honest man" who acts "from 'principle'" in refusing to bow to expediency in a given situation is *not* ignoring specific consequences, but insisting that the morality of an act should be judged not merely on the "consequences of an isolated case" but on the "probable effect" of such choices "in the long run."[30] Similarly, because the consequences of an act "include effects upon character, upon confirming and weakening habits" that will in turn determine future consequences, to stress the importance of motive is "equivalent to taking a broad view of future consequences." By this analysis, character is not an end-in-itself apart from consequences—indeed, the very notion of an "end-in-itself" falsifies the continuity of means and ends in the ongoing sequence of acts that constitute conduct. Rather, "virtues are ends because they are such important means" to the continued securing of beneficial consequences. Conversely, to stress the importance of consequences is not to deny the importance of motive, for "consequences give the only instruction we can procure as to the meaning of habits and disposition." Because we live in a growing and changing world, the "tendency" of a habit must be continually reevaluated. When changing consequences (or our improved recognition of consequences) "reveal unexpected potentialities in our habits," the meaning of a habit or a character trait changes: what may have been a virtue in one era or context may well be a vice in another. Thus "the work of intelligence in revising and readjusting habits, even the best of good habits, can never be foregone."[31]

"Character," then, describes the continuity of an individual's conduct: to know the quality of someone's character is to know how he or she is disposed to act and the tendency of those dispositions to create beneficial or detrimental consequences. Dewey here reveals marked affinities to Emerson, who describes character in similar terms as residing in the collective or cumulative tendency of a person's acts. The "varieties" of specific acts "are lost sight of at a little distance," Emerson argues: "One tendency unites them all. The voyage of the best ship is a zigzag line of a hundred tacks." Similarly, Dewey's claim that individual acts strengthen certain dispositions, reinforcing a given tendency or quality of character, is paralleled by Emerson's declaration that "the force of character is cumulative," so that "all the foregone days of virtue work their health into this." Dewey also sheds light on Emerson's affirmation, most notably in "Compensation," that a sufficient justice obtains in the contingent outcomes of our material world. When Emerson asserts, for instance, that "a character is like an acrostic," that "we pass for what we are," that a person "comes at last to be faithfully represented by every view you take of his circumstances," his claim is illuminated by Dewey's view that "tendency" describes a sufficient correspondence between character and outcome, the most correspondence that is possible given the contingencies of our pluralistic world. We must accept and work within such "modest probabilities" of character and result, Dewey argues: when "the world of actual experience does not guarantee" a total "identity of character and outcome," we must not take the familiar flight into positing "some truer ultimate reality which enforces an equation that is violated in this life"—a statement that recalls the satire of the Last Judgment with which Emerson opens "Compensation," and that could serve as a gloss for the oft-misunderstood argument of that essay.[32]

A second aspect of character must be addressed in order to flesh out an initial sketch of Dewey's treatment of the concept. For if character describes a cumulative continuity in an individual's conduct, it also comprehends, for Dewey, the ability through deliberation and choice to redirect, reorganize, and remake the habits that compose the self. This capacity, which emerges from the pluralism of the self described above, is captured in Dewey's definition of character as the "interaction," "integration," or "interpenetration" of the habits that constitute the self. The integration of habits may be extensive or limited; integration is "an achievement," and is "never total," and a person's actions may exhibit an unresolved conflict between various aspects of his selfhood. But *whatever* degree and quality of integration does exist—however a person's various habits modify each other at a given juncture—character determines and is revealed by a person's chosen course of action and its likely consequences or tendency. As Emerson puts it, "I suppose no man can violate his nature. . . . We pass for what we are. Character teaches above our wills. Men imagine that they communicate their virtue only by overt actions, and do not see that virtue or vice emit a breath every moment." Thus character plays a crucial role in deliberation, for the existing degree of harmony or interaction between our various habits determines *both* our ability to imagine various courses of action—"the more numerous our habits the wider the field of possible observation and foretelling," the "reason a baby can know little and an experienced adult know much when confronting the same things" is "because one has already formed habits which the other has still to acquire"—*and* our ability to choose among those possible courses. For a person's "estimate of future consequences" depends upon "what he now is," the dispositions he has cultivated; "only the man whose habits are already good can know what the good is."[33]

This pervasive dependence on habits does not, however, trap the self within a rigid determinism, for character is dynamic, not static: the capacity of choice that Dewey identifies as selfhood's defining feature resides in the "interpenetration" of habits: a habit, once formed, actively modifies other habits even when its activity is merely secondary or latent. For example, because it shapes our ability to gauge distances, the "habit of walking is expressed in what a man sees when he keeps still, even in dreams."[34] Because of this mutually modifying nature, habits can exert an inhibiting and redirecting force upon each other that enables the process of deliberation and the choice of an end that reorganizes habits into a new harmony or integration. Though our choice of an end is determined by the self we have already cultivated, we can choose among the various habits that compose our self—choose in our course of action to express and reinforce our "better self," as it were—thereby cultivating a transformed character in which desirable traits may be strengthened and undesirable ones sublimated. This capacity of remaking one's self in the process of projecting and pursuing new ends is itself a complex achievement of character to be pursued by cultivating habits of flexible, reasonable, and conscientious choice. In its richest and most vital sense, character is dynamic. For Dewey, as for Emerson, true stability and health of character can only be achieved by embracing these ongoing, interconnected processes of remaking one's self and one's environment, and seeking value in the growth of capacity and meaning that they facilitate.

These claims for the centrality of character are clarified when one traces the process of deliberation as Dewey describes it in *Human Nature and Conduct*. Viewing experience as primarily a matter of activity—of doing and undergoing—Dewey rejects the traditional view that knowing is coextensive with experience, that "consciousness," for instance, represents an awareness that duplicates or accompanies all the self's doings. Instead, following the lead of Charles Sanders Peirce,[35] Dewey defines the process of knowing or conscious reflection as a subset of experience, triggered by a problematic situation that impedes activity and concluding in a reorganization of the situation that restores activity. Habits, in their successful operation, are "too insistent and determinate to need to indulge in inquiry or imagination," so that "only a hitch in [habit's] workings occasions emotion and provokes thought." And yet, if habit "does not, of itself, know," habits still enable the process of knowing, so that consciousness "expresses functions of habits, phenomena of their formation, operation, their interruption and reorganization." Initially it is the blocking or impedance of habits that triggers reflection and "releases some impulse" that "tends to" break-up existing habits and "initiate a different and incompatible activity." Yet as this new impulse seeks an objective realization in reorganized conditions, "old habit supplies content, filling definite, recognizable subject matter":[36]

> Habits which were interfered with begin to get a new direction as they cluster about the impulse to look and see. The blocked habits . . . give him a sense of where he *was* going, of what he had set out to do, and of the ground already traversed. As he looks, he sees definite things, which are not just things at large but which are related to his course of action. The momentum of the activity entered upon persists as a sense of direction, of aim; it is an anticipatory project. In short, he recollects, observes and plans.[37]

The "discriminated and identified objects" that form the content of recollection, observation, and forecasting, all "represent habits turned inside out": they "exhibit both the onward tendency of habit and the objective conditions which have been incorporated within it."[38]

Dewey describes this survey of conditions and possible courses of actions as a "dramatic rehearsal" that is achieved through the inhibitory effect that habits have on each other, which inhibition allows various habits to express themselves in imaginative forecast:

> Deliberation is a dramatic rehearsal (in imagination) of various competing possible lines of action. . . . Each conflicting habit and impulse takes its turn in projecting itself upon the screen of the imagination. It unrolls a picture of its future history, of the career it would have if it were given head. Although overt exhibition is checked by the pressure of contrary propulsive tendencies, this very inhibition gives habit a chance at manifestation in thought. . . . Activity does not cease in order to give way to reflection; activity is turned from execution into intra-organic channels, resulting in dramatic rehearsal.[39]

Choice occurs when this dramatic rehearsal "hit[s] . . . upon an object which furnishes an adequate stimulus to the recovery of overt action . . . as soon as some habit, or some combination of elements of habits and impulse, finds a way fully open. Then energy is released. The mind is made up, composed, unified. . . . This decisive direction of action constitutes choice." Choice may, of course, be either unreasonable or reasonable. It may represent the continuing dominance of an unhealthy composite of habits, or the unproductive "suppression" or "surging, explosive discharge" of an "impulsive activity." However, it may also represent the achievement of a new and healthier harmonization of habits, in which an impulse released in the process of deliberation becomes "sublimated" as "a factor coordinated intelligently with others in a continuing course of action," as, for instance, a "gust of anger may, because of its dynamic incorporation into disposition, be converted into an abiding conviction of social injustice to be remedied." In such a desirable outcome, habit and impulse interact in an intelligent and reconstructive fashion: the release of impulse "renew[s] disposition and reorganize[s] habit," while those existing, reorganized habits guide impulse to an objective realization.[40]

This account of deliberation indicates how character serves as a powerful and necessary means to reconstructive change. As suggested above, it is the diversity of habits composing character that allows a person to project, in imaginative rehearsal, a variety of possible courses of action, and it is the mutually inhibiting and modifying interpenetration of these habits that first enables reflection by preventing any one habit from prematurely determining choice and then allows habits to be reharmonized in pursuit of a chosen end. This process of deliberation facilitates, Dewey argues, the legitimately individual or subjective contribution to mind— which resides in both the release of individual impulse that serves to "arouse thought" and "enliven belief"[41] and in the imaginative projection of habits as ideals or ends. Habits, when impeded, continue to act within the imaginative process of deliberation, thereby projecting ends that provide the impetus for renewed activity that can transform the environment:

> A hungry man could not conceive food as a good unless he had actually experienced, with the support of environing conditions, food as good. The objective satisfaction comes first. But he finds himself in a situation where food is denied in fact. It then lives in imagination. The habit denied overt expression asserts itself in idea. It sets up the thought, the ideal of food. This thought is not what is sometimes called thought, a pale bloodless abstraction, but is charged with the motor urgent force of habit. Food as a good is now subjective, personal. But it has its source in objective conditions and it moves forward to new objective conditions. . . . There is therefore demand for a changed environment, a demand which can be achieved only by some modification and rearrangement of old habits. . . . It is all of a kind with the doings of a man, who remembering a prior satisfaction of thirst and the conditions under which it occurred, digs a well. For the time being water in reference to his activity exists in imagination not in fact. But this imagination is not a self-generated, self-enclosed, psychical existence. It is the persistent operation of a prior object which has been incorporated in effective habit.[42]

As this passage makes clear, Dewey, in contrast to philosophies that celebrate individual mind as a transcendent or antecedent causal power, circumscribes significantly the scope of subjective imagination: it is the result or perpetuation of habits formed in previous objective conditions, and can have substantial force (as opposed devolving into escapist fantasy) only to the extent it again finds objective realization in habits that successfully reshape conditions.[43] Dewey insists, however, that to view individual intellectual capacities of "knowing, judgment," and "belief" as acquired results of experience, and not as some "separate original power and impulse of knowledge," is not to diminish the "value of knowledge when once it comes into existence," which is "so immense as to be called unique." Indeed, Dewey views individuality as an indispensable catalyst for creative change. The self is the means par excellence of all reconstructive action: habits are "the thing[s] . . . closest to us," the "means" most immediately "within our power," and the diverse and plastic array of capacities provided by the interpenetration of habits makes the self "the tool of tools, *the* means involved in all use of means."[44]

Yet to treat character as merely a means, however powerful, to producing desirable consequences is to misunderstand the relation between means and ends. As Dewey's model of deliberation suggests, present activity is not reorganized in order to achieve some distant end. Just the opposite is true: an end is chosen on the basis of its ability to "resolve entanglements in existing activity, restore continuity, recover harmony, utilize loose impulse and redirect habit."[45] Choice occurs when an end or course of activity is "hit upon" that sufficiently satisfies and unifies our present composition of habits and impulses; it is based on the present quality of dispositions as they are experienced in the "dramatic rehearsal" of deliberation:

> Joy and suffering, pain and pleasure, the agreeable and disagreeable, play their considerable role in deliberation. Not, however, by way of a calculated estimate of future delights and miseries, but by way of experiencing present ones. The reaction of joy and sorrow, elation and depression, is as natural a response to objects presented in imagination as to those presented in sense. . . . We do not think of future losses and expansions. We think, through imagination, of objects into which in the future some course of action will run, and we are *now* delighted or depressed, pleased or pained at what is presented. This running commentary of likes and dislikes, attractions and disdains, joys and sorrows, reveals to any man who is intelligent enough to note them and to study their occasions his own character.[46]

Deliberation is not, as classic Utilitarian theory would suggest, a matter of calculating the likely quantity of future pleasures so as to provide "an inducement to act." "The thing actually at stake in any serious deliberation is not a difference of quantity," but rather the *quality* of present activity as it is reshaped by a chosen end, the difference in quality between various courses of action as revealed in the "different dispositions they form and foster." In other words, choice is fundamentally about character: "what kind of person one is to become, what sort of self is in the making, what kind of a world is in the making."[47]

Indeed, character is at stake in a dual sense, for every meaningful choice not only determines the quality of one's present self, but, since the chosen course of action will strengthen some dispositions at the expense of others, shapes the quality of one's future self as well:

> [E]very such choice sustains a double relation to the self. It reveals the existing self and it forms the future self. That which is chosen is found congenial to the desires and habits of the self as it already exists. Deliberation has an important function in this process, because each different possibility as it is presented to the imagination appeals to a different element in the constitution of the self, thus giving all sides of character a chance to play their part in the final choice. The resulting choice also shapes the self, making it, in some degree, a new self.[48]

Pragmatism is often accused of lacking a tragic sensibility, yet Dewey describes the defining trait of selfhood[49] as an unavoidable act of choice between conflicting futures, a choice subject to contingency and inevitable loss. The "poignancy of situations that evoke reflection lies in the fact that we really do not know the meaning of the tendencies that are pressing for action," but we know there is real "conflict" between "qualitative incompatibilities": "one impulse carries us one way into one situation," while another leads us "to a radically different objective result." Dewey insists that deliberation cannot "do away with" this conflict, but only "attempt[s] to *uncover* the conflict in its full scope and bearing" as far as our fallible ability to forecast the future allows. That is, even the most intelligent choice is an "experiment," a gamble. In choosing one course of action, we enlist our energies in the attempt to create one kind of world and one kind of self, and while success is uncertain, what *is* certain is that we thereby preclude the realization of other possible worlds and selves. In William James's graphic metaphor, our most successful effort to realize certain portions of the ideal inevitably "butchers" others. In certain momentous life-decisions—as, for instance, "whether to be a merchant or school teacher, a physician or a politician"—it is clear that "with the difference in career belongs a difference in the constitution of the self." But even our "minor decisions," Dewey argues, though they "differ in acuteness and range," do not differ "in principle": "Our world does not . . . hang upon any one of them; but put together they make the world what it is in meaning for each one of us." In sum, while character "*is* an agency of accomplishing consequences, as is shown in the pains which the athlete, the lawyer, the merchant, takes to build up certain habits in himself," it is "not a *mere* means, an external instrument of attaining certain ends."[50] In a fundamental sense, character names the primary value we enjoy as humans—the nature of one's selfhood as it exists in the changing quality of present activity—that is at issue in any meaningful deliberation.

This claim that character is the true focus of deliberation is but one manifestation of Dewey's broader critique of the dualism of means versus ends, and of his subsequent melioristic assertion that the primary value of human experience lies in the growing quality of present activity. These two strands of Dewey's thought are crucial for understanding his stress on the role of character and community in morals. "Means" and "ends," Dewey notes, name different ways of treating a single act within the sequence of acts that compose conduct: "an end . . . is always both ends and means, the distinction being only one of convenience. Every means is a temporary end until we have attained it. Every end becomes a means of carrying activity further as soon as it is achieved." Ends are best thought of as "ends-in-view," Dewey contends: "They are not strictly speaking ends or termini of action at all," but rather "terminals of deliberation," "turning points *in* activity," "foreseen consequences which arise in the course of activity and which are employed to give activity added meaning and to direct its further course." In terms of function, then, "an end-in-view is a *means* in present action," reversing the dominant tendency to treat "present action" as a mere "means to a remote end." This common inversion of the true relation of means and ends "subordinat[es] . . . the living present to a remote and precarious future,"[51] seeking value in future outcomes that are subject to contingencies and circumstances beyond our control and ignoring the meaning that is most under our control, the growth or tendency of present activity:

> After all, the object of foresight of consequences is not to predict the future. It is to ascertain the meaning of present activities and to secure, so far as possible, a present activity with a unified meaning. . . . The best laid plans of men as well as of mice gang aglee; and for the same reason: inability to dominate the future. . . . Hence the problem of deliberation is not to calculate future happenings, but to appraise present proposed actions. We judge present desires and habits by their tendency to produce certain consequences. It is our business to watch the course of our action so as to see what is the significance, the import of our habits and dispositions. The future outcome

is not certain. . . . [But] *tendency* is a knowable matter[;] . . . we know what is the tendency of malice, charity, conceit, patience. We know by observing their consequences, by recollecting what we have observed, by using that recollection in constructive imaginative forecasts of the future, by using the thought of future consequence to tell the quality of the act now proposed.[52]

To focus on the meaning or tendency of present activity is in fact the surest way to secure, to the best of our limited human ability, the actual occurrence of good results. Again, however, Dewey insists that the value of present activity is not as a mere means to future results. The enhanced meaning of present activity is in a real sense the *only* value we ever possess or enjoy. "The present, not the future is ours," Dewey notes. "What sense is there in increased external control except to increase the intrinsic significance of living? The future that is foreseen is a future that is sometime to be a present. Is the value of that present also to be postponed to a future date, and so on indefinitely?"[53]

Dewey's analysis of the means-end relationship thus has radical implications for our conception of value, exhorting us to seek value not in projected future results, nor even in achieved results (save as they function as means to further enabling and enriching activity), but in the growing quality of meaning directly enjoyed in present activity as a result of our intelligent direction of conduct:

> The process of growth, of improvement and progress, rather than the static outcome and result, becomes the significant thing. Not health as an end fixed once and for all, but the needed improvement in health—a continual process—is the end and good. The end is no longer a terminus or limit to be reached. It is the active process of transforming the existent situation. Not perfection as a final goal, but the ever-enduring process of perfecting, maturing, refining is the aim in living. Honesty, industry, temperance, justice, like health, wealth and learning, are not goods to be possessed as they would be if they expressed fixed ends to be attained. They are directions of change in the quality of experience. Growth itself is the only moral "end."[54]

If ends are conceived as final goals to be attained, then the contingency and failure that besets our best efforts constitutes a serious cause for dismay and even pessimism. On this view, the only escape is to seek solace in the familiar—and yet, by Dewey's account, "ludicrous or tragic"— dualism that elevates ends into transcendental ideals which our efforts, subject to the finitude and contingency of material experience, cannot hope to realize. If, on the other hand, ideals are treated as ends-in-view, as tools for redirecting and reshaping the meaning of present activity, then attention shifts to a melioristic focus on the reality of progress—not on "failure to reach infinity," but on "positive attainment, actual enrichment of meaning and powers": "Good is always found in a present growth of significance in activity."[55]

Whatever moral term one highlights, the increased meaning of present activity attained through the intelligent choice of ends is a quality directly enjoyed in the present. Happiness, for instance, "is something now attained, even in the midst of pain and trouble, whenever recognition of our ties with nature and with fellow-men releases and informs our action." Progress also has an immediate reality in the moving and growing quality of activity. "We move on from worse and *into*, not just towards, the better," Dewey writes, "unless progress is a present reconstructing, it is nothing; if it cannot be told by qualities belonging to the movement of transition, it can never be judged." Similarly, liberty is not some abstract condition, but exists in the growth of meaning and liberation of capacity that is "actualized" when a person chooses the end that directs his or her activity—in the belief that such choice, and the action it determines, may make a difference in realizing one possible future as opposed to another.[56]

Such a melioristic emphasis on the growing meaning and capacity enjoyed in present activity regards the inevitably temporary and incomplete nature of every particular success not as a sign of failure, nor of the inherent moral deficiency of experience, but as providing salutary opportunities for continued deliberation, choice, and growth. Though the "most comprehensive deliberation leading to the most momentous choice only fixes a disposition which has to be continuously applied in new and unforeseen conditions, re-adapted by future deliberations," this does not "reduce moral life to the futile toil of a Sisyphus," Dewey affirms, for "continual search and experimentation to discover the meaning of changing activity, keeps activity alive, growing in significance." Indeed, like Emerson and James before him, Dewey argues that a world whose contingencies require ceaseless moral and intellectual effort is not merely sufficient to but in fact well suited to the needs of our agonistic human nature. To envision happiness in the static perfection of a fully and finally achieved end, is, Dewey claims—in a phrase that might be lifted directly from the pages of William James—"an insipid tedium" that "could satisfy only the most delicate of molly-coddles." To reject such visions of complete security and seek value instead in "the overcoming of obstacles," in the opportunities for growth that reside in our successes and defeats alike, makes "failure los[e] something of its fatality, and suffering yiel[d] fruit of instruction not of bitterness," and points the path to a happiness that is "stable . . . because it is dependent not upon what transiently happens to us but upon the standing disposition of the self" that "we actively bring with us to meet situations."[57]

Dewey here reveals one of his central inheritances from his romantic forebears Emerson and Thoreau, both of whom critiqued the prevalent tendency to pervert the true relation of means and ends, to sacrifice the quality of present activity by treating it as a mere means to the procuring of future—and too often merely materialistic—results.[58] Indeed, it is difficult not to hear, in the melioristic arguments from Dewey traced above, echoes of the Emersonian ethics explored in chapter 2. Echoes, for instance, of Emerson's honorific portrait of the "sturdy lad from New Hampshire or Vermont," who "does not postpone his life, but lives already," who refuses to subject his present growth to conventional standards of achieved success, but "in turn tries all the professions" in faith that "new powers shall appear." Or of Emerson's claim that "We must have an antagonism in the tough world for all the variety of our spiritual faculties, or they will not be born," that the obstacles and defeats our world presents us with are beneficial occasions for the cultivation and liberation of our capacities: "Passions, resistance, danger, are educators. We acquire the strength we have overcome. Without war, no soldier; without enemies, no hero. The sun were insipid, if the universe were not opaque." Or of Emerson's assertion that our only stable value or possession lies not in particular results of our labors, which are subject to contingency and loss, but in the growing and cumulative capacities we cultivate through our labors—in the "living property" "which a man is," and which "renews itself wherever the man breathes." Or, finally, of the affirmation (implied in all the above examples) that, though "people wish to be settled[,] . . . only so far as they are unsettled is there any hope for them." For in a changing world where even "good" traditions and habits become obsolete—where the "one fact that the world hates, that the soul *becomes* . . . for ever degrades the past, . . . confounds the saint with the rogue, shoves Jesus and Judas equally aside"—stability of character and happiness can only be achieved in embracing the ceaseless need for change; in "the power of self-recovery" found "only by . . . preferring truth to [the] past appreciation of truth" and by "alert acceptance of it, from whatever quarter."[59] For Emerson, as for Dewey, character in its honorific sense ultimately names both the cumulative, cultivated habit of pursuing the ongoing process of remaking one's self and environment, and the primary value we experience in that process.

Beyond "the Individual versus the Social": Character and Community in Morals

We are now poised to consider the central role that character plays in Dewey's theory of morals,[60] as well as how this emphasis on character shapes the vision of community that lies at the heart of his democratic ideal. Dewey's approach to morals is thoroughly naturalistic and experimental. Moral qualities and values emerge from the "objects and activities which develop out of natural desires and normal social relations."[61] Moral deliberation does not differ in kind from nonmoral deliberation, for morals are continuous with the aims and processes of all experimental inquiry: deliberation on the obstacles and possibilities that define a problematic situation and choice of an end that effectively restores activity. A choice is moral, Dewey contends, when it determines a difference in the quality of selfhood—a distinction that cannot be rigidly or finally drawn, since potentially any act may be judged to have significant enough consequences to define such a difference. Dewey's analysis of morals is also explicitly pluralistic: in contrast to traditional moral theories, each of which "postulate[s] one single principle as an explanation of moral life," he argues that moral experience cannot be subsumed under any one explanatory rubric. There are "independent" but interrelated factors "intertwined in all actual moral situations," each reflecting a different aspect of human experience and which often "can be at cross purposes" precisely "because each has a different origin and mode of operation."[62] Following the traditional divisions of moral theory, Dewey identifies three such independent factors: the good (which reflects the role of intelligent "deliberation upon desires and purposes"), the right (which reflects "demands that are socially authorized"), and virtues (which reflect the importance of "widespread approbation" and blame in shaping conduct).[63] As Steven Fesmire has noted,[64] Dewey is not suggesting that increasing the number of ethical categories from one to three can solve the problems attendant upon traditional attempts to articulate a unitary theoretical category. His point is more radical: that while the categories of traditional ethics (however one might want to enumerate them) all illuminate some real phase of the moral life, the independence of the factors they emphasize reflects an inherent element of conflict in morals that cannot be eliminated by *any* moral theory.[65] A moral philosophy that "frankly recognizes the impossibility of reducing all the elements in moral situations to a single commensurable principle," Dewey concludes, directs us away from the search for theoretical certainty and enjoins us instead to pursue flexible and imaginative experimental inquiry into particular ills and potential remedies in specific situations: it encourages people to "attend more fully to the concrete elements entering into the situations in which they have to act" and thereby allows them to form a "juster estimate of the force of each competing [moral] factor" as it operates in the "actual predicaments of conduct."[66] When deployed in such an experimental approach, moral theories provide invaluable analytic tools for interpreting concrete situations by highlighting the various factors at play in moral experience.[67]

Dewey's analysis of the various factors in morals is unified by two central concerns: first, the need to make morality "reflective" rather than merely "customary," informed by deliberation on the likely consequences of various options for reconstructing a particular social situation, rather than relying on arbitrary authority, dogmatic application of principle, or the positing of some absolute standard or law; and second, the need to harmonize individuals' personal interests with the interests of the many groups in which they live and act. These two main tasks of morals correspond, respectively, to what are in Dewey's view fundamental empirical facts of our human condition: namely, that we live in a moving, changing world in which all ideas and customs, having emerged to meet the demands of specific conditions, inevitably encounter novel conditions for which they are ill-suited, and that human beings can live only through association with other humans and must therefore reckon the demands and responses of other people as among the most important factors for evaluating any proposed line of conduct.

Character emerges in Dewey's morals as the practical solution to these twin tasks of morals.[68] As outlined above, Dewey describes character as a central means and end of the process of deliberation; thus it comes as no surprise that character figures prominently in his account of reflective morality. Dewey argues that the moral capabilities we designate by the terms "reason" and "conscience" are not, as is posited by many moral theories, ready-made endowments possessed by all individuals: though our human constitution includes a native *capacity* for them, reasonableness and conscientiousness are traits of character to be cultivated, complex habits of deliberating reasonably and conscientiously upon the consequences of one's actions. Dewey's emphasis on deliberation as an experimental process also shapes his account of basic moral goods. As we have seen, Dewey denies any dualism of motive-versus-consequences or means-versus-ends, locating morality in a habit's tendency to foster good consequences and, particularly, in the changing *quality* or tendency of character achieved by choosing an end-in-view that redirects activity and reorganizes the habits that compose one's self. Fundamental moral goods such as happiness and liberty, he argues, are realized precisely in this growing quality of present activity: they are components of a beneficial growth in selfhood or character attained through intelligent moral deliberation and choice.

Character also addresses the need to harmonize individual interests with ends that serve the common good. In identifying this necessity as "the very problem of morals," Dewey is careful not to perpetuate the familiar dualism of "the individual" versus "the social." The fact that humans exist only in and through association with other humans makes it nonsensical, he argues, to describe personal interests as inherently opposed to the interests of the social groups in which one lives; conduct always entails consideration of how one's own activity fits into some larger group or groups.[69] Yet if there is no dualism—no inherent conflict—between regard for one's self and regard for others, specific conflicts *do* arise: conflicting desires and our efforts to harmonize them are the very substance of our moral life. Character is fundamental to Dewey's ethics precisely because it names both the locus of these conflicts and the means to resolving them. Character, which is like "habit" a "double-barreled" term that expresses how environmental factors become incorporated in the dispositional makeup of the self, includes the ability of an individual, by choosing to enlist her efforts in the pursuit of ends that serve the common good, to strengthen the influence of those dispositions in her self, thereby cultivating a new self that finds its personal satisfaction in pursuing the common good.

It is crucial to note that these two dynamics of moral selfhood are, in Dewey's democratic vision, complementary. Thus, in describing "the very problem of morals" as the formation of "a voluntary self in which desires and affections centre in the values which are common; in which interest focusses in objects that contribute to the enrichment of the lives of all," Dewey clearly is *not* advocating the acquiescent molding of individual desires to the specific duties and virtues prescribed by the communities to which one belongs. His call for reflective rather than customary morality is based on the deeply Emersonian conviction that, because our world is a moving one in which "ideas of good and evil which were once true have to be modified as social conditions change," the only way to be a "good" self is to be a dynamic, changing self that questions conventional formulations of duty. One can be truly "conscientious," truly fulfill one's duty to others, only by continually testing the validity of the communally sanctioned principles and habits that have shaped one's character—by continually reassessing the consequences of one's acts and, when necessary, pursuing new ends that serve to remake that character.[70] Ultimately, then, the two main tasks of morals—the need to make morality reflective and to harmonize individual interests with ends that serve the common good—are comprehended in "character" conceived as the ongoing process of remaking self and environment: in the capacity of an individual to choose to enlist her efforts in the pursuit of ends that serve the common good and thereby cultivate a new self that finds its satisfactions in such common ends, and in the complementary capacity to cultivate the habit of conscientiously reevaluating and revising the ends that have hitherto defined that common good.

The centrality of character in Dewey's ethics clarifies the link between character and community with which I opened this chapter, for these complementary aspects of moral character correspond directly to the dynamics that characterize Dewey's model of democratic community: the twin requirements that individuals should seek personal cultivation in pursuing ends that serve the common good, and that each social group should find its interest served in enabling individuals to question and revise its principles and customs. Moreover, because for Dewey character comprehends both the subjective and the objective, the individual and the social aspects of selfhood, his emphasis on the cultivation of character points to a politics that rejects any dualism of "individual" versus "social" approaches to reform, that encompasses both the need to remake the social conditions that educate the habits of individual selfhood, and the necessary role of individual choice, imagination, and initiative in projecting and pursuing the ends that serve to remake those conditions.

The first factor in morals that Dewey addresses is "wisdom" or discernment of "the good": determination of those ends that are most worthy of pursuit. The key to wisdom, Dewey contends, lies in using experimental intelligence to choose those goods that are the most "inclusive" and "enduring," a standard that, as Dewey elaborates it, indicates how radically he departs from traditional ethical theories. Recall from Dewey's model of deliberation that choice occurs when a projected end satisfies some dominant habit or combination of habits, and that the function of an end—in which function its "goodness" must reside—is to restore activity and thereby determine the quality of character (the reorganized integration of habits) constituted by that restored activity. By this model, the most "enduring" and "inclusive" end is that which most successfully harmonizes the various dispositions that compose one's character. "Choice is reasonable," Dewey concludes, "when it induces us to act . . . with regard to the claims of each of the competing habits and impulses," when "the object of thought . . . stimulates by unifying, harmonizing, different competing tendencies," ideally in a fashion that effectively sublimates less beneficial dispositions. Dewey thus rejects the dualistic approach of traditional ethical theories that posit special moral faculties (such as reason, will, or conscience) different in kind from other habits of knowing, or that posit a separate, transcendent category of moral good that is intrinsically higher than mere "natural" pleasures (as in Kant's concept of the moral law). "In isolation," Dewey asserts, "one enjoyment cannot be said to be higher or lower than another"; "there is nothing intrinsically bad," for instance, "about raw impulse and desire," they only "become evil in contrast with another desire whose object includes more inclusive and more enduring consequences." There is no "absolute or inherent" contrast between "natural" and "moral" goods: moral goods are simply those pleasures that have withstood the process of reflection on their broader relations and consequences.[71]

Dewey would thus concur with the view, espoused in one version or another by many moral theories, that true happiness is that which accords with reason; his explanation of this connection, however, departs radically from more traditional views that locate happiness in renouncing merely "natural" desires to follow the higher dictates of reason and transcendent duty. "Rationality," as portrayed in Dewey's account of deliberation, "is not a force to evoke against impulse and habit," but rather names "the attainment of a working harmony among diverse desires." A chosen end is good not because it renounces desire, but because it harmonizes our existing desires in the most satisfactory, most enduring and inclusive, fashion: true happiness concerns the "difference in quality between an enduring satisfaction of the whole self and a transient satisfaction of some isolated element in the self." In this regard, Dewey's ethics recall Emerson's efforts in "Self-Reliance" to articulate a nonrenunciatory morality—his complaint, for instance, against virtues that are mere "penances" or "expiations" for "living in the world." Indeed, Dewey's claim that an end is good to the degree it successfully harmonizes the various dispositions that compose one's character provides an intriguing gloss on Emerson's brazen claim that "the only right is what is after my constitution, the only wrong what is against it." Similarly, while Dewey sees inhibition as essential to the deliberation and sublimation that enable the reconstruction of character, he insists that this inhibitory function is to be achieved not through an ascetic suppression of passions, but rather by cultivating a character with a diversity of passions that can modulate each other. "The man who would intelligently cultivate intelligence will widen, not narrow, his life of strong impulses while aiming at their happy coincidence in operation," Dewey contends: "More 'passions,' not fewer is the answer. . . . Variety of competing tendencies enlarges the world," and "brings a diversity of considerations before the mind." Here again it is evident why Dewey saw Emerson as an important precursor on the topic of character, as Dewey's view recalls Emerson's assertion in *The Conduct of Life* that self-cultivation or "culture" is a matter of "invoking the aid of other powers against the dominant talent"—that "a man has a range of affinities" that he can nurture to "modulate the violence of any master-tones that have a droning preponderance in his scale," not to "destroy" his "motherwit," but to effectively temper and direct it, "leav[ing] nothing but pure power."[72]

Thus Dewey argues, as he characteristically does about moral and intellectual capacities, that reason is not some "ready-made antecedent" faculty "which can be invoked at will," but a "laborious achievement of habit needing to be continually worked over." Reason is best conceived not as a substantive entity (which the prominence of nouns in our syntax too easily suggests), but as a quality of selfhood or action best described adjectivally or adverbially: to be a *reasonable* person is to have the habit of *reasonably* consulting and attempting to harmonize the full range of dispositions that compose one's self. Character, then, constitutes the practical path to happiness in at least two regards. First, the capacity for reasonable choice through which happiness is realized depends upon the cultivation of a "multitude of dispositions" that can be "manifested in deliberation" and upon training in the "method" of "their effectual organization into continuous dispositions of inquiry." In other words, the pursuit of happiness is fostered by social conditions that allow individuals to cultivate a diversity of habits and that train them to deploy those habits in the deliberative imagination of possible courses of action. Second, in line with his more general claim that the experience which forms a habit precedes the ability to deliberately project and choose an end—that the "act must come before the thought, and a habit before an ability to evoke the thought at will"—Dewey argues that the capacity for a reasonable happiness can be cultivated only by helping individuals to experience the pleasures of choosing more enduring and inclusive ends over ends that offer more immediate but shallow gratification, thereby strengthening their disposition to so choose in the future. The practical task of morals, in regards to wisdom and happiness, is to "utiliz[e] all possible occasions, when we are not in the presence of conflicting desires, to cultivate interest in," and "multiply occasions for the enjoyment of," "those goods which we do approve in our calm moments of reflection," so as to "integrate the office of the judge . . . into the formation of our very desires and thus learn to take pleasure in the ends which reflection approves."[73]

If wisdom means to seek a reasonable happiness by harmonizing the various dispositions that compose the self, this standard inevitably intersects with the two other, and more explicitly social, moral factors that Dewey identifies: duty and virtue. All three factors must be understood within the scope of "association" as the primary, inclusive fact of human conduct. Just as experience and habit refer to the inclusive fact of activity that comprehends both subjective and objective factors, so association comprehends both an individual's acts and the social groups in which those acts find their bases and meanings. The "idea that individuals are born separate and isolated and are brought into society only through some artificial device"—which idea underlies classic liberalism's dualistic opposition of "the individual" and "society"—is a "pure myth" that is patently refuted by the facts of human existence. "Social ties and connections are as natural and inevitable as are physical":[74]

> Individuals are interdependent. No one is born except in dependence on others. Without aid and nurture from others, he would miserably perish. The material of his intellectual subsistence, as well as of his physical, comes to him from others. As he matures, he becomes more physically and economically independent; but he can carry on his calling only through cooperation and competition with others. . . . Even when a person is alone he thinks with language that is derived from association with others.[75]

When "selfhood is taken for what it is, something existing in relationships to others and not in unreal isolation," it is evident that the interest which defines selfhood can contain no inherent conflict between "regard for self" and "regard for others," for these name "secondary phases of a more normal and complete interest: regard for the welfare and integrity of the social groups of which we form a part." Conduct always entails consideration of how one's activity fits into a larger group. "Interest in the social whole of which one is a member necessarily carries with it interest in one's own self," in one's "own place and work" within the group; conversely, "concern for one's own health, learning, [and] advancement," far from being opposed to social interest, is a necessary condition for contributing to any group, and hence a *"primary* responsibility placed upon each individual."[76]

Duty and virtue, as Dewey defines them, are outgrowths of this basic fact of association, describing ways in which our moral choices must take into account the needs and responses of other human beings. Because humans are so profoundly dependent upon cooperative interaction with other humans, "when we begin to forecast consequences, the consequences that most stand out are those which proceed from other people." Duty expresses the fact that we live in interdependence with other human beings who make demands upon us and upon whom we make demands. The concepts of "law" and the "right," Dewey contends, are simply generalizations of the various claims that people validly make upon each other. Duty is not, as Kantian theories would have it, some transcendent principle of right wholly superior to considerations of good consequences; instead, duty functions to "broaden" one's "conception" of "the area of consequences to be taken into account in forming ends and deciding what is Good" so that one is more likely to give "the same weight to his own good, as dictated by his own wants and purposes, as he gives to that of others." Similarly, the importance of virtues (and vices) in morals indicates the influential role that others' approval and disapproval plays in the formation of character. Motives, Dewey argues, are not essential and unchanging native drives that determine human behavior; they are formed (and re-formed) when the responses of others teach us the meaning of our acts: "others characterize an act with favorable or condign qualities which they impute to an agent's character . . . in order to encourage him in future acts of the same sort, or in order to dissuade him—in short, to build or destroy a habit. . . . After a time and to some extent, a person teaches himself to think of the results of acting this way or that before he acts." Accordingly, the true function of motives is not to fix blame for past acts (as, Dewey argues, is often mistakenly assumed). Their function is not "retrospective, but prospective": one is "held responsible in order that he may *become* responsible," so that "he may *become* a different kind of self and henceforth choose different sorts of ends." Thus, while he defines in generic terms the attributes of a moral self and the traits that make an interest a virtue, Dewey contends it is impossible to construct a hierarchy of virtues that define the unchanging traits of a good self, for virtues are the traits or dispositions of character that are encouraged within a particular culture or group, reflecting its customs, values, and social conditions.[77]

When these factors of duty and virtue are considered in light of Dewey's two larger concerns—making morality reflective rather than customary and harmonizing individual interest with the common good—character again emerges as the practical focus of morals. To begin with the latter concern, Dewey's approach avoids the dualism between personal interest and the greater moral good that hampers conventional moral theories— the type of dualism evident in the Kantian demand that personal interest be sacrificed to the absolute dictates of moral reason, or in hedonistic Utilitarianism's contradictory commitments to personal pleasure as the motive of all action and to a moral standard of maximizing the common good.[78] By contrast, because his model of character stresses that aspects of the social environment—including the accepted duties and virtues of one's social groups—are incorporated into the dispositional makeup of the self, Dewey denies any inherent conflict between egoism and altruism and focuses instead on the *practical* task of cultivating dispositions that effectively harmonize regard for self with regard for others. For instance, Dewey argues that duties are "involved" in the "inherent relationships persons sustain to one another"—relationships that define our selves. Thus a father "feels that" his duties to his child "are involved in the *parental relation*," that "because of this human relationship, something is owed to the child"; similarly, "friends owe something to one another because of the very nature of the friendly relation," and "citizens in a just state respond at their personal inconvenience to the demands of the state, not because the latter may bring physical pressure or mental coercion to bear upon them, but because they are members of organized society." Social responsibilities are not regrettable but necessary legal contrivances individuals reluctantly submit to so as to preserve their preexisting personal liberty—as the liberal metaphor of the social "contract" implies. We are "members" of human relationships in "such an intimate sense" that the demands others make upon us are not felt as "wholly alien" or "external impositions" even when a demand "runs contrary" to our "uppermost desire." The habits of regarding others that we cultivate in our relationships become deeply integral parts of our selves. One does not reckon one's duty to a child, for instance, in an abstract, calculating fashion: one *becomes* a parent—one *is* a parent—and the obligations inherent in this relation become a part of one's identity, so that "even if [a father] feels these to be a burden and seeks to escape from them, he flees from something which is part of himself and not from something imposed by external force."[79]

The extent to which Dewey's approach offers a radical alternative to traditional moral theories—and the explanatory power of his approach—is crystallized by a striking example from *Democracy and Education*:

> A physician who continues to serve the sick in a plague at almost certain danger to his own life must be interested in the efficient performance of his profession—more interested in that than in the safety of his own bodily life. But it is distorting facts to say that this interest is merely a mask for an interest in something else which he gets by continuing his customary services—such as money or good repute or virtue; that it is only a means to an ulterior selfish end. The moment we recognize that the self is not something ready-made, but something in continuous formation through choice of action, the whole situation clears up. A man's interest in keeping at his work in spite of danger to life means that his self is found *in* that work; if he finally

gave up, and preferred his personal safety or comfort, it would mean that he preferred to be *that* kind of a self. The mistake lies in making a separation between interest and self, and supposing that the latter is the end to which interest in objects and acts and others is a mere means. In fact, self and interest are two names for the same fact; the kind and amount of interest actively taken in a thing reveals and measures the quality of selfhood which exists.[80]

This example demonstrates how theories that posit "self-interest" as the primal motive behind all behavior, or that locate morality in an opposed altruistic capacity to renounce self-interest, ignore the fundamental unity of self and act. The "interest" at stake in any action significant enough to make it moral is not merely the attainment of an additional quantity of good for a completed self but the evolving quality of selfhood itself. The desire to be or remain the kind of person one has spent one's life striving to be may indeed be so deeply felt that it is worth risking or losing one's life to preserve one's identity. The appeal of Dewey's psychology becomes apparent when contrasted to the way dominant moral theories might account for the behavior—in one sense remarkable, and yet not uncommon—typified by Dewey's doctor. Our culture's view of morals is typically split between a liberal emphasis on self-interest and an opposing Kantian or Judeo-Christian emphasis on self-sacrifice or self-transcendence. According to this pervasive dualism, Dewey's doctor, having pursued a medical career that is a mere means to the true motive of self-interest (fame, wealth, etc.) and, if he lives in a liberal-capitalist[81] culture, having been taught that such pursuit of personal gain, far from being inconsistent with the general welfare, is the best means to promote it, is suddenly confronted with a situation that requires him to renounce this habitual motive and obey a stern dictate of self-sacrifice—a renunciation allegedly grounded in innate capacities of conscience, reason, or will (perhaps fortified by Sunday sermons) that allow him to apprehend his duty and follow it. The schizophrenic incoherence of this account as a realistic description of human behavior would be laughable if not for the fact that its various components enjoy such widespread acceptance and influence in our culture.

Dewey offers a far more credible explanation, viewing the doctor's behavior as the evidence of a well-cultivated moral character: the ability to locate one's personal interest in pursuit of ends that benefit others (even at the risks one's life) results from past experiences in which one enjoyed the quality of satisfaction such choices yield, until the subsequent disposition to find satisfaction in such pursuits eventually became a habitual part of one's self. Whereas traditional moral theories seek to transcend the gap between egoism and altruism by positing a sheer act of moral will, Dewey argues that no such gap exists and that regard for self and regard for others can be harmonized through the practical choices and concrete experiences that cultivate character. While people may not often face the type of dire situation confronting Dewey's doctor, the function of character in the example is paradigmatic. "Many an individual," Dewey notes, "solves the problem" of "instituting an identity or equation between personal and general happiness" in a similar fashion:[82]

> He does so not by any theoretical demonstration that what gives others happiness will also make him happy, but by voluntary choice of those objects which do bring good to others. He gets a personal satisfaction or happiness because his desire is fulfilled, but his desire has first been made after a definite pattern. . . . He has achieved a happiness which has *approved* itself to him, and this quality of being an approved happiness may render it invaluable, not to be compared with others. By personal choice among the ends suggested by desires of objects which are in agreement with the needs of social relations, an individual achieves a *kind* of happiness which is harmonious with the happiness of others.[83]

Dewey here offers an important alternative to two of our culture's most dominant theories of the tension between personal desires and the common good—the classic liberal account, with its optimistic faith in an inherently rational human subject, and the contrastingly pessimistic account offered by Freudian psychology. Liberalism denies any real conflict between self-interest and social duty, arguing not only that an innate, rational self-interest is sufficient to bind individuals together in a "social contract," but also that the "rational" pursuit of personal profit, working through the operations of "natural" economic laws, is sufficient to maximize the (pecuniary) welfare of all. Rejecting this vision of rationality, Freud depicts socialization as a painful process of sublimating irrational primal drives that dooms human beings to a state of unresolved psychic conflict and unhappiness.[84] Dewey's model of the moral self avoids both of these extremes: though he denies any *inherent* dualism between self-interest and the common good, he insists, in opposition to liberalism, that *particular* conflicts between personal desires and duties to others are only-too-real aspects of specific moral situations and cannot be resolved by the "invisible hand" of beneficent market forces. Yet if moral conflicts are real, they are not irremediable: in opposition to Freud, Dewey contends that humans *are* capable of harmonizing conflicting duties and desires so as to achieve a fulfilling, reasonable happiness.

Dewey's dissent from these more traditional philosophies reflects his emphasis on the central role habit plays in human nature, which leads him to view both the liberal and Freudian accounts as too essentialist, as falsely positing some inherent trait(s)—whether liberalism's "reason" or Freud's irrational drives—as the primary explanatory force behind all conduct. Describing native human impulses as vague and unformed until interaction with environing social conditions shapes them into habits, a Deweyan psychology rejects Freud's model of primal irrational drives that can at best be held at bay in an uneasy psychic truce, affirming that human nature is much more plastic and responsive to an educative remaking than the Freudian view allows.[85] Dewey similarly rejects liberalism's claim that the ability to harmonize personal desires with the common good reflects an innate rationality, insisting instead that the ability to deliberate and choose *reasonably* is a function of habits that can and must be taught, learned, and chosen. This view thus points toward what is arguably Dewey's central critique of classic liberal individualism: namely, that creating a just and humane society is not merely a matter of protecting the liberties and interests of already-formed individuals, but of cultivating individuality, of reconstructing social conditions so as to educate individuals in the habits of moral selfhood. Dewey's model of character thus leads to a balanced view of reform, one that avoids both a naive optimism and a debilitating pessimism by affirming, on the one hand, that human nature *can* be educated, and, on the other hand, that it *must* be educated, that intelligent and painstaking attention must be given to reforming social conditions with an eye to their pervasive influence on character.

The central role that such cultivation of character plays in Dewey's ethics is evident in the model of selfhood described in the passage above, which asserts the ability of character—the deliberate cultivation of desires and habits based on intelligent evaluation of their tendency and quality—to satisfy the intersecting demands of the independent factors at play in morals: to satisfy the demands of duty and virtue by strengthening one's disposition to choose "objects which are in agreement with the needs of social relations," while harmonizing these demands with the other desires that compose the self, thereby enabling a reasonable happiness. Dewey acknowledges that such a character is an achievement, the result of intelligent effort and choice, on the part of both an individual and the society that educates him, to remake personal dispositions: "He gets a personal satisfaction or happiness because his desire is fulfilled, but his desire has first been made after a definite pattern." But Dewey insists this effort to remake the self is *not* a sacrifice or compromise of individual happiness to social duty: the achievement of such a self represents for Dewey the most reasonable, inclusive happiness precisely because it combines both cooperation with others in pursuit of common ends and the exercise of individual choice in selection of those ends.

Indeed, in Dewey's democratic vision these are the two factors that most imbue one's activity with enhanced quality and meaning. Satisfying the claims others make on us is not only consistent with a rational happiness, but a necessary ingredient in it. Because we are inherently social beings for whom relationships with other humans form intimate and pervasive aspects of personal identity, the choice to pursue aims that serve the common good invests one's present activity with an intrinsic and immediately enjoyed quality that constitutes, for Dewey, the most precious and secure type of happiness available to us. "The final happiness of an individual resides in the supremacy of certain interests in the make-up of character," he asserts: "namely, alert, sincere, enduring interests in the objects which all men can share. . . . [T]his kind of happiness alone is not at the mercy of circumstance. No amount of outer obstacles can destroy the happiness that comes from lively and ever-renewed interest in others and in the conditions and objects which promote their development."[86] Yet it is also crucial to note Dewey's accompanying emphasis on the exercise of individual choice: if pursuit of ends that harmonize one's personal good with the interests of others yields an intrinsically valuable quality of happiness (which presumably holds true even in social systems where cooperation reflects mere obedience to rigid custom), such happiness can achieve its richest value only when common ends are voluntarily chosen, not externally imposed. It is not merely that an individual is free, as noted in the example above, to exercise "personal choice" among a variety of possible ends "which are in agreement with the needs of social relations," nor is it enough that an end should be approved in terms of being consistent with a social standard; it must have "*approved* itself to him." An end must be the result of a process of moral deliberation in which an individual actively participates,[87] and must be verified to that individual's own judgment by the subsequent quality of happiness experienced—which "quality of being an approved happiness may render it invaluable, not to be compared with others."

The role of individual choice becomes even more prominent when Dewey considers the factors of duty and virtue in light of his second unifying concern—the need to make morality reflective. While it is a basic fact of human life that we must acknowledge the claims that others make on us (duties) and the types of acts that win their approval (virtues), the validity of any *particular* duty or virtue, Dewey contends, must be open to interrogation and revision by the operations of experimental inquiry. Duty must not be treated as a rigid, absolute rule that "take[s] precedence of all human claims"; rather, as an expression of the generally accepted claims that humans make upon each other, duty properly functions as a tool for experimental inquiry into concrete problems, as "a reminder to consider human claims in a large way" that "make[s] us sensitive to the relations and claims involved in particular situations." Similarly, virtues should not simply reflect the prevailing prejudices of a community; moral inquiry should strive "to discover what *should* be esteemed so that approbation will follow what is decided to be *worth* approving." Though a "generalized sense of duty" can make us more alert to the claims of others, and a generalized sense of right can provide a standard for evaluating whether an end is worthy of approbation, neither can specify what particular end might be most worthy of pursuit: that can be determined only by experimental inquiry into the concrete ills and possible remedies immanent in a given situation, and by choice that is based upon such deliberation and subject to revision in light of subsequent results.[88]

Accordingly, Dewey asserts that our capacity to satisfy duties to others and pursue virtuous actions springs not from some innate faculty of conscience, but reflects a practical achievement of character that, once again, is most appropriately conceived in adjectival or adverbial terms— our task is to cultivate the habit of *conscientiousness*, of deliberating *conscientiously* (broadly, impartially, and intelligently) on how various courses of action might impact others: "moral deliberativeness, when it is habitual," entails "scrupulous attention to the potentialities of any act or proposed aim. . . . Genuine conscientiousness has an objective outlook; it is intelligent attention and care to the quality of an act in view of its consequences for general happiness."[89] The common misconception of conscience as an innate faculty stems in part, Dewey argues, from a failure to recognize that intuitive moral responses, while seemingly innate, are in fact habitual. Reflective judgments or "valuations" from past experiences become so habitual that they operate unreflectively as immediate "valuings"[90]—as an adult whose experience allows her to foresee imminent harm in a situation feels an immediate moral impulse to act where an untutored child is oblivious of any moral import. In line with his broader view that habit both forms the basis of human intelligence and threatens, in its rigidity, to hinder human intelligence, Dewey suggests that the habitual availability of moral judgments provides, on the one hand, a tremendous economy of power that allows us to apply the lessons of past experience without a potentially paralyzing need for deliberation, and, on the other hand, entails the constant threat that habits of judgment derived from past conditions will be dogmatically applied to altered situations where they are no longer valid.

Hence, Dewey approves Aristotle's injunction that "only the good man is a good judge of what is truly good," that "it takes a fine and well-grounded character to react immediately with the right approvals and condemnations," but adds two crucial emendations. First, that "there is no such thing as a good man—in an absolute sense," that every person has habitual "prejudices" and "unconscious biases" making him or her "unduly sensitive to some values" and "indifferent to others," so that "spontaneous 'intuitions' of value have to be entertained subject to correction, confirmation and revision, by personal observation of consequences"; and, second, the corollary qualification that "the better" a person is "the more likely he is to be perplexed as to what to do in novel, complicated situations." A moral person is always seeking to recognize consequences (existing or potential) that reveal the limits of her existing principles and habits: the "truly conscientious person not only uses a standard in judging, but is concerned to revise and improve [her] standard," is "on the *lookout*" for occasions that require her to revise her estimation of the quality or tendency of the dispositions that define her existing character—and, by choosing new ends, to remake that character. Furthermore, a truly good person views this not as an onerous necessity, but embraces it as an opportunity to seek better ends and create a better self: she is "on the outlook for something *better*, . . . for good not already achieved."[91]

While Dewey here insists, in Emersonian fashion, that true social responsibility requires the liberty of individual conscience and self-remaking, the freedom to reject conventional notions of duty and form new ends, he also insists that the converse is true—the individual liberty that is realized in self-remaking requires social responsibility. Indeed, in marked contrast to traditional liberal views that equate liberty with a freedom from social responsibilities or that posit an "antecedent basis" for responsibility in some "metaphysical" "freedom of the will," Dewey contends that "freedom in its practical and moral sense . . . is connected with possibility of growth, learning and modification of character, just as is responsibility." The unity of self and act, of motive and consequence, means that responsibility and liberty are in fact two names for the same process: liberty, like conscientiousness, resides in the capacity to learn from experience and deliberately choose new ends—and in so doing choose what kind of self to be. As previously discussed, Dewey argues that motives are inherently *prospective*: "One is held responsible in order that he may *become* responsible"; we apprise another of the tendency and quality of her acts so that she may choose better ends and so become a better self. This possibility for learning, growth, and change also describes liberty. In broad terms that recall the meliorism of William James, Dewey argues that freedom requires a world pluralistic or indeterminate enough so that our choices may help realize one potential future rather than another: "To foresee future objective alternatives and to be able by deliberation to choose one of them and thereby weight its chances in the struggle for future existence, measures our freedom." Much as James, in "Pragmatism and Religion," asserts that "our acts" are "our turning places, where we seem to ourselves to make ourselves and grow," where we realize our evolving selves as we act to realize our cherished ideals in our own corner of the universe, so Dewey describes freedom as existing in our capacity to choose what kind of self to be in the present by choosing what kind of future world to strive for—in short, in the capacity of character to remake itself. Liberty, like conscience and reason, is "not a native gift or an endowment but is acquired." In taking responsibility for the consequences or tendencies of one's acts, liberty is "actualized" not as an end achieved, but, in accord with Dewey's analysis of the true function of ends-in-view, as a growing quality of present activity and character: "We do not use the present to control the future. We use the foresight of the future to refine and expand present activity. In this use of desire, deliberation and choice, freedom is actualized."[92]

Thus, just as a truly conscientious self is "on the lookout" for opportunities to revise its habitual ends and dispositions, so the "growing, enlarging, liberated self" "welcomes untried situations," "goes forth to meet new demands and occasions, and readapts and remakes itself in the process." Indeed, whether the focus be on happiness, conscientiousness, or liberty, Dewey reaches the conclusion that the essential distinction in morals is that between "the static and the dynamic self," between "the accomplished self" "constituted by habits already formed" and "the opportunity" and "need" to "go beyond what one has been": "the good person is precisely the one who is most conscious of the alternative, and is the most concerned to find openings for the newly forming or growing self."[93] Here again one is struck by Dewey's profound debt to Emerson, specifically to his celebration of "transition," "abandonment," and the virtue of becoming "unsettled," to his contention that the only secure value in life is found in leaving behind the false security of achieved results—and the selfhood they define—for new challenges and growth. Indeed, if one seeks a rationale for Dewey's claim, in his 1903 address, that Emerson's twin commitments to character and to the trial by present experience capture an essential basis or spirit of democracy, one might best look to the arguments traced above: to Dewey's assertion that conscientiousness and liberty—fulfilling one's duties to others and achieving a liberation of one's personal capacities—come together in the cultivated habit of submitting all existing customs and ideas, and therefore one's achieved self, to the remakings of experimental intelligence.

This analysis of the inextricable link between liberty and responsibility also indicates how Dewey anticipates ethical concerns raised by Kenneth Burke and Ralph Ellison, concerns explored in chapter 6. Dewey's contentions that conscientiousness requires continuous inquiry into the changing or unacknowledged consequences of one's actions, and that there is "no such thing" as a wholly good person fully aware of the implications of his habits, are echoed by Burke's call for a "comic ethics" that charitably recognizes how every individual is "necessarily mistaken," unaware of the blindnesses and complicities of his position within the complex fabric of our social interconnection. Similarly, when Burke balances this charitability with an uncompromising call to acknowledge how one's local actions are "identified" with their more remote or indirect consequences on others, he essentially adopts a Deweyan view that the quality of one's acts (and selfhood) is defined by their tendency to create beneficial or detrimental consequences. In other words, one literally cannot know the quality of one's acts, and the quality of one's self—and hence, cannot choose what kind of self to be, in which choice liberty resides—without attending conscientiously to the complex and indirect consequences of one's activity within a larger communal context.[94] As Ellison's narrator eloquently encapsulates matters in a climactic scene from *Invisible Man,* when he challenges a wealthy (faux-Emersonian) philanthropist to recognize how their destinies are connected across the inequities of American society: "if you don't know *where* you are, you probably don't know *who* you are." In this regard, Dewey, Burke, and Ellison all resist the idea that an individualized vocation or activity can achieve an autonomous moral integrity—as Emerson's rhetoric at times seems to assert, as when he brashly claims, "I may . . . absolve me to myself" by following "my own stern claims and perfect circle." Yet if Dewey insists that an ethical individualism requires careful attention to how one's acts impact others, he locates this in a habit of conscientious self-reconstruction that is, as outlined above, deeply Emersonian. In this respect too, Dewey prefigures Ellison, who argues that the only "antidote" to the tragic "hubris" that plagues a narrow individualism is an Emersonian ethic of "consciousness, consciousness, *consciousness*" in service of "a more refined conscientiousness."[95]

The Politics of Deweyan Character: Education, Democracy, Community

Dewey's assertion of the centrality of character clarifies several important political dimensions of his thought, dimensions that indicate in broad terms the enduring political appeal of his pragmatism and that illuminate more specifically his analysis, in *The Public and Its Problems* and *Individualism Old and New,* of the task of reconstructing individuality and community in the era of corporate industrial society. First, the "double-barreled" nature of character indicates how Dewey provides an alternative to the stale dualism between "individual" and "institutional" approaches to social reform.[96] If the practical task of morals is to reconstruct character, such reconstruction can never be purely individual or social, but comprehends *both* the need to reconstruct social conditions so as to shape and reshape individuals' habits *and* the crucial role that individual desire, imagination, and choice play in so reconstructing social conditions. This dialectic dynamic of reform is among the most politically valuable aspects of Dewey's thought, for it combines a mandate for institutional reform with an insistence on the necessity of individual responsibility, and balances an affirmation of the possibility of reform with a sober acknowledgment of its difficulty.

To identify habit, as Dewey does, as the basic process or building-block of selfhood, is to assert that all human motives—indeed, the capacity to choose or even envision an end—depend on acquired dispositions shaped by environing conditions. Dewey thus rejects the notion that reform can be initiated by, or grounded in, an individual capacity for moral choice that is antecedent to and independent of existing social conditions, rejects any simplistic notion that "an individual in any system can have a righteous will" and that social conditions, while affecting "the external execution of the motive," do not shape "the motive itself." "We change character from worse to better," he asserts, "only by changing conditions. . . . We cannot change habit directly: that notion is magic. But we can change it indirectly by modifying conditions, by an intelligent selecting and weighting of the objects which engage attention and which influence the fulfillment of desires." Yet, as this reference to changing character through "intelligent selection" of objects indicates—and as the ideas explored throughout this chapter should make clear—Dewey's emphasis on the pervasive role that social conditions play in shaping character does not reduce to a social determinism, but instead promotes a vigorous, melioristic affirmation of individual freedom and responsibility. To insist that the capacity for wise, reasonable, and conscientious personal choice is an emergent *result* within experience (and not some antecedent faculty of will) is not to deny its unique role once it emerges. "All morality," Dewey notes, "is both individual and social": social because the "material of personal reflection and of choice comes to each of us from the customs, traditions, institutions, policies and plans of these large collective wholes," yet ineluctably "personal in that social problems have to be faced by individuals, and decisions reached in the forum of individual minds have to be carried into effect by individual agents, who are in turn personally responsible for the consequences of their acts." Though our ability to envision and choose new ends is always limited by the habits cultivated in existing social conditions, that limited capacity for choice offers a real and, in Dewey's melioristic view, sufficient freedom to determine the quality of one's own identity: "the contention is not in the least that our will, the body of our desires and purposes, is subservient to social conditions," for "as soon as we become aware of [engrained social habits], we like or dislike their effects; we actively approve and support them; we tolerate them, we are willing to have them exist rather than take the trouble to change them; or we are moved to active opposition. In any case, there is human complicity, an assumption of responsibility." If it is unrealistic "magic" to believe that "an individual in any system can have a righteous will," it is equally false to assume a contrasting lack of agency: "in whatever occupation he finds himself," to the degree an individual can imagine and pursue alternative courses of action, "he lives in situations that are in some respect flexible and plastic," so that "the first move in recovery of an integrated individual is accordingly with the individual himself."[97]

In thus balancing an acknowledgment of the shaping power of social environment with an assertion of individual freedom and responsibility, Dewey's model of character avoids two opposing errors common to more traditional philosophies. On the one hand, he avoids the error—typified by classic liberalism's "negative" view of liberty as requiring only "freedom from oppressive legal and political measures"—of ignoring the need to create social conditions that provide individuals with an effective freedom grounded in the control of resources required to execute a chosen course of action: "No man and no mind was ever emancipated merely by being left alone," he insists, "Removal of formal limitations is but a negative condition; positive freedom is not a state but an act which involves methods and instrumentalities for control of conditions." On the other hand, he avoids the error (to which collectivist philosophies are prone) of assuming that institutional reform takes precedence over individual responsibility, that individual freedom must or can wait until the conditions to enable it are realized. From Dewey's perspective, this is to misunderstand the function of ends, to think of freedom as a final goal to be achieved rather than as a growing quality of present activity actualized through the choice to enlist one's energies in attempts to remake environing conditions. This "recognition that good is always found in a present growth of significance in activity protects us," Dewey asserts, "from thinking that welfare can consist in a soup-kitchen happiness, in pleasures we can confer upon others from without," from thinking that we can promote the liberty or happiness of others "except through liberating their powers" by "engaging them in activities that enlarge the meaning of life": that is, by offering them the opportunities to participate in the cooperative pursuit of common ends.[98]

Dewey's emphasis on the shaping force of social conditions carries a second major political advantage, in that it allows him simultaneously to affirm the possibility for reform and to acknowledge its difficulty. Dewey's social psychology of habit offers an important alternative to influential schools of thought that treat "social customs" as "direct and necessary consequences of specific impulses." Two prominent examples are classic liberalism, whose case for laissez-faire, limited government (as the *only* form of government suited to preserving individual liberty and the social benefits that accrue from it) is based upon the assumption of an innate rational propensity to pursue self-interested acquisition, or the Freudian approach, which views all morality as a necessary restriction on humankind's inherent libidinous and aggressive instincts. By contrast, to take Dewey's stance that human impulses are vague and unformed until "social institutions and expectations shape and crystallize" them "into dominant habits," is to stress the extreme plasticity of human nature and affirm the possibility of reform—to deny that any type of government or social organization is final or absolute, necessitated by some inherent or unchanging instinct of human nature. However, Dewey's position does not translate, as some critics have alleged, into an overly optimistic assessment of the prospects for reforming human nature. For the corollary of Dewey's assertion that reforming social conditions *can* remake human nature is that such social reform is a necessary, and difficult, requirement for remaking character. If habit—as the ability to form new dispositions—constitutes the plasticity of human nature, it is also true that the intrinsically assertive nature of existing habits and customs represents a powerful inertial force that must be overcome in any efforts at reform. While Dewey chides conservatives for citing the "practical unalterability of human nature," he also critiques those reformers who assert that customary practices, because merely conventional, are easily transformed: in fact, Dewey argues, while there is indeed nothing absolute about customs, while they are ultimately plastic, "it is precisely custom which has the greatest inertia," introducing "a force of lag in human life" that is "enormous."[99]

Here, too, the broad contours of Dewey's approach harken back to Emerson, who in his essay "Politics" asserts that "society is fluid," that the changing habits and demands of present activities can remake any and all inherited customs and traditions: "institutions," "though they existed before we were born," are "not aboriginal," and since "every law and usage" was originally an "expedient to meet a particular case," they are "all alterable." Yet if our changing habits *can* transform institutions, Emerson notes, this implies the corollary fact that real and lasting institutional change occurs only when the collective habits of a citizenry have truly outgrown old customs. The law, Emerson argues, is only "the expression of what cultivation exists in the population which permits it," so that "the State must follow, and not lead the character and progress of the citizen"[100]—an argument which finds a striking update in Dewey's *Human Nature and Conduct*:

> A social revolution may effect abrupt and deep alterations in external customs, in legal and political institutions. But the habits that are behind these institutions and that have, willy-nilly, been shaped by objective conditions, the habits of thought and feeling, are not so easily modified. They persist and insensibly assimilate to themselves the outer innovations. . . . The force of lag in human life is enormous. . . . Habits of thought outlive modifications in habits of overt action. The former are vital, the latter, without the sustaining life of the former, are muscular tricks. Consequently as a rule the moral effects of even great political revolutions, after a few years of outwardly conspicuous alterations, do not show themselves till after the lapse of years. A new generation must come upon the scene whose habits of mind have been formed under the new conditions. . . . Where general and enduring moral changes do accompany an external revolution it is because appropriate habits of thought have previously been insensibly matured. The external change merely registers the removal of an external superficial barrier to the operation of existing intellectual tendencies.[101]

A passage like this suggests why Dewey's social psychology holds such promise for addressing recalcitrant human problems—such as racism,[102] or the militarism that James says has been "bred" into "our bone and marrow,"[103] or, for that matter, the corrosively narrow pursuit of personal profit that liberalism attributes to an innate motive of acquisitive self-interest.[104] For Dewey insists that such attitudes are not purely individual (as, for instance, some minimize racism as merely individual, not institutionalized, prejudice), nor inherent instincts of human nature (as a Freudian psychology might view war as the inevitable result of primal aggressive instincts),[105] but rather are deeply engrained, self-perpetuating, collective habits in the full "double-barreled" sense of that term—in that social conditions profoundly and pervasively shape individuals' "habits of thought and feeling," which habits in turn retard efforts to transform those conditions. Dewey's approach treats such problems as susceptible to meliorating reconstruction, but also alerts us to the daunting scope of the reconstructive task involved.

Accordingly, the task of cultivating character that is central to Deweyan reform is both individual and social, a process in which social conditions are reconstructed with primary attention to their educative influence, creating individuals whose reconstructed habits, in turn, exert an idealizing or transforming effect on social conditions. As Dewey describes this dialectic (here in regards to how our consciousness of social ties and duties evolves), "We are not caught in a circle; we traverse a spiral in which social customs generate some consciousness of interdependencies, and this consciousness is embodied in acts which in improving the environment generate new perceptions of social ties, and so on forever." Dewey's insistence that reform must be grounded in a reconstruction of the social conditions that educate individuality constitutes a significant departure from the stance often imputed to Emerson, which is that reform must be initiated or driven by personal reformation—though, as I argue in chapter 2, such a reading distorts Emerson's views on reform. In this respect, Dewey's most relevant precursor in the American "transcendentalist" tradition may be Emerson's friend and colleague Margaret Fuller, who argues in *Woman in the Nineteenth Century* for a "parallel movement" in individual and institutional reform. She dramatizes this synthesis as a debate between Goethe's Romanticism and Fourier's socialism: "Fourier says, As the institutions, so the men! . . . Goethe thinks, As the man, so the institutions!" To which she responds: "Ay! but Goethe, bad institutions are prison walls and impure air that make him stupid. . . . And thou, Fourier, do not expect to change mankind at once. . . . If these attempts are made by unready men, they will fail."[106]

"Character" is one of Dewey's names for this dialectic process of reforming self and environment; another, more encompassing term is "education." In part, Dewey believes that reform must be initiated (or can be most effectively initiated) in the explicitly educative efforts carried on in schools, both because young people's characters are comparatively plastic and unformed, and because schools may offer an environment "freed from extraneous associations and from the pressure of wage-earning" in which students can experience modes of associated endeavor "typifying social callings" as "intrinsically valuable." This is not some ivory-tower vision of education: indeed, Dewey rejects the notion that "we can change character and mind by direct instruction and exhortation" or "apart from a change in industrial and political conditions." But it *is* possible, he argues, to "produce in schools a projection in type of the society we should like to realize, and by forming minds in accord with it gradually modify the larger and more recalcitrant features of adult society."[107] In other words, if schools help students cultivate habits of enjoying the intrinsically valuable qualities of shared experience and endeavor, these habits will be frustrated when students subsequently find themselves in narrower, less humane systems of social interaction; such frustrated habits (as Dewey's model of deliberation stipulates) provide the impetus for recognizing the shortcomings of existing social arrangements, the desire to transform them, and the means for projecting or imagining new ends to guide their reconstruction.

While the explicitly educative function of schools holds an important position in Dewey's politics, his view of character as an ongoing process of reconstructing self and environment leads him to view education as *the* quintessentially human occupation[108] and to conceive education in the broadest sense as comprehending the continuous shaping influence exerted by all aspects of one's social environment. The "fundamental fact in social life and in personal character," he contends, is that "the formation of habits of belief, desire and judgment is going on at every instant under the influence of conditions set by men's contact, intercourse and associations with one another"; if we do not deliberately and intelligently attend to these educative influences, we leave them to mere accident and custom. Ultimately, then, a Deweyan politics mandates the reform of *all* social arrangements in an attempt to make them fully educative of the habits of moral selfhood and fully liberating of individuals' capacities: "When self-hood is perceived to be an active process," and "it is also seen that social modifications are the only means of the creation of changed personalities," Dewey affirms, "institutions are viewed in their educative effect:—with reference to the types of individuals they foster," and "their value" is measured by "the extent to which they educate every individual into the full stature of his possibility." This primary commitment to education constitutes for Dewey the "moral meaning" of democracy considered not merely as a political system, but as a way of life, a "principle" that "holds as much of one form of association, say in industry and commerce, as it does in government":[109]

> The best guarantee of collective efficiency and power is liberation and use of the diversity of individual capacities in initiative, planning, foresight, vigor and endurance. Personality must be educated, and personality cannot be educated by confining its operations to technical and specialized things, or to the less important relationships of life. Full education comes only when there is a responsible share on the part of each person, in proportion to capacity, in shaping the aims and policies of the social groups to which he belongs. This fact fixes the significance of democracy. It cannot be conceived . . . as a consecration of some form of government which has already attained constitutional sanction. It is but a name for the fact that human nature is developed only when its elements take part in directing things which are common, things for the sake of which men and women form groups—families, industrial companies, governments, churches, scientific associations and so on.[110]

This definition of democracy indicates how the model of character traced above is inherently democratic. For democracy, Dewey argues, describes that dynamic in which individuals voluntarily identify with common ends, *and* social groups find their interest in having their customs revised and reinvigorated by the power of individual choice and imagination. These two aspects of democracy correspond directly with Dewey's assertion that the solution to the two main tasks of morals lies in the cultivation of character—in the cultivated habits of finding personal fulfillment in pursuit of ends that benefit others, and of conscientiously evaluating and revising the habits and ends previously accepted as good.

This commitment to democracy and/as education—specifically, the assertion that full education requires "a responsible share on the part of each person, in proportion to capacity, in shaping the aims and policies of the social groups to which he belongs"—brings us to the third in Dewey's trio of overlapping master terms, "community." In concluding this chapter on Dewey's model of the moral self, it remains to consider two issues. The first is how his concept of character and his ideal of community are intimately connected and reciprocal—a topic which takes us full circle to the question with which we began: how a democratic concept of character that has its roots in Emerson can result in a rationale for community. The second concerns how Dewey's vision of community—properly understood as a pragmatic ideal, a tool for melioristic reconstruction of existing conditions—sets the context for *Individualism Old and New* and *The Public and Its Problems*, where he gives his most detailed analyses of the prospects for reconstructing individualism and community. In regards to both these issues, it is helpful to quote at length the definition of democracy-as-community from the latter work:

> From the standpoint of the individual, [democracy as a social idea] consists in having a responsible share according to capacity in forming and directing the activities of the groups to which one belongs and in participating according to need in the values which the groups sustain. From the standpoint of the groups, it demands liberation of the potentialities of members of a group in harmony with the interests and goods which are common. . . .
>
> Regarded as an idea, democracy is not an alternative to other principles of associated life. It is the idea of community life itself. It is an ideal in the only intelligible sense of an ideal: namely, the tendency and movement of some thing which exists carried to its final limit, viewed as completed, perfected. Since things do not attain such fulfillment but are in actuality distracted and interfered with, democracy in this sense is not a fact and never will be. But neither in this sense is there or has there ever been anything which is a community in its full measure, a community unalloyed by alien elements. The idea or ideal of a community presents, however, actual phases of associated life as they are freed from restrictive and disturbing elements, and are contemplated as having attained their limit of development. Wherever there is conjoint activity whose consequences are appreciated as good by all singular persons who take part in it, and where the realization of the good is such as to effect an energetic desire and effort to sustain it in being just because it is a good shared by all, there is in so far a community. The clear consciousness of a communal life, in all its implications, constitutes the idea of democracy.[111]

Community so defined depends upon character in several important ways. "Associated or joint activity" is again the inclusive fact of human existence with which Dewey begins, but "no amount of aggregated collective action of itself constitutes a community": community exists "only when the consequences of combined action are perceived and become an object of desire and effort."[112] Community requires recognition of consequences that define the common good and requires that securing these consequences should become an effective and voluntary motive of individuals' behavior. This describes a process of (among other things) cultivating character: a process, as outlined above, of cultivating the habits of conscientiously inquiring into how one's actions impact others and of finding personal satisfaction in the pursuit of ends that benefit others. Conversely, key aspects of Dewey's model of character necessitate a communal context—specifically, his analyses of basic moral goods such as happiness, conscientiousness, and liberty. Recall, from the preceding discussion, that the unity of motive and consequence means that one cannot know the quality of one's acts or the quality of selfhood they define—and, since liberty describes the ability to choose the quality of one's acts and self, one cannot be free—without attending to the consequences of one's acts on others. Recall, too, Dewey's claim that to acknowledge consequences affecting others and one's corresponding duties to them is never simply a personal sacrifice, but a fulfillment of relationships that intimately define one's self, and his subsequent conclusion that the most secure and inclusive happiness available to us resides in the growth of meaning we experience in striving with others after common ends. Lastly, recall that liberty and happiness reside in a growing quality of present activity that depends upon the choice of an end-in-view to redirect one's activity and remake one's character, which choice requires the kind of community Dewey describes above: a social group that encourages and enables each of its individual members to take "a responsible share according to capacity in forming and directing the activities of the groups to which one belongs." If liberty and happiness are, for Dewey, ultimately products of personal responsibility and choice, it is only in the context of a growing or emerging community that such choice finds its basis and meaning.

The fact that Dewey stresses the status of democracy and community *as ideals*—and all this implies about their function within a Deweyan model of experimental inquiry and reform—is crucial for understanding Dewey's approach to the reconstruction of individualism and community. Dewey defines democracy and community as ideals in the pragmatic sense of an imaginative projection from existing circumstances, "some thing which exists carried to its final limit, viewed as completed, perfected." That democracy so idealized, like "community in its full measure," "is not a fact and never will be" is not a cause for pessimism, but is wholly consonant with Dewey's melioristic view of the function of ends:

> The action of deliberation, as we have seen, consists in selecting
> some foreseen consequence [an end-in-view] to serve as a stimulus

to present action. It brings future possibilities into the present scene and thereby frees and expands present tendencies. But the selected consequence is set in an indefinite context of other consequences just as real as it is, and many of them much more certain in fact. The "ends" that are foreseen and utilized mark out a little island in an infinite sea. The limitation would be fatal were the proper function of ends anything else than to liberate and guide present action out of its perplexities and confusions. But this service constitutes the sole meaning of aims and purposes. . . . The "ideal" as it stands in popular thought, the notion of a complete and exhaustive realization, is remote from the true function of ends.[113]

Ideals considered as specific ends-in-view are essentially tools for analyzing present conditions and reorganizing present activities. Because they are grounded in, and extend from, existing conditions, ends apprise us of possibilities immanent in existing conditions and, by projecting these possibilities in some more fully realized form, provide objects that effectively restore, reorganize, and give meaning to our activity. Ends similarly serve to apprise us of defects or obstacles in the current situation that must be remedied or overcome. The fact that our efforts to realize ends are never fully successful, always require the projection of revised ends, and bring to light or into existence new complications and problems, does not negate the progress and the liberation of capacity that are actualized in this ongoing process of experimental inquiry and reconstruction.[114] Ideals can also be more broadly envisioned or defined—as Dewey's ideals of democracy and community are—in which case they function not as specific ends-in-view but as principles or standards. A standard cannot specify what specific ends-in-view are realistically attainable or worthy of pursuit; those can emerge only from intelligent deliberation on the possibilities and problems of a particular situation. Yet a standard still functions as a tool for analyzing present conditions, for it helps us to generate and choose among ends-in-view—by alerting us to those aspects of our current situation that fall short of the standard and those which best approximate it—and it helps us to evaluate actual outcomes and revise our ends-in-view accordingly. Understood in this context, Dewey's articulation of a democratic ideal that has never been and never will be fully realized is not indulgence in some hopeless fantasy (indeed, it is difficult to find a more trenchant critic of impractical or fantastic idealism than Dewey), but indicates the practical path to democracy: so long as the ideal of democracy-as-community provides us with an effective standard for generating new ends-in-view, democracy is actualized in the liberation of capacity, the exercise of self-determining choice, and the growth of socially shared meaning that individuals enjoy by enlisting their energies in cooperative efforts to construct a more democratic society.

In this sense, Dewey notes, the "democratic ideal poses, rather than solves, the great problem: How to harmonize the development of each individual with the maintenance of a social state in which the activities of one will contribute to the good of all the others."[115] And it is in this spirit that Dewey's twin ruminations on community and individuality, *The Public and Its Problems* and *Individualism Old and New*, must be understood. Dewey does not attempt to prescribe what form a democratic state must take, nor what a reconstructed democratic individuality or personality might look like—indeed, he insists that it is impossible to do so, that new social arrangements and new forms of personality can only emerge through experimental efforts to reconstruct present conditions. But he does undertake what *is* both a possible and necessary first step toward such a reconstruction of individualism and community: namely, using the democratic ideal as a tool for analyzing current conditions—in Dewey's case, the corporate industrial order of the 1920s—in order to identify the existing obstacles to, and the existing possibilities for, creating more democratic communities and cultivating more democratic forms of individuality.

FIVE

"THE LOCAL IS THE
ULTIMATE UNIVERSAL"

Dewey on Reconstructing Individuality and Community

In 1926, when John Dewey delivered and revised the series of lectures that would be published as *The Public and Its Problems*, the future of individualism in American culture weighed heavily on his mind. In "William James in Nineteen Twenty-Six," he wondered aloud about James's melioristic ethic of individualized vocation—as typified in James's vision in "Pragmatism and Religion"—of individuals willing to stake themselves in the uncertain struggle to realize ideals in "the parts of the world to which [they] are closest":[1] had James described "an abiding, an indestructible, possession of American life," or merely "summed up an age, the pioneer age, . . . when it was passing from the actual scene"? Had the type of "intellectual and moral individuality" James envisioned been rendered obsolete by the "organization and regimentation appropriate to the technology of mass production"? "Merely to ask the questions," Dewey remarked in an uncharacteristically glum tone, "occasions a certain depression."[2]

Dewey's most direct answer to his own questions comes in *Individualism Old and New* (originally serialized in *The New Republic* in 1929 and 1930), yet this work is best understood in tandem with *The Public and Its Problems,* a broader reflection on the nature of the state and the prospects for democracy as both a form of government and an ideal of community to be realized in all areas of human association. For the task of reconstructing individuality—and specifically a democratic individuality—is only one aspect of (or an analytical distinction within) the larger project of reconstructing the diverse forms of associated activity so that they might better embody a communal dynamic. It is a cornerstone of Dewey's social thought that human beings do not exist apart from association with other humans; individuality emerges and can be reshaped only within the specific forms of association in which individuals live and form their habits. Further, the ideal of community that, for Dewey, defines democracy applies not only to an individual's relation to the various groups to which he or she belongs, but also to each group's interaction with other groups in the larger society. Accordingly, two requirements that are essential to the model of a conscientious and liberating self outlined in chapter 4 are also necessary for achieving a communal relationship between various groups: namely, knowledge of the consequences (especially those affecting others) that define the meaning of an activity, and the ability, on the basis of such knowledge, to control that meaning by choosing the ends that redirect the activity and reshape its tendency. As discussed above, community exists to the extent that such knowledge of the consequences of our actions reveals a broader common interest that is made the motivating object of individuals' and local groups' activities, and to the extent that the broader social group (however widely defined) identifies its interest in helping all groups and individuals to share equally in shaping the aims and enjoying the fruits of associated activity.

The *Public and Its Problems* and *Individualism Old and New* argue that these conditions of community—knowledge of the consequences that define an activity's meaning and significant ability to shape the ends that direct activity—have been eroded by the corporate forms of social organization ushered in by the scientific and industrial revolutions. This new social order, Dewey argues, has extended the consequences of our associated activities far beyond the scope of the local, face-to-face communities in which we most immediately live and act, making it immensely difficult to recognize, let alone control, those consequences adequately. At the same time, the fact that an increasingly collective system of production has remained tied to an outdated system of individual property has alienated the vast majority of workers from meaningful control over and understanding of the larger ends that direct their labor, thereby stripping their individuality of a socially integrated meaning. Accordingly, when Dewey analyzes the social conditions of 1920s America in order to assess the obstacles to, and the immanent possibilities for, a revitalized community and individuality, he frames the issue as follows: can inquiry into the consequences of our complex networks of association help identify and empower the public which has a shared interest in regulating those consequences, forging a "great community" capable of restoring to *local* communities the meaning and control necessary to make labor educative and liberating, so that the modern industrial economy might become the basis of a new democratic culture, the crucible for a new type of democratic personality?

In tracing how *The Public and Its Problems* and *Individualism Old and New* explore these questions, I will stress the following aspects of Dewey's approach, all of which reflect what is most distinctive and radical about his social thought—his commitment, above all else, to a fully experimental method of social inquiry. First, while he argues that restoring the local communities that foster a socially integrated individuality will require new agencies[3] for regulating the collective forces of modern society, Dewey insists that these agencies can emerge *only* when experimental inquiry provides clearer knowledge of the consequences of existing social conditions that require regulation on the public's behalf. Second, this experimentalism—as expressed in Dewey's theory of the public and the state—leads him to reject classic liberal individualism for imposing an ahistorical absolutism that obscures the plasticity of human nature and the relativity of social institutions. Dewey is adamant, however, that this critique of liberal individualism does not endorse an opposing and equally absolutist collectivism. Indeed, he describes experimentalism as the means to a new individualism: one that rejects classic liberalism's negative conception of liberty and its rigid laissez-faire opposition to public regulation, in favor of a broad commitment to creating the positive conditions of individual liberty and equality by whatever means— whether personal and voluntary or more collectively organized—are best suited to each particular situation. Third, in line with his general model of reform, Dewey asserts that the reconstruction of individuality can occur only as a mutually transforming, interactive process between evolving social conditions and the actions of growing, changing individuals. Lastly, even as he argues for new political agencies capable of regulating the corporate forces of modern industrial society, Dewey insists that such political action is only a means to the more fundamental goals of achieving democracy as a way of life, which must be realized in local communities, and of liberating individuals' capacities, which must always in a crucial sense remain a matter of individual responsibility and choice.[4]

Invaded Communities and Lost Individuals: Individualism in a New Age of Human Relations

The prospects for a renewed democratic individuality, Dewey argues, are largely defined by "the outstanding fact of modern life"—the ways in which the industrial revolution, especially in its phase of corporate con-glomeration, has radically transformed the terms of human interaction, drawing local communities into a "vast" and "impersonal" network of social cooperation:

> The new technology applied in production and commerce resulted in a social revolution. The local communities without intent or forecast found their affairs conditioned by remote and invisible organiza-tions. The scope of the latter's activities was so vast and their impact upon face-to-face associations so pervasive and unremitting that it is no exaggeration to speak of a "new age in human relations." The Great Society created by steam and electricity may be a society, but it is no community. The invasion of the community by new and rela-tively impersonal and mechanical modes of combined human behav-ior is the outstanding fact of modern life. In these ways of aggregate activity the community, in its strict sense, is not a conscious partner, and over them it has no direct control.[5]

As indicated by this description of local groups "invaded" by "remote and invisible organizations" beyond their control, Dewey's main concern is that the modern system of socioeconomic interaction has undermined basic conditions of community: the ability to recognize and control the consequences that define the meaning and quality of an activity as it fits into a larger social context. "An inchoate public is capable of organiza-tion," Dewey notes, "only when indirect consequences are perceived, and when it is possible to project agencies which order their occurrence." Such recognition and control has been rendered far more difficult by a system of "forces so vast, so remote in initiation, so far-reaching in scope and so complexly indirect in operation, that they are, from the standpoint of the members of the local social units, unknown": consequences "are suffered, but they cannot be said to be known, for they are not, by those who experience them, referred to their origins."[6]

By disempowering local communities, Dewey argues, the vast and impersonal forms of modern association have also undermined an authentic, socially integrated individuality. "Assured and integrated individuality," he contends, "is the product of definite social relationships and publicly acknowledged functions": the meaning of an individual's acts (and hence the moral quality of character or selfhood they define) depends upon their tendency to create beneficial or harmful consequences. So long as the consequences of the system of modern industry are not fully recognized in their collective import nor controlled in the public interest—"so long as the results of industry as the determining force in life are corporate and collective while its animating motives and compensations are so unmitigatedly private"—the individuality of those involved, as defined by the social meaning of their labor, is "submerged" or lost. This is most obvious in the case of wage laborers: the "one central fact" of our "economic regime," Dewey claims, is that "most of those who are engaged in the outward work of production and distribution of economic commodities . . . execute plans which they do not form, and of whose meaning and intent they are ignorant—beyond the fact that these plans make a profit for others and secure a wage for themselves." Wage laborers "have no share—imaginative, intellectual, emotional—in directing the activities in which they physically participate."[7] Less evident is that this impoverishment of individuality also affects those who seem to enjoy an exalted personal power in the current system:

> Judged by this standard, even those who seem to be in control, and to carry the expression of their special individual abilities to a high pitch, are submerged. They may be captains of finance and industry, but until there is some consensus of belief as to the meaning of finance and industry in civilization as a whole, they cannot be captains of their own souls—their beliefs and aims. . . . Their reward is found not in what they do, but in a deflection of social consequences to private gain. . . . No complete satisfaction is possible where such a split exists. Hence the absence of a sense of social value is made up for by an exacerbated acceleration of the activities that increase private advantage and power.[8]

Even those individuals who exert enormous individual control over and reap enormous individual profit from the collective systems of activity, Dewey claims, achieve a narrow form of individuality that fails to fulfill a fully humane social function, that lacks the fullness of meaning which occurs only when one's talents and social position are enlisted in the service of a recognized common good.

It is crucial to note that Dewey is not blaming the impoverishment of American individuality simply upon the advent of industrial technology or the collective order of human relations that followed in its wake; the problem, he argues, is our failure to recognize the true social meaning and utilize the attendant possibilities of these developments.[9] This is a point that separates Dewey from some of his contemporaries on the American intellectual Left, most notably Lewis Mumford, whose study *The Golden Day* (also published in 1926) had accused pragmatism— James's especially, and to a lesser extent Dewey's—of focusing on means to the exclusion of critical reflection on valuable ends or ideals, of concentrating on the instrumentalities of existing conditions instead of on ideals that could transcend and transform those conditions, and of thereby rationalizing "acquiescence" to the machine age and its evils. While he painted pragmatism as a symptom of the Gilded Age, Mumford by contrast valorized the decades before the Civil War as a golden age when American society had escaped the materialism of the pioneer age but not yet succumbed to the materialism of the machine age, a sociocultural balance Mumford saw as fostering the transformative power of individual imagination epitomized by writers such as Emerson, Melville, and Whitman.[10]

In response to this charge voiced by Mumford—and by Randolph Bourne before him[11]—that pragmatism's emphasis on instrumentalities precluded necessary attention to ideals or ends, Dewey reaffirmed his stance that careful and creative attention to existing conditions as means for imagining and realizing ends-in-view is the necessary condition for an effective idealism.[12] Accordingly, Dewey's attitude toward the ascendant industrial order does indeed differ fundamentally from Mumford's. "Certain changes do not go backward," he argues, and while there is "no way to 'restrain' or turn back the industrial revolution and its consequences," to accept existing social conditions as an accomplished fact is not to acquiesce in them as final, but rather to view the present (in the spirit of both Emerson and James) as the material out of which a new and different future will have to be built.[13] Unlike Mumford, who paints the advent of the machine age as an unmitigated tragedy for the human spirit, Dewey views it as containing both ills to be remedied *and* "immanent" "possibilities" for imagining and realizing new, more humane ends.[14] The technologies of the industrial age, Dewey insists, are instrumentalities that can be used for good or ill:

> What actually happens in consequence of industrial forces is dependent upon the presence or absence of perception and communication of consequences, upon foresight and its effect upon desire and endeavor. Economic agencies produce one result when they are left to work themselves out on the merely physical level. . . . They have a different outcome in the degree in which knowledge of consequences is equitably distributed, and action is animated by an informed and lively sense of a shared interest.[15]

Far from an acquiescent stance, this is a melioristic affirmation of contingency and the consequent power of intelligently informed choice and desire to influence the direction and outcome of social change. Indeed, Dewey argues it is the *failure* to accept existing conditions as the necessary starting point for reform, the failure to project ideals that have a basis in actual conditions, that threatens effective activism: "Ideals and standards formed without regard to the means by which they are to be achieved and incarnated in flesh are bound to be thin and wavering" at best, and at worst constitute an indulgent and impotent escapism. In what is clearly a swipe at Mumford (among others), he notes there is "no greater sign of the paralysis of the imagination," nothing more "childish" than "the animism" that argues "the machine itself is the source of our troubles," and nothing more futile than the nostalgia of "American critics of the present scene . . . devising modes of escape" by "tak[ing] flight in their imagination to India, Athens, the Middle Ages, or the American age of Emerson, Thoreau and Melville." If "our own civilization . . . is to achieve and manifest a characteristic culture" capable of cultivating a truly democratic type of personality, Dewey concludes, "It will come by turning a machine age into a significantly new habit of mind and sentiment, or it will not come at all." The task of reconstructing individualism, then, is one of "utiliz[ing] . . . the realities of a corporate civilization to validate and embody the distinctive moral element in the American version of individualism: Equality and freedom expressed not merely externally and politically but through personal participation in the development of a shared culture."[16]

The State Must Always Be Rediscovered:
Dewey's Democratic Experimentalism

This vision of equality and freedom achieved "through personal participation in the development of a shared culture" indicates again that, for Dewey, fostering a democratic individualism requires reconstructing community—requires a democratic method for regulating the corporate forces of modern society so that they might empower rather than obscure local communities. The thoroughgoing experimentalism that Dewey brings to this task is evident in his theory of the public and the state articulated in *The Public and Its Problems*.[17] Consistent with his rejection of any fixed or final causes outside the transactions of experience, Dewey grounds his theory of the state only on the "objective fact" of human association: that "human acts have consequences upon others, that some of the consequences are perceived, and that their perception leads to subsequent efforts to control action so as to secure some consequences and avoid others." Subsequently distinguishing private consequences that "affect the persons directly engaged in a transaction" from indirect ones that "affect others beyond those immediately concerned," Dewey argues that when such indirect consequences are recognized as "extensive and enduring" enough to warrant regulation, "whether by inhibition or promotion," a public is identified "consist[ing] of all those who are affected by the indirect consequences of transactions" and in whose interest they are to be regulated. A state emerges when a public organizes itself sufficiently to ensure that governmental agencies effectively regulate those consequences on its behalf.[18]

Such a "purely formal" or functional definition, Dewey argues, is as far as theory can go in stipulating what the state should be.[19] The particular form a state should take depends upon the public consequences of associated behavior in a given situation and upon viable means for regulating those consequences effectively. In short, the question of identifying a public and creating the governmental agencies to regulate the terms of social interaction in its interest is inherently a matter for experimental social inquiry:

[W]hat the public may be, what the officials are, how adequately they
perform their function, are things we have to go to history to discover.... In no two ages or places is there the same public. Conditions make the consequences of associated action and the knowledge
of them different.... The formation of states must be an experimental process. The trial process may go on with diverse degrees of blindness and accident, ... [o]r it may proceed more intelligently, because
guided by knowledge of the conditions which must be fulfilled. But
it is still experimental. And since the conditions of action and of inquiry and knowledge are always changing, the experiment must always be retried; the State must always be rediscovered.[20]

Just how radically Dewey's approach departs from traditional political
philosophies is evident if one contrasts it to the theory of the state presented by either classic Lockean liberalism or traditional Marxism, both
of which posit fixed causes that predetermine the state's development.
Liberalism, by positing an autonomous self possessing individual liberty
prior to society, subsequently dictates that a legitimate state must be as
limited as possible, so as to protect but never encroach on this inherently individual liberty; Marxism, by positing class struggle as the prime
mover driving history inexorably towards the inevitable teleology of
communism, depicts the state as inherently an instrument of class domination that is destined to whither away.[21]

In marked contrast, Dewey describes the notion "that social 'evolution' has been either from collectivism to individualism or the reverse"
as "sheer superstition." The meaningful alternative is not between individualism and collectivism, he contends, but between absolutism and
experimentalism. "The person who holds the doctrine of 'individualism'
or 'collectivism,'" he argues, "has his program determined in advance,"
indulging in an absolutism that "appl[ies] a hard and fast doctrine which
follows logically from his preconception of the nature of ultimate causes"
and thereby abdicating the "responsibility of discovering the concrete
correlation of changes ... [and] events through their complicated careers." The antidote to such opposing dogmatisms is an experimentalism which holds that "the question of what transactions should be left
as far as possible to voluntary initiative and agreement and what should
come under the regulation of the public is a question of time, place and
concrete conditions that can be known only by careful observation and
reflective investigation. For it concerns consequences": "At one time and
place a large measure of state activity may be indicated and at another

time a policy of quiescence and *laissez-faire*." The only certainty, in Dewey's view, is the fact of change itself and the necessity that the state "must always be rediscovered."[22]

This experimentalism that separates Deweyan democracy from classic liberalism has roots in Emerson's similarly radical insistence on the need to remake institutions to fit the needs of an ever-changing present. Recall Emerson's claims in his essay "Politics" that "society is fluid" with "no roots and centres"; that "every law and usage was a man's expedient to meet a particular case," and thus must be revised as our activities and circumstances change; that "Our statute is a currency, which we stamp with our own portrait," which "soon becomes unrecognizable, and in process of time will return to the mint"; that "as fast as the public mind is opened to more intelligence, the code is seen to be brute and stammering," and that this "education of the general mind never stops." Significantly, Emerson insists that even the revered institutions of American democracy enjoy no validity apart from historical conditions: "In this country, we are very vain of our political institutions" that we "ostentatiously prefer to any other in history," failing to see that "They are not better, but only fitter for us" because "in coincidence with the spirit of the age." Emerson's conclusion here prefigures Dewey's contention that the tendency to treat the founding documents of the US government as sacred and immutable poses one of the major obstacles to revitalizing our democracy.[23]

The experimentalism expressed in Dewey's theory of the public undergirds his entire approach to the process by which a democratic community and individuality might be reconstructed. The "remote," "far-reaching," and "complexly indirect" corporate forces that have "invaded" local communities make it difficult to recognize and understand the consequences that define a public: "It is not that there is no public, no large body of persons having a common interest in the consequences of social transactions," but that there is "too much public, a public too diffused and scattered and too intricate in its composition," or more accurately "too many publics, for conjoint actions which have indirect, serious and enduring consequences are multitudinous beyond comparison" with "little to hold these different publics together in an integrated whole."[24] The "prime difficulty," therefore,

> is that of discovering the means by which a scattered, mobile and manifold public may so recognize itself as to define and express its interests. This discovery is necessarily precedent to any fundamental

change in the machinery [of government.] ... The problem lies deeper; it is in the first instance an intellectual problem: the search for the conditions under which the Great Society may become the Great Community. When these conditions are brought into being they will make their own forms. Until they have come about, it is somewhat futile to consider what political machinery will suit them.[25]

While new governmental agencies (or powers) are needed to regulate the consequences of our modern society in the public interest, an adequate knowledge of the consequences requiring regulation and of the potential means for their regulation can emerge only through more substantial and sustained experimental inquiry into existing social conditions: "The prime condition of a democratically organized public," Dewey concludes, "is a kind of knowledge and insight which does not yet exist."[26] The most a work of political theory can do is to clarify the task: as Dewey attempts to do in *The Public and Its Problems* by defining the problem of creating a democratic state as first-and-foremost a problem of discovering the public, and then by addressing the experimental method needed to effect this discovery.

Accordingly, the closing chapters of *The Public and Its Problems* outline necessary conditions for an experimental social inquiry, which Dewey treats under two main headings. First, a fully experimental approach— one whose "concepts," "principles" and "theories" have been "shaped and tested as tools of inquiry," and one whose "policies and proposals for social action" are "treated as working hypotheses . . . subject to ready and flexible revision in the light of observed consequences"—would require a true "freedom of social inquiry and of distribution of its conclusions." By this, Dewey is quick to specify, he means not merely a negative freedom *from* government constraints on opinion or expression, but a *positive* freedom that entails command of the resources to put ideas into experimental practice: the "method of democracy" requires a "positive toleration" in which "free inquiry" is "not merely grudgingly tolerated," but "opportunity at different times and places . . . [is] given for trying different measures."[27]

Second, the experimental social inquiry needed to identify and empower the public depends upon a full and free communication. Indeed, Dewey argues that,

> Communication of the results of social inquiry is the same thing as the formation of public opinion. This marks one of the first ideas

framed in the growth of political democracy as it will be one of the last to be fulfilled. For public opinion is judgment which is formed and entertained by those who constitute the public and is about public affairs. Each of these two phases imposes for its realization conditions hard to meet.[28]

If social inquiry is to support judgment that is both "about public affairs" and "formed and entertained by those who constitute the public," it must be based on genuine two-way communication between the public and those intellectuals whose expertise is germane to the public interest. Unless their inquiry is meaningfully informed and shaped by the public, experts cannot intelligently analyze existing social conditions or propose policies: "the wise cease to be wise," Dewey insists, in so far as "they become a specialized class . . . shut off from knowledge of the needs which they are supposed to serve." Conversely, the results of inquiry cannot become knowledge in the fullest sense until they are possessed and used by the public, for while experts can provide insight into causes, consequences, and possible remedies, they cannot decide questions of values, uses, and ends: "their expertness is not shown in framing and executing policies, but in discovering and making known the facts upon which the former depend."[29] Only the public itself (communicating through genuinely representative officials[30]) can rank existing needs and choose which ends are worthy of pursuit.[31] Rebutting Walter Lippmann's claim that the technical complexity of modern social problems has made government-by-experts inevitable, relegating public opinion to a periodic electoral referendum on the incumbent experts,[32] Dewey affirms that a genuine public opinion remains feasible: "It is not necessary that the many should have the knowledge and skill to carry on the needed investigations" but only that they should "have the ability to judge of the bearing of the knowledge supplied by others upon common concerns." "A mechanic can discourse of ohms and amperes as Sir Isaac Newton could not in his day," he notes, and "Many a man who has tinkered with radios can judge of things which Faraday did not dream of"—examples which show Dewey, like Emerson before him, locating a leveling, democratic force in the receptivity of human intelligence that allows individuals so easily to appropriate the ideas of inventors and geniuses.[33]

However, if the communication necessary to a truly public opinion is possible, Dewey insists that it will be difficult, "one of the last" ideals of democracy "to be fulfilled" (as he puts it in the passage quoted above).

Among the "hard conditions" required to realize such communication, Dewey singles out the need for radical change in the media: the need for journalism to reject "the triviality and 'sensational' quality of so much of what passes as news" and to focus instead on interpreting the social consequences of events and on cultivating an artful mode of presentation that would make the findings of social inquiry accessible to a general public. This hope of "a genuine social science" that "would manifest its reality in the daily press" will be frustrated, Dewey suggests, so long as the media are controlled by and run as powerful business interests, so long as the "gathering and sale of subject-matter having a public import is part of the existing pecuniary system." Lastly, forging a public opinion that could provide the basis for a recovered community requires new symbols to communicate the shared public interest, so that it may become operative intellectually and emotionally as a shaping motive in the activities of individuals in their local communities.[34]

Individualisms Old and New: The Experimentalist Alternative to Classic Liberalism

This need for an experimental method of social inquiry—which figures so prominently in the prescription for discovering a democratic public and restoring community offered in *The Public and Its Problems*—is also central to Dewey's analysis of the prospects for reconstructing individualism. Achieving such an experimentalism would require overcoming what Dewey describes as deeply engrained "emotional" and "intellectual" habits of absolutism that lead "the mass of men" to resist applying to "human concerns" the experimental method they "have got used to" in "physical and technical matters."[35] Such habits of mind are both reflected in and perpetuated by traditional political theories, which, Dewey notes, "have shared in the absolutistic character of philosophy generally," asserting a "non-historical" "finality and foreverness in their theories" by positing fixed entities (whether the ideal state or a model of essential human nature) beyond the transactions of experience.[36] This absolutism of traditional social thought obscures the mutually transforming dynamic between individuality and its environing social conditions—obscures the plastic capacity of human nature to form different habits when social conditions are remade, and obscures the fact that seemingly rigid social institutions are themselves relative and plastic, not necessitated by some unchanging human psychology—and thereby hinders experimental efforts to reconstruct both social conditions and human personality.

Reconstructing individualism thus would require (among other things) rejecting the absolutist logic of "historic" individualist philosophy that has served to justify the existing economic and political order and perpetuate the habits of individuality it promotes. This absolutism is most evident, Dewey argues, in classic liberalism's dualism of "the individual" versus "society," the former endowed with "natural" rights and economic drives, the latter a set of "artificial" arrangements that threaten to impinge on individual liberty and distort the beneficent operations of "natural" economic "laws." In both its economic and political forms, this dualism mandates a laissez-faire distrust of any governmental regulations that limit individuals' pursuit of personal gain or limit the operation of "natural" economic laws that allegedly translate such self-interested pursuits into maximized wealth for all. The historical origins of this doctrine are not far to seek, Dewey suggests: the economic forces unleashed by the scientific and industrial revolutions conflicted with the "existing laws and customs" of an "agrarian" and "feudal" culture that seemed (at least to those in position to benefit from the new economic forces) to constrain "human initiative, energy, and inventive skill," while traditional forms of governmental and ecclesiastical authority "were felt—and at the time with good reason—to mark arbitrary limitations on the legitimate freedom of individuals." "Since it was necessary, upon the intellectual side, to find justification for the movements of revolt, and since established authority was upon the side of institutional life," by far the "easiest" and most radically effective ideological recourse "was to go back to the naked individual, to sweep away all associations as foreign to his nature and rights save as they proceeded from his own voluntary choice, and guaranteed his own private ends." This "appeal to the individual as an independent and isolated being" was not logically necessary, Dewey argues—"revolts against prior governmental forms" could have been justified "in an assertion of the rights of groups" upon which "the state could not legitimately encroach." Moreover, if the stark opposition of a free individual versus oppressive institutions provided an expedient political weapon, the extremity of this conceptualization predictably devolved into dogmatism: "It was an easy step" from revolt against *particular* repressive forms of government "to the idea that all government by its very nature tends to be repressive," and thus a historically specific "revolt against old and limiting associations was converted, intellectually, into the doctrine of independence of any and all associations."[37]

By perpetuating this dualistic formulation, Dewey stresses, classic liberalism has badly distorted popular conceptions of individuality, human association, and liberty. First, by positing an individual independent of association, it promotes a psychology that is patently false to the facts of human existence: "The idea of a natural individual in his isolation possessed of full-fledged wants, of energies to be expended according to his own volition, and of a ready-made faculty of foresight and prudent calculation is as much a fiction in psychology as the doctrine of the individual in possession of antecedent political rights is one in politics." Second, it promotes an impoverished view of society. Whereas liberalism depicts society as an artificial and regrettable necessity that individuals reluctantly join so as to protect their preexistent interests, Dewey describes association as providing the necessary basis of all human life and the opportunity for shared meaning that constitutes our fullest and most secure happiness. Similarly, whereas liberalism depicts society as a contrivance for "cater[ing] to" the desires of an individual that is "already given" and complete, Dewey describes it as the medium in which one achieves individuality. Social arrangements are not merely "means for obtaining something for individuals," but "means of *creating* individuals": "man is not merely *de facto* associated, but he *becomes* a social animal in the make-up of his ideas, sentiments and deliberate behavior. *What* he believes, hopes for and aims at is the outcome of association and intercourse."[38]

Third, liberalism presents a false and merely negative view of liberty. Freedom, Dewey claims, does not consist in an individual freeing herself from all associations (which is an impossibility) but in obtaining release from the oppressive or restricting effects of *some* groups so as to allow a freer and more liberating participation in *others*: "Liberty is that secure release and fulfillment of personal potentialities which take place only in rich and manifold association with others." When individuals "find themselves cramped and depressed by absorption of their potentialities in some mode of association," life "has been impoverished, not by a predominance of 'society' in general over individuality, but by a domination of one form of association . . . over other actual and possible forms." People "may think they are clamoring for a purely personal liberty, but what they are doing is to bring into being a greater liberty to share in other associations, so that more of their individual potentialities will be released and their personal experience enriched." By contrast, because it defines liberty as an inherent possession of the autonomous individual—and not, as Dewey describes it, as a growth in capacity and meaning one achieves in association with others—liberalism promotes the negative view that "all men need is freedom *from* oppressive legal and political measures," which view "neglect[s] the necessity of studying and regulating . . . conditions so that a nominal freedom can be made an actuality."[39]

Fourth, liberalism precludes public efforts to create such conditions of an effective liberty by articulating a severely restricted and dogmatic vision of legitimate governmental regulation. To insist upon a doctrinaire policy of laissez-faire, to contend that "the great aim in political life is to limit the encroachments of governments in order to secure the liberty of citizens," is tantamount, Dewey argues, to "an abdication of effort at intelligent control." Viewed in light of Dewey's claim that the scope and means of public regulation must be experimentally adapted to the needs of present conditions, liberalism's faith "that an *a priori* conception of the intrinsic nature and limits of the individual on one side and the state on the other will yield good results once for all" can only appear as "absurd." This absolutism is especially unfortunate, Dewey suggests, given the irony that the industrial revolution, even as it gave rise to liberal individualism, was rapidly undermining the type of individual autonomy liberalism celebrated: "'the individual,' about which the new philosophy centered itself, was in process of complete submergence in fact at the very time in which he was being elevated on high in theory." The endurance of the liberal conception of individuality, Dewey argues, has saddled our culture with a philosophy of "enormous ineptitude . . . to meet the needs and direct the factors of the new age."[40]

The purpose in thus critiquing "historic" individualism, Dewey is careful to stress, is "not to indicate that some anti-'individualistic' principle is correct" or endorse some equally dogmatic "collectivistic formula and program." Far from rejecting individualism per se, Dewey envisions a new individualism that fulfills "the genuinely spiritual element" of the individualistic tradition—"the ideal of equality of opportunity and of freedom for all"—which would require replacing the absolutism of liberal individualism with experimental efforts to create the social conditions that could give these ideals substance. The "ethical formula" of individualism—the "greatest possible freedom of individuals as long as that freedom is not used to the detriment of equal or *similar* liberty on the part of other individuals"—has enduring value, he argues, but only if reinterpreted as rejecting liberalism's merely "legalistic" and "formal" equality in favor of a more "realistic" and "material" standard:[41]

> What is meant by *like* or *equal* freedom? If it signified materially alike, equal in actual power, it would be difficult to take objection with it. The formula would be compatible with the efforts of organized society to *equalize conditions*. It would, for example, justify public action to secure to all an education which would effect a complete development of their capacities, so that they might meet one another on a plane of knowledge and trained intelligence as nearly even as possible. It would justify legislation to equalize the standing of those now at a disadvantage because of inequality in physical power, in wealth, in command of the machinery of employment. It would justify, in other words, a vast amount of so-called social legislation which the individualistic theory as usually held condemns.[42]

An individualism that had as its core this goal of effective liberty and equality would seek, above all, to create social conditions that would afford all persons an equal opportunity to participate in the associated activities through which individuals' capacities are educated and liberated. So conceived, "individualism" describes an integral component of democracy considered as a way of life or the ideal of community—namely, the commitment to create forms of association that "educate every individual into the full stature of his possibility." Such an individualism could *only* be realized through experimental inquiry into the educative effect of existing social conditions, by asking "what the specific stimulating, fostering, and nurturing power of each specific social arrangement may be": "Just what response does *this* social arrangement, political or economic, evoke, and what effect does it have upon the disposition of those who engage in it? Does it release capacity? If so, how widely? . . . What sort of individuals are created?" It would also require experimental inquiry into the most effective available means for constructing alternative forms of association. A new individualism, as Dewey envisions it, could not be defined by any *form* of social organization—neither identified with a laissez-faire reliance on private initiative nor opposed to more public and organized forms of associated activity—but would instead consist in using the ideal of a democratic, communally integrated individuality to direct the experimental process of social reform.[43]

This experimental approach provides the context for understanding the specific diagnoses and recommendations that Dewey offers in *Individualism Old and New*. While he had argued in *The Public and Its Problems* that it is impossible to predict what forms of governmental agency will be needed to regulate the public consequences of the new corporate age—that when the conditions enabling "a scattered, mobile and manifold public" to "so recognize itself as to define and express its interests" have been realized, they will "make their own forms"—Dewey *is* willing in *Individualism Old and New* to offer the broad prescription that some form of increased public control over industry is needed to make the conditions of industrial labor serve the democratic goal of educating and liberating individuality. This conclusion follows directly from arguments already outlined. Take Dewey's view that liberty entails the ability to choose the ends that define the quality of one's activity and selfhood; add his related claim that personality is fully educated only when each individual is afforded "a responsible share[,] ... in proportion to capacity, in shaping the aims and policies of the social groups to which he belongs"; lastly, acknowledge the "central fact" of modern industrial life, that most workers "have no share—imaginative, intellectual, emotional—in directing the activities in which they physically participate," and the conclusion is clear that "only by economic revision can the sound element in the older individualism—equality of opportunity—be made a reality." The undisputed fact shaping our options for the future is that the growth of industrial capitalism has ushered in a new network of human relations shaped by corporate institutions of unprecedented scope and power. The fundamental questions we face—summed up in Dewey's chapter heading "Capitalistic or Public Socialism?"—regard who will regulate the consequences of these vast corporate forces and for what purpose: will they be managed for monetary profit by individuals enjoying private ownership and control, or managed in the public interest through a democratic, participatory process that values "the educative influence of economic and political institutions" over "their immediate economic consequences"?[44]

In an American context, be it Dewey's of 1930 or ours of today, proposals involving a significant degree of socialism are in danger of being pigeonholed, dismissed, or vilified. Not surprisingly, Dewey takes explicit pains to distinguish the experimental nature of his proposed goals and methods from political assumptions that remain mired within a false dualism of individualism versus collectivism:

Because of the bankruptcy of the older individualism, those who are aware of the break-down often speak and argue as if individualism were itself done and over with. I do not suppose that those who regard socialism and individualism as antithetical really mean that individuality is going to die out or that it is not something intrinsically precious. But in speaking as if the only individualism were the local episode of the last two centuries . . . they slur over the chief problem—that of remaking society to serve the growth of a new type of individual. There are many who believe that socialism of some form is needed to realize individual initiative and security on a wide scale. . . . But they too often seem to assume that the result will be merely an extension of the earlier individualism to the many.

Such thinking treats individualism as if it were something static, having a uniform content. It ignores the fact that the mental and moral structure of individuals, the pattern of their desires and purposes, change with every great change in social constitution. Individuals who are not bound together in associations . . . are monstrosities. It is absurd to suppose that the ties which hold them together are merely external and do not react into mentality and character, producing the framework of personal disposition. . . . The habit of opposing the corporate and the collective to the individual . . . distracts attention from the crucial issue: How shall the individual refind himself in an unprecedentedly new social situation, and what qualities will the new individualism exhibit? . . . [T]he problem is not merely one of extending to all individuals the traits of economic initiative, opportunity and enterprise; . . . it is one of forming a new psychological and moral type.[45]

Dewey's primary concern here is to assert the mutually transforming dynamic that exists between human nature and its environing social conditions, and to insist that the resultant plasticity of both makes the process of reconstructing individuality and community radically open-ended. Human nature is plastic: the specific forms of association in a given culture or community shape "the mental and moral structure of individuals," the habitual "desires and purposes" that constitute character. Reforming the conditions of human association thus is not a means for fulfilling the static needs of completed individuals, but a means for recreating individuality, for promoting "a new psychological and moral type" with *new* desires and purposes.

Accordingly, Dewey's call for increased public control of industry is not intended merely to "exten[d] . . . to the many" the pecuniary rewards that would satisfy the acquisitive habits inculcated by "the earlier

individualism," nor to establish a quantitative equality of material reward, but to foster a *qualitative* equality of opportunity to participate in
the associated endeavors through which individuals' capacities are developed and their actions imbued with social meaning:

> Sharing a good or value in a way which makes it social in quality is not
> identical with dividing up a material thing into physical parts. To par-
> take is to *take* part, to *play* a role. . . . Its proper analogue is not physical
> division but taking part in a game, in conversation, in a drama, in fam-
> ily life. It involves diversification, not sameness and repetition. . . . Each
> contributes something distinctive from his own store of knowledge,
> ability, taste, while receiving at the same time elements of value con-
> tributed by others. . . . One person is morally equal to others when he
> has the same opportunity for developing his capacities and playing his
> part that others have, although his capacities are quite unlike theirs.[46]

To the extent we can make such a communal equality of participation
the guiding principle of our social organizations, Dewey argues, it will
be possible to cultivate a truly democratic individuality, one characterized not by "ideas of pecuniary profit," but by a "pattern of thought and
desire . . . enduringly marked by consensus with others" and by "cooperation in all regular human associations."[47]

While Dewey stipulates that greater public control over industry is a
necessary starting point in the process of reconstructing individualism,
he insists that it is *only* a starting point in a process of reform that must of
necessity be experimental and open-ended. It is important to note that he
is not calling for some totalizing form of collectivism that would extend
over all areas of life. The boundary between public and private, he argues,
must be continually reevaluated and redrawn: which consequences are
deemed important enough to warrant public regulation will vary with
changing conditions. Moreover, the types of social organization appropriate as the *means* to such regulation are also a matter for experimental
inquiry. "Public" cannot be equated with "collective" nor "private" with
"individualistic," for a scheme of social organization relying more on
personal control and initiative may, depending upon conditions, be the
best vehicle for achieving a public good: for example, most Americans
view public schools as crucial to promoting a democratic equality of opportunity, yet, Dewey reminds us, a "ruling class and the government
may use the schools" to "turn out minds in a common mold . . . favorable
to their own special interest" and to "suppress freedom of inquiry," and

"under such conditions, there is justification for upholding, on moral grounds" the view that private schools better serve the public interest.[48] Thus Dewey's call for greater public control over the vast corporate forces that dominate the industrial economic regime is wholly consistent with the maintenance or even extension of more voluntary, personalized forms of organization in other areas of social life—including areas that are primarily economic.

Similarly, Dewey rejects the notion, assumed by the teleological narrative of classic Marxism, that collective forms of social control constitute the ideal end of social reform. Reconstructing individuality is part of the larger process of social reform in which changing social conditions and changing habits of personality transform each other in a dialectic that has no fixed end. Since habits are formed through individuals' interactions with their specific social environments, it is foolish to think that a new individuality can be forged unless the conditions of associated activity are remade so as to instill new habits: "disintegrated individuals can achieve unity only as the dominant energies of community life are incorporated to form their minds," Dewey insists, and to "attempt to cultivate [such unity] first in individuals and then extend it to form an organically unified society is fantasy." Neither can reform be conceived or pursued as a discrete sequential process in which reconstructed individuality will be produced by changed conditions. For if the social environment necessarily shapes individuality, once it emerges individuality in turn exerts a transforming force on that environment. As outlined in chapter 4, the subjective phase of mind supplies initiative and imagination that are essential to the intelligent choice of reconstructive ends: the frustration of individuals' habits triggers and drives the process of deliberation, and the "interpenetration" of habits that constitutes character allows individuals to project and choose among a variety of ends-in-view, thereby redirecting activity and reorganizing the habits that compose character. This "positive and constructive energy of individuals, as manifested in the remaking and redirection of social forces and conditions, is itself a social necessity." Thus reform consists in an unending process of mutual transformation in which no final form of *either* human personality or social organization can be posited. Both "reformers" and "conservatives" alike too often assume that efforts to reeducate personality must be governed by "a mental picture of some desired end, personal and social, which is to be attained." In contrast,

Dewey notes, a truly "experimental social method" would have to "surrender . . . this notion," and reject any fixed ideal of *reconstructed* individuality for a faith in *reconstructing* individuality—that is, for a faith in an ongoing process of self-reconstruction that facilitates an open-ended process of institutional reform: "Every care would be taken to surround the young with the physical and social conditions which best conduce, as far as freed knowledge extends, to release of personal potentialities. The habits thus formed would have entrusted to them the meeting of future social requirements and the development of the future state of society."[49]

Consequently, just as *The Public and Its Problems* argues it is impossible to predetermine what forms a new democratic state might take, so in *Individualism Old and New* Dewey declines to predict "the form which [an] emergent individualism will assume," noting, "Indeed, I do not see how it can be described until more progress has been made in its production." However, if "it is still impossible to foresee in detail what would happen if a system of cooperative control of industry were generally substituted for the present system," one *can* predict, Dewey claims, that "there would be an enormous liberation of mind" as "desire for related knowledge, physical and social, would be created and rewarded" and "initiative and responsibility would be demanded and achieved." Moreover, "one can say without hesitation" that so long as the conditions of industrial labor are *not* made cooperative in a meaningful sense, so long as "multitudes are excluded from occasion for the use of thought and emotion in their daily occupations," "we shall attain only the personal cultivation of a class, and not a characteristic [democratic] American culture." Dewey's vision for reconstructing individuality hinges, then, on two convictions. The first is that a new democratic individualism can be constructed if (and *only* if) the conditions of human association in an era of industrial production are made cooperative and hence educative of individuals' capacities—that "a new culture expressing the possibilities immanent in a machine and material civilization will release whatever is distinctive and potentially creative in individuals." The second is that the reconstruction of individuality will be realized as an ongoing *process*, in which individuals nurtured in a more communal network of associations will continually remake themselves as they remake social institutions: "individuals thus freed will be the constant makers of a continuously new society," Dewey affirms, and in so remaking "the moving present" we will "create ourselves as we create an unknown future."[50]

The Primacy of the Local: Reconstructing Individuality
as a Democratic Way of Life

Perhaps most importantly, Dewey's call for new political agencies commensurate with the corporate forces of the machine age must be understood in relation to the pluralism and meliorism of his broader ethical vision: in relation, specifically, to his pluralistic insistence on local
community as the most vital scene of character formation and moral
choice, and to his melioristic contention that the true function of ideals
or ends is to enrich the meaning of present activity that constitutes the
primary value we enjoy as humans. In the concluding pages of both *The
Public and Its Problems* and *Individualism Old and New*, Dewey reasserts
the primacy of the local, arguing that new forms of collective political
organization, while necessary for realizing a democratic culture and individuality, can never be sufficient to the task. Achieving democracy as a
way of life is ultimately a local responsibility, dependent upon individuals choosing how best to contribute to and redirect the activities of the
groups to which they belong so that these might more closely embody
a communal dynamic. And in this respect achieving liberty ultimately
remains an individual responsibility, as well: it is in the exercise of this
inescapable personal choice that individual liberty is realized and the
quality of individuality remade. Rejecting any dualism between "collective" and "individual" efforts at reform, Dewey insists that when conditions require us to focus on "large-scale" social "arrangements" and the
collective or organized forms of action necessary to reform them, this
does *not* mean that individual imagination, initiative, and responsibility
are replaced by some mysterious collective agency. Quite the opposite
is true: when questions of broad social institutions "are uppermost,"
it "makes morals more acutely personal than they were when custom
ruled":

> It forces the need of more personal reflection, more personal knowl-
> edge and insight, more deliberate and steadfast personal convictions,
> more resolute personal attitudes in action—more personal in the sense
> of being more *conscious* in choice and more voluntary in execution. It
> would then be absurd to suppose that "social morals" meant a swal-
> lowing up of individuality in an anonymous mass, or an abdication
> of personal responsibility in decision and action. It signifies that the
> social conditions and social consequences of personal action (which
> always exist in any case), are now brought to explicit consciousness

so that they require searching thought and careful judgment in a way practically unprecedented formerly. . . . [P]ersonal conduct is so complicated by social conditions that a person has to decide about the latter in order to reach a conclusion in the former.[51]

Accordingly, while establishment of a "great" or global community can provide greater knowledge of, and control over, the broader contexts in which local communities participate, such knowledge attains full meaning *only* as it is applied in the choices and efforts of individuals within those local contexts.

In arguing that political empowerment of the "Great Community" is necessary to restore meaning and control to local communities, Dewey carefully distinguishes between political democracy and democracy as a way of life—and stresses the limits of what specifically political forms of association can accomplish. According to Dewey's analysis, the state is *not* "all absorbing and inclusive," but a "distinctive and restricted social interest": the organized public regulating through its representative officials the indirect consequences of associated behavior. Democracy as a "social idea" of community to be achieved in "all modes of human association" is "a wider and fuller idea than can be exemplified by the state even at its best." Democracy in this primary form cannot be achieved merely through political organization, but involves a more fundamental process of educating character: community requires that a group afford each of its members the active role in common endeavors that will cultivate his or her individual capacities, *and* requires in turn that the pursuit of ends that serve the common good becomes intimately woven into each individual's dispositional makeup. Community in this "deepest and richest sense," Dewey concludes, "must always remain a matter of face-to-face intercourse," a product of the enduring and intimate local relationships that provide the "chief agencies" "by which dispositions are stably formed and ideas acquired which la[y] hold on the roots of character." A "great" community, Dewey concludes, "can never possess all the qualities which mark a local community," but it can provide the necessary conditions for local community by "ordering the relations and enriching the experience of local associations"—that is, by increasing knowledge of and control over the larger social contexts in which local groups participate.[52] If at the level of a global community shared public interests could be adequately recognized and agencies of cooperative control instituted, then "local communal life" might be "reestablished" with a fullness, variety and freedom of possession and enjoyment of meanings and goods unknown in the contiguous associations of the past. For it will be alive and flexible as well as stable, responsive to the complex and world-wide scene in which it is enmeshed. While local, it will not be isolated. Its larger relationships will provide an inexhaustible and flowing fund of meanings upon which to draw, with assurance that its drafts will be honored.[53]

The establishment of a Great Community would facilitate a more equitable sharing and humane use of the material benefits generated by our global systems of interdependence. However, the fact that Dewey lists "meanings" before "goods" indicates that the equality he envisions is, once again, primarily a *qualitative* equality of participation and shared meaning. Above all, then, the establishment of a Great Community would allow individuals in local groups to understand more fully how their activities contribute to the larger global society and allow them to participate more meaningfully in the control and redirection of their activities within that larger social context.

Individualism Old and New's call for greater public control of industry must be understood in this light: as an effort to restore meaning and control to local communities—to those "face-to-face" relations in which the habits of individual character are cultivated—and to thereby create the conditions in which "lost" individuals can recover a socially integrated individuality. Even more explicitly than *The Public and Its Problems*, *Individualism Old and New* stresses the limits of politics, that creating new forms of public regulation can support but never replace the more basic task of achieving democracy as a way of life. Politics is not "fundamental," Dewey insists, but "accessory": "A certain amount of specific change in legislation and administration is required in order to supply the conditions under which other changes may take place in non-political ways."[54] Dewey again argues that the most crucial function of political association is to restore a sense of socially integrated *meaning* to local communities and the activities of their individual members:

> The psychological effect of law and political discussion is enormous. Political action provides large-scale models that react into the formation of ideas and ideals about all social matters. One sure way in which the individual who is politically lost, because of the loss of objects to which his loyalties can attach themselves, could recover a composed mind, would be by apprehension of the realities of industry and finance as they function in public and political life. . . . While,

as I have already said, political action is not basic, concentration of attention upon real and vital issues such as attend the public control of industry and finance for the sake of social values would have vast intellectual and emotional reverberations. . . . Politics is a means, not an end. But thought of it as a means will lead to the thought of the ends which it should serve. It will induce consideration of the ways in which a worthy and rich life for all may be achieved. In so doing, it will restore directive aims and be a significant step forward in the recovery of a unified individuality.[55]

Dewey's treatment of politics here reflects his reconception of the means-ends relationship. As discussed in chapter 4, Dewey rejects the common view that present activity is a means to achieving future ends, and argues instead that ends are in fact means to enriching present activity—that ends function not as ideals to be fully attained, but as a provisional ends-in-view whose primary value is in giving new direction and meaning to present activity. Similarly, Dewey challenges the common assumption that political association entails subordinating local activities to larger group ends, that meaning resides in the attainment of generalized common aims. Precisely the reverse is true, he suggests: the function of political association is to establish common ends that will restore meaning and direction to local activities, and meaning resides in the growing quality of local, present activity that accrues when individuals' chosen courses of action are informed by more intelligent and humane ends. As he puts it above, establishing "public control of industry and finance for the sake of social values" would provide "objects to which [the lost individual's] loyalties can attach themselves." Restoring "directive aims" on this "large-scale" of concerted public action will "react into the formation of ideas and ideals about all social matters," guiding the local choices and actions through which individuals form and remake their characters and thus facilitating "the recovery of a unified individuality."

But if political action can thus be "a significant step" in the recovery of an integrated individuality, Dewey insists that the attainment of an integrated and liberating self must ultimately remain a matter of individual responsibility. Long before the slogan "think globally; act locally" became a progressive mantra, Dewey argued that while political association can restore a broader context of social meaning and provide a wider knowledge of consequences and new common aims to inform local activity, individuals must still translate this knowledge into chosen courses of action adapted to the needs and possibilities of the actual conditions in which they find themselves: "Wholesale creeds and all-inclusive ideals are impotent in the face of actual situations; for doing always means the doing of something in particular."[56] In Dewey's pluralistic vision, the demands of and resources for action are always shaped by the uniqueness of each particular situation and the individuals who participate in it:

> We are given to thinking of society in large and vague ways. We should forget "society" and think of law, industry, religion, medicine, politics, art, education, philosophy—and think of them in the plural. For points of contact are not the same for any two persons. . . . All these callings and concerns are the avenues through which the world acts upon us and we upon the world. There is no society at large, no business in general. Harmony with conditions is not a single and monotonous uniformity, but a diversified affair requiring individual attack.
>
> Individuality is inexpugnable because it is a manner of distinctive sensitivity, selection, choice, response and utilization of conditions. For this reason, if for no other, it is impossible to develop integrated individuality by an all-embracing system or program. No individual can make the determination for anyone else; nor can he make it for himself once and forever. A native manner of selection gives direction and continuity, but definite expression is found in changing occasions and varied forms. The selective choice and use of conditions have to be continually made and remade. Since we live in a moving world and change with our interactions in it, every act produces a new perspective that demands a new exercise of preference. If, in the long run, an individual remains lost, it is because he has chosen irresponsibility; and if he remains wholly depressed it is because he has chosen the course of easy parasitism.[57]

Asserting that each individual bears an inescapable responsibility for recovering his or her own individuality is tantamount to affirming that individual liberty exists, for, as outlined in chapter 4, Dewey locates our capacity for freedom in the ability to accept responsibility for the consequences of one's actions, to use those consequences to reevaluate the quality of existing habits, and on the basis of such knowledge to pursue new ends that will form and strengthen new habits. Liberty, in sum, names the ability to choose what kind of self to be in the present by choosing what kind of future to pursue. As Dewey argues in the passage above, this process of choice that is the defining characteristic of selfhood is inescapably local and particular. Individuality emerges in the interaction between an individual—with an existing set of habits, desires, talents, values, impulses, and attractions that reflect her own unique history—and the unique set of social contexts and conditions that define her possibilities for action. It is the response that our acts find in environing conditions that reveals to us the quality of our selfhood. Thus liberty is not some metaphysical endowment, but an *achievement* that can be attained only by engaging the particular conditions with which one is faced, by choosing to pursue new ends that promise to move those conditions towards a desired future: "conditions are not fixed. . . . Their movement is not destined to a single end. . . . Many outcomes may be projected, and the movement may be directed by many courses to many chosen goals, once conditions have been recognized for what they are. By becoming conscious of their movements and by active participation in their currents, we may guide them to some preferred possibility. In this interaction, individuals attain an integrated being."[58] To have an "integrated" self, then, means to be integrated into existing conditions, to find one's identity in—or stake one's identity on—intelligent efforts to influence the course of change in one's own corner of the world. Such integration is not a static achievement, but an ongoing process of remaking one's self and surroundings, and "recovery" of individuality is a matter not of returning to some essential self, but of pushing on through present difficulties and defeats to reattain one's harmony or equilibrium in a new (and hopefully improved) situation.[59]

In thus describing the reconstruction of self and world as "a diversified affair requiring individual attack"—a process occurring via the many "avenues through which the world acts upon us and we upon the world" in which we "create ourselves as we create an unknown future"—Dewey reaffirms the pluralistic vision that William James offers in the closing pages of *Pragmatism*, the vision of individuals working to realize ideals in "the parts of the world to which we are closest," with each "such ideal realized" constituting "one moment in the world's salvation." Dewey even offers his own alternative to James's religious rhetoric: "To gain an integrated individuality, each of us needs to cultivate his own garden," Dewey contends, "But there is no fence about this garden: it is no sharply marked-off enclosure. Our garden is the world, in the angle at which it touches our own manner of being." Dewey suggests here, as he does in various of his works, that our local efforts gain an ideality or even religious significance from their implication in the interconnected pluralistic universe in which we live. As noted at the outset of this chapter,

Dewey had questioned whether a Jamesian ethics of individualized vocation could still be relevant in a modern world increasingly structured
by large, impersonal systems of interaction; the analyses he pursued in
The Public and Its Problems and *Individualism Old and New* strengthened
his conviction that the community which educates individuality, and the
individual acts which serve to remake community, must both remain,
in their most vital sense, local. Because it is ultimately on the local level
that we live our moral lives—that we translate knowledge of sometimes
remote consequences into chosen courses of action that define the quality of our characters—Dewey describes "the local" as "the ultimate universal, and as near an absolute as exists."[60]

Yet if one can hear Jamesian echoes in the conclusion of *Individualism
Old and New*, it is not James but Emerson whom Dewey invokes, signal-
ing his awareness that his own ethics find significant roots in the American precursor he shared with James, and drawing on Emerson's cultural
authority to position his own program for reconstructing individuality
as extending a valued tradition of American democratic thought. Dewey
enlists Emerson to reaffirm two central themes of *Individualism Old and
New*. First, that a truly democratic culture can be forged only by "accepting the corporate and industrial world in which we live" and realizing its
immanent possibilities, which Dewey presents as embodying the Emersonian faith that the present contains new creative energies and possibilities out of which the future must be created—that it "is in vain" (in the
words of Emerson's that Dewey quotes) to "look for genius to reiterate its
miracles in the old arts" and that "beauty and holiness" must be found "in
new and necessary facts" of "the field and road-side," the "shop and mill."
Second, noting that "the same Emerson who said that 'society is everywhere in conspiracy against its members' also said, and in the same essay,
'accept the place the divine providence has found for you, the society of
your contemporaries, the connection of events,'" Dewey cites Emerson
as supporting his own contention that the recreation of self which all individuals must pursue can be achieved only by engaging the local conditions in which each individual finds himself—that these "moving and
multiple associations" are "the only means by which the possibilities of
individuality can be realized."[61] More broadly, since a transactional model
of experience and selfhood provides the basis for Dewey's social thought,
the fact that he locates in "Self-Reliance" not an atomistic or "transcendent" self, but a dynamic self that exists only in its creative interactions

with environing conditions, shows Dewey in 1930 reaffirming the claim he made twenty-seven years earlier in his address on Emerson—that he found in Emerson's philosophy a coherent articulation of principles essential to his own vision of democracy as a way of life.

The enduring relevance of Dewey's approach to reconstructing individualism can be suggested from several perspectives. First, though Dewey insists that we live in a moving world in which ideas and practices must be continually readapted to changing conditions, and thus would be the first to insist that his diagnosis of the prospects for reconstructing individualism in 1930 cannot be expected to meet the needs of our contemporary situation, it is remarkable how many of the specific obstacles to restoring community and individuality that he identified still face us today—many in exacerbated form. What Dewey described as a "central fact" in the crisis of democratic culture, that "most of those who are engaged in the outward work of production and distribution of economic commodities have no share—imaginative, intellectual, emotional—in directing the activities in which they physically participate," remains as true in our "postindustrial" economic era as it was in Dewey's day.[62] Dewey's call for more extensive socialized control over industry, made in the depths of the Great Depression, may seem quaint and outdated to those who view our current politicoeconomic landscape, since the fall of the Berlin Wall, as the shining triumph of liberal freedom. But by diagnosing the deep rifts in the lives of most Americans—between the instrumental and aesthetic aspects of experience, between working-hours largely drained of meaning beyond the securing of a paycheck, and leisure-time devoted to compensating for this lack through a consumerist pursuit of sensationalized pleasure[63]—and by asserting that we can heal such alienations only to the extent that we make our forms of association truly cooperative, affording individuals the participatory control needed to make their labor individually fulfilling and socially meaningful, Dewey's ideal of democracy as a way of life still offers a radical critique of and alternative to our existing socioeconomic regime.

Similarly, if the local communities in which individuals might attain a socially integrated individuality had been, by Dewey's day, undermined by vast and impersonal forms of associated activity "remote in initiation," "far-reaching in scope," and "complexly indirect in operation," the reach and complexity of such forces has only been increased by the new types of economic, cultural, and technological interdependence currently described as "globalization." There have been efforts to establish new international government agencies to regulate the consequences of our global interdependence—such as the United Nations[64] and the World Trade Organization—but their efforts still occur within the considerable constraints of traditional nationalist and liberal-capitalist frameworks. Although events such as the protests at the 1999 WTO meetings in Seattle, or at various G8 meetings since 2000, might indicate a growing awareness of the consequences of our globalized society—and some sense of solidarity with others affected by those consequences—it would be hard to argue that the public has even begun to recognize itself in anything like the degree to which Dewey demands. That is to say, our problem, Dewey would likely tell us, remains foremost an *intellectual* problem of developing an adequate knowledge of our evolving forms of social interaction and their consequences.

Moreover, the main conditions that Dewey listed as necessary to organize a public capable of regulating the forces of our global society—a truly experimental method of social inquiry and the free and full communication such inquiry requires—remain stubbornly elusive. Dewey's hopes for media that serve as vibrant communicators of a "genuine social science" have not been realized, as new technologies that seemed to promise a more global and diverse marketplace of information and ideas—such as twenty-four-hour satellite news outlets and the Internet—have largely remained under the control of increasingly large corporate conglomerates, purveyors of the kind of consumerism and sensationalism that Dewey deplored. We are also far from overcoming the absolutistic habits of thought that Dewey saw as preventing an experimental approach to social issues—as is evidenced not only by the disturbing presence of fundamentalist extremism (in both the United States and globally), but by the persistence in mainstream American politics of a sterile dichotomy between "individualist" and "collectivist" approaches, that is evident, especially on socioeconomic issues,[65] in the dogmatic laissez-faire liberalism of the conservative Right and the inability of the Left to articulate a compelling alternative beyond a watered-down version of New Deal social programs.

It takes but a few such observations to show that much of Dewey's critique remains all-too relevant in our new century. Dewey's continuing importance as a theorist of democratic individuality, however, lies not in the specific problems or remedies he identifies—indeed, he admits in *The Public and Its Problems* that his requirements for creating a genuine public opinion will to some "seem close to [a] denial of the possibility." It reflects instead, as outlined in the close of chapter 4, the broad political benefits of Dewey's model of reform as a dialectic process with no fixed end in which human nature and its environing conditions mutually transform each other. First, that it allows him simultaneously to assert the possibility of reform and acknowledge its difficulty. And, second, that it allows him to define success in melioristic terms: to affirm that the "good is always found in a present growth of significance in activity," that value does not reside in the complete realization of some projected ideal (be it liberty, democracy, community, or individuality), but rather in the growing quality and meaning of activity that is immediately enjoyed in the present as we use such ideals to redirect our activities, reorganize our habits, and remake our social institutions.[66]

Dewey's analysis of the prospects for reconstructing individuality combines precisely such a tough-minded realism about the difficulty of reform with a melioristic definition of value that precludes pessimism and affirms human agency. On the one hand, Dewey tells us there is no short-cut to reconstructing individualism: it requires nothing less than the effort to reconstruct all areas of human association (government, churches, schools, businesses, community organizations, families, etc.) so as to make them more communal and democratic—more participatory, more educative and liberating of individuals' capacities. Moreover, such an effort is by its nature unending. We live in a moving world where the consequences of associated activity that define the common interest and define the quality of the dispositions that constitute character are always changing. In such a world, the public is always to be rediscovered, community and moral selfhood are always to be remade, and the tasks of inquiry, communication, and education—all facilitated by individuals' acts of deliberation and choice—necessary to such reconstruction are unending. On the other hand, the fact that these ideals are continually to be pursued and never to be fully realized does not imply that an integrated individuality is therefore endlessly deferred. The goal is not *reconstructed* individuality as some fixed ideal whose completed realization must wait upon the reconstruction of society into a fully functioning community; such a notion misunderstands the true function of ideals as means to redirect and enrich present activity. Instead, Dewey affirms our ability to achieve a *reconstructing* individuality in the present: as soon as one strives to deliberate more intelligently on the consequences of one's actions and to choose new ends that promise to harmonize more fully individual satisfaction with the common good, one begins to recover an integrated individuality that is actualized in the growing meaning and liberation of capacity enjoyed in one's present activity.

I have stressed, throughout chapters 4 and 5, how this vision of Dewey's reaches back to Emerson and James. Key aspects of Dewey's thought also provide a context for situating the ethical concerns of Kenneth Burke and Ralph Ellison, to whom the final chapter of this study is devoted. I have already linked Dewey's model of "conscientiousness" to Burke's and Ellison's assertions that one's identity is inextricably defined by the often indirect and unrecognized ways one's activities impact others. A related connection to Burke and Ellison is suggested by the argument in *The Public and Its Problems* that the full and free communication needed to discover the public and forge a great community will require new symbols adequate to convey the significance of our interconnections, "so that genuinely shared interest in the consequences of interdependent activities may inform desire and effort and thereby direct action." "Communication can alone create a great community," Dewey insists, for though "the ties which hold men together in action are numerous, tough and subtle[,] . . . they are invisible and intangible," so that "the thoughts and aspirations congruous with them are not communicated, and hence are not common." "Our Babel," he concludes, "is not one of tongues, but of the signs and symbols without which shared experience is impossible."[67] The entire corpus of Burke's writings can be considered as an attempt to meet the need that Dewey here articulates. Burke's commitment to promoting rhetorical persuasion over violence leads him to articulate the twin ethical mandates of confronting the ways in which one's social position places one into conflict with others and of recognizing the shared interests that unite us across social divisions. Burke's "grammar" of motives and his advocacy of literature as "equipment for living" can be seen as attempts to assemble—from the resources of philosophy and literature—the symbolic tools that can support this task of ethical communication. Similarly, Ellison's great novel of twentieth-century America, *Invisible Man*, can be read as an attempt to provide, in the career of Ellison's nameless narrator, a symbol for just such a Burkean ethics, and a symbol for the interconnectedness of American identity that is both defined by, and reaches across, the stubborn structures of racial oppression that continue to mar our democracy. Such affinities between their visions of democratic selfhood reveal Dewey, Burke, and Ellison as working with and through a common Emersonian inheritance—an inheritance that for Ellison, as we shall see, was itself an example of the complex interconnections of democratic identity.

PART THREE

A TRAGICOMIC ETHICS
IN THE EMERSONIAN VEIN

Kenneth Burke and Ralph Ellison

SAYING YES AND SAYING NO

Individualist Ethics in Ellison and Burke

The writings of Ralph Ellison constitute one of American literature's most sophisticated explorations of the doubleness that W. E. B. Du Bois described as central to African-American identity. While Du Bois testified to the African-American's "longing" to overcome the social and psychic divisions imposed by American society, to "merge his double self into a better and truer self," he envisioned that "truer" self as one in which the doubleness of African and American elements would coexist: "In this merging he wishes neither of the older selves to be lost. He would not Africanize America, for America has too much to teach the world and Africa. He would not bleach his Negro soul in a flood of white Americanism, for he knows that Negro blood has a message for the world."[1] Similarly, Ellison always asserted that, as an artist and an individual, he was heir to both a distinctive African-American culture and to the American heritage within the Western European tradition. "I was taken very early," he recalled of his youth, "with a passion to link together all I loved within the Negro community and all those things I felt in the world which lay beyond." As an aspiring musician, for example, Ellison "felt no need to draw a line between the two traditions" of jazz and classical music: "the idea was to master both." Even in segregated America, Ellison found that, "culturally, everything was mixed": "we wanted to share both: the classics and jazz, the Charleston and the Irish reel, spirituals and the blues, the sacred and the profane." Without minimizing the "all too real" obstacles designed to deny blacks opportunities, he insisted on the complexity of the experience that African-Americans achieved in spite of and in resistance to those obstacles. Consequently, he criticized writers such as Richard Wright for portraying African-Americans as too determined, too defeated, by their social environment.[2]

The individualism behind this critique of Wright is itself a prime example of Ellison's desire to "master both" traditions, a product of that border space of doubleness where things are "culturally mixed," where traditional "American" institutions become inflected by the unique perspective of African-American experience.[3] Ellison's individualism draws on a central Emersonian tradition of American individualism, yet revises that tradition by placing it firmly within the context of American race relations. I hope to illustrate this genealogy by exploring a complex scene of intertextual allusion: Ellison's satire of Emerson in *Invisible Man*. Critics have tended to read this satire as evidence of Ellison's scathing rejection of Emersonian individualism.[4] Such a reading accepts—and constructs Ellison as accepting—the very traditional and resilient interpretation that Emerson's philosophy ignores the material and historical reality of evil. In contrast, I want to argue that Ellison's parody is aimed at a highly mediated version of Emerson—the Emerson canonized in Lewis Mumford's 1926 study *The Golden Day*, an influential precursor to F. O. Matthiessen's *American Renaissance*. Moreover, even as Ellison lampoons this canonical Emerson, the ethic of self-expressive action dramatized by the career of his narrator extends a pragmatic tradition of individualism running from Emerson through writers such as William James and Kenneth Burke. The canonical portrait of an idealist Emerson who affirms the transcendent autonomy of the individual mind too often has obscured the more pragmatic self described in Emerson's writings, a self that exists only within the limitations of the material world, including the pervasive limitations of culture, society, and language, and therefore a self that is always socially implicated and indebted. It is this Emersonian tradition, concerned with the individual's complex relations to social resources and responsibilities, that Ellison extends. Thus *Invisible Man*'s parody of Emerson is best read, I believe, as a dual gesture of critique and affiliation:

Ellison rejects a canonical Emersonianism, and the political blindnesses commonly associated with it, in order to appropriate the ethical possibilities of a more pragmatic Emersonian individualism.[5]

While Mumford is the mediating figure in *Invisible Man*'s parody of Emerson, Ellison's affiliation to a more pragmatic Emerson can be traced through the mediating figure of Ellison's friend Kenneth Burke, whom Ellison claimed had a large influence on *Invisible Man*.[6] Both Ellison and Burke reject a narrowly individualistic version of Emersonianism by insisting that an ethic of self-expressive activity, or self-culture, must include a political component of social responsibility. In this regard, they reassert a focus Emerson himself affirmed, for, as I argued in chapter 2, Emerson too rejected the notion that the pursuit of self-culture relieved one of responsibility to address social inequalities. Such rearticulations of Emersonianism offered from within the pragmatic tradition are far more cogent, I would argue, than more traditional interpretations that depict Emerson as an absolute idealist or an apologist for capitalism. Moreover, following Du Bois's and Ellison's insistence that the African-American experience is quintessentially American, I would argue that a truly "American" sense of an Emersonian tradition must include African-American writers, like Ellison, who have both claimed and reshaped that tradition.[7]

Named Ralph Waldo Ellison by his father, Ellison could hardly help but feel Emerson as an imposing American precursor. Indeed, Emerson occupies a prominent position in *Invisible Man*: Mr. Norton, a white New England industrialist and a philanthropic trustee of the black state college that the narrator attends, repeatedly recommends Emerson's philosophy to the narrator. Norton particularly dwells on the idea of "fate," which he says links him to the narrator: "You are my fate," he insists, "upon you depends the outcome of the years I have spent in helping your school."[8] Ellison heavily ironizes Norton's vision of his connection to black youth, making it clear that his philanthropy is blatantly self-aggrandizing:

> I have wealth and a reputation and prestige—all that is true, but your great Founder had more than that, he had tens of thousands of lives dependent upon his ideas and upon his actions. What he did affected your whole race. In a way, he had the power of a king, or, in a sense, of a god.[9]

It is a desire for such god-like power that underlies Norton's concept of destiny connecting him to the narrator: "Through you and your fellow students I become, let us say, three hundred teachers, seven hundred trained mechanics, eight hundred skilled farmers, and so on." In contrast, Norton's actual effect on the narrator is disastrous: he asks the narrator to drive him on a tour of the countryside, where he hears a story of incest from a black farmer, Jim Trueblood, that mirrors Norton's incestuous feelings for his own daughter and pushes him to a physical collapse. When Norton calls for whiskey to restore himself, the narrator takes him to a local saloon and bordello, named, significantly, The Golden Day. Here Norton meets a group of black war veterans on furlough from a local asylum who treat him with anger and disdain, anger that boils over into a riot. Norton's self-serving vision of himself, and of black-white relations, thus receives a shock, while the narrator gets expelled from college, upbraided by the college president, Dr. Bledsoe, for being stupid enough to show a white person the reality of black experience. Nor is this all. The narrator, sent North with what he thinks are letters of recommendation from Bledsoe, seeks employment from a character *named* "Mr. Emerson," whom the narrator does not meet, but at whose office he sees Bledsoe's letter, which reveals that the college and its white trustees have conspired to expel him permanently, to "hope him to death, and keep him running."[10]

Not surprisingly, readers often see these allusions as a bitter indictment of Emersonian individualism. Alan Nadel, in his insightful study of *Invisible Man*'s allusions to American literature, argues that the inaccessible Mr. Emerson represents the abstract idealism of Emerson's philosophy, while Mr. Norton represents the absurdity of attempting to apply these ideals to real life. This parody rejects Emerson, Nadel concludes, as an "author of false hopes" who is unable "to recognize evil . . . [in] the complicated form it takes in the actual world." The limitation of such an interpretation is that it largely accepts *Invisible Man*'s parodic characters as a sincere and accurate criticism of Emerson's philosophy. It is, after all, a highly mediated version of Emerson that is being lampooned: Mr. Norton's vague platitudes confidently cite Emerson to validate his role as industrialist and philanthropist, but Ellison's satire surely invites us to discount this self-serving appropriation. Indeed, Nadel's footnotes include a remark from a letter that Ellison wrote Nadel, in which he cautions that he was not satirizing Emerson's "oracular stance" but rather "some of the bombast that has been made of his pronouncements."[11] The narrator's relation to Mr. Norton is indeed crucial for understanding how *Invisible Man* both extends and revises Emerson's ethics, yet we should resist concluding that the parody of Norton's "bombastic" reduction of Emerson indicates Ellison's true relation to Emerson.

The need for such interpretive caution is heightened by the fact that it is not only Norton but also Lewis Mumford who mediates the version of Emerson satirized by Ellison. The name of the whorehouse to which the narrator takes Norton, The Golden Day, clearly directs our attention to Mumford's study of the same title. The "golden day" is Mumford's name for the years 1830–60, which he celebrates as an era in which writers like Emerson, Thoreau, Whitman, Melville, and Hawthorne transformed the material facts of American life into higher expressions of artistic or spiritual truth. What is remarkable about Mumford's book is the pessimism and nostalgia of its historical narrative—an interpretation stressed both by Nadel and by James Livingston's excellent study of pragmatism.[12] Mumford portrays his golden day as a fleeting cultural moment when the American mind had escaped the materialism of the pioneer, but not yet become mired in the materialism of the Gilded Age: "That world was the climax of American experience. What preceded led up to it: what followed, dwindled away from it." In this scheme, America's development into an industrial society, accelerated by the Civil War, can appear only as a tragic fall in which the American imagination succumbed to the materialism of the machine age. Mumford locates this imaginative failure in the literature of realism and naturalism, and especially in the philosophy of William James, whose focus on utility, Mumford charges, amounts to a "pragmatic acquiescence" to material reality.[13]

What Ellison seems to be parodying, then, is Mumford's idealized construction of Emerson and his narrative of the relation between American literature and history.[14] Most obviously, by turning The Golden Day into a whorehouse for disenfranchised black soldiers, Ellison is ridiculing Mumford's history: 1830–1860 was no golden day for African-Americans. Mumford makes only passing reference to the sectional struggle over slavery which increasingly dominated the American scene in the 1840s and 1850s, and his only real interest in the Civil War is that it hastened the industrialization that ended his "golden day": "the war was a struggle between two forms of servitude, the slave and the machine. The machine won, and the human spirit was almost as much paralyzed by the victory as it would have been by the defeat." By contrast, Ellison, in his 1946 essay "Twentieth-Century Fiction and the Black Mask of Humanity," praises writers such as Emerson, Thoreau, Whitman, Melville, and Twain not for the imaginative transcendence of history that Mumford valorizes, but for confronting the central dilemma of American history embodied in the oppressed humanity of the African-American.[15]

Nadel provides a cogent interpretation of Mumford's role in *Invisible Man*'s literary allusions, arguing that Ellison's whorehouse symbolizes the historical reality repressed by Mumford's study. Unfortunately, when Nadel moves on to assess Ellison's allusions to Emerson, Mumford vanishes from his account. Having persuasively argued that Ellison encourages us to reject Mumford's reductive literary history, Nadel himself is content to rehearse very conventional interpretations of Emerson. In his reading of Ellison's characters Mr. Norton and Mr. Emerson, Nadel paints Emerson as an absolute optimist who effaces evil—either by celebrating a transcendent ideal beyond material reality, or by celebrating the material as ideal, blithely ignoring the less-than-ideal aspects of that reality. The problem here is not in Nadel's interpretations of Ellison's characters; these seem right on the mark—*if* one reads the characters as lampooning stereotypical misreadings of Emerson, if one recalls Ellison's claim to be satirizing the "bombast that has been made of" Emerson. Nadel acknowledges but then erases this basic, yet crucial, distinction: he admits that Norton's platitudes are distortions of Emerson, but then argues Norton's absurd applications reveal absurdities in Emerson.[16] For example, Nadel sees Norton's reductive notion of "fate" as an extension of Emerson's reductiveness:

> [Emerson] asserts that Fate is Nature, which is good, and failure to see that good in any given event is the failure of human understanding to penetrate the underlying natural cause; . . . The implication here is that all human remedy and redress is attitudinal. Some may regard this as rationalizing, but that may not be a bad choice for problems which admit no other solution. The problem with this philosophy is that it does not differentiate—in fact encourages not differentiating—between natural evils and correctable human error. Such a lack of distinction enables wealthy Mr. Norton to oversimplify Emerson.[17]

Nadel is correct in noting that Emerson's philosophy is "attitudinal"; indeed, as I argue below, the attitudinal aspect of his ethics is one of the central pragmatic views connecting Emerson to Burke and Ellison. However, when Nadel claims that Emerson's philosophy is merely attitudinal, that it fatalistically renounces acts that might redress correctable evils, it is Nadel and not Emerson who is failing to "differentiate."

In particular, how can the concept of "fate" that Mr. Norton espouses (and Nadel accepts) be squared with the fact that Emerson throughout his writings exhorts people to action that will both realize their human potential and reshape the world around them? Emerson's essay "Fate," belying its title, explicitly rejects fatalism in favor of activism. Even as Emerson acknowledges that "limitation" is a central "element running through entire nature,"[18] he affirms that creative change occurs within and against the limits of the material world:

> Fate has its lord; limitation its limits; is different seen from above and from below; from within and from without. For, though Fate is immense, so is power, which is the other fact in the dual world, immense. If Fate follows and limits power, power attends and antagonizes Fate.[19]

Emerson insists that power and limitation are inextricably linked, that particular limits are transcended, that today's obstacle may be the occasion for or source of tomorrow's power. Listing examples of dangerous and limiting natural forces—water, cold, steam, electricity, disease—Emerson stresses that such forces at the least serve as stimulants to human ingenuity, while at best they are "convertible by intellect into wholesome force": "The water drowns ship and sailor, like a grain of dust. But learn to swim, trim your bark, and the wave which drowned it, will be cloven by it, and carry it, like its own foam, a plume and power." As this makes clear, Emerson neither ignores evil, nor fatalistically accepts it: instead, he accepts a world of limits in order to affirm our limited, yet sufficient, ability to act on and transform that world: "We can afford to allow the limitation, if we know it is the meter of the growing man."[20]

Given the history of Emerson's critical reception,[21] however, it is not surprising that readers—even ones as astute as Nadel—should accept Ellison's parodic figures of Mr. Norton and Mr. Emerson as an accurate and sincere critique of Emerson. Emerson traditionally has been accused of a "transcendentalist" fascination with the absolute that ignores or subsumes the tragic limits of existence. Curiously, this supposed absolutism has been described as taking two nearly contradictory forms. As the title of Stephen E. Whicher's influential study *Freedom and Fate* suggests, critics have charted a shift in the course of Emerson's career, from a naive idealism that celebrates the individual's access to absolute unity and power, to a more sober skepticism or fatalism that celebrates the absolute forces of nature that determine and limit our individual acts. This conventional construction of two Emersons clearly parallels the two figures in Ellison's parody: Mr. Emerson, with his inaccessible idealism, and Mr. Norton, with his naively benign vision of our actual fates.

The key question is, how much sense does it make to conclude that Ellison is endorsing these conventional readings of Emerson? The biting energy that *Invisible Man* expends on parodying Emerson suggests an anxiety of influence that should encourage us to look past its apparent rejection of Emerson in order to see other, more significant connections between the two writers. In discussing his literary namesake, Ellison acknowledged just such a complex sense of indebtedness to Emerson. As a youth, Ellison changed his middle name from Waldo to an anonymous "W" and "avoided [Emerson's] works like the plague." As an adult artist, however, he stressed that he "did not destroy" but "only suppressed" that "troublesome middle name of mine": "I could suppress the name of my namesake out of respect for the achievements of its original bearer, but I cannot escape the obligation of attempting to achieve some of the things which he asked of the American writer."[22]

When Ellison's allusions are seen as directed at Mumford's literary history, his satire can be read as rejecting its idealized portrait of Emerson, even as his novel extends a pragmatic tradition of individualism that has its roots in Emerson. In opposing Emersonian transcendence to Jamesian acquiescence, Mumford replicates essentially the same split that critics have posited in Emerson's career—from the naive prophet of "freedom" to the stern prophet of "fate." Those who read Emerson in such absolutist terms—whether it be, like Mumford, to praise him for transcending historical limits, or, like Nadel, to blame him for ignoring them—erase the pragmatic Emerson who had such an important influence on James, Burke, and Ellison. There is, of course, a countertradition in American criticism that views Emerson as a founding figure in American pragmatism—one that starts with both John Dewey and James, and extends through more contemporary critics like Burke, Richard Poirier, and Stanley Cavell.[23] *Invisible Man*'s parody of and its indebtedness to Emerson place Ellison in this pragmatic tradition as well. If Ellison sends

Mr. Norton to The Golden Day saloon in order to reject Mumford's ide-alized Emerson, and thus affiliate himself with another, more politically useful Emerson, then one place to look for such an affiliation is precisely in those pragmatic aspects of Emerson's individualism that are effaced by Mumford's narrative.

Specifically, I want to focus on two aspects of the individualist ethics that connect Emerson to Ellison and Burke, aspects which can be termed "tragic" and "comic," following Burke's definitions of those attitudes. Though often accused of ignoring tragic limits, Emerson in fact insists that our acts are always limited by the cultural media with which they must be articulated and the material environment they strive to re-shape.[24] As cultural beings, our dependence on inherited ideas and tools is so profound that even our efforts to reform or transcend traditional constructs must make use of tradition: "so deep is the foundation of the existing social system" that people "are under the necessity of using the Actual order of things, in order to disuse it." Moreover, though our acts can change our environment, any changes in turn become part of a new environment that re-acts upon us: "Every spirit makes its house; but afterwards the house confines the spirit."[25] To see one's acts in this perspective, as expressing both one's will and the limits on that will, is, Burke argues, a tragic vision:

> The act, in being an assertion, has called forth a counter-assertion in the elements that compose its context. And when the agent is enabled to see in terms of this counter-assertion, he has transcended the state that characterized him at the start. In this final state of tragic vision, intrinsic and extrinsic motivations are merged. That is, although purely circumstantial factors participate in his tragic destiny, these are not felt as exclusively external, or scenic; for they bring about a *representative* kind of accident, the kind of accident that belongs with the agent's particular kind of character.[26]

Emerson expresses a similar insight when he claims that the individual "comes at last to be faithfully represented by every view you take of his circumstances." Emerson's individualist ethic of self-expressive action, or self-culture, is a response to these tragic limits on the self. It is against the resistances of our environment that we know and develop our indi-viduality: "We must have an antagonism in the tough world for all the

variety of our spiritual faculties, or they will not be born." Viewing individuals as alienated from both the sources and products of their acts,
Emerson locates our primary value, our only inalienable "property," in
the development of self we achieve through the act of doing: "that which
a man is does by necessity acquire, and what the man acquires is living
property." "The goods of fortune may come and go like summer leaves,"
Emerson writes, but "what a man does, that he has."[27]

But if Emerson locates value in the individual's self-expressive acts, his
ethics also attend to social obligations. This is because for Emerson—as
for the pragmatists who follow him—the self is inescapably *social*. For
example, when Emerson in "Self-Reliance" exhorts the reader to "Trust
thyself," the gloss he provides may surprise some: "Accept the place the
divine providence has found for you, the society of your contemporaries, the connection of events." The self here exists through its social
and historical engagements, by participating in the "events" that define
a historical moment. Emerson is acutely aware that human intelligence
is cultural; perhaps his central insight, and preoccupation, is that our
acts and even our perceptions depend on what he often calls "history" or
"society"—in short, on language. There is a social division of labor inherent in the cultural sources of all human acts. No person can perform
all the actions culture makes available; each must focus on some specialized area of activity. Accordingly, though Emerson exhorts us to "do
your work, and I shall know you," he celebrates those individuals who let
culture work for them, who best manipulate the resources supplied by
others. In his essay on Shakespeare, he describes "the greatest genius" as
"the most indebted man": "he finds himself in the river of the thoughts
and events, forced onward by the ideas and necessities of his contemporaries"; "all have worked for him, and he enters into their labors."[28]

Emerson's model of the self thus acknowledges that our individual
acts are socially indebted and imply a social responsibility. At moments,
he attempts to deal with this social implication by asserting that a rigorous and sincere pursuit of the work or vocation that best utilizes and
develops one's talents is a moral end that sufficiently fulfills one's duties
to others:

> You may fulfil your round of duties by clearing yourself in the *di-
> rect*, or in the *reflex* way. Consider whether you have satisfied your
> relations to father, mother, cousin, neighbour, town, cat, and dog,
> whether any of these can upbraid you. But I may also reject this reflex

standard, and absolve me to myself. I have my own stern claims and perfect circle.[29]

Indeed, extending this audacious claim that one can absolve one's self through the "stern claims" of individualized work, Emerson insists that we have our most beneficial effect on others through the example of our individualized action. Arguing that our most precious and stable value lies in developing our individual faculties, Emerson asserts that others can truly aid us only by pushing us to our own work. "Activity is contagious," he writes in "The Uses of Great Men": "Men are helpful through the intellect and the affections. Other help I find a false appearance."[30] Though he has complex and conflictual attitudes toward community, Emerson views the influence of others as essential to the self. This is evident in his intense preoccupation with friendship and the inspiration we draw from geniuses. In Emerson's vision, the healthy community would be one in which active individuals would inspire and antagonize each other through their diverse activities.[31]

It is on such issues that both Burke and Ellison reject a narrowly individualistic inference that might be—and too often is—drawn from certain of Emerson's ideas and utterances, in order to align themselves with a vision of Emersonian individualism that affirms a necessary synthesis between individualized self-culture and social responsibility. In opposition to the idea that individual acts—despite their social indebtedness—can attain an autonomous or independent moral integrity, Burke argues that an individualist ethics must include more directly political gestures of communication and self-analysis. Responsibility cannot be measured only by the isolated requirements of a specialized vocation. "The human agent, *qua* human agent, is not motivated solely by the principles of a specialized activity. . . . Any specialized activity participates in a larger unit of action. 'Identification' is a word for the autonomous activity's place in this wider context, a place with which the agent may be unconcerned"— but *should* be concerned. That is, the ethics of an activity cannot be measured solely by an individual's intentions or competence: "one's morality as a specialist cannot be allowed to do duty for one's morality as a citizen." Rather, we must consider how our individual acts participate in larger social contexts, contexts that may imbue our efforts with consequences we did not intend. He illustrates this point with a brutal pastoral metaphor that strikes at the heart of a narrow professionalism: "The shepherd, *qua* shepherd, acts for the good of the sheep, to protect them from discomfiture and harm. But he may be 'identified' with a project that is raising the sheep for market." Burke, for example, often critiques the complicity between science and the military-industrial complex: one can be an excellent physicist, in terms of technical proficiency, and yet be helping to create weapons of mass murder. The need to rethink individual responsibility, Burke repeatedly reminds us, has become imperative in our time, the "extreme division of labor under late capitalist liberalism having made dispersion the norm and having transformed the state of Babel into an ideal," making it increasingly easy to absolve one's self of any broad responsibility, even as the destructive power of technology has made it increasingly urgent that people confront injustice and conflict in a peaceful fashion.[32]

Burke here shares Mumford's concern over the dangers posed by modern technology while moving beyond Mumford's reactionary response to those dangers.[33] Burke acknowledges that the "generic divisiveness" inherent in humankind's nature as a "symbol-using animal" is exacerbated by the "state of high occupational diversity" existing in modern industrial societies—communist as well as capitalist. Yet instead of imagining (as Mumford does) a self that imaginatively transcends the material conditions of modern society, Burke pragmatically envisions an ethical self that is capable of dealing with such divisions. To view people as inevitably existing in a state of social division, Burke argues, need not require us to see humans as essentially alienated, combative, or deceptive: we may also choose to see people as essentially *rhetorical*—as "humane word-slingers" committed to "persuasion by words, rather than by force."[34]

The complex and divisive social context of our individual acts, Burke insists, requires a "comic" ethics. Both comedy and tragedy provide ways of understanding human limitation, but, Burke stresses, they differ crucially in their attitudes toward individualism. Tragedy, which he links to historical eras of nascent individualism, portrays human limitation in relation to natural and supernatural forces such as "fate" or "the Gods," viewing individualism—and its attendant ethical blindnesses—in terms of criminal transgression or "hubris." In contrast, comedy deals with the limitations of "man in society": it analyzes human motives with "the maximum of forensic complexity" required by "sophisticated social structures," viewing individualization as an inescapable result of the diversity of social roles and positions[35]:

> The progress of humane enlightenment can go no further than in picturing people as not *vicious* but as *mistaken*. When you add that people are *necessarily* mistaken, that *all* people are exposed to situations in which they must act as fools, that *every* insight contains its own special kind of blindness, you complete the comic circle, returning again to the lesson of humility that underlies great tragedy.[36]

A comic awareness of human limitation endorses a pluralistic tolerance of diversity and conflict. Every social position has its own special kind of blindness: thus, people are "necessarily mistaken," but not necessarily "vicious." Our conflicts with others do not result only from overt ill will: the diversity of occupation and lifestyle inherent in culture ensures that people will have different and conflicting needs. Accordingly, a comic ethics provides a mandate for rhetoric, for confronting our differences and communicating across them: it encourages "charitability" toward the motives of those who differ from us—indeed, the alternative is an assumption of universal cunning and hypocrisy that would make social cooperation impossible. However, Burke also insists that charitability must not be "gullibility": we must denounce overt deception and oppression, and crucially, we must strive to recognize how our own social position may subtly implicate us in conflicts with others. Burke's concept of "identification" combines these dual rhetorical responsibilities: we must "identify" with others across social divisions, while also confronting how our own position may "identify" us with divisive social forces—like the shepherd who is "identified" with the slaughterhouse.[37]

If Burke provides a rationale for critiquing those moments in Emerson that seem to assert the moral autonomy of individual action, his comic ethics at the same time extend a pragmatic tradition leading back, through William James, to Emerson. In *Attitudes toward History*, Burke argues that Emerson, Whitman, and James offer "perhaps the three most well-rounded . . . frames of acceptance in American literature." Frames of acceptance are ways of describing and approaching reality: they "name both friendly and unfriendly forces" and "fix attitudes that prepare for combat." A frame of acceptance is "not the same as *passiveness*," Burke insists, for it articulates attitudes of both acceptance and rejection, saying "yes" and saying "no," naming those things we can or must accept and those we can or must struggle to change. For Burke, pragmatism exemplifies a "well-rounded" frame because it refuses to accept limitation without also affirming our ability to act in response to those limits—an attitude he locates in the Jamesian motto that "Where resignation *must* be, it will be 'provisional' . . . afford[ing] 'ground and leisure to advance to new philanthropic action.'" This activist attitude closely parallels the logic of Emerson's essay "Fate" discussed above and, indeed, Burke cites Emerson as a precursor to James. Emerson's doctrine of "compensation"—the idea that "in all evil, there is inevitably some compensatory good"—does not ignore evil, Burke argues, but articulates a pragmatic response to evil, a "project for living" that views the limits of our world as occasions for action: "Calamities arise, and by compensation, they force us to turn them into benefits, lest we perish."[38]

It is a desire to strike a pragmatic stance of acceptance and rejection towards the ethical blindnesses of individualism that motivates Burke's comic balance between "charitability" and "gullibility." To accept charitably that all individuals are "necessarily mistaken"—implicated in social conflicts of which they are unaware—is not simply to excuse or exonerate them. Precisely the opposite is true: the comic frame, by insisting that individuals are always in danger of being mistaken, obligates us to scrutinize the various ways our lives are "identified" in larger social contexts. Burke pragmatically "accepts" the inevitability of social conflicts in order to adopt an activist mandate of confronting and resolving those conflicts: his comic frame "promotes the realistic sense of one's limitations, . . . yet the acceptance is not passive."[39] Indeed, the Emersonian roots of Burke's comic ethics become evident when one compares his view of people as necessarily mistaken to Emerson's description of the individual in "Experience":

> The individual is always mistaken. He designed many things, and drew in other persons as coadjutors, quarrelled with some or all, blundered much, and something is done; all are a little advanced, but the individual is always mistaken. It turns out somewhat new, and very unlike what he promised himself.[40]

While Emerson is capable of brazenly asserting that "I may . . . absolve me to myself," he is also—as this passage from "Experience" shows—acutely conscious of the ways in which the individual's actions participate in larger social processes of change over which no individual has complete control. If Burke rejects the former Emersonian mood, his comic ethics still extend the Emersonian project of critically analyzing the inescapably social context of individual action.

Ellison perhaps most clearly illustrates his affiliation to the individualist ethics of both Emerson and Burke in a speech he delivered to Harvard alumni in 1974. Ellison opens by expressing his uncanny sense of the ironies involved in speaking at the university where his literary namesake delivered the famous Divinity School address, an unease compounded, Ellison reports, when "I received a letter from Harvard addressed to Ralph Waldo Emerson! Lord but what tenacious memories you Harvards have!"[41] This anecdote provides a winning humorous gambit to warm up the audience, but lurking in the joke is a serious point about the relationships between individuals, and across social divisions, in a pluralistic society:

> Now that I stand before you, how fortunate for me that my unmistakable pigmentation shines forth no less as sign than as symbol. I assure you that even though I've insisted for years that our American obsession with practical joking was originally not intentional, but arose out of the incongruities abounding in a man-and-mammy-made society set up within an unexplored and alien land, it was still somewhat shocking to find, under the most decorous of circumstances, the image of a Negro American made to show forth through the ghostly (and I hope benign) lineaments of a white philosopher and poet.[42]

This striking image of double-consciousness, Ellison's "Negro" face "showing forth" through Emerson's "ghostly lineaments," abounds in possible meanings. We hear a writer expressing his sense of appropriating a precursor's voice or, more uncomfortably, having that precursor speak through him—an anxiety of influence here complicated by race. Following Houston Baker's lead, we can hear Ellison self-consciously donning a "Western critical mask" in his pronouncements about literature. Above all, one hears Ellison's sense of the unexpected intersections of identity in America's pluralistic culture: what "show[s] forth" in this image is not only the stubborn perception of race that divides Ellison from Emerson, but also the shared aspects of cultural identity that reach across racial categories. Ellison's "shock" is a shock of recognition, for his connection to Emerson aptly reflects the democratic and individualist ideals shared by the two writers, ideals that led African-American fathers to name their sons Ralph Waldo. "There were, and are, a number of [Negro youngsters] named Waldo," Ellison notes in "The Novel as a

Function of American Democracy": and, "amusing as this is, it reveals something of how the insight and values of literature get past the usual barriers in society and seep below the expected levels."[43]

Ellison uses his uncanny affiliation with Emerson as an opening example of the complex social relationships that any truly democratic individualist ethics must take into account. A recurrent theme in Ellison's work is that if America is ever to fulfill its democratic promise, individuals will need to recognize more fully how they are connected to each other—both by the social relations of inequality that create conflict, and by the shared democratic ideals that might spur us to remedy those inequities. Ellison's Harvard speech invokes such connections, exemplified in the memorial to Harvard's Civil War dead that links Ellison and his audience in the unfinished struggle for civil rights. This vision of America embodies the social complexity of Burke's comic frame—and its potential for conflict and miscommunication: "Such mysteries arise out of the difficulty of communicating across the hierarchical divisions of American society, and a great deal of our misunderstanding springs from our failures of communication."[44]

Similarly, as Ellison describes the individualist ethics required by this pluralistic complexity, he explains his connection to Emerson in terms that closely parallel Burke's comic and tragic frames. Much as Burke warns that insidious motives can be "identified" with seemingly benign acts, so Ellison also focuses on the potential ethical blindnesses of individualism. Discussing the familiar notion of "American innocence" often applied to Emerson—the "tendency to ignore the evil which can spring from our good intentions"—Ellison argues that "innocence" is a misnomer for the ethical dilemmas of individualism, which are better understood in a tragic terminology of "hubris" and "nemesis." Crucially, however, Ellison is not rehearsing the commonplace that Emerson naively ignores evil. On the contrary, he insists that "neither tragic arrogance nor insolence is limited to Americans": echoing Burke's comic assumption of inevitable "mistakenness," Ellison asserts that "these flaws arise from the nature of the human animal and from the limitations encountered by human consciousness when asserting itself against the vast multiplicity of the universe." Moreover, while he admits that Emersonian individualism is liable to this human "forgetfulness [that] leaves us vulnerable to *nemesis*," he twice cites Emerson as exemplifying the "conscience," "consciousness," and "conscientiousness" that offers the only remedy to such ethical lapses:[45]

[R]emember that the antidote to *hubris*, to overweening pride, is irony, that capacity to discover and systematize clear ideas. Or, as Emerson insisted, the development of consciousness, consciousness, *consciousness*. And with consciousness, a more refined conscientiousness, and most of all, that tolerance which takes the form of humor, for when Americans can no longer laugh at each other, they have to fight one another.[46]

Revealing his close affinity to Burke, Ellison here asserts that the best ethical response to the potentially tragic results of our human limitations is a comic "consciousness" of the complexity of human motives, with its accompanying humorous "tolerance" (Burke's charitability) towards conflict. Even as Ellison warns against the threat of ethical blindness implicit in a narrowly construed Emersonian individualism, he lays claim to an Emersonian sense of the complexity of the individual's social implication—affiliating himself with the Emerson who knew that "the individual is always mistaken," or, in Ellison's words, the Emerson who was well "aware of the labyrinth in which Americans walk."[47]

Ellison's use of a Burkean terminology of tragedy and comedy to discuss Emerson suggests that our reading of *Invisible Man*'s parody of Emerson should be informed by Ellison's claim that his fiction expresses a "tragicomic"[48] attitude toward life:

There is a value for the writer in trying to give as thorough a report of social reality as possible. . . . [T]he small share of reality which each of our diverse groups is able to snatch from the whirling chaos of history belongs not to the group alone, but to all of us. It is a property and a witness which can be ignored only to the danger of the entire nation.[49]

Ellison's mandate to give "as thorough a report of social reality as possible" is a tragic ethic of self-expression in the Emersonian vein, locating value in the character we achieve in a struggle against the resistances of our environment. In his essays and interviews, Ellison repeatedly voices the deeply Emersonian idea that expressing the complexity of one's experience is a moral duty that requires nonconformism. "I learned that nothing could go unchallenged," he relates, especially the "formulas" of "historians, politicians, sociologists," and even the "older generation of Negro leaders and writers," formulas which threatened to "deprive both humanity and culture of their complexity."[50] By expressing the particularity of one's individual and communal experience, one can disrupt the

totalizing ideological narratives which would render that experience invisible. Ellison here revises Emerson by broadening self-expression into
an act of social communication and political assertion. Self-expression
is a way to take personal responsibility for making one's own invisibility
visible; it is also a social act that reveals the reciprocity of human responsibility. To make one's own invisibility visible is to challenge others
to "see" that invisibility and acknowledge how their identity and social
position depend on the invisibility of others. Here Ellison, like Burke,
adds a social, or "comic," component to his individualist ethics, insisting
that self-expression must serve as an act of political communication: it is
a "property and witness" that "belongs not to the group alone," a reality
that all in a democratic society must acknowledge.

Invisible Man charts its narrator's progression toward this tragicomic model of self-expression, a progression that can be traced in
the narrator's relationship with Mr. Norton. As Ellison observes in his
"Working Notes for Invisible Man," Jim Trueblood—the farmer whose
tale of incest forces Norton and the narrator to retreat to the Golden
Day bordello—serves as one model of a possible "tragicomic" attitude
and as an indicator of how far Norton and the narrator must travel
to achieve a more accurate knowledge of themselves and their relation
to one another. "Life is either tragic or absurd," Ellison claims, "but
Norton and the boy have no capacity to deal with such ambivalence."[51]
Houston Baker has argued that Trueblood's tragicomic ambivalence
lies in his status as a trickster/blues figure who rejects the logic of guilt
and punishment/castration implicit in the dominant Western tragic
myths.[52] Trueblood's attitude towards his transgression is "comic" in
Burke's terms: seeing himself not as "vicious" but "mistaken," Trueblood gains comic insight into the complex social context of his act.
As Baker insists, the entire Trueblood episode is deeply implicated in
the socioeconomic relations of the Jim Crow South: Trueblood's incest
occurs, for example, because a lack of firewood has forced daughter
and parents to sleep together for warmth. Moreover, by telling his tale
for eager white audiences, Trueblood gains insight into—and even
some control over—the workings of race and class that define his social
situation. In rejecting the symbolic castration of mainstream Western
culture, Baker argues, Trueblood resists the social castration visited
on black men in Ellison's America.[53] Exploding Norton's placid vision of the "fate" connecting him to African-Americans, Trueblood's

tragicomic tale exposes the reality of race relations existing behind the college's ideology of racial uplift.

Yet Trueblood is a problematic model of tragicomic ethics, for, as Baker acknowledges, he gains his insight and control only by donning a minstrel mask for his white auditors, playing a stereotype whose function, Ellison insisted, "was to veil the humanity of Negroes" and thereby "repress the white audience's awareness of its moral identification with its own acts and with the human ambiguities pushed behind the mask."[54] The resonances between Ellison's and Burke's terminology here are salient: an attitude which allows people to obscure how their acts "identify" them with others is an ethical failure. Baker reads Trueblood's shortcomings as Ellison's acknowledgment that it is perhaps impossible for the African-American artist to escape such compromises—that there is no pure space for African-American expression free of the distortions of the market and racism. Baker's argument here is very convincing. Indeed, Ellison's narrator comes to learn that even in his heady career as a political orator he has not escaped Trueblood's dilemma: like Trueblood's tale, the narrator's speeches are manipulated for the purposes of a white audience (the Brotherhood's leadership). Yet Baker's conclusion does not take into account the fact that Ellison's narrator does attempt, in his final confrontation with Norton, an act of tragicomic expression that avoids the compromises of the minstrel mask.

The narrator's development in the novel can be read as a preparation for the tragicomic mode of action he adopts in his final encounter with Norton. The narrator learns that he must assert the particularity of his experience against the competing ideologies of racial uplift and economic determinism that he encountered at the black college and in his experience with the socialist "Brotherhood," respectively. This requires narrating how those ideologies rendered him "invisible"—he becomes visible only by naming his invisibility. The narrator's presence in the Prologue and Epilogue, as someone who has gained insight through narrating his experience, is the true culmination of the novel—a fact critics have often discussed,[55] and Ellison himself indicated by describing his narrator as progressing from "invisibility to visibility" and "from ranter to writer." Many readers have been troubled by the fact that this act of self-narration is also an act of "hibernation": the insight achieved through naming one's own invisibility seems to require an ironic detachment and paralysis. The narrator is driven "underground" by the bitter realization that even when he felt he was most effectively expressing the particular plight of the black community—as during his speech at Tod Clifton's funeral, or when he helped Harlem residents burn down the tenement in which they lived—his acts were manipulated and lost in larger political struggles. "I . . . had been a tool," he writes, "A tool just at the very moment I had thought myself free." Thus, despite his insistence that his "hibernation" is a "covert preparation for a more overt action," and despite his decision to emerge from his hole, his ironic awareness of his past invisibility seems to preclude future actions that would not involve him in a similar invisibility—a similar futility and vulnerability to manipulation. Indeed, the narrator acknowledges this possible connection between insight and paralysis, when he describes himself, as he enters his hibernation, as "caught like Trueblood's jaybird that yellow jackets had paralyzed in every part but his eyes."[56]

The narrator's claim that his act of self-narration does not lead to an ironic paralysis can be read, I want to suggest, as a pragmatic assertion that a tragicomic awareness of our human limits does not discourage action, but rather encourages us to act in response to those limits. As I argued above in relation to Emerson, a tragic attitude affirms that we express our humanity only by engaging the resistant world, even though such engagement implies a loss of autonomy. Ellison's narrator exemplifies this tragic view. The deepest despair of his hibernation is symbolized in a nightmare, in which Jack and the Brotherhood, Mr. Emerson, Norton, and Bledsoe—"*all of whom*," the narrator says, "*had run me*" and "attempt[ed] to force [their] picture of reality upon me"—make the narrator "*free of illusions*" by castrating him. This dream suggests that one cannot escape illusion simply by avoiding action: one could avoid illusion only if one could be stripped (castrated) of all human desire. Thus the narrator finds it impossible to remain in an ironic detachment: "I couldn't be still even in hibernation. Because, damn it, there's the mind, *the mind*. It wouldn't let me rest." Being human *requires* acting, even though we know acting will involve us in blindnesses and embarrassments. The narrator accepts "all past humiliations" as "precious parts of my experience": to accept your particular history, even its humiliations, is to affirm the character you have developed in coping with that history.[57] Ellison here adopts the agonistic view of identity that is central to Emerson's ethic of self-reliance—the idea that "we must have an antagonism in the tough world for all the variety of our spiritual faculties, or they will not be born."

Yet Ellison, characteristically, stresses the social component of a democratic individualism. He insists that to accept a tragic history is also to align yourself with the resources of a particular cultural heritage—with a set of attitudes, styles, myths, symbols, rhetorical strategies, and political concerns:

> What I have tried to commemorate in fiction is that which I believe to be enduring and abiding in our situation, especially those human qualities which the American Negro has developed despite, and in rejection of, the obstacles and meannesses imposed on us. . . . [S]o much which we've gleaned through the harsh discipline of Negro American life is simply too precious to be lost. I speak of the faith, the patience, the humor, the sense of timing, the rugged sense of life and the manner of expressing it which all go to define the American Negro. These are some of the things through which we've confronted the obstacles and meannesses of which you speak, and which we dare not fail to adapt to changed conditions lest we destroy ourselves. . . . I am unwilling to see those values which I would celebrate in fiction as existing sheerly through terror; they are a result of a tragicomic confrontation of life.[58]

The tragic side of Ellison's tragicomic ethics is expressed in the view he takes here toward communal identity. He of course wants to eradicate the injustices imposed on African-Americans, but at the same time, he wants to celebrate and preserve the character, the cultural sensibility, forged in the experience of resisting those injustices. As a number of critics have noted,[59] and as Ellison always insisted, *Invisible Man* is not simply the story of the narrator's disastrous infatuation with the ideologies of racial uplift and socialism; it is also an exploration of the rich African-American traditions available to him, embodied by his grandfather, Trueblood, the Vet, Mary, Brother Tarp, Tod Clifton, Frederick Douglass, and Louis Armstrong, as well as the more troubling examples of Bledsoe, Rinehart, and Ras the Exhorter/Destroyer.

One characteristic of the African-American sensibility that Ellison valued highly was the ability to "suffer the injustice which race and color are used to excuse without losing sight of either the humanity of those who inflict that injustice or the motives, rational or irrational, out of which they act." This claim brings us to the "comic" side of Ellison's tragicomic ethics. In describing the African-American ability to confront racial conflict while acknowledging a human connection across that conflict, Ellison parallels Burke's definition of the "comic" balance between "charitability" and "gullibility." In fact, Ellison credited Burke with a large influence on the structure of *Invisible Man*, claiming that the narrator's development followed the Burkean progression from "purpose, to passion, to perception"—"purpose" being an act, "passion" the resistance or limitation that act meets, and "perception" the self-knowledge an actor gains in seeing the extent and limit of his or her act.[60]

Ellison's self-proclaimed debt to Burke is significant for what it suggests about the narrator's "hibernation" in *Invisible Man*.[61] Burke—in a passage Ellison himself quotes in his essay "An Extravagance of Laughter"—insists that the progression to a comic "perception" of the limits of every action does not lead to an ironic paralysis, but enables people to act more consciously. By becoming "student[s] of [themselves]" including on those "occasions when [they have] been tricked or cheated," people can be "*observers of themselves, while acting*"; the "ultimate" comic attitude "would not be *passiveness*, but *maximum consciousness*." Ellison's narrator echoes this logic, when he says: "I'm shaking off the old skin. . . . I'm coming out, no less invisible without it, but coming out nevertheless . . . since there's a possibility that even an invisible man has a socially responsible role to play."[62] In shaking off the skin of his old delusions, the narrator has accepted that new actions will risk new delusions; he will emerge "no less invisible," but more conscious of the invisibility against which he must struggle. The ironic consciousness that the narrator attains is not a sign of paralysis: instead, it signals his pragmatic acceptance that the self is never finished (much less absolute) but is a fluid and provisional work in progress—that continued growth can occur only through subsequent acts and the embarrassments they entail.

Instead of being a retreat from social action, the self-expression that Ellison's narrator achieves in his hibernation is, like Burke's "identification," a social act of communication, confrontation, and self-analysis. Ellison stresses this by including in his Epilogue one "overt action" that the narrator does undertake in his hibernation—his final confrontation of Mr. Norton.[63] Since it occurs in the subway, this action clearly depends on the ironic awareness the narrator has achieved "underground." In this prominent encounter, the narrator revises the notion of "fate" that Norton had espoused at the black college. Norton's assertion that his "destiny," as a philanthropist, depends on the success of those he helps, is not only transparently egocentric; more importantly, it reflects an ideology of social uplift that falsifies his true connection to the narrator. This ideology renders the narrator "invisible" because it ignores the reality of segregated America. It also effaces Norton's true identity, allowing him to deny how his status as a white industrialist implicates him in the systemic oppression of people like the narrator. In their final meeting, Norton, lost on the subway platform but too ashamed to ask a white person for directions, approaches the narrator, whom Norton does not remember:

> "Don't you know me?" I said.
> "Should I?" he said.
> "You see me?" I said, watching him tensely.
> "Why, of course—Sir, do you know the way to Centre Street?"
> "So. Last time it was the Golden Day, now it's Centre Street. You've retrenched, sir. But don't you really know who I am?"
> "Young man, I'm in a hurry," he said, cupping a hand to his ear. "Why should I know you?"
> "Because I'm your destiny."
> "My destiny, did you say?" He gave me a puzzled stare, backing away. "Young man, are you well? Which train did you say I should take?"
> "I didn't say," I said, shaking my head. "Now, aren't you ashamed?"
> "Ashamed? ASHAMED!" he said indignantly.
> I laughed, suddenly taken by the idea. "Because, Mr. Norton, if you don't know *where* you are, you probably don't know *who* you are. So you came to me out of shame. You are ashamed, now aren't you?"[64]

In this exchange—which ends with the narrator erupting in laughter and Norton escaping into a subway train—the narrator's response to Norton exemplifies a model of social connectedness that imposes responsibilities of communication and self-analysis on both parties. With the subway setting symbolizing the narrator's underground self-awareness and Norton's blindness, the narrator attempts to make Norton see the dynamic of invisibility that truly connects their destinies. By naming his invisibility, the narrator accepts the responsibility of self-expression: "after years of trying to adopt the opinions of others I finally rebelled. I am an *invisible* man."[65] Crucially, this act of self-expression imposes similar responsibilities of self- and social-awareness on Norton: Norton cannot know "who he is" until he acknowledges "where he is"—until he acknowledges how his social position is "identified," in Burke's sense, with the forces that render others invisible.

The narrator here displays Burke's comic balance of connection and confrontation, or, in Ellison's own terms, the dual ability to see the "injustice" and "humanity" of one's oppressor. Even in rejecting Norton's notion of "fate," he acknowledges that their identities are indeed connected. In one sense, he is approaching Norton in a spirit of kindness: he really is trying to help the lost Norton find his way, to know his true social and individual identity. This is no easy claim of democratic fraternity, but a complex assertion of the connection between oppressor and oppressed. As the narrator explains elsewhere in the Epilogue:

> I condemn and affirm, say no and say yes, say yes and say no. . . . I sell you no phony forgiveness, I'm a desperate man—but too much of your life will be lost, its meaning lost, unless you approach it as much through love as through hate. So I approach it through division. So I denounce and I defend and I hate and I love.[66]

The vocabulary of "yes and no" resounds throughout Invisible Man. The narrator learns the futility of saying "yes" to dominant ideologies—like Norton's and the Brotherhood's—that render him invisible, but when he attempts to sabotage the Brotherhood by following his grandfather's advice to "overcome 'em with yeses, undermine 'em with grins, agree 'em to death and destruction," the results are equally disastrous.[67] Trueblood's minstrel performance, as well as Bledsoe and the Vet, constitute other unsatisfactory models of "yessing" duplicity. The narrator's final confrontation of Norton offers an alternative to these strategies of duplicity, a way to say "yes" and "no" in a direct political act of communication—to assert the democratic connection of all American citizens and confront the systemic discrimination that separates us. Finally, this attempt to say "yes" and "no" echoes Burke's balance of acceptance and rejection, linking the ethics of Ellison's novel with a comic attitude that is "charitable" but not "gullible" in confronting social divisions and conflicts.

It is in this individualist ethics of self-expression, and not in the parodic figures of Mr. Norton and Mr. Emerson, that Ellison's most vital appropriation and rearticulation of Emerson lies. In "Twentieth Century Fiction and the Black Mask of Humanity," Ellison argues that American literature has failed to offer meaningful models of democratic individualism precisely because it too often has rendered invisible the humanity of those excluded from America's promise of freedom. Ellison asserts that the "individualist" impulse to rebel against society's constrictions and corruptions must be "dialectically" tempered by a "humanist" acceptance of the social order: specifically, the individual must accept his or her own responsibility for the social order and its injustices. As an example of such a balance, he cites the famous moment from *The Adventures of Huckleberry Finn* when Huck decides to "emancipate" Jim. By having Huck accept "the judgment of his superego—that internalized representation of the community—that his action is evil," Twain suggests that the individualist desire to reject the injustices of society is inescapably compromised by our profound implication in society: "Huck Finn's acceptance of the evil implicit in his 'emancipation' of Jim represents Twain's acceptance of his personal responsibility for the condition of society." All too frequently, Ellison claims, the social protest voiced by American literature remains "shallow" because it "seldom turns inward upon the writer's own values; almost always it focuses outward, upon some scapegoat with which he is seldom able to identify himself as Huck Finn identified himself with the scoundrels who stole Jim, and with Jim himself."[68] Ellison here insists that an individualist ethics must include Burkean acts of "identification." We can only understand our own democratic identity—our freedoms, our tyrannies, and our responsibilities—if we understand how our social position "identifies" us with social structures that oppress others: a truth that has found its most powerful symbol, Ellison argues, in the figure of the enslaved or disenfranchised African-American.

Ellison's discussion of American literature illuminates his dual attitude toward the possibilities of Emersonian individualism. On the one hand, he asserts that individualism must guard against a false sense of independence: he critiques the American tendency towards "[narrow] artistic individualism" that devolved, in writers such as Hemingway, into personalized myths of merely individual tragedy. *Invisible Man*'s parody denounces the Emerson appropriated by this tradition of individualism, which evades the historical and social connections that define the American self. Yet Ellison is simultaneously reclaiming a different Emerson: he lists Emerson as among those nineteenth-century American writers who were led by their commitment to individualism—by the "passion for personal freedom" and "revolt against the old moral authority"—to reconceive "the Negro as a symbol of Man."[69] Like Burke, Ellison is drawn to the Emerson whose obsession with "self-reliance" is based on the pragmatic insight that the individual's actions are always socially implicated and indebted. Ellison's writings suggest that the positive promise of American individualism can be realized only if the Emersonian ethic of nonconformist self-expression includes the political task of exploring

our connections to and conflicts with others—only if the danger of individualist "hubris" is tempered by an Emersonian ethic of "consciousness,
conscience, and conscientiousness." This tension is summed up in the
distance between Emerson's brazen claim, that "I may . . . absolve me to
myself," and the hard-won sense of democratic identity expressed by Ellison's narrator when he wonders, in the novel's famous closing line, "Who
knows but that, on the lower frequencies, I speak for you?"[70]

This echoing final question voiced by Ellison's narrator, and his assertion that "there's a possibility that even an invisible man has a socially
responsible role to play," provide fitting notes on which to end this study,
for these utterances encapsulate central insights about democratic individuality as it is reconceived in the pragmatic tradition I have traced out.
Ellison's challenge to his readers, to hear in the "lower frequencies" of his
narrator's voice a shared democratic fate, insists that selfhood is inherently relational: that our individual identities, shaped by the shared social
contexts in which we live, are fundamentally interconnected and interdependent. That the qualities of experience and selfhood other individuals achieve shape the social context that lends meaning to one's own acts
and self; that in cultivating a life that expresses one's own individuality,
one is inevitably speaking "for" and to others in one's communities; and
that the silencing or stunting of others' lives inescapably impoverishes
the moral meaning of our own lives. That the task of cultivating one's
self, and thereby contributing to the shared experiences of one's communities, entails an obligation to ensure that others enjoy opportunities
to play socially responsible roles that allow them to "speak" their selves
for themselves, and for and to us. And, finally, that, in James's terms, we
must listen for "the cries of the wounded" on those lower frequencies of
human interaction: must attend to the experiences and opportunities of
others who may—in obvious or in subtle, indirect ways—be excluded or
marginalized by our own activities.[71]

These ethical commitments of a pragmatic individualism constitute
a significant alternative to the dominant tradition of liberal individualism, which stresses independent, autonomous subjects pursuing personal fulfillment primarily defined by acquisition of material wealth and
liberation *from* public responsibilities. While the political Right valorizes this vision as the engine of economic enterprise and the antidote to

oppressive governmental regulation, and the Left decries it as a corrosive force that threatens our social fabric, pragmatic theorists of democratic individuality urge us to change radically the terms of debate. As I have stressed throughout this book, the keys to this alternative lie in the pluralism and experimentalism of pragmatism's ethical vision. A pluralistic model of experience describes selfhood as the process of interaction between a human creature and her environment: an educative process in which the habits that compose character are cultivated in and through our associations with others, and a transformative process in which an individual contributes to common efforts to remake her social and natural environments. Individuality, in its fullest sense, is not simply the sheer fact of personhood, but a quality of selfhood to be achieved—the successful cultivation of a self that realizes an individual's native gifts. Accordingly, pragmatism rejects classic liberal individualism's negative project of protecting "naturally" free individuals from "artificial" social constraints, and embraces the constructive project of creating forms of association that will help educate democratic individuals. As Dewey puts it, social arrangements are not merely "means for obtaining something for individuals," but "means of *creating* individuals." "Liberty is that secure release and fulfillment of personal potentialities which take place only in rich and manifold association with others," and so is found not in escape from social engagements (which is humanly impossible), but in persons replacing restricting forms of association for healthier ones in which "more of their individual potentialities will be released and their personal experience enriched."[72]

This transactional model of selfhood also leads pragmatists to reject those views that see individualism as inherently opposed to community or meaningful collective efforts at reform. Individuality, in the pragmatic tradition running from Emerson to Dewey and beyond, is a fundamental end and means of any democratic community. Providing individuals opportunities to cultivate their most vital selves is a primary moral standard by which a democratic society should be judged, and the diverse capacities of individuals provide elements of insight, imagination, initiative, and conscience necessary to revitalize a group's endeavors and remake its customs. In a very real sense, to deny some persons a "socially responsible role," to render them, like Ellison's narrator, "invisible," is not only to efface and stunt their individuality, but to impoverish the social context in which *all* individuals must pursue their lives. As Ellison insists, "the small share of reality which each of our diverse groups is able to snatch from the whirling chaos of history" is "a property and a witness" that "belongs not to the group alone, but to all of us."[73] In this sense, in his protest from and against his invisibility, Ellison's narrator does indeed speak for all.

If this pluralistic vision leads pragmatists to assert that cultivating individuality is a fundamental and enduring democratic commitment, their pluralism also leads them to an experimentalism which insists that our conceptions of individuality and democracy are themselves contingent, and must of necessity continue to evolve. Pluralism posits a moving, changing world, in which ideas, customs, and institutions developed in one set of circumstances inevitably grow obsolete in others; in which human actions transform conditions, an interaction that in turn re-acts to create new habits of human personality. A world, in short, in which both human nature and its environing conditions are substantially plastic. Our forms of social organization and governmental regulation, our ideals and values—including central principles like "democracy" and "individualism"—must all must be flexible and revisable to meet the conditions and demands of our changing world. Thus, to be a pragmatic individualist is to insist that individualism need not—indeed, inevitably *will not*—continue to mean what it has meant in the centuries between John Locke's time and our own. To the extent that we find the tenets of classic liberal individualism to be rigid, absolutist, or reactionary, we have an obligation *and* opportunity to create new conceptions and practices of democratic individuality. To conflate individualism-as-it-has-been with individualism-as-it-could- or will-be is to lapse into ahistorical absolutism. As Dewey puts it, to take "the bankruptcy of the older individualism" as an indication that "individualism were itself done and over with," to proceed "as if the only individualism were the local episode of the last two centuries," is to "slur over the chief problem—that of remaking society to serve the growth of a new type of individual."[74]

This experimentalist approach to the task of remaking individualism imposes rigorous ethical demands on communities and the individuals living within them. In stark contrast to the laissez-faire stance of classic liberalism, pragmatic individualism mandates that a democratic society must pursue an ongoing effort to remake—or reconstruct—all areas of human association in order to make them more democratic, more able to educate and liberate individuals' capacities by allowing them to participate meaningfully in the choice and pursuit of common ends. Conversely, individuals bear a responsibility to cultivate their own talents in a fashion that contributes to common goals—not trusting to the specious operations of an "invisible hand," but pursuing the dictates of one's own talents or genius, working to realize one's own dearest-held ideals, *and* attending conscientiously to the consequences our acts have upon others. Pragmatism holds to the fallibilist view that both individuals and communities are inevitably subject to mistakes and blindnesses. As James insists, we must never forget that in striving to realize our ideals we necessarily "butcher" other possibilities—perhaps cherished by other beings. Thus, as Dewey and Burke argue, we must conscientiously scrutinize how our acts impact others, and adopt a charitable (but not gullible) comic tolerance when others are blind *to us*. Moreover, since a pluralist experimentalism requires that morality be reflective, not customary, that the goodness of a community's customs and ideals must be continually reevaluated in the trials of experience, democratic selves must be ready to follow the dictates of individual conscience against conventional moralities when those become sources of injustice. Hence, Emerson's or Ellison's emphasis on nonconformist individuality harmonizes, in ways not usually acknowledged, with Dewey's definition of democracy-as-community.

The enduring appeal of this pragmatic approach lies in the fact that it both soberly acknowledges the scope of the task before us, and affirms in melioristic terms the sufficient meaning and success to be gained in engaging that task. Creating a vital democracy, and a truly democratic individualism, requires nothing less than reconstructing all areas of human association—economic, governmental, political, educational, familial, sexual, etc.—and in the process creating new forms of human personality. Moreover, as Dewey acknowledges, our best efforts will never fully realize the democratic ideal. Yet the function of ideals, from a pragmatic view, is to serve as goals that redirect and refocus our present activity, imbuing it with new purpose, quality, and meaning. If ideals such as democracy, liberty, and individuality are never fully achieved, they *are* realized in the liberation of capacity, the exercise of self-determining choice, and the growth of socially shared meaning that individuals enjoy by enlisting their individual talents in cooperative efforts. As Dewey asserts, "We use the foresight of the future to refine and expand present activity," and "in this use of desire, deliberation and choice, freedom is actualized."[75] When a person engages the problems and possibilities of the situation in which he finds himself, and strives to realize ends consonant with the common good, he begins to attain or recover what Dewey terms an "integrated" individuality—integrated both into a meaningful relation with environing conditions, and into the shared experience of the groups in which he lives.[76] This hope for a recovered individuality can be heard in the voice of Ellison's narrator when he resolves, despite his repeated humiliations and effacements, to leave his hibernation for new engagements: "I'm shaking off the old skin. . . . I'm coming out, no less invisible without it, but coming out nevertheless . . . since there's a possibility that even an invisible man has a socially responsible role to play." This melioristic faith in the sufficient value we find in our ability to change and grow reaches back to Emerson's injunction that we should seek power in transition and becoming; in his exhortation to "Trust thyself," by engaging "the place the divine providence has found for you, the society of your contemporaries, the connection of events"; and in his affirmation that the person willing to commit his or her self to new ventures and their risks of failure "does not postpone his life, but lives already."[77]

While they offer us no fixed vision of what a reconstructed individualism or democracy would look like—for these always remain to be remade to meet the changing needs of our lives and world—the proponents of a pragmatic individualism do assure us of our ability to recover a more vital, integrated individuality by engaging democratic and experimental efforts to remake the conditions of our lives. Moreover, as we face the constraints posed by the legacy of liberal individualism, they would teach us that there is no way out but through: so long as we retain a democratic commitment to the value of individuality, we have no option but to reconsider how a new individualism might be forged *out of* our present, *in* our future. And so long as we fail to use the full resources of experimental inquiry and shared endeavor to create more fully democratic communities in which individuals can thrive, we will still remain under Emerson's indictment that individualism "has never been tried." As we do take up the task, we will find in the pragmatic tradition from Emerson to Ellison both a resource and a provocation.

Notes

In citing works in the notes, short titles have generally been used after the first reference to a text. Works frequently cited have been identified by the following abbreviations:

E&L   Ralph Waldo Emerson, *Essays and Lectures* (New York: Library of America, 1983).

CE   Ralph Ellison, *The Collected Essays of Ralph Ellison*, ed. John F. Callahan (New York: Modern Library, 1995).

IM   Ralph Ellison, *Invisible Man* (New York: Random House 1972 [1952]).

JMN   *The Journals and Miscellaneous Notebooks of Ralph Waldo Emerson*, ed. William H. Gilman, *et al.*, 16 vols. (Cambridge, Ma.: Harvard University Press, 1960–82).

LW   *John Dewey: The Later Works: 1925–1953*, ed. Jo Ann Boydston, 17 vols. (Carbondale: Southern Illinois University Press, 1981–90).

MW   *John Dewey: The Middle Works: 1899–1924*, ed. Jo Ann Boydston, 15 vols. (Carbondale and Edwardsville: Southern Illinois University Press, 1976–83).

W1878   *William James, Writings 1878–1899* (New York: Library of America, 1992).

W1902   *William James, Writings 1902–1910* (New York: Library of America, 1987).

INTRODUCTION: "INDIVIDUALISM HAS NEVER BEEN TRIED":
TOWARD A PRAGMATIC INDIVIDUALISM

1. The epigraphs for this chapter are taken from the following: Alexis de Tocqueville, *Democracy in America*, abr. ed., ed. Thomas Bender, trans. Henry Reeve, as revised by Frances Bowen and Phillips Bradley (New York: Modern Library, 1981 [1945]), 395. William James, notes for 1905 lecture series "Characteristics of an Individualistic Philosophy," quoted in Robert D. Richardson, *William James: In the Maelstrom of American Modernism*

(Boston: Houghton Mifflin, 2006), 459. John Dewey, *Individualism Old and New*, in *LW*, 5:80. Ralph Waldo Emerson, *JMN*, 10:154.

2. As I drafted this introduction, in September 2009, President Obama had just delivered a speech to the joint houses of Congress on health care reform, in which he argued for retaining the healthy individualistic skepticism toward big government solutions, while also arguing that at times large collective efforts at regulation are necessary. In this sense, Obama is articulating a flexible and pragmatic approach that is broadly in the spirit of the experimentalism described in this introduction (and throughout this study), although I would not claim that Obama's vision is specifically pragmatic in the senses I draw from writers like Emerson, James, and Dewey. For more specific considerations of whether Obama's politics align with the school of American pragmatic philosophy, see Michael Eldridge, "Barack Obama's Pragmatism," http://www.obamaspragmatism.info/ (accessed 30 September 2009), and James T. Kloppenberg, *Reading Obama: Dreams, Hope, and the American Political Tradition* (Princeton, N.J.: Princeton University Press, 2010). As I revise this introduction, fresh evidence of how the Right, by contrast, deploys the rhetorical power of individualism in a dogmatic stance against government regulation appears in the official Republican response to Obama's 2011 State of the Union address, in which Rep. Paul Ryan asserted that "'the pursuit of happiness' depends upon individual liberty; and individual liberty requires limited government" ("Republican Response to State of the Union Address," *The Washington Post*, www.washingtonpost.com/wp-dyn/content/article/2011/01/25/AR2011012506905.html [accessed 25 January 2011]).

3. In Dewey's terms, everything is a process or "event," one particular career of interactions occurring in relation to myriad other processes of interaction. See my chapter 4.

4. William James, *Pragmatism*, in *W1902*, 601.

5. For a discussion of James's theory of truth, see my chapter 3.

6. William James, *The Principles of Psychology*, 2 vols. (New York: Dover, 1950 [1890]), 2:368.

7. John Dewey, *Reconstruction in Philosophy*, in *MW*, 12:186.

8. See note 8 to chapter 4, below.

9. "The person who holds the doctrine of 'individualism' or 'collectivism,'" Dewey argues, "has his program determined in advance," and indulges in an absolutism that "appl[ies] a hard and fast doctrine which follows logically from his preconception of the nature of ultimate causes" and thereby abdicating the "responsibility of discovering the concrete correlation of changes . . . and events through their complicated careers" (John Dewey, *The Public and Its Problems*, in *LW*, 2:361).

10. Ralph Waldo Emerson, "Man the Reformer," in *E&L*, 146.

11. This key verb is deployed by Locke in section 127 of "Of the Ends of Political Society and Government" (chapter 9, book 2 of his *Two Treatises of Government*, ed. Peter Laslett [Cambridge: Cambridge University Press, 1963], 369). The key sections of book 2 that outline the metaphysical and political argument I summarize here are chapters 2, 5, and 7–9. The critique I outline here is articulated by Dewey. See my fuller discussion in chapter 5.

12. For example, see in note 2 above the classic liberal axiom that equates individual liberty with limited government, as asserted by Republican representative Paul Ryan.

13. Dewey, *Public and Its Problems*, 340; *Individualism Old and New*, 48–49.

14. John Dewey and James H. Tufts, *Ethics*, in *LW*, 7:335.

15. A recent study that parallels my central contention that a viable model of individualist ethics can be distinguished from, and against, classic liberal individualism is Kwame Anthony Appiah's *The Ethics of Identity* (Princeton, N.J.: Princeton University Press, 2005). Appiah locates in the liberalism of John Stuart Mill several key concepts that also characterize the Emersonian-pragmatic tradition I explore: namely, the assertion that individuality is not merely a means, but a primary social good or end; the critique of an inherent opposition between individual and society; the assertion that the self is inherently social and relational; the belief that individuality (individual liberty, fulfillment, happiness) necessarily includes relationships and obligations to others; and, lastly, the conviction that the role of the state is not merely to safeguard a preexisting individual liberty, but more positively to provide individuals with the means of self-cultivation. See chapter 1, "The Ethics of Individuality." That Appiah's ethics, derived from Mill, should in important ways parallel the American tradition I explore helps explain why William James dedicated *Pragmatism* to Mill.

16. Tocqueville, *Democracy in America*, 397, 395.

17. The relevant sections in which Tocqueville articulates this central argument are the second book, chapters 2, 4, 5, and 15.

18. Ibid., 400, 402.

19. Ibid., 137–8.

20. Ibid., 416, 417, 416, 143–4.

21. The book's title is itself drawn from Tocqueville. See Robert N. Bellah, Richard Madsen, William M. Sullivan, Ann Swidler, and Steven M. Tipton, *Habits of the Heart: Individualism and Commitment in American Life* (Berkeley: University of California Press, 1985), 37. For Tocqueville's original use of this phrase, see *Democracy in America*, 179.

22. Bellah, et al., *Habits of the Heart*, viii, 143, 51.

23. Indeed, Bellah lauds the tradition of classic American philosophy, from Charles Peirce and Dewey to W. E. B. Du Bois, Jane Addams, and Charlotte Perkins Gilman, for a social realism that asserts the primacy of association and thereby rejects the ontological individualism of Lockean liberalism. Bellah even acknowledges that James was a trenchant critic of Lockean model of self-interest. See *The Good Society* (New York: Knopf, 1991), 294–95. (By contrast, Bellah's treatment of Emerson is reductive and dismissive. See *Habits of the Heart*, 55–56.) It is significant, for the purposes of the contrast I draw between pragmatism and Bellah's brand of communitarianism, that while Bellah cites Dewey for his affirmation of community, he does not note or stress either Dewey's emphasis on the process of inquiry nor the individualistic strands of Dewey's vision of community.

24. Robert N. Bellah, "The Vocation of a Christian University in a Globalized World," in *Prism*, vol. 5 (Tacoma, WA: Humanities Division of Pacific Lutheran University, 2002), 6–8.

25. Ibid., 7; Bellah, et al., *Habits of the Heart*, 283, 142.

26. This line of argument from *The Public and Its Problems* is discussed in my chapter 5.

27. Indeed, George Kateb has offered an even more trenchant argument that communitarian critiques of individualism are inherently antidemocratic. Kateb locates democratic individualism (as a "normative doctrine" that informs a "set of practices") in the Athenian claim that "all people—at least all citizens—count or matter apart from their roles, functions, or place in society," and locates this "central individualist idea" as well in Emerson's affirmations that "a self is more than role or function or place and that therefore one may take on many roles experimentally," and that "there is a self beyond even these engagements, a self that at last carves out an area for its distinctive work and busies itself above all in the receptive and appreciative apprehension of experience." Asserting that such individualist beliefs are inherent to democracy, and that communitarians espouse an opposing normative belief—one that praises "tradition" and "authority" and asserts that "individuals exist for society, not the reverse"—Kateb argues that communitarian critiques of individualism voiced by Bellah, Christopher Lasch, Alasdair MacIntyre, Michael Sandel, Charles Taylor, and Michael Walzer, are "antidemocratic, even though the thinkers I have mentioned would deny that imputation." Specifically, he rejects their shared communitarian "supposition that democracy could exist without individualism . . . that individualism could disappear or be drastically purged and democracy still remain and grow ever stronger." Kateb concludes that "the value of communitarian critics is not to offer supplementary values but rather to provoke disquiet with individualist values and to further the attempt to refine

them. Communitarian values cannot be absorbed into democracy without compromising democracy, but they can help to diminish complacency. The work of refining democratic individualism is not the business of communitarians" (George Kateb, "Democratic Individualism and Its Critics," *Annual Review of Political Science* 6 [June 2003]: 275, 279, 300–304).

28. See Reinhold Niebuhr, *The Self and the Dramas of History* (New York: Scribner's, 1955), 137–38; John Patrick Diggins, *The Promise of Pragmatism: Modernism and the Crisis of Knowledge and Authority* (Chicago: University of Chicago Press, 1994); and Cornel West, *The American Evasion of Philosophy: A Genealogy of Pragmatism* (Madison: University of Wisconsin Press, 1989). For a defense of Dewey's vision of human nature, and his subsequent politics, against such criticisms, see my chapter 4. For a discussion of West's critiques of Emerson and James, see my chapters 2 and 3.

29. Lewis Mumford and Randolph Bourne voiced the most influential versions of these indictments. See Lewis Mumford, *The Golden Day: A Study in American Experience and Culture* (New York: Boni and Liveright, 1926); and Randolph Bourne, "The Twilight of the Idols," in *The Radical Will: Selected Writings, 1911–1918*, ed. Olaf Hansen (Berkeley: University of California Press, 1977), 336–48. See my chapter 5 for a discussion of Dewey's politics in relation to Mumford. For a discussion of Ellison's parody of Mumford's version of Emersonianism, see chapter 6.

30. William James, "The Moral Philosopher and the Moral Life," in *W1878*, 609.

31. James, *Pragmatism*, 611.

32. Dewey, *Public and Its Problems*, 328. See my chapter 4 for a discussion of this link from Emerson to Dewey. For an example of a typical (and typically reductive) reading of self-reliance as undermining community, see Bellah, et al., *Habits of the Heart*, 55–56, 81.

33. See, for example: M. C. Otto, "On a Certain Blindness in William James," *Ethics* 53:3 (April 1943): 184–91; James Campbell, *The Community Reconstructs: The Meaning of Pragmatic Social Thought* (Champaign: University of Illinois Press, 1992); and West's *American Evasion of Philosophy*. For a discussion of Campbell and Otto's opposition of James's individualism versus Dewey's politics, see my chapter 3.

34. Ralph Waldo Emerson, "The American Scholar," in *E&L*, 62.

1. WHAT'S THE USE OF READING EMERSON PRAGMATICALLY?: THE EXAMPLE OF WILLIAM JAMES

1. William James, *Pragmatism*, in *W1902*, 487.

2. Though this chapter primarily focuses on James and Emerson, let me note in passing the following definition of philosophy from John Dewey's

essay "Philosophy and Democracy": "philosophy is a form of desire, of effort at action—a love, namely of wisdom; . . . it is an intellectualized wish, an aspiration subjected to rational discriminations and tests, a social hope reduced to a working program of action. . . . By wisdom we mean not systematic and proved knowledge of fact and truth, but a conviction about moral values, a sense for the better kind of life to be led. Wisdom is a moral term. . . . As a moral term it refers to a choice about something to be done, a preference for living this sort of life rather than that. It refers not to accomplished reality but to a desired future which our desires, when translated into articulate conviction, may help bring into existence" (*MW*, 11:43–44).

3. Ralph Waldo Emerson, "Fate," in *E&L*, 943.

4. James, *Pragmatism*, 542.

5. See Michael Lopez, *Emerson and Power: Creative Antagonism in the Nineteenth Century* (Dekalb: Northern Illinois University Press, 1996), 3–52; and Charles E. Mitchell, *Individualism and Its Discontents: Appropriations of Emerson, 1880–1950* (Amherst: University of Massachusetts Press, 1997), 1–72.

6. Mitchell, *Individualism and Its Discontents*, 35.

7. For a discussion of Mumford's portrayal of Emerson, see my chapter 6. For a broader discussion of Mumford as a critic of William James's pragmatism, see James Livingston, *Pragmatism and the Political Economy of Cultural Revolution, 1850–1940* (Chapel Hill: University of North Carolina Press, 1994), 225–55.

8. Herman Melville, marginalia in personal copy of Emerson's *Essays, Second Series*, in *The Portable Melville* (New York: Viking, 1952), 600–601. Henry James, "Emerson," in *The American Essays of Henry James*, ed. Leon Edel (Princeton, N.J.: Princeton University Press, 1989 [1956]), 51–76. George Santayana, "Emerson," in *Emerson: A Collection of Critical Essays*, ed. Milton R. Konvitz and Stephen E. Whicher (Englewood Cliffs, N.J.: Prentice-Hall, 1962), 31–8, and "The Genteel Tradition in American Philosophy," in *Pragmatism and Classical American Philosophy*, 2nd ed., ed. John J. Stuhr (New York: Oxford University Press, 2000), 348–59. Van Wyck Brooks, *America's Coming of Age* (New York: Huebsch, 1915). Irving Howe, *The American Newness: Culture and Politics in the Age of Emerson* (Cambridge, Ma.: Harvard University Press, 1986). David Marr, *American Worlds since Emerson* (Amherst: University of Massachusetts Press, 1988). John Updike, "Emersonianism," in *Odd Jobs: Essays and Criticism* (New York: Knopf, 1991), 148–68. Lopez and Mitchell insightfully survey many of these various critics' responses to Emerson: on Henry James and Santayana, see *Emerson and Power*, 30–38; on T. S. Eliot, see *Individualism and Its Discontents*, 6, and *Emerson and Power*, 20, 24; on Brooks, see *Individualism and Its Discontents*, 49–52; on Howe see *Emerson and Power*, 24; on Updike, see *Emerson and*

Power, 19, 76, and *Individualism and Its Discontents,* 189–90. On Giamatti, see *Emerson and Power,* 122–23.

9. Stephen E. Whicher, *Freedom and Fate: An Inner Life of Ralph Waldo Emerson* (Philadelphia: University of Pennsylvania Press, 1953).

10. Sacvan Bercovitch, "Emerson, Individualism, and the Ambiguity of Dissent," *South Atlantic Quarterly* 89 (1990): 623–62. Robert Milder has replicated a similar dichotomy by positing Emerson's transformation from a "social revolutionary" of the nonconformist variety, in his earlier writings, to a "liberal accomodationist" and "laissez-faire apologist" in his later writings. See "The Radical Emerson?" in *The Cambridge Companion to Ralph Waldo Emerson,* ed. Joel Porte and Saundra Morris (New York: Cambridge University Press, 1999), 51, 67. Myra Jehlen, *American Incarnation: The Individual, the Nation, and the Continent* (Cambridge, Ma.: Harvard University Press, 1986), 85, 108–110. Christopher Newfield, *The Emerson Effect: Individualism and Submission in America* (Chicago: University of Chicago Press, 1996). Dana Nelson, "Representative/Democracy," paper delivered at the Modern Language Association Convention, 30 December 1998, San Francisco. Richard F. Teichgraeber III, *Sublime Thoughts and Penny Wisdom: Situating Emerson and Thoreau in the American Market* (Baltimore: Johns Hopkins University Press, 1995), xvi.

11. Kenneth Burke, *Attitudes toward History* (Los Altos, Ca.: Hermes, 1959 [1937]); *A Grammar of Motives* (Berkeley: University of California Press, 1969 [1945]); and "I, Eye, Ay—Emerson's Early Essay 'Nature': Some Thoughts on the Machinery of Transcendence," in *Emerson's Nature: Origin, Growth, Meaning,* ed. Merton M. Sealts Jr. and Alfred R. Ferguson (Carbondale: Southern Illinois University Press, 1979 [1969]), 150–63. Frederic Carpenter, "William James and Emerson," *American Literature* 11 (March 1939): 39–57.

12. Stanley Cavell, "Thinking of Emerson," in *The Senses of Walden: An Expanded Edition* (San Francisco: North Point Press, 1981), 129. Also see *Emerson's Transcendental Etudes* (Palo Alto, Ca: Stanford University Press, 2003); *Conditions Handsome and Unhandsome: The Constitution of Emersonian Perfectionism* (Chicago: University of Chicago Press, 1990); *In Quest of the Ordinary: Lines of Skepticism and Romanticism* (Chicago: University of Chicago Press, 1988); and *This New Yet Unapproachable America: Lectures after Emerson after Wittgenstein* (Albuquerque, N.M.: Living Batch, 1989). Richard Poirier, *Poetry and Pragmatism* (Cambridge, Ma.: Harvard University Press, 1992), and *The Renewal of Literature: Emersonian Reflections* (New York: Random House, 1987). Harold Bloom, *Agon: Towards a Theory of Revisionism* (New York: Oxford University Press, 1982), 116, 113–14. For other critics who have placed Emerson in a pragmatic tradition, see Russell Goodman, *American Philosophy and the Romantic Tradition* (New York: Cambridge University Press, 1991); John J.

McDermott, "Spires of Influence: The Importance of Emerson for Classical American Philosophy," in *Streams of Experience: Reflections on the History and Philosophy of American Culture* (Amherst: University of Massachusetts Press, 1986), 29–43; David Robinson, *Emerson and the Conduct of Life: Pragmatism and Ethical Purpose in the Later Work* (New York: Cambridge University Press, 1993); and Cornel West, *The American Evasion of Philosophy: A Genealogy of Pragmatism* (Madison: University of Wisconsin Press, 1989).

13. Stanley Cavell, "What's the Use of Calling Emerson a Pragmatist?" in *The Revival of Pragmatism: New Essays on Social Thought, Law, and Culture*, ed. Morris Dickstein (Durham, N.C.: Duke University Press, 1998), 79.

14. Richard Poirier, "Human, All Too Inhuman," *The New Republic*, 2 February 1987, 30.

15. See, for example, Ralph Barton Perry, *The Thought and Character of William James*, 2 vols. (Boston: Little, Brown, 1936), 1:39–63, 140–45; Carpenter, "William James and Emerson"; and F. O. Matthiessen, *The James Family* (New York: Knopf, 1961), 431–34.

16. Carpenter, "William James and Emerson," 40–41. James's copies of Emerson's works are held in the rare books collection of Harvard University's Houghton Library. I have provided references to specific volumes from James's collection only when citing particular instances of James's marginalia.

17. William James to Henry James, 3 May 1903, and Frances R. Morse, 26 May 1903, in *The Letters of William James*, 2 vols., ed. Henry James III (1926; reprint, New York: Kraus Reprint Co., 1969), 2:190, 194.

18. See Carpenter, "William James and Emerson." The other heading Carpenter stresses is one marked "RWE," which Carpenter believes designates passages that James saw as indicative of Emerson's singular sensibility.

19. Ralph Waldo Emerson, "Self-Reliance," in *E&L*, 271–72.

20. George Kateb, *Emerson and Self-Reliance* (Thousand Oaks, Ca: Sage, 1995), 6–7.

21. Emerson, "Fate," 943.

22. Ralph Waldo Emerson, "Circles," in *E&L*, 412.

23. Using a similar interpretive logic, Lopez argues that Emerson's Nietzschean ethics of antagonism and overcoming constitute the "deep structure, or elemental pattern in his thought, a pattern that can be found underlying even those passages in which he seems most monistic," *Emerson and Power*, 4.

24. Kateb, *Emerson and Self-Reliance*, 95.

25. Ralph Waldo Emerson, "The Poet," in *E&L*, 464; "Address, Delivered before the Senior Class in Divinity College, Cambridge, Sunday Evening, July 15, 1838," in *E&L*, 91.

26. For a discussion of the address and its aftermath, see Robert D. Richardson, *Emerson: The Mind on Fire* (Berkeley: University of California Press, 1996), 288–300.

27. David Robinson offers a lucid and valuable discussion of how Unitarian theology helped shape Emerson's Romantic ethic of self-culture. By extension, Robinson's argument helps us see Unitarianism as one of the precursors to American pragmatism. See *Apostle of Culture: Emerson as Preacher and Lecturer* (Philadelphia: University of Pennsylvania Press, 1982).

28. Lopez, *Emerson and Power*, 211, 9. For a list of works on Emerson and science, see William Rossi, "Emerson, Nature, and Natural Science," in *A Historical Guide to Ralph Waldo Emerson*, ed. Joel Myerson (New York: Oxford University Press, 2000), 139n6.

29. Ralph Waldo Emerson, "The American Scholar," in *E&L*, 56, 59. James apparently applied this Emersonian reading lesson to Emerson himself, for in his copy of Emerson's *Miscellanies*, James wrote in the margin beside this passage, "True of R. W. E." Marginalia in William James's personal copy of Ralph Waldo Emerson's *Miscellanies: Embracing Nature, Addresses, and Lectures* (Boston: Ticknor and Fields, 1868 [1855]), Houghton Library, Harvard University (WJ 424.25.12), 87.

30. This issue of how to read the monistic versus pluralistic aspects of Emerson's thought is approached from a different direction by John Lysaker, who charts a tension between Emerson's optimistic "theodicy," which asserts nature inevitably works toward benefical ends, and an emerging post-theological vision that he also sees articulated in Emerson's thought. See *Emerson and Self-Culture* (Bloomington: Indiana University Press, 2008), 81–118.

31. Mitchell, *Individualism and Its Discontents*, 82–83.

32. James's definition of pragmatism is actually threefold. He describes it as "primarily a method of settling metaphysical disputes that otherwise might be interminable" by "interpret[ing] each notion by tracing its respective practical consequences"; second, as an "attitude of orientation," of *"looking away from first things, principles, 'categories,' supposed necessities; and of looking towards last things, fruits, consequences, facts"*; and, third, as a "genetic theory" of truth (*Pragmatism*, 506, 510, 515). See my chapter 3 for a more detailed discussion of James's pragmatism.

33. Ibid., 510.

34. For example, considering the philosophical question of "design in nature," James argues: "The old question of *whether* there is design is idle. The real question is *what* is the world, whether or not it have a designer—and that can be revealed only by the study of all nature's particulars. . . . What sort of design? and what sort of designer? are the only serious questions,

and the study of facts is the only way of getting even approximate answers" (Ibid., 536).

35. James, *Pragmatism*, 538; "The Dilemma of Determinism," in W1878, 588–89; *A Pluralistic Universe*, in W1902, 776; "Dilemma of Determinism," 568–70.

36. The argument that I summarize here pulls together ideas articulated by James in a variety of works, most notably: the essays "The Sentiment of Rationality," "The Will to Believe," and "The Dilemma of Determinism," collected in *The Will to Believe*, and the "One and the Many" and "Pragmatism and Religion" chapters from *Pragmatism*.

37. James, *Pragmatism*, 556; "Dilemma of Determinism," 570.

38. James, *Pragmatism*, 546–48, 551–52, 553.

39. See McDermott, "Spires of Influence," 32, 38–9, for an insightful discussion of James's address. Though his focus differs from mine, McDermott shares my conclusion that James's address remains in some respects condescending toward Emerson. Surveying the public pronouncements that four classic American philosophers—James, Dewey, Santayana, and Royce—made on Emerson and his intellectual legacy, McDermott himself identifies two significant lines of influence between Emerson and American pragmatism: first, Emerson's commitment to a "practical" and "experiential" approach to inquiry that eschews theoretical solutions for efforts to "live" in an "ameliorative and perceptive way." Second, and more intriguingly, McDermott claims that Emerson actually "anticipated the doctrine of 'radical empiricism,'" specifically in the way he asserts the reality and "primary importance of relations over things" and "hold[s] to an aggressive doctrine of implication." Given his identification of these proto-pragmatic aspects of Emerson's philosophy, McDermott finds James's address "disappointing" in "regard to the question of the influence of Emerson on James," and bemoans the fact that James "never undertook a systematic study of Emerson, especially as directed to his notions of experience, relations, and symbol. James would have found Emerson far more 'congenial' and helpful than many of the other thinkers he chose to examine. A detailed study of Emerson as an incipient radical empiricist is a noteworthy task for the future."

40. William James, "Address at the Centenary of Ralph Waldo Emerson, May 25, 1903," in W1902, 1121.

41. Burke, *Grammar of Motives*, 74–77; "I, Eye, Ay," 154.

42. William James, *The Varieties of Religious Experience*, in W1902, 36; "Address at the Centenary," 1124.

43. James, "Address at the Centenary," 1124–25.

44. "Emerson," in *The Works of William James: Manuscript Essays and Notes* (Cambridge, Ma.: Harvard University Press, 1988), 315–19. The original notebook is held in the special collections of Harvard University's Houghton

Library (Notebook No. 20 in bMSAm 1092.9, "Emerson / Common Sense / Miller—Bode."). The editors of *Manuscript Essays and Notes* date the "Emerson" portion of the notebook at 1905, which seems an obvious error, since the portion of the notebook dealing with Emerson is clearly a draft for the 1903 address. It appears the editors mistakenly dated the entire contents of this notebook based on James's discussion of Dickinson Sergeant Miller and Boyd Henry Bode, which they date at 1905–1908 (*Manuscript Essays and Notes, xxx*).

45. For James's meliorism, see *Pragmatism*, 538, 612–19. For Dewey's meliorism, see John Dewey, *Experience and Nature*, in *LW*, 1: chapter 10, esp. 313–15, 324–26; and *Reconstruction in Philosophy*, in *MW*, 12:181–82. For a discussion of James's meliorism and how it is prefigured in Emerson's essay "Fate," see James M. Albrecht, "'The Sun Were Insipid, if the Universe Were Not Opaque': The Ethics of Action, Power, and Belief in Emerson, Nietzsche, and James," *ESQ* 43 (1997): 144–48.

46. "The Sentiment of Rationality," published in the 1897 collection *The Will to Believe*, combines two separate addresses originally delivered in 1879 and 1880.

47. William James, "The Sentiment of Rationality," in *W1878*, 520–21, 522.

48. James, "Address at the Centenary," 1122; *Pragmatism*, 612–13.

49. Emerson, "Self-Reliance," 259, 262, 265.

50. Ibid., 259.

51. Ibid., 259.

52. Ralph Waldo Emerson, "Spiritual Laws," in *E&L*, 311; "Self-Reliance," 281.

53. Ralph Waldo Emerson, "Nature," in *E&L*, 549, 551; "The Uses of Great Men," in *E&L*, 626; "Self-Reliance," 265–66.

54. Ralph Waldo Emerson, "Nominalist and Realist," in *E&L*, 577. For a similar claim, see Emerson's "Plato; or, the Philosopher," in *E&L*, 637–38. For similar arguments in James, see "Sentiment of Rationality," 505–6; and *Some Problems of Philosophy*, in *W1902*, 1010, 1020, 1034. James clearly inclines toward the nominalist camp in arguing that "Conceptions, 'kinds' are teleological instruments. No abstract concept can be a valid substitute for a concrete reality except with reference to a particular interest in the conceiver," that "*the only meaning of essence is teleological, and that classification and conception are purely teleological weapons of the mind*. The essence of a thing is that one of its properties which is so *important for my interests* that in comparison with it I may neglect the rest," "Sentiment of Rationality," 509; *The Principles of Psychology*, 2 vols. (New York: Dover, 1950 [1890]), 2:335.

55. Emerson, "Nominalist and Realist," 585–86.

56. Ibid., 580–81.

57. Emerson, *JMN*, 7:342.

58. In his introduction to *Attitudes toward History*, entitled "James, Whitman, Emerson," Burke argues that the tradition these writers represent

constitutes perhaps the most "well-rounded" ethical "frame" in American literature, for they typify the pragmatic refusal to accept limitation without also affirming our ability to act in response to those limits. Burke illustrates this attitude with the Jamesian motto, "Where resignation *must* be, it will be 'provisional,' . . . afford[ing] 'ground and leisure to advance to new philanthropic action,'" *Attitudes toward History*, 3.

59. Emerson, "Nominalist and Realist," 583. For James's quotation of this passage, see "Address at the Centenary," 1121.

60. Quoted in Perry, *Thought and Character*, 1:144.

61. James, *Pragmatism*, 491–92.

62. However, as McDermott argues, there are significant ways in which Emerson does anticipate James's radical empiricism. See note 39 above.

63. Cavell, "What's the Use of Calling Emerson a Pragmatist?," 79. Interestingly, in his 1903 address on Emerson, Dewey was more willing than James to credit Emerson with a rigorous consistency of philosophical vision (see note 5 to my chapter 4), anticipating Cavell's argument that Emerson's brand of "philosophy" eschewed the illusory quest for certainty that, Dewey felt, plagued traditional philosophy. For a discussion of Dewey's address on Emerson, see my chapter 4.

64. Emerson, "History," in *E&L*, 237.

65. Emerson's essay "History" repeatedly asserts the protopragmatic view that the meaning of events from the past—as preserved in narratives and artifacts—is always defined by the symbolic or interpretive use to which we can put those narratives and artifacts in the present. For instance:

> Time dissipates to shining ether the solid angularity of facts. No anchor, no cable, no fences, avail to keep a fact a fact. Babylon, Troy, Tyre, Palestine, and even early Rome, are passing already into fiction. The Garden of Eden, the sun standing still in Gibeon, is poetry henceforward to all nations. Who cares what the fact was, when we have made a constellation of it to hang in heaven an immortal sign?

This assertion that the meaning of historical artifacts does not (or cannot) reside in their ability to re-present a foregone reality leads Emerson to focus instead on the meanings that historical artifacts hold in the present: "The fact narrated must correspond to something in me to be credible or intelligible." Thus, even Emerson's provocative claim that "there is properly no history, only biography," which has been taken as a sign of his ahistorical absolutism, in fact has a distinctly pragmatic logic ("History," 240, 238, 240).

66. Emerson, "American Scholar," 58. The full sentence in "History" in which the phrase James underlined occurs is: "Let it suffice that in the light of these two facts, namely, that the mind is One, and that nature is

its correlative, history is to be read and written" (255). William James, Marginalia in personal copy of Ralph Waldo Emerson's *Essays, First Series*. Boston: Fields, Osgood, 1869. Houghton Library, Harvard University. (*AC85J2376z869e), 255. Marginalia in personal copy of Emerson's *Miscellanies*, 88.

67. Emerson, "History," 255–56.

68. James, *Principles*, 1:241, 243–46; *Pragmatism*, 595. For an excellent discussion of the Emersonian affinities in such passages, see Poirier, *Renewal of Literature*, 14–18, 47–48.

69. James, *Pragmatism*, 509. Poirier, *Renewal of Literature*, 14–19, 33.

70. Dewey, "Emerson," in *MW*, 3:191.

2. "LET US HAVE WORSE COTTON AND BETTER MEN": EMERSON'S ETHICS OF SELF-CULTURE

1. William James, *Pragmatism*, in *W1902*, 509.

2. Ralph Waldo Emerson, "Fate," in *E&L*, 953; "Friendship," in *E&L*, 351; "Man the Reformer," in *E&L*, 140.

3. For a recent study that explores the centrality of self-culture in Emerson's thought, see John Lysaker, *Emerson and Self-Culture* (Bloomington: Indiana University Press, 2008). Lysaker's study is admirable both for the Cavellian seriousness with which he regards Emerson as a still-relevant philosopher, and for the insight and nuance of his readings. Lysaker describes self-culture as the task of creating a life that "eloquently" expresses one's character, which entails translating the "impersonal" determinants of selfhood—including the "temperamental" and "ecstatic" dictates of genius (such as "involuntary perceptions") and the social sources of human intellect—into the "personal" (those efforts and experiences that "no one else can assume for us"): translating, that is, the impersonal sources of genius into "practical power" in and through our personal activities. Lysaker elaborates on the Emersonian virtues required for self-culture (such as self-trust and an "aversion to apology"); on the centrality of friendship in Emerson's ethical vision; on an "ethos of the moment" that opens us to new possibilities of action and growth; and on the ways in which self-culture, far from being incompatible with reform, in fact impels and demands it (see note 145 below). Though his focus, key terms, and interpretations differ from mine, Lysaker's articulation of self-culture is consonant with the models of democratic individuality I trace in Emerson and his pragmatic descendants.

4. The epigraph to this section is from Emerson's journal, June–July 1842, in *JMN*, 8:182–83.

5. Ralph Waldo Emerson, "The Conservative," in *E&L*, 178.

6. Ralph Waldo Emerson, "History," in *E&L*, 240.

7. Ralph Waldo Emerson, "Circles," in *E&L*, 407–8.

8. Ibid., 407, 403–4; Ralph Waldo Emerson, *Nature*, in *E&L*, 13; "Circles," 404.

9. Emerson, *Nature*, 7.

10. Emerson more explicitly argues for this continuity of nature and culture in the "Commodity" chapter of *Nature*, where he writes that "the useful arts are reproductions or new combinations by the wit of man, of the same natural benefactors," the "process and the result" of nature (ibid.,12). Also see his 1844 essay "Nature," where he writes: "We talk of deviations from natural life, as if artificial life were not also natural. . . . If we consider how much we are nature's we need not be superstitious about towns, as if that terrific or benefic force did not find us there, also, and fashion cities. Nature who made the mason, made the house" ("Nature," in *E&L*, 548).

11. Ralph Waldo Emerson, "Self-Reliance," in *E&L*, 279; "The Transcendentalist," in *E&L*, 198.

12. Emerson, *JMN*, 5:218.

13. Emerson, "Circles," 404.

14. Ralph Waldo Emerson, "The Poet," in *E&L*, 463; "Circles," 403, 405, 407; "Self-Reliance," 271.

15. Ralph Waldo Emerson, "Spiritual Laws," in *E&L*, 311.

16. Ralph Waldo Emerson, "The American Scholar," in *E&L*, 57; "Self-Reliance," 275; "Circles," 413; "Self-Reliance," 281, 266, 278, 282.

17. Emerson, *Nature*, 28.

18. Myra Jehlen, *American Incarnation: The Individual, the Nation, and the Continent* (Cambridge, Ma.: Harvard University Press, 1986), 108–110. For an interpretation that, contrary to Jehlen's reading, outlines the deeply pragmatic aspects of "Discipline," see Michael Lopez, *Emerson and Power: Creative Antagonism in the Nineteenth Century* (Dekalb: Northern Illinois University Press, 1996), 58–66.

19. Ralph Waldo Emerson, "Compensation," in *E&L*, 285–86.

20. Emerson, "Compensation," 289.

21. Ibid., 296.

22. Ibid., 291, 297.

23. Ibid., 298.

24. Ibid., 298. Friedrich Nietzsche, *The Twilight of the Idols and The Anti-Christ*, trans. R.J. Hollingdale (New York: Penguin, 1990 [1968]), 33.

25. Emerson, "Spiritual Laws," 314; *Nature*, 48; "Fate," 946.

26. Kenneth Burke, *A Grammar of Motives* (Berkeley: University of California Press, 1969 [1945]), 38–39.

27. For other works that acknowledge the tragic aspect of Emerson's philosophy, see Lopez, *Emerson and Power*; Gertude Reif Hughes, *Emerson's Demanding Optimism* (Baton Rouge: Louisiana State University Press, 1984); and Newton Arvin, "The House of Pain: Emerson and the Tragic Sense," *Hudson Review* 12, no. 1 (Spring 1959): 37–53. For an assertion that pragmatism, more broadly, has a tragic sensibility, see Sidney Hook, *Pragmatism and the Tragic Sense of Life* (New York: Basic Books, 1974).

28. Emerson, "Compensation," 298.

29. Kenneth Burke, *Attitudes toward History* (Los Altos, Ca.: Hermes, 1959 [1937]), 18–19.

30. Ralph Waldo Emerson, "The American Scholar," in *E&L*, 60; "History," 254–55.

31. Emerson, "History," 253–54, 237; "The Uses of Great Men," in *E&L*, 620.

32. Emerson, "Self-Reliance," 259, 260.

33. Emerson, "Spiritual Laws," 310.

34. Ibid., 310–11.

35. Ibid., 310.

36. Emerson, "History," 240.

37. Emerson, "Self-Reliance," "Circles," 403; "Uses of Great Men," 623.

38. Emerson, "American Scholar," 57; "Uses of Great Men," 620, 622, 620.

39. Emerson, "Uses of Great Men," 616–17.

40. Emerson, "Self-Reliance," 275.

41. Emerson, "Circles," 414.

42. Emerson, *JMN*, 2:387.

43. Emerson cites the steam engine's ability to "lengthen" time and "shorten" space in "Fate" (959).

44. Emerson, "Self-Reliance," 271.

45. Emerson, "Self-Reliance," 264; "Shakspeare; or, the Poet," in *E&L*, 710.

46. Emerson, "Shakspeare," 710–11.

47. Ralph Waldo Emerson, "Power," in *E&L*, 971, 984, 981.

48. Ralph Waldo Emerson, "Wealth," in *E&L*, 1010–11.

49. Emerson, "Power," 983.

50. Emerson, "American Scholar," 54.

51. Ralph Waldo Emerson, "Culture," in *E&L*, 1018, 1015.

52. Ibid., 1016–17.

53. As George Kateb puts it, "Receptivity is the highest form of self-reliance" (*Emerson and Self-Reliance* [Thousand Oaks, Ca.: Sage, 1995], 6).

54. Ibid., 153, 163, 33, 28–29, 4, 14.

55. Emerson, "Self-Reliance," 261. As Emerson writes in "The Poet": "Words are also actions, and actions are a kind of words" (450).

56. Emerson, "American Scholar," 62.

57. Kateb, *Emerson and Self-Reliance*, 186–7, 197–202.

58. See "Emerson/Nietzsche," ed. Michael Lopez, *ESQ: A Journal of the American Renaissance*, 43 (1997). Also see Lopez, *Emerson and Power*; and George Stack, *Nietzsche and Emerson: An Elective Affinity* (Columbus: Ohio University Press,1993).

59. Friedrich Nietzsche, *On the Genealogy of Morals and Ecce Homo*, trans. Walter Kaufmann (New York: Vintage, 1969 [1967]), 49. Nietzsche quotes this phrase (and the entire excerpt from Aquinas) in Latin; the translation of this phrase from Latin is Kaufmann's.

60. For a definition of "ressentiment," see *Genealogy of Morals*, 36–37.

61. Nietzsche, *Genealogy of Morals*, 123.

62. Ibid., 117; 67; and 97–146 passim.

63. Friedrich Nietzsche, *The Gay Science*, trans. Walter Kaufmann (New York: Vintage, 1974), 176–77. Similarly, in section 335, Nietzsche ridicules the idea that all individuals could share or agree on an unconditional moral judgment (*Gay Science*, 263–66).

64. Emerson, "Self-Reliance," 263.

65. Ibid., 261–62.

66. Ibid., 272, 259–60.

67. Ibid., 274.

68. Ibid., 273, 274.

69. Nietzsche, *Gay Science*, 270.

70. For example, see the passage from Emerson's essay "Experience" (beginning, "The life of truth is cold") discussed in the next section of this chapter.

71. As I discuss in the next section of this chapter, Emerson admits in "Self-Reliance" that it is hard to refuse the demands of conventional morality: "Every decent and well-spoken individual affects and sways me more than is right," he complains, and, after indulging in an imagined tirade against a "foolish philanthropist," he sheepishly admits, "I confess with shame I sometimes succumb and give the dollar" (262–63).

72. Nietzsche, *Genealogy of Morals*, 142.

73. The term Nietzsche uses, "Selbstaufhebung," implies dual meanings of "self-cancellation" and "self-preservation."

74. Ralph Waldo Emerson, "Considerations by the Way," in *E&L*, 1083, 1085.

75. Ibid., 1085–86.

76. Ibid., 1086.

77. Nietzsche, *Gay Science*, 244.

78. Nietzsche, *Genealogy of Morals*, 111, 108, 107.

79. The ethics that Nietzsche describes in this passage have strong affinities to those of the Emerson described by Joel Porte in the chapter titled "Economizing" from his study *Representative Man: Ralph Waldo Emerson in His Time* (New York: Oxford University Press, 1979): 247–82. Focusing mainly on *The Conduct of Life*, Porte examines how Emerson uses financial and sexual tropes to describe the process of sublimating and refocusing one's energies.

80. See *Emerson and Thoreau: Figures of Friendship*, ed. John T. Lysaker and William Rossi (Bloomington: Indiana University Press, 2010), and Lysaker, *Emerson and Self-Culture*, 141–67.

81. Emerson, "Uses of Great Men," 621.

82. Emerson, "Friendship," 351.

83. Emerson, "Circles," 406.

84. Ibid., 406.

85. Ralph Waldo Emerson, "New England Reformers," in *E&L*, 601.

86. Ibid., 602–3.

87. Emerson, "Uses of Great Men," 621–22.

88. Ibid., 627.

89. Emerson, "Circles," 408.

90. The earlier passages are: "The nonchalance of boys who are sure of a dinner, and would disdain as much as a lord to do or say aught to conciliate one, is the healthy attitude of human nature"; and "they teach us to abide by our spontaneous impression with good-humored inflexibility then most when the whole cry of voices is on the other side" ("Self-Reliance," 261, 259). For an excellent discussion of the issues of stylistic performance in passages such as these in Emerson, see Richard Poirier, *The Renewal of Literature: Emersonian Reflections* (New York: Random House, 1987), 49, 147–48, 196.

91. Emerson, "Self-Reliance," 262–63.

92. Poirier, *Renewal of Literature*, 49.

93. Emerson, "Self-Reliance," 273–74.

94. Ralph Waldo Emerson, "Experience," in *E&L*, 490.

95. In fairness, it should be noted that Nietzsche's scorn of human weakness similarly implies a faith in and admiration for the human capacity for growth and change. Thus Nietzsche describes man as *"the* sick animal," because he is also "the bravest of animals," the "great experimenter with himself" who has "dared more, done more new things, braved more and challenged fate more than all the other animals put together." The "existence on earth of an animal soul turned against itself, taking sides against itself, was something so new, profound, unheard of, enigmatic, contradictory, and *pregnant with a future* that the aspect of the earth was essentially altered" (*Genealogy of Morals*, 121, 162, 85).

96. Emerson, "Compensation," 296–97.

97. Emerson, "Self-Reliance," 260.

98. Emerson, "Uses of Great Men," 630, 623.

99. Ibid., 617, 629.

100. Ibid., 629–30.

101. For a dissenting opinion on this issue, see Cornel West, who argues that Emerson's philosophy was fatally limited by a racialist conception of personality (*The American Evasion of Philosophy: A Genealogy of Pragmatism* [Madison: University of Wisconsin Press, 1989], 34–35).

102. Emerson, *JMN*, 9:299–300. For a similar argument, consider the following passage from Emerson's "The Fortune of the Republic": "The genius of the country has marked out our true policy. Opportunity of civil rights, of education, of personal power, and not less of wealth; doors wide open. If I could have it,—free trade with all the world without toll or custom-houses, invitation as we now make to every nation, to every race and skin, white men, red men, yellow men, black men; hospitality of fair field and equal laws to all. Let them compete, and success to the strongest, the wisest and the best. The land is wide enough, the soil has bread for all" (*The Complete Works of Ralph Waldo Emerson* [New York: AMS Press, 1979 (1904)], 541).

103. Emerson, "New England Reformers," 599.

104. See, for example, Yehoshua Arieli, *Individualism and Nationalism in American Ideology* (Cambridge, Ma.: Harvard University Press, 1965), 277–89; and Sacvan Bercovitch, "Emerson, Individualism, and the Ambiguities of Dissent," *South Atlantic Quarterly* 89 (1990): 629–30, 636–37, 644.

105. See the concluding section of chapter 4 for a discussion of Dewey's views on the practical function of democracy as an ideal.

106. Emerson lived from 1803–82, Marx from 1818–83.

107. Robert D. Richardson reports that Emerson's "only recorded contact with the writings of Karl Marx" was reading "a signed piece by Marx in the *New York Tribune* for 22 March 1853, called 'Forced Emigration'" (*Emerson: The Mind on Fire* [Berkeley: University of California Press, 1996], 508).

108. "Ode, Inscribed to W. H. Channing," in *Ralph Waldo Emerson: Collected Poems and Translations* (New York: Library of America, 1994), 62–63.

109. Emerson, "Self-Reliance," 281.

110. Karl Marx, *Capital: A Critique of Political Economy*, ed. Friedrich Engels, trans. Samuel Moore and Edward Aveling (New York: Random House, Modern Library), 82–87, 90–91, 94–96, 389–91. According to Marx, a "definite social relation between men . . . assumes, in their eyes, the fantastic form of a relation between things." He insists that the value of a product is a function of the amount of human labor required to produce it: "In the midst of all the accidental and ever fluctuating exchange-relations between the products,

the labour-time socially necessary for their production forcibly asserts itself like an over-riding law of nature." Thus the value of the product of any individual producer is a socially produced value—a function of the society's division of labor—and the fluctuations of market value should be viewed as reflecting the "quantitative proportions in which society requires" "all the different kinds of private labour." The most just way to distribute wealth, Marx argues, is on the basis of the individual's share in the total labor-time of society. By contrast, the capitalist form of commodity exchange portrays this social value as the private property of the individual—as the private product of his or her labor: "It is, however, just this ultimate money form of the world of commodities that actually conceals, instead of disclosing, the social character of private labour, and the social relations between the individual producers." Marx argues that this alienation of social value is further exacerbated by wage labor and capitalist production. Unlike an independent producer, who owns the means of production and sells a commodity, a wage laborer owns only his or her own labor-power, and the capitalist who owns the means of production sells the commodity produced by the worker's labor.

111. Emerson, "New England Reformers," 593–94.

112. Emerson, "Man the Reformer," 137.

113. Ibid., 138.

114. Ibid., 144–45.

115. Ibid., 145.

116. Emerson, *JMN*, 9:189.

117. Emerson, "Compensation," 296.

118. Emerson, "Man the Reformer," 142.

119. Recall Emerson's argument from "Compensation," discussed earlier in this chapter, that any person who merely exploits the labor of others commits ethical suicide, purchasing a merely material gain at the cost of sacrificing his or her own self-culture: "he has resisted his life, and fled from himself, and the retribution is so much death."

120. Ralph Waldo Emerson, "The Method of Nature," in *E&L*, 115–16.

121. Emerson, "Self-Reliance," 274.

122. Ibid., 261.

123. Emerson, "Wealth," 989, 991.

124. John Dewey, *Democracy and Education*, in *MW*, 9:128; also see 125–30.

125. Emerson, "Man the Reformer," 145.

126. See Henry D. Thoreau, *Walden, Civil Disobedience, and Other Writings*, 3rd ed., ed. William Rossi (New York: W. W. Norton, 2008), 233. In echoing Pontius Pilate, Thoreau is acknowledging the difficulty of achieving an individual moral integrity, of truly washing one's hands of the injustices of society.

127. Emerson, "Man the Reformer," 139.

128. Margaret Fuller, *Woman in the Nineteenth Century*, ed. Larry J. Reynolds (New York: W. W. Norton, 1998), 74.

129. See Richard F. Teichgraeber III, *Sublime Thoughts and Penny Wisdom: Situating Emerson and Thoreau in the American Market* (Baltimore: Johns Hopkins University Press, 1995). Also see Sam McGuire Worley's argument that Emerson and Thoreau practice a mode of "immanent social criticism," which "observes and advises from the authority of a position within a culture rather than a position of superiority or detachment outside it" (*Emerson, Thoreau, and the Role of the Cultural Critic* [Albany: State University of New York Press, 2001], 125).

130. West, *American Evasion of Philosophy*, 17, 18, 34, 40.

131. Bercovitch, "Emerson, Individualism," 655, 656, 650–51, 641.

132. Len Gougeon, *Virtue's Hero: Emerson, Antislavery and Reform* (Athens: University of Georgia Press, 1990). As both Gougeon and Charles Mitchell document, the image of Emerson as an idealist aloof from politics was originally valorized by those, such as Emerson biographer Oliver Wendell Holmes and Harvard president Charles W. Eliot, who wanted to construct an Emerson compatible with the genteel Brahmin tradition, and later accepted by those who would cite this purported aloofness as proof of Emerson's obsolescence. For Gougeon's discussion of Holmes's and Eliot's attempts to minimize or ignore Emerson's political activity, as well as the counter-efforts of those like Thomas Wentworth Higginson who argued for a more accurate version of Emerson's reformist efforts, see *Virtue's Hero*, 7–17 and 340–48. For a discussion of how the vision of a "genteel" Emerson valorized by Holmes and Eliot later became the basis for later critics to dismiss Emerson, see Charles E. Mitchell, *Individualism and Its Discontents: Appropriations of Emerson, 1880–1950* (Amherst: University of Massachusetts Press, 1997), 6–7 and 12–72 passim.

133. Gougeon, *Virtue's Hero*, 271.

134. Ibid., 144–45. It is worth noting that Gougeon here replicates Myra Jehlen's argument that Emerson's idealistic belief in a benevolent world contains a deterministic renunciation of human action, since, in a world governed by an irresistible beneficent progress, our human actions are unnecessary.

135. Ibid., 272.

136. Kateb, *Emerson and Self-Reliance*, 177–78.

137. Kateb's concerns here parallel in important ways Richard Rorty's argument that the demands of collective action necessarily consign individual freedom to a private and mental realm. Rorty's position is to "drop the demand for a theory which unifies the public and private," and instead

"treat the demands of self-creation and of human solidarity as equally valid, yet forever incommensurable" (*Contingency, Irony, Solidarity* [New York: Cambridge University Press, 1989], xv). Kateb's "mental" self-reliance, in other words, has clear affinities to Rorty's "liberal irony." While they both see an individual mental liberty as having crucial ethical benefits—Kateb's receptivity fostering an appreciation for the diverse particulars of our world, Rorty's irony making one less likely to dominate or inflict suffering on others—their visions of individual freedom also reinforce a dualistic opposition between the self and society that differs significantly from the ideal of democratic individuality-in-community running from Emerson, through James and Dewey, to Ellison.

138. Emerson, "New England Reformers," 596.

139. Emerson, "Man the Reformer," 146.

140. Ralph Waldo Emerson, "Politics," in *E&L*, 559–60.

141. Emerson, "Circles," 408; "The Poet," 449; "Self-Reliance," 267.

142. Emerson, *JMN*, 9:136–137, 425.

143. Emerson, *JMN*, 11:361.

144. Emerson, *JMN*, 9:127.

145. Emerson, *JMN*, 9:430. Along similar lines, Lysaker argues that, because the self is inextricably implicated in myriad relations and dependencies with others, the eloquence or quality of one's life requires attending to our impacts on others and the qualities of selfhood they have the opportunity to attain. Thus, Emersonian self-culture impels and requires individuals to advance reform on two levels: first, through the contagious influence that our own character or ethos, our way of acting in the world, exerts on those with whom we intimately interact; and second, in broader social terms, through working to reform social relations so that all individuals have meaningful opportunities for self-culture. "In the pursuit of an eloquent life," Lysaker elaborates, "we should take responsibility for our influences as best we can . . . self-culture asks us to be role-models . . . how we conduct our lives is what will serve as a guide for others," and it entails "a commitment to establishing conditions that facilitate the upbuilding of humanity here and now as well as in the future." Hence, "self-culture not only doesn't eschew activism and state-based initiatives, but directs us toward them, and precisely in order to fulfill its goal of an eloquent life. We would be mistaken, therefore, if we found an antinomy between self-culture and politics, or self-culture and social reconstruction" (*Emerson and Self-Culture*, 172–73, 175, 194). I take Lysaker's argument here to be consonant with various issues I discuss in this chapter: Emerson's model of friendship and community, his ruminations on the ethical issues involved in the social division of labor; and his stances on politics and reform. Lysaker's claims here also dovetail with my discussion

in chapter 4 of Dewey's insistence that the quality of one's selfhood is defined by the consequences of one's actions—including their consequences on others, and (in chapter 6) of Burke's insistence that individual acts are "identified" with remoter, indirect consequences of our social interaction.

146. Emerson, "Politics," 563–64.

147. Ralph Waldo Emerson, "Lecture on Slavery," 25 January 1855, in *Emerson's Antislavery Writings*, ed. Len Gougeon and Joel Myerson (New Haven, Conn.: Yale University Press, 2002), 103.

148. Ralph Waldo Emerson, "An Address on the Emancipation of the Negroes in the British West Indies," 1 August 1844, in *Antislavery Writings*, 28.

149. For a description of a transcendentalist emphasis on "moral suasion," with its insistence that "only individual moral reform could ameliorate social problems," see Gougeon, "Historical Background," in Emerson, *Antislavery Writings*, xi, and *Virtue's Hero*, 34–35. Gougeon argues that an optimistic faith in "the fatalistic evolution of goodness," aided primarily by individuals acting "in ways appropriate to themselves," is "reflected in virtually all of Emerson's abolition speeches in the 1840s"; however, he also argues that events in the 1840s made Emerson "painfully aware of the conspicuous failure of individual moral suasion in ameliorating the problem," and sees the August 1844 address, which "accept[s] the notion that slavery was such a special and aggressive evil that organized and focused opposition was necessary," as a major turning point in Emerson's politics (*Virtue's Hero*, 144–45, 68, "Historical Background," xxxix).

150. In this 1844 address, Emerson was already arguing that the Union was not worth preserving if it meant complicity with slavery; indeed, citing the outrages suffered by Massachusetts, he claims "The Union is already at an end" (*Antislavery Writings*, 25).

151. For a detailed account of Emerson's evolving views on abolition, see Gougeon's *Virtue's Hero*, and "Historical Background," in *Emerson's Antislavery Writings*, xi–lvi. Also see Teichgraeber, *Sublime Thoughts*, chapters 2, 4, and 6.

152. My use of the term "melioristic" stands in opposition to Gougeon's use of the phrase "inevitable, ameliorative fate," which implies that progress is guaranteed, while James's definition of meliorism specifically stresses the contingent nature of progress. This Jamesian meliorism is much more consonant, I would argue, with Emerson's tragic view of progress.

153. Teichgraeber, *Sublime Thoughts*, 90–112.

154. Ibid., 112.

155. Emerson, "Address on the Emancipation," in *Antislavery Writings*, 20.

156. Ibid., 21.

157. Ibid., 22, 17, 22, 26.

158. Ralph Waldo Emerson, "The Fugitive Slave Law," 7 March 1854, in *Antislavery Writings*, 83, 84, 85, 86–7, 88–89.

159. For a discussion of this final claim in the context of Emerson's views on religion, see David Robinson, "Emerson and Religion," in *The Historical Guide to Ralph Waldo Emerson*, ed. Joel Myerson (New York: Oxford University Press, 2000), 169–70.

160. Emerson, *JMN*, 5:477.

3. MOMENTS IN THE WORLD'S SALVATION: JAMES'S PRAGMATIC INDIVIDUALISM

1. The epigraph is from an outline for the concluding lecture in the series "Characteristics of an Individualistic Philosophy," 1905; quoted in Robert D. Richardson, *William James: In the Maelstrom of American Modernism* (Boston: Houghton Mifflin, 2006), 459. The Swift James refers to here is Morrison I. Swift, mentioned prominently in the opening pages of *Pragmatism*. For the significance that James's audiences would have attached to Swift, a radical anarchist writer and political organizer, see Deborah Coon, "One Moment in the World's Salvation: Anarchism and the Radicalization of William James," *Journal of American History* 83, no. 1 (1996): 70–71.

2. For an excellent overview of James's career as a public philosopher, see George Cotkin, *William James: Public Philosopher* (Urbana: University of Illinois Press, 1989).

3. James himself adopted this term in the subtitle to his anthology *The Will to Believe*.

4. See my discussion of Dewey's "William James in Nineteen Twenty-Six," in chapter 5. However, as I explore in chapters 4 and 5, Dewey in his own work affirmed that a reconstructed individualism was necessary for realizing a more vital democratic culture. In a 1942 essay Dewey explicitly rejected his earlier worries that James's individualism might be the outdated vestige of an earlier era. Instead, Dewey praises James for a pluralistic (not atomistic) model of the self, and argues that the "pluralism" and "temporal relationism" of James's individualism remains an important intellectual resource in a world seeking to create democratic alternatives to totalitarianism ("William James and the World Today," in *LW*, 15:3, and 3–8 passim).

5. See my discussion of M. C. Otto's early, and trenchant, version of this criticism, in the concluding section of this chapter. Cornel West, for example, argues that "Like Emerson, [James] is prohibited by his individualism from taking seriously fundamental social change; instead, he opts for a gradualism supported by moral critique," a "perspective" that West rejects as "one of political impotence" (*The American Evasion of Philosophy: A Genealogy of Pragmatism* [Madison: University of Wisconsin Press, 1989], 60). James

Campbell approvingly echoes Otto's distinction between James and Dewey, arguing that "James could still—as Dewey could no longer—focus upon the importance of the individual considered apart from the group and the socioeconomic factors of life." Campbell aligns Dewey with "other Pragmatic social thinkers" who "emphasiz[e] the social aspect to the downplaying of the individual, whereas James's emphasis is just the reverse." Though Campbell stresses the need for *both* an "ethics of fulfillment" and an "ethics of reform," he concludes that "James's ethics of fulfillment is not translatable into an ethics of reform" (*The Community Reconstructs: The Meaning of Pragmatic Social Thought* [Urbana: University of Illinois Press, 1992], 16–17). Also see H. S. Thayer, *Meaning and Action: A Critical History of Pragmatism*, 2nd ed. (Indianapolis, Ind.: Hackett, 1981 [1968]), 441–43. In arguing that Dewey, with his focus on "the individual-in-context," "would have characterized James as a spokesman for the 'old individualism' of an eighteenth-century laissez-faire, atomistic, pre-industrial social philosophy," Thayer insists on a distinction that Dewey himself explicitly renounced in his 1942 essay "William James and the World Today" (see note 4 above).

Other critics offer more sympathetic analyses of James's individualism, arguments more consonant with my own emphases and conclusions. Deborah Coon stresses that James's individualism was not a throwback from America's premodern past, but rather a response to the specifically modern forms of "bigness" that increasingly dominated America around the turn of the twentieth century—corporations, imperialism, and militarism (see "One Moment in the World's Salvation"). George Cotkin also offers a sympathetic reading of James's "discourse of heroism," and argues that James used his model of individuality to confront serious ethical dilemmas of his age, such as imperialism. Cotkin concludes that James's "idea of the Promethean, reformist individual in his doctrine of meliorism" "avoided some important political questions," and resulted in a political vision that "remains vague and unimpressive in various ways," yet Cotkin approvingly quotes James T. Kloppenberg's view that James "helped to nurture the seeds of a new political sensibility, which reached fruition in the writings of John Dewey and other like-minded American radicals between 1890 and 1920" (*William James: Public Philosopher*, chapters 5 and 6; 170–72). Gerald E. Myers at times dismisses James's meliorism as naively optimistic, yet he argues for a nuanced assessment of James's individualism, stressing that James held a "transactionist theory" of the relation between "person and environment," saw "the individual" and "the community" as "dialectically related," and accordingly affirmed "that one who upholds an ethic of democratic individualism is obligated to take part in social or political change" (*William James: His Life and Thought* [New Haven, Conn.: Yale University Press, 1986], 415, 412, 410, 430).

James O. Pawelski and Richard M. Gale offer two competing studies of James's model of the self. In *The Divided Self of William James* (New York: Cambridge University Press, 1999), Gale argues that the pluralistic-naturalistic tendencies of James's thought (a "promethean pragmatist" vision) exist in fundamental and irresolvable conflict with the more mystic and religious ("anti-promethean") aspects of his thought. Pawelski, in *The Dynamic Individualism of William James* (Albany: State University of New York, Press, 2007) offers a cogent overview of three aspects of James's individualism: sociological, psychological, and metaphysical. Emphasizing the integration of perception, conception, and volition in James's reflex action model, Pawelski argues—against Gale—that James articulated, in his later writings, an "integrated individualism" that comprehends and manages the tensions Gale sees as unresolved.

6. Richardson, *William James*, 458.

7. John E. Smith, *The Spirit of American Philosophy* (New York: Oxford University Press, 1963), 43.

8. See ibid., 47–55, for an excellent overview of how James was reacting against the model of experience articulated by the tradition of British empiricism.

9. In *Principles of Psychology* James professed to maintain a dualistic concept of mind and matter, and located the evidence of a dualistic subject in the will—specifically, in the effort of attention the self can put forth to keep an unpleasant, but necessary, idea before the mind. However, as Dewey cogently argued, most aspects of James's *Principles* serve to undermine this dualistic account of the subject, and James himself, in the 1904 essay "Does 'Consciousness' Exist?" explicitly rejected a dualism of subject and object, reinterpreting "consciousness" not as an entity outside experience, but a function within it ("The Vanishing Subject in the Psychology of James," in *LW*, 14:155–67). This progression in James's thinking, I would contend, warrants treating will in a similar fashion, as a function within experience or a quality of certain acts in experience. Such treatment is not only consistent with James's later thought, but with Dewey's definition of character as composed of the interpenetration of habits, and his description of the highest mental facts (such as conscience) as complex habits or qualities of activity.

10. See James's definition of radical empiricism in *The Meaning of Truth*, which includes the "postulate . . . that the only things that shall be debatable among philosophers shall be things definable in terms drawn from experience" (*W1902*, 826).

11. Dewey's critique of classic liberal individualism is discussed in chapter 5.

12. William James, *Pragmatism*, in *W1902*, 508, 503.

13. James articulates this definition of rationality in "The Sentiment of Rationality," in *W1878*, 504–39.

14. James, *Pragmatism*, in *W1902*, 495.

15. Ibid., 506, 508.

16. Ibid., 508–9, 510, 515, 513, 512.

17. Ibid., 574, 599.

18. William James, "Remarks on Spencer's Definition of Mind as Correspondence," in *W1878*, 903, 908.

19. William James, *A Pluralistic Universe*, in *W1902*, 776–77.

20. Dewey's model of experience is discussed in chapter 4.

21. William James, *The Meaning of Truth*, in *W1902*, 826.

22. James, *Pragmatism*, 600–601. For James's list of "tender-minded" versus "tough-minded" traits, see 491.

23. Ibid., 592, 598.

24. Ibid., 584–85.

25. William James, "The Will to Believe," in *W1878*, 472; "Sentiment of Rationality," 520, 533; *Pragmatism*, 508. James carefully distinguishes the role belief plays in different kinds of truths—for instance, distinguishing moral beliefs from scientific beliefs. However, even in scientific inquiry, he stresses the way our purposes and satisfactions necessarily enter into the process: the imagination and intuition of a scientist in developing hypotheses; the actions on the basis of that hypothesis that reveal and help create new facts that verify the hypothesis; and even the broad desire for scientific truth itself is a human purpose or belief. Similarly, James acknowledges the existence of many facts that our beliefs and actions will never change, such as "The future movements of the stars or the facts of past history," that are "determined now once and for all, whether I like them or not. They are given irrespective of my wishes" ("Sentiment of Rationality," *W1878*, 529).

26. James, *Pragmatism*, 528–40; "The Dilemma of Determinism," in *W1878*, 591.

27. James, *Pragmatism*, 542. For James's analyses of monism and determinism versus pluralism, see *Pragmatism*, 541–57, and "Dilemma of Determinism," 569–76, 588–92.

28. James, "Dilemma of Determinism," 578–79; *Pragmatism*, 612.

29. James, "Dilemma of Determinism," 588–89; *Some Problems of Philosophy*, in *W1902*, 1054.

30. James, "Dilemma of Determinism," 590; *Pragmatism*, 548; *Some Problems*, 1052; "Sentiment of Rationality," 524, 518; "Dilemma of Determinism," 583.

31. See John Dewey, "The Development of American Pragmatism," in *The Essential Dewey: Volume I, Pragmatism, Education, Democracy*, ed. Larry

Hickman and Thomas M. Alexander (Bloomington: Indiana University Press, 1998), 9.

32. James, "Will to Believe," 463, 473.

33. James, "Sentiment of Rationality," 531–33.

34. James, *Pragmatism*, 601, 540.

35. The other political tropes James uses to describe pragmatism have a similar tenor, using analogies that stress a democratic decentralization: a "pluralistic world" is "more like a federal republic than like an empire or a kingdom," he asserts, and the notion of a "universe with such as *us* contributing to create its truth," James notes ironically, will appear to those of the rationalist temper as radical as "Home-rule for Ireland," or "self-government" for "the Filipinos" (*Pluralistic Universe*, 776; *Pragmatism*, 601).

36. James, "Sentiment of Rationality," 536–37, 529.

37. See James's critique of Spencer in "Great Men and Their Environment," in *W1878*, 618–46. On Coon, see note 5 above.

38. James, "Sentiment of Rationality," 519.

39. The other half of this claim, as I interpret it, is expressed in "The Moral Philosopher and the Moral Life": namely, that "good" and "obligation" both refer to the desires or demands that sentient beings feel, all of which desires, according to James, morals must take into account in the effort to create the most "inclusive" whole. "Obligation respondent to demand," then, describes the relation between individuals and the world in this dual sense: that we are obligated and able to do what the universe demands of us, *and* that our desires and demands on the universe are legitimate—worthy of consideration, even though they cannot all be fulfilled. See the discussion of "The Moral Philosopher and the Moral Life" in the concluding section of this chapter.

40. James, "Sentiment of Rationality," 524, 521.

41. William James, *The Principles of Psychology*, 2 vols. (New York: Dover, 1950 [1890]). See chapter 10, "The Consciousness of Self," 1:291–410.

42. The epigraph is a handwritten note at the head of the "Habit" chapter in James's personal copy of *Psychology: Briefer Course*; quoted in Richardson, *William James*, 315.

43. John Dewey, "William James as Empiricist," in *LW*, 15:11. For Dewey's discussions of the importance and influence of *Principles*, see "Development of American Pragmatism," 9–10; "From Absolutism to Experimentalism," in *Essential Dewey*, 1:20; "William James as Empiricist"; and "Vanishing Subject," 155–67.

44. See Dewey's "The Vanishing Subject in the Psychology of James" for a detailed account of how James, despite his official profession of a dualism of Subject-Object and mental-material, in fact describes the self as existing almost completely in the objective interactions of the human organism

and its environment. My entire reading of James's *Principles* is influenced by Dewey's analysis, though my specific focus and observations overlap little with his. See Gale, *Divided Self of William James*, 335–51, for a critique of Dewey's attempt to see James as only a step away from a fully naturalistic account of the self.

45. Dewey, "Vanishing Subject," 158; "James as Empiricist," 13; "Development of American Pragmatism," 10; "James as Empiricist," 12, 11; "Vanishing Subject," 167, 161.

46. James, *Principles of Psychology*, 1:6, 8.

47. James, *Principles of Psychology*, 1:141, 139, 284, 285, 287; 2:335; 1:224, 402.

48. Ibid., 1:288–89.

49. For a discussion of how this kind of concern for the alien otherness of experience, and the experiences of alien beings, might constitute a pragmatic contribution to the debate over the moral status of animals, see James M. Albrecht, "'What Does Rome Know of Rat and Lizard?': Pragmatic Mandates for Considering Animals in Emerson, James, and Dewey," in *Animal Pragmatism: Re-Thinking Human-Nonhuman Relationships*, ed. Erin McKenna and Andrew Light (Bloomington: Indiana University Press, 2004), 19–42.

50. William James, "The Importance of Individuals," in *W1878*, 648.

51. See, for example, James's contrast of how dogs—with their canine bodies and brains—would perceive and construct a different reality in a Vatican sculpture gallery than would human inhabitants, "Brute and Human Intellect," in *W1878*, 929–30.

52. James, *Pragmatism*, 558–71; *Principles of Psychology*, 1:289.

53. See the "Reasoning" chapter in James, *Principles of Psychology*, 2:325–71.

54. James, *Principles of Psychology*, 2:336n, 343.

55. William James, "Great Men and Their Environment," 642–43.

56. James, *Principles of Psychology*, 2:344.

57. Ibid., 2:365.

58. Hence James's commentary on the remark of his carpenter acquaintance. As James notes, "It is not only the size of the difference which concerns the philosopher, but also its place and kind. An inch is a small thing, but we know the proverb about an inch on a man's nose," "Importance of Individuals," 648.

59. William James, "What Makes a Life Significant," in *W1878*, 861–62.

60. James, *Principles of Psychology*, 1:243; *Pragmatism*, 509; "A World of Pure Experience," in *W1902*, 1180–81.

61. Richard Poirier, *The Renewal of Literature: Emersonian Reflections* (New York: Random House, 1987) and *Poetry and Pragmatism* (Cambridge, Ma.: Harvard University Press, 1992).

62. James, *Principles of Psychology*, 1:253–55.

63. James's phenomenological claim that intuitive insights often spring from the vaguer "fringes" of focused attention—and his consequent call to reinstate the vague in our mental life—has been corroborated by recent neuroscience research on how brain activity occurs in the left and right hemispheres. "At first, the brain lavishes the scarce resource of attention on a single problem. But, once the brain is sufficiently focussed, the cortex needs to relax in order to seek out the more remote associations in the right hemisphere, which will provide the insight. . . . [T]he insight process is an act of cognitive deliberation—the brain must be focussed on the task at hand—transformed by accidental, serendipitous connections. We must concentrate, but we must concentrate on letting the mind wander" (Jonah Lehrer, "The Eureka Hunt," *The New Yorker*, 28 July 2008, 43). Also see note 80 below.

64. James, *Principles of Psychology*, 2:561, 564, 568–69, 534.

65. Ibid., 2:579.

66. Ibid., 2:578–79.

67. See James, "Great Men," 619–22 and "Importance of Individuals," 647–52.

68. James, "Importance of Individuals," 651; *Principles of Psychology*, 1:453.

69. James, *Principles of Psychology*, 2:579.

70. "Thus social evolution is a resultant of the interaction of two wholly distinct factors—the individual, deriving his peculiar gifts from the play of physiological and infra-social forces, but bearing all the power of initiative and origination in his hands; and, second, the social environment, with its power of adopting or rejecting both him and his gifts. Both factors are essential to change. The community stagnates without the impulse of the individual. The impulse dies away without the sympathy of the community." James, "Great Men," 629–30.

71. James, "Great Men," 626–29.

72. See note 70 above.

73. James, "Great Men," 632.

74. Ralph Waldo Emerson, "The Uses of Great Men," in *E&L*, 629–30. See chapter 2 for a discussion of this aspect of Emerson's individualism.

75. John Dewey, "Time and Individuality," in *Essential Dewey*, 1:223.

76. For a discussion of the role of habit in Dewey's social psychology, see my chapter 4.

77. James, *Principles of Psychology* 1:104, 105, 107, 112–114; 2:402, 368.

78. Ibid., 1:104, 125, 108; 2:391.

79. Ibid., 2:392–93.

80. For a discussion of Dewey's model of reasonable deliberation, see my chapter 4.

Contemporary neuroscience research has confirmed both James's and Dewey's arguments that our "rational" decision processes result from an attempt to coordinate competing habitual or emotional impulses in the brain. See Jonah Lehrer, interview by Terry Gross, *Fresh Air*, National Public Radio, 2 March 2009.

81. James, *Principles of Psychology*, 1:120, 121.

82. Ibid., 1:121, 232–33 (also see 107), 127, 120, 288.

83. Ibid., 2:580.

84. Ibid., 1:122.

85. Ibid., 1:124–25.

86. Ibid., 2:463; 1:123; 2:401, 441. "Striking while the iron is hot," James argues, in general means focusing education on childhood and youth, that period in which our brains and instincts are most plastic, and our habits still unformed. "Could the young but realize how soon they will become mere walking bundles of habits, they would give more heed to their conduct while in the plastic state" (ibid., 2:401, 1:127). Youth, as the saying goes, is wasted on the young.

87. Ibid., 2:437.

88. See James's *Principles of Psychology*, chapter 10, on "The Consciousness of Self," and chapter 26, on "Will." For Dewey's astute analysis, see "Vanishing Subject."

89. James, *Principles of Psychology*, 1:594, 2:580, 1:126–27.

90. Ibid., 1:319, 322.

91. See James's letter, cited in note 121 below.

92. William James, "The Moral Philosopher and the Moral Life," in *W1878*, 596; *Pragmatism*, 514.

93. James, "Moral Philosopher," 601.

94. Ibid., 603. This definition of obligation explains the second half of what James means when he says that individualism means "in morals— obligation respondent to demand." For James, individualism is rational to our moral needs because it describes a universe in which, first, every individual being's desires are legitimate demands to be considered in our moral calculations, and second, we can have faith that, since our actions can help create a more moral future, our individual powers are sufficient to meet the moral demands the universe places upon us.

95. Ibid., 602.

96. Ibid., 617, 607–8.

97. Ibid., 610.

98. Ibid., 608–9.

99. James, *Pragmatism*, 611.

100. James, "Moral Philosopher," 613–14.

101. Ibid., 609.

102. For James's discussion of subjectivism, see "Dilemma of Determinism," 580–84.

103. James, "Moral Philosopher," 611.

104. Ibid., 609, 611, 610.

105. Ibid., 613.

106. Ibid., 613.

107. James, *Pragmatism*, 611–12.

108. Ibid., 612–13.

109. Ibid., 617–618.

110. James, "Sentiment of Rationality," 536, 533.

111. James, *Pragmatism*, 618, 616–17.

112. Ibid., 618, 612–13.

113. James, "Sentiment of Rationality," 536–37.

114. James, "Moral Philosopher," 615. In a complementary vein, James argues that a sense of participating in larger communal contexts supports an individualist ethics by *relieving* our sense of responsibility: by allowing us to feel that, having done our part, we can justifiably rest in our reliance on the other parts of the universe to do theirs.

115. Ibid., 615. James's peculiar religious synthesis attempts to meet two conflicting ethical needs that he felt acutely: the need, on the one hand, for the reassurance of a divinity who registers and sympathizes with our moral efforts, and the need, on the other, to avoid the theoretical problem of evil implicit in the idea of an omnipotent, providential deity. Many readers are likely to find James's synthesis unsatisfying. His idea of a *limited* deity, while preserving his pluralistic vision of a universe with genuine contingency, is so far from conventional monotheistic notions as to appear weak to the conventionally religious (as James himself admitted). Conversely, those who—like Dewey—espouse a thoroughly naturalistic metaphysics and ethics are likely to see James's theism as tender-minded backsliding. However, as James acknowledged, his pluralistic ethics are coherent in a purely naturalistic metaphysics (see "Moral Philosopher," 605), and for the purposes of my study, these naturalistic applications of James's philosophy are sufficient. Not all critics share my view that James's religious beliefs are so incidental to his pragmatism. Pawelski argues that James's religious commitment to a metaphysical individuality makes his individualism more "radical" and fully satisfying of human needs than the individualism of Emerson, whose positing of an over-soul "renders individuality illusory" on a metaphysical level (*Dynamic Individualism of William James*, 126–28). Gale, by contrast,

sees James's religiosity as a substantial barrier separating his pragmatism from Dewey's naturalism (*Divided Self of William James*, 335–51).

116. For an excellent discussion of this aspect of James's ethics, see Charlene Haddock Seigfried, "James: Sympathetic Apprehension of the Point of View of the Other," in *Classic American Pragmatism: Its Contemporary Vitality*, ed. Sandra B. Rosenthal, Carl R. Hausman, and Douglas R. Anderson (Urbana: University of Illinois Press, 1999), 85–98.

117. William James, "On a Certain Blindness in Human Beings," in *W1878*, 841.

118. Ibid., 860.

119. William James, "What Makes a Life Significant," 861–62.

120. James, "On a Certain Blindness," 847; "What Makes a Life Significant," 862.

121. Letter from William James to Mrs. Henry Whitman, 7 June 1899, in *The Letters of William James*, 2 vols., ed. Henry James III (1926; reprint, New York: Kraus Reprint Co., 1969), 2:90.

122. M. C. Otto, "On a Certain Blindness in William James," *Ethics* 53, no. 3 (April 1943): 184–91. In "What Makes a Life Significant," which forms the basis for Otto's critique, James asserts that "Society has . . . undoubtedly to pass towards some newer and better equilibrium, and the distribution of wealth has doubtless slowly got to change," but then adds that such changes will not "make any *genuine vital difference*, on a large scale, to the lives of our descendants," because the "solid meaning of life is always the same eternal thing—the marriage, namely, of some unhabitual ideal, however special, with some fidelity, courage, and endurance; with some man's or woman's pains.—And whatever or wherever life may be, there will always be the chance for that marriage to take place" (878). Of this argument, Otto concludes: it is "almost impossible" to read James "otherwise than as indorsing the fixity of social classes and teaching that the lower-placed individual can make the most of himself by adopting the social creed of St. Paul: 'I have learned, in whatever state I am in, therewith to be content.' . . . The bearing of the economic pattern of society on general human happiness simply did not assume for him the status of a philosophic problem" (187).

123. Otto, "On a Certain Blindness in William James," 189. The phrase Otto quotes here is from Emerson, not James.

124. Ibid., 190.

125. Two notable examples are Campbell's *The Community Reconstructs* and West's *American Evasion of Philosophy*. Campbell praises "The Moral Equivalent of War" for stressing "the importance of the social structure and group psychology to the ethical realm," and for acknowledging that "an important prerequisite of living a good life is first making the world a better

place"—a reading consonant with my own. However, Campbell sees this as an exception in James's thought ("Although James's moral thought largely undercuts the possibility of social reconstruction, his discussion of war . . . is happily another story"), whereas I see it as evidence of the broad continuity between James's and Dewey's pragmatic approaches to individualism and reform (*The Community Reconstructs*, 19–21).

126. James, *Pragmatism*, 512–13; "The Moral Equivalent of War," in W1902, 1289.

127. James, "Moral Equivalent," 1288.

128. Gerald E. Myers similarly notes that "the pacifist must overcome any initial blindness to the feelings of the military minded" (*William James: His Life and Thought*, 444). These democratic and pacifistic elements of James's pragmatic rhetorical strategy mark a significant line of connection between him and Kenneth Burke, who argues that the commitment to rhetoric—to become "humane word-slingers"—constitutes the only viable alternative the all-too-dominant model of humans as killers (*A Rhetoric of Motives* [Berkeley: University of California Press, 1969 (1950)], 72).

129. James, "Moral Equivalent," 1287.

130. John Dewey, "The Pragmatic Acquiescence," in *LW*, 3:151. For a discussion of Dewey's exchange with Mumford, see my chapter 5.

131. James, "Moral Equivalent," 1281, 1283, 1290, 1293, 1290.

132. Cotkin, for instance, calls it a "weak, albeit psychologically innovative and instructive, response to the problems posed by war" (*William James: Public Philosopher*, 150). Myers, similarly, praises "the notion that there may be a moral equivalent for the pugnacious impulse," but calls James's proposal "naive": "it could never function as the panacea that James claimed it to be" (*William James: His Life and Thought*, 444).

133. Letter from John Dewey to Scudder Kylce, 29 May 1915. Quoted in Myers, *William James: His Life and Thought*, 602n151. Myers quotes Jo Ann Boydston as claiming "that this is the only remark about James in Dewey's correspondence that might be construed as negative."

134. John Dewey, *Human Nature and Conduct*, in *MW*, 14:80, 81–2.

135. John Dewey, *Individualism Old and New*, in *LW*, 5:120–21.

4. CHARACTER AND COMMUNITY: DEWEY'S MODEL OF MORAL SELFHOOD

1. The epigraphs for this chapter are taken from the following: John Dewey, *The Public and Its Problems*, in *LW*, 2:328; "Emerson—The Philosopher of Democracy," in *MW*, 2:191.

2. For overviews of Dewey's early pragmatic philosophy and his years as a progressive educational reformer in Chicago, see Robert B. Westbrook, *John Dewey and American Democracy* (Ithaca, N.Y.: Cornell University Press,

1991), 59–194; and Alan Ryan, *John Dewey and the High Tide of American Liberalism* (New York: W. W. Norton, 1995), 124–53.

3. Dewey, *Public and Its Problems*, 362. Dewey's assessment of the characteristics of, and requirements for, an experimental and democratic method of social inquiry are discussed in more detail in my chapter 5. For discussions of Dewey's theory of social inquiry and its political implications, see James Campbell, "Democracy as Cooperative Inquiry," in *Philosophy and the Reconstruction of Culture: Pragmatic Essays after Dewey*, ed. John J. Stuhr (Albany: State University of New York Press, 1993), 17–34; and James Gouinlock, *Excellence in Public Discourse: John Stuart Mill, John Dewey, and Social Intelligence* (New York: Teachers College Press, 1986).

4. John Dewey and James Hayden Tufts, *Ethics*, in *LW*, 7:329. Though Dewey and Tufts coauthored *Ethics*, in their preface they indicate their separate authorship of different sections of the book. The chapters on ethical theory from which I draw were all written by Dewey, and for ease of citation only Dewey is cited as the author in subsequent notes.

5. On the question of Emerson's status as a philosopher, Dewey writes: "It is said that Emerson is not a philosopher. I find this denegation false or true according as it is said in blame or praise—according to the reasons proferred. When the critic writes of lack of method, of the absence of continuity, of coherent logic, and, with the old story of the string of pearls loosely strung, puts Emerson away as a writer of maxims and proverbs, a recorder of brilliant insights and abrupt aphorisms, the critic, to my mind, but writes down his own incapacity to follow a logic that is finely wrought" ("Emerson," 184). For a discussion of James's occasional condescension toward Emerson's capacity as a philosopher, see my chapter 1 above.

6. Dewey, "Emerson," 188–89, 187, 189–90, 190.

7. Cornel West argues that Dewey is offering a "creative misreading" of Emerson, that Dewey's ostensible portrait of Emerson is really a self-portrait (*The American Evasion of Philosophy: A Genealogy of Pragmatism* [Madison: University of Wisconsin Press, 1989], 72–76). While Dewey is undoubtedly constructing an Emerson who is usable for and consistent with his own philosophy, I take him at his word when he claims both that Emerson's philosophical vision has intellectual consistency and an enduring moral relevance for democracy. To dismiss his claims is, I would contend, condescending to both Dewey and Emerson, and dismisses the ways in which pragmatists like Dewey and James allow us to reconsider Emerson's legacy.

8. Dewey refers to democracy as a "way of life" in "Democracy and Educational Administration," in *LW*, 11:217; cited in John J. Stuhr, "Democracy as a Way of Life," in *Philosophy and the Reconstruction of Culture: Pragmatic*

Essays after Dewey, ed. John J. Stuhr (Albany: State University of New York Press, 1993), 37–58, which provides an excellent overview of this broader view of democracy. See also Dewey, *Public and Its Problems,* 325.

9. John Dewey, *Democracy and Education,* in *MW,* 9:92, 105.

10. Dewey, *Public and Its Problems,* 327–28. A more detailed discussion of this Deweyan ideal of community is offered in the concluding section of this chapter.

11. John Dewey, *Experience and Nature,* in *LW,* 1:63–65.

12. "Ends are, in fact, literally endless, forever coming into existence as new activities occasion new consequences. 'Endless ends' is a way of saying that there are no ends—that is no fixed self-enclosed finalities" (John Dewey, *Human Nature and Conduct,* in *MW,* 14:159). See also *Reconstruction in Philosophy,* in *MW,* 12:119–21.

13. Dewey, *Reconstruction in Philosophy,* 112–13.

14. Ibid., 142–46. As Dewey puts it, things "*are* what they can do and what can be done with them," 146.

15. Because knowing is, in Dewey's pragmatic account, a process that is triggered by problematic elements that impede ongoing activity in a given situation, the ultimate goal of knowing is to restore a harmonious adaptation between an organism and its environment so that activity may be restored and its quality enhanced. The "actual end of desire" is "a re-unification of activity and the restoration of its ongoing unity," while the "object" of desire (the change in conditions that knowing aims to bring about) is a *means* to restored activity (*Human Nature,* 172).

16. Dewey, *Experience and Nature,* 18–19.

17. Ibid., 19.

18. Dewey, *Democracy and Education,* 173, 171; *Experience and Nature,* 18–19; *Reconstruction in Philosophy,* 131–32, 150; *Experience and Nature,* 34.

19. Dewey, *Reconstruction in Philosophy,* 128–29.

20. Ibid., 129.

21. Dewey, *Human Nature,* 31, 15–16, 21–22; *Ethics,* 171.

22. Dewey, *Human Nature,* 68; *Democracy and Education,* 46–49, 53–54; *Human Nature,* 66–67.

23. Although Dewey describes the ability to form habits as the source of our human plasticity, he acknowledges that habits, as insistent "demands for certain kinds of activity," tend, "if unchecked," toward an unthinking efficiency of action (*Human Nature,* 21, 121).

24. Ibid., 76–77. Dewey here describes a duality similar to that James articulates in *Pragmatism,* where he asserts the superabundance of older truth "no longer malleable to human need," the "dead heart of the living tree" that has "grow[n] stiff with years of veteran service and petrified in

men's regard." Although James affirms "how plastic even the oldest truths nevertheless really are," he acknowledges the tremendous conservative force such "older truths" wield: "Their influence is absolutely controlling. Loyalty to them is the first principle—in most cases it is the only principle; for by far the most usual way of handling phenomena so novel that they would make for a serious rearrangement of our preconceptions is to ignore them altogether, or to abuse those who bear witness for them" (*W1902*, 515, 513).

25. Ralph Waldo Emerson, "The Uses of Great Men," in *E&L*, 620. Dewey acknowledged this affinity between his and Emerson's emphases on the plasticity of human nature. He cites Emerson's respect for the potential latent in human "immaturity" at the end of chapter 4 in *Democracy and Education*, which celebrates our "dependence" upon traditions as the source of the plasticity of human nature (57).

26. Dewey, *Human Nature*, 88; Ralph Waldo Emerson, "The American Scholar," in *E&L*, 60; Dewey, *Human Nature*, 25, 20.

27. For a cogent discussion of selfhood as an event whose very essence is contingency, pluralism, and temporality, see "Time and Individuality," in *The Essential Dewey: Volume I, Pragmatism, Education, Democracy*, ed. Larry Hickman and Thomas M. Alexander (Bloomington: Indiana University Press, 1998), 217–26. See my chapter 3 for a discussion of this essay.

28. Dewey *Human Nature*, 90, 96, 41.

29. Dewey, *Ethics*, 285–86, 173; *Human Nature*, 37, 34, 37.

30. Dewey, *Human Nature*, 37. Dewey makes essentially the same argument about Kant's "categorical imperative," arguing that the true rationale behind Kant's standard—whether one could will one's own behavior to be universalized—is not an argument for acting regardless of consequences, but for considering consequences as broadly and impartially as possible (*Ethics*, 221–23).

31. Dewey, *Human Nature*, 35, 38.

32. Ralph Waldo Emerson, "Self-Reliance," in *E&L*, 266; "Spiritual Laws," in *E&L*, 314. Dewey, *Human Nature*, 37. For a discussion of "Compensation," see my chapter 2.

33. Dewey, *Human Nature*, 39–40, 30; Emerson, "Self-Reliance," 265–66; Dewey, *Human Nature*, 123, 128, 142, 26.

34. Dewey, *Human Nature*, 29.

35. For Peirce's ground-breaking pragmatic that inquiry is triggered by "real and living doubt" in a specific problematic situation and that the "settlement of opinion" is "sole end of inquiry," see Charles Sanders Peirce, "The Fixation of Belief," in *Pragmatism and Classical American Philosophy: Essential Readings and Interpretive Essays*, 2nd ed., ed. John J. Stuhr (New

York: Oxford University Press, 2000), 71 and 67–76 passim. Dewey's analysis of knowing or conscious reflection is also consonant with William James's argument in "Does 'Consciousness' Exist?" which denies the reality of "consciousness" as a separate mental reality or realm, and redefines it as a function between different experiences, in *W1902*, 1141–58.

36. Dewey, *Human Nature*, 124–25, 126.

37. Ibid., 127.

38. Ibid., 127.

39. Ibid., 132–33.

40. Ibid., 134, 135, 108, 117.

41. Ibid., 118.

42. Ibid., 39–40.

43. Also see the subsequent discussion of "mind as individual" (ibid., 62). This description of the subjective element of mind as an "intermediary" phase in the process of the reconstruction of experience receives a more detailed treatment in *Experience and Nature*, 170–71 and 162–90 passim.

44. Dewey, *Human Nature*, 130, 29; *Experience and Nature*, 189.

45. Dewey, *Human Nature*, 139.

46. Ibid., 140.

47. Ibid., 139, 150.

48. Dewey, *Ethics*, 286–87.

49. Dewey argues that "choice is the most characteristic activity of a self" (*Ethics*, 286).

50. Dewey, *Human Nature*, 150. William James, "The Moral Philosopher and the Moral Life," in *W1878*, 609. Dewey, *Human Nature*, 150; *Ethics*, 287.

51. Dewey, *Democracy and Education*, 113; *Human Nature*, 154–55, 156, 185.

52. Dewey, *Human Nature*, 143–44.

53. Ibid., 144, 183.

54. Dewey, *Reconstruction in Philosophy*, 181.

55. Dewey, *Human Nature*, 198–99, 202.

56. Ibid., 182, 195 (my emphasis), 213–15.

57. Dewey, *Human Nature*, 144–45; *Reconstruction in Philosophy*, 182; *Human Nature*, 200; *Ethics*, 198. For an example of the Jamesian tone Dewey echoes here, see "The Dilemma of Determinism," where James derisively dismisses certain popular representations of paradises and utopias as "lubberlands" of "unexampled insipidity" (*W1878*, 583).

58. Thoreau's most developed version of this critique is, of course, the "Economy" chapter of *Walden*.

59. Emerson, "Self-Reliance," 275; "Man the Reformer," in *E&L*, 140; "Considerations by the Way," in *E&L*, 1084; "Self-Reliance," 281; "Circles," in *E&L*, 413; "Self-Reliance," 271; "Circles," 407.

60. Gregory F. Pappas offers an excellent concise overview of Dewey's ethics, arguing that he offers a metatheoretical critique of the limits and proper uses of moral theory, a descriptive focus on the "generic traits" of "moral experience," and a normative suggestion of "how we can improve our appreciation of morally problematic situations"—which three emphases are "intertwined" throughout his writings and "cannot be understood in isolation" from one another. Dewey's normative vision, Pappas concludes, is of a "moral life that is 'intelligent,' 'aesthetic,' and 'democratic'" ("Dewey's Ethics: Morality as Experience," in *Reading Dewey*, ed. Larry A. Hickman [Bloomington: Indiana University Press, 1998], 100–101, 115). Steven Fesmire emphasizes the crucial role of imagination in Dewey's ethics, suggesting that the type of imaginative and discriminating attention to the actual conditions of moral situations that Dewey requires is best conceived as a kind of "moral artistry" (*John Dewey and Moral Imagination: Pragmatism in Ethics* [Bloomington: Indiana University Press, 2003]). James Gouinlock situates Dewey's moral philosophy as an extension of his naturalistic metaphysics, his model of experience, and his subsequent vision of philosophic method (*John Dewey's Philosophy of Value* [New York: Humanities Press, 1972]). Jennifer Welchman focuses on the development of Dewey's ethical thought leading up to and culminating in his 1908 *Ethics*, a period in which he abandoned his early neo-Hegelian idealism for a pragmatic approach (*Dewey's Ethical Thought* [Ithaca, N.Y.: Cornell University Press, 1995]).

61. Dewey, *Ethics*, 263. The moral category of the good emerges from the central role of "natural desires" in experience: that is, from the basic facts that every organism requires in its interaction with its environment consummatory achievements that allow its life to continue, and that because an organism's actions exert a transforming effect on its environment, its present actions play a role in enabling or precluding what satisfactions can be pursued in the future. These basic facts carry, for those beings capable of deliberating on future consequences, the attendant need and opportunity to choose which competing ends to pursue and desires to satisfy ("Three Independent Factors in Morals," in *LW*, 5:281–82). The categories of the Right and the Virtues have their origin in basic aspects of human association: respectively, that "Men who live together inevitably make demands on one another" that eventually become codified as "generally acceptable" and "reciprocal" duties, and that "Individuals praise and blame the conduct of others," which responses from other humans have an "influential" effect on shaping conduct (Ibid., 284, 285–86).

62. Dewey, *Ethics*, 274; "Three Independent Factors," 280, 287, 280.

63. Dewey, "Three Independent Factors," 286. The traditional divisions of moral theory are as follows: the "good" or wisdom corresponds to

consequentialist moral theories, the "right" corresponds to deontological theories, and "approbation" corresponds to virtue theories. As noted in the body of this chapter and in note 64 below, Dewey's selection of these three categories is not intended to impute any absolute validity to them: it is simply a useful organizational strategy that allows Dewey to use the insights of traditional moral theory to describe important aspects of moral experience while simultaneously arguing that no single theory can pretend to any comprehensive explanatory power.

64. Fesmire made this point at his session on "Pragmatist Ethics—Theory and Practice," at the Society for the Advancement of American Philosophy's Summer Institute in American Philosophy, in Eugene, Oregon, 6–7 July 2004. Fesmire noted that, in the 1930 panel discussion that is transcribed as an appendix to "Three Independent Factors in Morals," Dewey is cited as explicitly acknowledging that "he exaggerated, for the purposes of discussion, the differences among the three factors" (*LW*, 5:503).

65. Dewey writes: "uncertainty and conflict are inherent in morals. . . . One has to manage forces with no common denominator" ("Three Independent Factors," 280).

66. Ibid., 288.

67. As Pappas notes, "Dewey thought that the purpose of disclosing the limitations of moral theory is to determine the functions it might be able to perform. 'Theory having learned what it cannot do, is made responsible for the better performance of what needs to be done' [*MW* 4:45]" ("Dewey's Ethics," 103). See Dewey's *Ethics*, 275–83 for the pragmatic argument that a moral principle has its origin in experience as "a generalized statement of what sort of consequences and values tend to be realized in certain kinds of situations," and thus, properly used, "*is a tool for analyzing a special situation*" (276, 280).

68. For an introduction to the role of character in Dewey's morals that is consonant with many of the arguments I pursue in this chapter, see Pappas, "Dewey's Ethics," 106, 110–11, 114–15.

69. Dewey, *Ethics*, 302, 294, 298–300.

70. Ibid., 302–3, 268, 271–73, 306–7.

71. Dewey, *Ethics*, 206; *Human Nature*, 135; *Ethics*, 207; *Human Nature*, 129–31; *Ethics*, 197, 187, 207. Dewey here extends the naturalistic approach to morals that William James outlines in "The Moral Philosopher," 600–603. For a discussion of James's essay, see my chapter 3.

72. Dewey, *Human Nature*, 136; *Ethics*, 197. Emerson, "Self-Reliance," 263, 262. Dewey, *Ethics*, 189, 206; *Human Nature*, 136–37; Emerson, "Culture," in *E&L*, 1015–18.

73. Dewey, *Human Nature*, 136–37, 25; *Ethics*, 208, 196. Dewey's contention that entities like reason, liberty, or conscience should be conceived

adverbially or adjectivally, not as substantive entities, extends William James's insight (articulated in the "Stream of Thought" chapter of the *Principles of Psychology*) that the syntactical structure of our language distorts our conception of reality: specifically, that the tendency of nouns to emphasize the substantive aspects of experience obscures the transitional aspects of experience *as a process.*

74. Dewey, *Ethics*, 227.

75. Ibid., 227.

76. Ibid., 300, 299, 300.

77. Dewey, *Human Nature*, 217–18; *Ethics*, 227–28, 224–25; *Human Nature*, 84–85, 217; *Ethics*, 304–5. Dewey argues that no catalogue or hierarchy of unchanging virtues can be compiled, for the nature of an interest is that it includes both a disposition and an object to which it attaches. Virtues are thus tied to the specific objects and conditions of various cultural and historical moments. Similarly, Dewey enumerates the qualities of a moral self only in generic terms corresponding to his chosen independent factors in morals: a "good self" is "*wise* or prudent" in its ability to choose "inclusive satisfaction," "*faithful* in acknowledgment of the claims involved in its relations with others," and "*conscientious*" in having "the active will to discover new values and to revise former notions" (*Ethics*, 255, 256–57, 285). As Pappas argues, Dewey's "cardinal virtues" are the "habits he identified with moral 'intelligence'" necessary to "determine what morality requires *here* and *now*": habits such as "sensitivity, conscientiousness, sympathy, and open-mindedness" ("Dewey's Ethics," 114).

78. Dewey, *Ethics*, 240.

79. Ibid., 218, 228.

80. Dewey, *Democracy and Education*, 361–62.

81. In fairness to Adam Smith, a founding figure in economic liberal individualism, it should be noted his argument from *The Wealth of Nations* (that "natural" economic forces translate individuals' pursuit of personal profit into a force that maximizes wealth for people in all countries and all economic strata) represents only half of his vision. His earlier work, *The Theory of Moral Sentiments* (1759), stressed the importance of innate moral faculties such as conscience and sympathy (not rational calculation of economic self-interest) as providing the basis for society. Typically, our culture has appropriated only that part of Smith's argument that so conveniently justifies the pursuit of individual profit within a capitalist system.

82. Dewey, *Ethics*, 248.

83. Ibid., 248.

84. I am thinking here, primarily, of Freud's argument in *Civilization and Its Discontents*, trans. and ed. James Strachey (New York: W. W. Norton,

1969 [1930]) that conscience is formed through the superego's ability to redirect aggressive impulses back against themselves, so that the socialized self, far from being the picture of rationality liberalism posits, controls its primal, transgressive urges only at the cost of an internalized psychic violence.

85. Freud, of course, does view psychic conflicts as remediable in that primal (libidinal and aggressive) drives can and must be sublimated: but because he views these drives as inherent and dominant constituents of human nature, such sublimation leaves an ineradicable residue of fundamental conflict (and unhappiness) at the core of the Freudian psyche. While Dewey insists on the tragic reality of conflicts between *particular* ends, desires, and dispositions, his approach would reject as essentialist the Freudian notion of a *fundamental* conflict that defines selfhood. For a concise overview of Dewey's differences from Freudian psychoanalysis, see Westbrook, *John Dewey and American Democracy*, 290–92.

86. Dewey, *Ethics*, 302.

87. As Dewey puts it in *Democracy and Education*: "In the degree in which men have an active concern in the ends that control their activity, their activity becomes free or voluntary and loses its externally enforced and servile quality" (269).

88. Dewey, *Ethics*, 229, 235–36, 232, 237, 246–47, 280–81. Dewey argues that "right" names the fact that, if one is fair and impartial, one must acknowledge that "nothing is good for himself which is not also a good for others," that another's claim is valid *if* it is the kind of claim or support that we would desire for ourselves. Or, alternatively, "Right expresses the way in which the good of a number of persons, held together by intrinsic ties, becomes efficacious in the regulation of the members of a community." The concept of "the right" functions as a standard—stipulating that a chosen end or satisfaction must be one that "at the same time brings satisfaction to others, or . . . at least harmonizes with their well-being in that it does not inflict suffering upon them"—and as such does *not* specify what ends should be chosen as worthy of pursuit (ibid., 225, 228, 247).

89. Dewey, *Ethics*, 272–73. Or, as he puts it in *Human Nature*: "The moral is to develop conscientiousness, the ability to judge the significance of what we do, not by means of direct cultivation of something called conscience, or reason, or a faculty of moral knowledge, but by fostering those impulses and habits which experience has shown to make us sensitive, generous, imaginative, impartial in perceiving the tendency of our inchoate dawning abilities. Every attempt to forecast the future is subject in the end to the auditing of present concrete habit and impulse. Therefore the important thing is the fostering of those habits and impulses which lead to a broad, just, sympathetic survey of situations" (143).

90. Dewey, *Ethics*, 266–67.

91. Ibid., 271, 272, 271, 273. "Conscientiousness," Dewey concludes, means having "the active will to discover new values and revise former notions" (ibid., 285).

92. Dewey, *Ethics*, 304–5; *Human Nature*, 214. William James, *Pragmatism*, 612–13; Dewey, *Ethics*, 306; *Human Nature*, 215. Dewey offers a parallel analysis of the relation between individual will and responsibility in *Experience and Nature*, where he describes the uniquely subjective aspect of experience as a kind of "partnership" between a human being and the objective conditions of his or her environment, in which an individual assumes responsibility for the tendency or consequences of a certain portion of experience, even though he or she in no way fully controls the outcome. Subjectivity is thus not some preexistent or ubiquitous faculty, but a result that emerges in experience, a unique and powerful addition to experience by introducing the possibility of reconstructive deliberation, choice, and action.

93. Dewey, *Ethics*, 306–7.

94. Kenneth Burke, *Attitudes toward History* (Los Altos, Ca.: Hermes, 1959 [1937]), 41–42; *A Rhetoric of Motives* (Berkeley: University of California Press, 1969 [1950]), 27–29. See, for example, Dewey's criticism in *Human Nature* of the all-too-common "refusal to note the plural effects that flow from any act, a refusal adopted in order that we may justify an act by picking out that one consequence which will enable us to do what we wish to do" while "ignoring all the collateral 'ends' of his behavior" that are "equally real" (158).

95. Ralph Ellison, *IM*, 578; Emerson, "Self-Reliance," 274; Ralph Ellison, "Address to the Harvard College Alumni, Class of 1949," in *CE*, 425. For a discussion of Emerson's claim that "I may . . . absolve me to myself" in the context of his larger philosophy, see my chapter 2.

It is important to note that while Dewey does insist that conscientious attention to the quality of one's acts can be maintained only through intelligent deliberation on the complex and changing consequences of those acts upon others, he elsewhere in his 1938 *Ethics* makes a remark that suggests a much more charitable gloss on Emerson's claim that one may legitimately focus one's efforts on the "stern claims and perfect circle" of one's own vocation: "In general, conduct, even on the conscious plane, is judged in terms of the elements of situations without explicit reference either to others or to oneself. The scholar, artist, physician, engineer, carries on the great part of his work without consciously asking himself whether his work is going to benefit himself or some one else. He is interested in the *work* itself; such objective interest is a condition of mental and moral health. It would be hard to imagine a situation of a more sickly sort than that in which a person thought that every act performed had to be actuated consciously by regard for the welfare of others" (*Ethics*, 297).

96. Indeed, Dewey presents *Human Nature* as, among other things, an attempt to offer an alternative to these two competing "schools" of reform (9).

97. Dewey, *Ethics*, 340; *Human Nature*, 18–19; *Ethics*, 327, 318, 317, 342, 341; *Individualism Old and New*, in *LW*, 5:120. In *Human Nature*, Dewey asserts that "rationality of mind is not an original endowment but is the offspring of intercourse with objective adaptations and relations"—"But when it has been generated it establishes a new custom, [an active demand for reasonableness in other customs], which is capable of exercising the most revolutionary influence upon other customs. . . . [P]ersonal rationality or reflective intelligence [is] . . . the necessary organ of experimental initiative and creative invention in remaking custom" (55–56). Similarly, in *Reconstruction in Philosophy*, he writes that "philosophic reconstruction . . . will regard intelligence not as the original shaper and final cause of things, but as the purposeful energetic re-shaper of those phases of nature and life that obstruct social well-being. It esteems the individual not as an exaggeratedly self-sufficient Ego which by some magic creates the world, but as the agent who is responsible through initiative, inventiveness, and intelligently directed labor for re-creating the world, transforming it into an instrument and possession of intelligence" (108).

98. Dewey, *Human Nature*, 210; *Public and Its Problems*, 340; *Human Nature*, 202.

99. Dewey, *Human Nature*, 86, 76–77. The liberal arguments I refer to here are best expressed in Locke's *Second Treatise on Civil Government* and Adam Smith's *Wealth of Nations*. The Freudian argument is best encapsulated in *Civilization and Its Discontents* (see notes 84 and 85 above). For examples of the critique that Dewey (and pragmatism more generally) holds an overly optimistic view of the power of intelligence to educate and reform human nature, and an inadequate theory of the operations of power, see Reinhold Niebuhr, *The Self and the Dramas of History* (New York: Scribner's, 1955), 83, 115, 137–38, 144; and John Patrick Diggins, *The Promise of Pragmatism: Modernism and the Crisis of Knowledge and Authority* (Chicago: University of Chicago Press, 1994).

100. Ralph Waldo Emerson, "Politics," in *E&L*, 559. For a discussion of this passage, see my chapter 2.

101. Dewey, *Human Nature*, 77–78.

102. Shannon Sullivan has offered an intriguing analysis of racism from an analytical perspective that draws on both pragmatism and psychoanalysis

(*Revealing Whiteness: The Unconscious Habits of Racial Privilege* [Blooming-
ton: Indiana University Press, 2006]).

103. William James, "The Moral Equivalent of War," in *W1902*, 1283. For
a discussion of "The Moral Equivalent of War" and Dewey's reactions to it,
see my chapter 3.

104. If persons in our society pursue activities disproportionately motivated by a narrow desire for personal profit, Dewey argues, this is not the
result of some innate acquisitive drive, but rather a habit shaped by existing
conditions in our economic regime: "Money is a social institution; property
is a legal custom; economic opportunities are dependent upon the state of society; the objects aimed at, the rewards sought for, are what they are because
of social admiration, prestige, competition and power. If money-making is
morally obnoxious it is because of the way these social facts are handled, not
because a money-making man has withdrawn from society into an isolated
selfhood or turned his back upon society. His 'individualism' is not found
in his original nature but in his habits acquired under social influences"
(*Human Nature*, 218).

105. See Freud's public letter "Why War?" written in an exchange with
Albert Einstein, about the causes of war and the prospects for eradicating
it. Citing his theory of the two fundamental human instincts—the libidinal
or erotic and the aggressive or destructive—Freud asserts that the latter explains why "it is so easy to make men enthusiastic about a war." After asserting that there is "no use in trying to get rid of men's aggressive inclinations,"
Freud points to the pacifism of people like himself and Einstein as evidence
of the ongoing psychological evolution of human beings: the "process of
evolution of culture" that "for incalculable ages mankind has been passing through," consisting of a "strengthening of the intellect, which is beginning to govern instinctual life" and which enables "a progressive displace-
ment of instinctual aims and a restriction of instinctual impulses." "War
is in the crassest opposition to the psychical attitude imposed on us by the
cultural process," and as a result of this long and slow development, Freud
concludes, many people find they "cannot help" but "rebel against war": "We
are pacifists because we are obliged to be for organic reasons." Freud says it
is impossible to predict "how long" we will "have to wait before the rest of
mankind become pacifists too." Thus, while Freud does admit the possibility of reforming human nature, his model of primal human impulses that
are susceptible to a gradual process of cultural evolution (that Freud likens
to "the domestication of certain species of animals") stands in marked contrast to Dewey's social psychology, which views human impulses as much
more plastic, capable of being redirected through the (admittedly difficult)
work of reforming the social conditions in which we form our habits ("Why

War?" in *The Modern World*, Classics of Western Thought series, 4th ed., vol. 3, ed. Edgar E. Knoebel [New York: Harcourt, Brace, Jovanovich, 1992 (1964)], 546–559).

106. Dewey, *Human Nature*, 225; Margaret Fuller, *Woman in the Nineteenth Century*, ed. Larry J. Reynolds (New York: W. W. Norton, 1997 [1845]), 46, 74. As Dewey writes in *The Public and Its Problems*, in regards to an educational method informed by a more scientific psychology: "such a change in educational methods would release new potentialities, capable of all kinds of permutations and combinations, which would then modify social phenomena, while this modification would in its turn affect human nature and its educative transformation in a continuous and endless procession" (359).

107. Dewey, *Human Nature*, 89; *Democracy and Education*, 208, 325–26.

108. See Dewey, *Human Nature*, 184–86.

109. Dewey, *Human Nature*, 222; *Reconstruction in Philosophy*, 192, 186, 200.

110. Dewey, *Reconstruction in Philosophy*, 199–200.

111. Dewey, *Public and its Problems*, 327–28.

112. Ibid., 330.

113. Dewey, *Human Nature*, 179.

114. As Erin McKenna has shown, Dewey's analysis of ideals allows us to rethink the concept and function of utopia, providing a pragmatic rationale for a "process model" of utopia that provides an alternative to both the more familiar "end-state" model of utopia (that posits a fixed ideal of society) and the revolutionary "anarchist" model (*The Task of Utopia: A Pragmatist and Feminist Perspective* [Lanham, Md.: Rowman and Littlefield, 2001]).

115. Dewey, *Ethics*, 350.

5. "THE LOCAL IS THE ULTIMATE UNIVERSAL": DEWEY ON
RECONSTRUCTING INDIVIDUALITY AND COMMUNITY

1. William James, *Pragmatism*, in *W1902*, 613.

2. John Dewey, "William James in Nineteen Twenty-Six," in *LW*, 2:159, 161, 159. In a 1942 essay titled "William James and the World Today," Dewey explicitly rejected his earlier worries that James's individualism might be the outdated vestige of an earlier era, and reaffirmed his sense of the enduring political importance of James's philosophy (see note 4 to chapter three, above). Dewey's 1926 essay is a review of the Modern Library edition of *The Philosophy of William James*. Dewey locates the essence of James's individualist ethic by quoting from Horace Kallen's introduction to that edition: James offered, Kallen wrote, an affirmation "of the will to believe at one's own risk in the outcome of an enterprise the success of which is not guaranteed in advance," and within this context, offered "an assertion of the autonomy and naturalness of the individual; of his freedom to win to such success or

excellence as is within his scope, or on his own belief, in his own way, by his own effort, at his own risk during his unending struggle to live in this changing world which was not made for him, this altogether *un*-guaranteed world" ("James in Nineteen Twenty-Six," 159).

3. I use "agencies" here not in the common sense of a governmental bureau or department, but rather in the broad sense of "powers" or "means."

4. Two works that offer thorough discussions of Dewey's approach to reconceiving individuality and community are James Campbell, *The Community Reconstructs: The Meaning of Pragmatic Social Thought* (Urbana: University of Illinois Press, 1992) and Alfonso J. D'Amico, *Individuality and Community: The Social and Political Thought of John Dewey* (Gainesville: University of Florida Press, 1978). Both of these studies' readings of Dewey are consonant with my own, although, as I argue in chapter 3, Campbell's emphasis on the "social" or communal side of pragmatism underestimates the importance of a reconstructed democratic individualism in Dewey's social vision, and posits too rigid an opposition between an individualistic Emerson and James, on the one hand, and Dewey's more "social" vision on the other.

5. John Dewey, *The Public and Its Problems*, in *LW*, 2:296. Dewey takes the phrase a "new age in human relations" from Woodrow Wilson's *The New Freedom*, a book constructed out of Wilson's campaign speeches from the 1912 presidential election. The term "great society" he borrows from Graham Wallas's 1914 book of the same title (*Public and Its Problems*, 295, 404). In arguing that the new economic corporatism of modern life required new governmental agencies to regulate it, Dewey was voicing a position that had become a commonplace of mainstream American political discourse in the 1912 election. Theodore Roosevelt's Progressive Party platform had explicitly endorsed an activist government to deal with the monopoly powers of the modern economy, while William Howard Taft's Republican Party platform had maintained a more conservative laissez-faire position; Wilson's "new freedom" was offered as an alternative to split the difference, and Wilson argued that the threat posed by the corporate forces of the modern economy should be remedied by a restoration of free competition, a position that appealed more to the states' rights sensibilities of the Democratic Party. (For a recent study of the election of 1912, see James Chace, *Wilson, Roosevelt, Taft and Debs—The Election That Changed the Country* [New York: Simon and Schuster, 2004].) Needless to say, Dewey's own conclusions about the implications of these transformations in modern economic and social life, and his subsequent prescriptions for achieving a vital democracy, are far more radical than anything Wilson or Roosevelt ever endorsed.

6. Dewey, *Public and Its Problems*, 316–17.

7. John Dewey, *Individualism Old and New*, in *LW*, 5:67, 69, 104.

8. Ibid., 67.

9. "With an enormous command of instrumentalities, with possession of a secure technology" at our command, "we glorify the past, and legalize and idealize the *status quo*, instead of seriously asking how we are to employ the means at our disposal so as to form an equitable and stable society. This is our great abdication" (ibid., 48).

10. Mumford accuses pragmatism (and Gilded Age culture in general) of "idealizing the real"—that is, of celebrating the vision of progress and value defined by existing industrial and technological means instead of articulating ideals capable of transforming actual conditions—and of thereby abdicating the task of a true idealism, the effort to realize the ideal. As Mumford puts it: "The mission of creative thought is to gather into it all the living sources of its day, all that is vital in the practical life, . . . and, recasting these things into new forms and symbols, to react upon the blind drift of convention and habit and routine. . . . What is valid in idealism is the belief in this process of re-molding, re-forming, re-creating, and so humanizing the rough chaos of existence. That belief had vanished. . . . As Moncure Conway had said: we must idealize the real. There was the work of a Howells, a Clemens, a James. It was an act of grand acquiescence. . . . This generation had lost the power of choice; it bowed to the inevitable" (*The Golden Day: A Study in American Experience and Culture* [New York: Boni and Liveright, 1926], 166). As I discuss in chapter 6, the existence of slavery, which Mumford minimizes almost to the point of ignoring it, is a glaring blind-spot in his image of antebellum American society as a "golden" age of organic sociocultural balance.

11. Mumford quotes Randolph Bourne to make his case against Dewey. The main thrust of Mumford's critique—here in words borrowed from Bourne—is: "To those of us . . . who have taken Dewey's philosophy almost as our American religion, it never occurred that values could be subordinated to technique. . . . And Dewey, of course, always meant his philosophy, when taken as a philosophy of life, to start with values. But there was always that unhappy ambiguity in his doctrine as to just how values were created, and it became easier and easier to assume that just any growth was justified and almost any activity valuable so long as it achieved its ends. The American, in living out his philosophy, has habitually confused results with product, and been content with getting somewhere without asking too closely whether it was the desirable place to get. . . . You must have your vision, and you must have your technique. The practical effect of Dewey's philosophy has evidently been to develop the sense of the latter at the expense of the former" (*The Golden Day*, 265–66). For the full version of this famous critique, see Randolph Bourne, "The Twilight of the Idols," in *The Radical Will: Selected Writings, 1911–1918*, ed. Olaf Hansen (Berkeley: University of California Press, 1977), 336–48.

12. The crux of this disagreement is crystallized in a public exchange
between Dewey and Mumford, on the heels of *The Golden Day*, that was
originally published in *The New Republic*. (The exchange, as well as relevant
excerpts from *The Golden Day*, are reprinted in Gail Kennedy, ed. *Pragmatism and American Culture* [Boston: D. C. Heath, 1950], 49–57). Dewey had
argued, in *Reconstruction in Philosophy*, and in agreement with both Bourne
and Mumford, that the existing instrumentalities of modern technology
and industry had not been sufficiently or intelligently focused on achieving
humane ends: "That up to the present the application of the newer methods
and results has influenced the means of life rather than its ends; or, better put, that human aims have so far been affected in an accidental rather
than in an intelligently directed way, signifies that so far the change has been
technical rather than human and moral, that it has been economic rather
than adequately social. Put in the language of Bacon, this means that while
we have been reasonably successful in obtaining command of nature by
means of science, our science is not yet such that this command is systematically and preeminently applied to the relief of human estate" (*MW*, 12:103).
Both Bourne and Mumford acknowledged that Dewey *intended* instrumentalism to serve humane values, they simply argued (on the basis of historic
evidence) that it was incapable of doing so. "Mr. Dewey seems to believe,"
Mumford argues, "that the 'ends' or 'ideals' will come into existence of
themselves, if only we pay careful attention to the means. I do not share this
belief; and in view of what has happened during the last three centuries, it
seems to me one of bland complaisance or blind optimism" ("The Pragmatic
Acquiescence: A Reply," in Kennedy, *Pragmatism and American Culture*, 56).

Dewey offers two rejoinders. First, he reiterates that the very concept of
instruments implies "ends to which they are put" and "values for which tools
and agencies are to be used," and that to stress the importance of "science and
technology" as instruments is to assert that they are *not* primary or "final,"
"not the truth or reality of the world and life." Second, he reaffirms his view
that the greatest threat to humane ends lies not, as Mumford claims, in too
much attention to instruments, but in our *failure* to attend to the instrumentalities that supply the only means by which new and humane ends might be
imagined and realized. Dewey writes: "The ideal values which dignify and
give meaning to human life have themselves in the past been precarious in
possession, arbitrary, accidental and monopolized in distribution, because
of lack of means of control; by lack, in other words, of those agencies and
instrumentalities with which natural science through technologies equips
mankind. Not all who say Ideals, Ideals, shall enter the kingdom of the ideal,
but those who know and who respect the roads that conduct to the kingdom"
("The Pragmatic Acquiescence," in Kennedy, *Pragmatism and American*

Culture, 53). For an excellent discussion of the Dewey-Mumford exchange, see Robert B. Westbrook, "Lewis Mumford, John Dewey, and the 'Pragmatic Acquiescence," in *Lewis Mumford: Public Intellectual*, ed. Thomas P. Hughes and Agatha C. Hughes (New York: Oxford University Press, 1990). 301–22.

13. Dewey, *Individualism Old and New*, 63, 74.

14. Ibid., 69. James Livingston cogently argues that it is Mumford's nostalgia for an allegedly more organic antebellum America that is truly acquiescent or politically impotent, whereas pragmatism's acceptance of the industrial revolution as a fait accompli leads to a more effective, and ultimately more radical, political stance. See *Pragmatism and the Political Economy of Cultural Revolution, 1850–1940* (Chapel Hill: University of North Carolina Press, 1994), esp. 225–55. Livingston focuses mainly on William James as embodying this pragmatic politics.

15. Dewey, *Public and Its Problems*, 333.

16. Ibid., 323 ; Dewey, *Individualism Old and New*, 87, 101, 100, 57.

17. For excellent overviews of Dewey's arguments in *The Public and Its Problems*, see James Gouinlock's introduction in Dewey, *LW*, 2:xxiii–xxxvi, and Robert B. Westbrook, *John Dewey and American Democracy* (Ithaca, N.Y.: Cornell University Press, 1991), 300–318.

18. Dewey, *Public and Its Problems*, 243–45, 252, 253, 276–77. Dewey's insistence that public regulation may be concerned with "inhibition or promtion" of consequences affecting the public good is an important distinction, for it posits a legitimate public interest in regulating social interactions not only to prevent harmful consequences that might impinge on the liberties of other individuals (to which function laissez-faire liberal individualism wants to limit government), but also to promote beneficial consequences that enable individuals to liberate their capacities—for example, by providing universal access to quality education or health care. I use the terms "recognized" and "identified" because a public may exist without being known; that is, the indirect consequences of associated activity may not be adequately understood, and so may define a public that is unacknowledged, inchoate, or undiscovered.

19. Ibid., 256. This generic definition does imply a standard for a good state: "namely, the degree of organization of the public which is attained, and the degree in which its officers are so constituted as to perform their function of caring for public interests" (256).

20. Ibid., 256.

21. For Lenin's discussion of Engels's description of the "withering away" of the state, see V. I. Lenin, "State and Revolution," in *The Modern World*, Classics of Western Thought series, 4th ed., vol. 3, ed. Edgar E. Knoebel (New York: Harcourt, Brace, Jovanovich, 1988), 585–96. For a discussion of

how Dewey's pragmatism led him to critique Marxism, see Westbrook, *John Dewey and American Democracy*, 465–76.

22. Dewey, *Public and Its Problems*, 356, 361, 356, 281.

23. Ralph Waldo Emerson, "Politics," in *E&L*, 559–60, 563. Dewey, *Public and Its Problems*, 326–27, 341. See my chapters 2 and 4 for related discussions of Emerson's essay "Politics" and affinities between his and Dewey's views of reform.

24. Dewey, *Public and Its Problems*, 316–17, 320.

25. Ibid., 327.

26. Ibid., 339.

27. Ibid., 362, 339–40; Dewey, *Ethics*, 329. In calling for such a "positive toleration" that goes beyond merely tolerating freedom of opinion and expression, Dewey articulates an important difference between his democratic model of social inquiry and the liberal defense of freedom of opinion John Stuart Mill articulates in *On Liberty*. For a detailed comparison of Dewey's and Mills's positions, see James Gouinlock, *Excellence in Public Discourse: John Stuart Mill, John Dewey, and Social Intelligence* (New York: Teachers College Press, 1986).

28. Dewey, *Public and Its Problems*, 345–46.

29. Ibid., 364, 365. Dewey argues that "a thing is fully known only when it is published, shared, socially accessible" (345).

30. Dewey is quite explicit about the need for this distinction: there is no such thing as a "mysterious collective agency" that is capable of acting; even when a collective or public interest is being claimed or expressed, it is always individuals who act in their capacity as public officials. Accordingly, he argues that the primary problem of representative government or democracy is ensuring that officials do actually act in the public interest and he stresses the subsequent need to improve the level of public debate through which the public's views, values, and choices are communicated to elected officials. See *Public and Its Problems*, 247, 283, 365.

31. As Dewey puts it in an aptly pedestrian metaphor: "The man who wears the shoe knows best . . . where it pinches, even if the expert shoemaker is the best judge of how the trouble is to be remedied" (ibid., 364).

32. See John Dewey, "Practical Democracy" (a review of Lippmann's *The Phantom Public*), in *LW*, 2:213–20. On how Dewey's debate with Lippmann shaped *The Public and Its Problems*, see Westbrook, *John Dewey and American Democracy*, 294–300; and Alan Ryan, *John Dewey and the High Tide of American Liberalism* (New York: W. W. Norton, 1995), 216–20.

33. Dewey, *Public and Its Problems*, 365–66. The following examples are representative of this recurrent theme in Emerson: "He that is once admitted to the right of reason is made a freeman of the whole estate. What Plato has

thought, he may think; what a saint has felt, he may feel; what any time has befallen any man, he can understand"; "All that Shakspeare says of the king, yonder slip of a boy that reads in the corner feels to be true of himself"; and "How easily we adopt their labors! Every ship that comes to America got its chart from Columbus. Every novel is a debtor to Homer. Every carpenter who shaves with a foreplane borrows the genius of a forgotten inventor. Life is girt all around with a zodiac of sciences, the contributions of men who have perished to add their point of light to our sky" ("History," in *E&L*, 237, 238–39; "The Uses of Great Men," in *E&L*, 620).

34. Dewey, *Public and Its Problems*, 347, 348–49, 323–24, 332.

35. Ibid., 341.

36. Ibid., 357.

37. Dewey, *Ethics*, 331–32, 333; *Public and Its Problems*, 289–90; *Ethics*, 333; *Public and Its Problems*, 289. Dewey describes individualism as committing a dogmatic or absolutist fallacy, whereby "the temporary phenomenon is taken as an illustration of an eternal truth, and the needs of a particular situation frozen into a universal principle" (*Ethics*, 326).

38. Dewey, *Public and Its Problems*, 299; *Experience and Nature*, in *LW*, 1:59–60; *Reconstruction in Philosophy*, in *MW*, 12:190–91; *Public and Its Problems*, 251.

39. Dewey, *Public and Its Problems*, 354–55, 329, 356; *Human Nature and Conduct*, in *MW*, 14:210.

40. Dewey, *Ethics*, 333–34; *Public and Its Problems*, 276, 294, 295. *Individualism Old and New* repeatedly stresses the fact that outdated and absolutistic tenets of classic liberal individualism are perhaps the greatest impediment to envisioning and realizing a new type of democratic individuality that is consonant with, and can be fostered by, the conditions of corporate industrial society. "A stable recovery of individuality waits upon an elimination of the older economic and political individualism," Dewey argues, "an elimination which will liberate imagination and endeavor for the task of making corporate society contribute to the free culture of its members." "Traditional ideas" of individuality "are more than irrelevant," he claims, "They are an encumbrance; they are the chief obstacle to the formation of a new individuality integrated within itself and with a liberated function in the society wherein it exists." Along similar lines, he asserts: "The chief obstacle to the creation of a type of individual whose pattern of thought and desire is enduringly marked by consensus with others, and in whom sociability is one with cooperation in all regular human associations, is the persistence of that feature of earlier individualism which defines industry and commerce by ideas of private pecuniary profit" (75–76, 86, 84).

41. Dewey, *Ethics*, 335–36; *Individualism Old and New*, 48–49; *Ethics*, 334–35. Similarly, though he rejects the classic or "historic" form of liberalism,

Dewey argues that liberalism should not be abandoned, but reconstructed. Toward this end, in *Liberalism and Social Action* he argues that liberalism's core principles—its commitment to liberty, equality and fraternity—have an enduring value if redefined in a manner consistent with the pragmatic ideals of experimental social inquiry and democracy as a communal way of life.

42. Dewey, *Ethics*, 335.

43. Dewey, *Reconstruction in Philosophy*, 186, 192–93.

44. Dewey, *Public and Its Problems*, 327; *Reconstruction in Philosophy*, 199; *Individualism Old and New*, 104, 76, 103.

45. Dewey, *Individualism Old and New*, 80–81.

46. Dewey, *Ethics*, 345–46.

47. Dewey, *Individualism Old and New*, 84.

48. Dewey, *Public and Its Problems*, 244; *Ethics*, 336.

49. Dewey, *Individualism Old and New*, 73, 72, 109; *Public and Its Problems*, 360.

50. Dewey, *Individualism Old and New*, 89, 104–5, 109, 123.

51. Dewey, *Ethics*, 319. As noted in chapter 4, Dewey insists that morals are *always* both individual and social. He uses the distinction between "personal" and "social" morals merely to indicate "the kind of moral questions which are uppermost"—"personal" morals referring to periods when "social life is stable" so that "the problems of morals have to do with the adjustments which individuals make to the institutions in which they live," while morals become more "social" when "social life is in a state of flux," and "moral issues . . . centre in the value of social arrangements, of laws, of inherited traditions that have crystallized into institutions" (*Ethics*, 319, 314–15).

52. Dewey, *Public and Its Problems*, 252–53, 325, 367.

53. Ibid., 370.

54. Dewey, *Individualism Old and New*, 96.

55. Ibid., 96, 98.

56. Ibid., 120.

57. Ibid., 120–21.

58. Ibid., 112.

59. This idea of "recovery" illuminates Emerson's assertion that "We must hold hard to this poverty, however scandalous, and by more vigorous self-recoveries, after the sallies of action, possess our axis more firmly" ("Experience," in *E&L*, 490).

60. Dewey, *Individualism Old and New*, 123; James, *Pragmatism*, 612–13; Dewey, *Individualism Old and New*, 122–23; *Public and Its Problems*, 369. Dewey describes the religious ideality of local experience in *Human Nature and Conduct*, in *Experience and Nature*, and, most thoroughly, in *A Common*

Faith. For Dewey, this religious aspect of experience is wholly naturalistic, requiring no positing of supernatural deity. See my chapter 3 for a discussion of how James, by contrast, defends a supernatural god as necessary to—and consistent with—a melioristic ethics in a pluralistic universe.

61. Dewey, *Individualism Old and New*, 122–23. Dewey actually misquotes the second of these three passages in a manner that softens the extremity of Emerson's claim, which reads: "Society everywhere is in conspiracy against *the manhood of every one of* its members" ("Self-Reliance," 261; emphasis added).

62. Dewey, *Individualism Old and New*, 104.

63. Ibid., 103–4.

64. In his updated introduction to the 1946 edition of *The Public and Its Problems*, Dewey cited the United Nations as evidence "that there is developing the sense that relations between nations are taking on the properties that constitute a public, and hence call for some measure of political organization" (*LW*, 2:375).

65. One cannot, of course, fully explain the current divide between the Right and Left in American politics as the contrast between a laissez-faire liberalism and a (watered-down) New Deal–variety belief in government regulation and intervention. This contrast *is* most accurate and applicable in terms of questions of socioeconomic justice, with the American Right opposing a progressive income tax, stronger environmental and workplace-safety regulations, public health-care funding, increased funding of public education, etc., on the grounds of preventing an excessive level of governmental "interference" or "socialism" that would stifle economic initiative and growth and impose a tyrannical restraint on individual liberty and local, state government. On other issues, however, such as women's reproductive freedoms or increased government authority to conduct domestic surveillance, it is the Right which favors more government intervention (even at the cost of creating new bureaucracies), while the Left decries such government intervention as infringing on individual liberties.

66. Dewey, *Public and Its Problems*, 351; *Human Nature*, 202.

67. Dewey, *Public and Its Problems*, 332, 323–24.

6. SAYING YES AND SAYING NO: INDIVIDUALIST ETHICS IN ELLISON AND BURKE

1. W. E. B. Du Bois, *The Souls of Black Folk*, in *Three Negro Classics* (New York: Avon, 1965 [1903]), 215.

2. Ralph Ellison, "That Same Pain, That Same Pleasure," in *CE*, 71, 68–69, 70, 72. "I came to understand, in other words, that all that stood between me and writing symphonies was not simply a matter of civil rights, even

though the civil rights struggle was all too real" (72). For Ellison's criticisms of Wright, see "That Same Pain," 73–75; "Richard Wright's Blues," in *CE*, 128–44; and "The World and the Jug," in *CE*, 155–88.

3. Paul Gilroy offers a similar theory of culturally mixed identity that cuts across racial and national lines. He depicts the "transcultural, international cultural formation" of the African diaspora—characterized by "hybridity" and "homelessness," by "routes" instead of "roots"—as a "counter-culture" to the dominant Western paradigm of enlightenment/modernity and its underlying dualism of purity and exclusion. Gilroy does not offer a sustained discussion of Ellison, focusing instead on writers, like Du Bois and Wright, whose trans-Atlantic expatriation catalyzed their sense of transcultural identity. See *The Black Atlantic: Modernity and Double Consciousness* (Cambridge, Ma: Harvard University Press, 1993), 4, 2, 111–12, 2, 45–46, 17–19. There are, nonetheless, clear affinities between Ellison's and Gilroy's views of black cultures as existing in spaces at once inside and outside of mainstream Western culture (following Du Bois's model of "double-consciousness")—spaces characterized both by exclusion and by a freedom to appropriate and mix cultural styles. Ellison uses the autobiographical trope of the Oklahoma "territory" to describe his border space, while Gilroy uses the international space of the Atlantic and the ships that traversed it. See Ralph Ellison, "Going to the Territory," in *CE*, 600–605; and Gilroy, *Black Atlantic*, 16–17.

4. This interpretation has gained ascendancy in the work of recent critics such as Alan Nadel (discussed in the body of this chapter) and Kun Jong Lee. Following Cornel West's lead, Lee argues that Ellison's satire is aimed at the inability of Emerson's individualism to deal with the reality of racism; see Lee, "Ellison's *Invisible Man*: Emersonianism Revised," *PMLA* 107 (1992): 331–44. The first wave of critics to assess Ellison's allusions to Emerson focused mainly on literary or philosophical affinities between the two writers, instead of on Ellison's political revision of Emerson. See Leonard J. Deutsch, "Ralph Waldo Ellison and Ralph Waldo Emerson: A Shared Moral Vision," *CLA Journal* 16 (1972): 159–78; William W. Nichols, "Ralph Ellison's Black American Scholar," *Phylon* 31 (1970): 70–5; and Earl H. Rovit, "Ralph Ellison and the American Comic Tradition," *Wisconsin Studies in Contemporary Literature* 1.3 (1960): 34–42. My own approach is offered as an alternative to each of these trends, one that acknowledges both the philosophical tradition connecting Ellison and Emerson, and the way in which Ellison turns this inheritance to his own political concerns. Since this chapter was originally published, several critics have explored further the lines of influence from Emerson to Ellison (and sometimes, through Burke). Lawrence Buell reads Emerson's influence on Ellison as an example of Emersonian (anti)mentorship (*Emerson* [Cambridge, Ma: Harvard University Press, 2003], 315–25).

Michael Magee concurs with my emphasis on the "intensity of connections between Emerson, Burke, and Ellison," but stresses Burke's concept of language as symbolic action, which, Magee argues, undergirds "Ellison's view of pragmatism and jazz as related forms of democratic symbolic action" (*Emancipating Pragmatism: Emerson, Jazz, and Experimental Writing* [Tuscaloosa: University of Alabama Press, 2004], 191n23). And Jack Turner argues that Ellison, by extending the Emersonian ethic of "moral and intellectual awakening" to include an "honest confrontation" of race, "did not simply rehabilitate the Emersonian project, but revolutionized it" ("Awakening to Race: Ralph Ellison and Democratic Individuality," *Political Theory* 36, no. 5: 656–67).

5. For a different analysis of Ellison's individualism, see Jerry Gafio Watts, *Heroism and the Black Intellectual: Ralph Ellison, Politics, and Afro-American Intellectual Life* (Chapel Hill: North Carolina University Press, 1994). Focusing not on Ellison's fiction, but on his career as an African-American intellectual and on his public statements about the purposes and responsibilities of art, Watts discusses Ellison in light of the conflict between "hyperpoliticized" and "depoliticized" approaches to African-American cultural studies. Though he admires Ellison for championing the complexity of African-American cultural and individual experience against a reductive Marxism or Black Nationalism, Watts critiques Ellison's individualism for veering too far in the opposite direction. Ellison's cultural pluralism and his commitment to a vision of the exceptional, heroic individual as a measure of freedom and possibility, Watts argues, remain trapped in a bourgeois, meritocratic elitism that ignores, or underestimates, the determining force that structures of inequality have upon the individual; see pages 11, 57, 71, 62, 105, 96, 81–85, 108. While Watts offers a valuable discussion of Ellison's debate with Irving Howe (and Richard Wright) over the politics of literary practice, his conclusion that Ellison retreats into an apolitical individualism is too determined by the polemics of this debate. My reading of the individualist ethics dramatized in *Invisible Man*, and of the responsibilities of democratic art that Ellison outlines in "Twentieth Century Fiction and the Black Mask of Humanity," are intended to show that Ellison had a more coherent, and politically engaged, vision of individualism—and literary practice—than Watts seems to allow.

6. Ralph Ellison, "The Art of Fiction: An Interview," in *CE*, 218–19. For a selection of pieces that discuss Ellison's connection to Burke, see Ralph Ellison, "The Essential Ellison," *Y'Bird Reader* (Autumn 1977): 130–59; Kenneth Burke, "Ralph Ellison's Trueblooded *Bildungsroman*" in *Speaking for You: The Vision of Ralph Ellison*, ed. Kimberly W. Benston (Washington, D.C.: Howard University Press, 1987), 349–59; Sandra Adell, "The Big E(llison)'s

Texts and Intertexts: Eliot, Burke, and the Underground Man," *CLA Journal* 37 (June 1994): 377–401; Robert O'Meally, "On Burke and the Vernacular: Ralph Ellison's Boomerang of History," in *History and Memory in African-American Culture*, ed. Genevieve Fabre and Robert O'Meally (New York: Oxford University Press, 1994), 244–60; Timothy L. Parrish, "Ralph Ellison, Kenneth Burke, and the Form of Democracy," *Arizona Quarterly* 52 (Autumn 1995): 117–48; Donald Pease, "Ralph Ellison and Kenneth Burke: The Nonsymbolizable (Trans)Action," *boundary 2* 30, no. 2 (2003), 65–96; Danielle Allen, "Ralph Ellison on the Tragi-Comedy of Citizenship," in *Ralph Ellison and the Raft of Hope: A Political Companion to "Invisible Man,"* ed. Lucas E. Morel (Lexington: The University Press of Kentucky, 2004), 37–57; and Magee, *Emancipating Pragmatism*.

7. See chapter 1 for my discussion of how critics such as Sacvan Bercovitch, Myra Jehlen, and Christopher Newfield offer political critiques that accept and perpetuate the traditional dichotomies of Emerson criticism. Cornel West has offered the most ambitious attempt to map a genealogy of American pragmatism that includes African-American writers. West does not include either Burke or Ellison in his study. Moreover, West is ultimately dismissive of the political potential of the Emerson-James trajectory of pragmatism, arguing that both thinkers are hindered by a "bourgeois" commitment to individualism that prevents them from "taking seriously fundamental social change." West further argues that Emerson's commitment to egalitarianism is seriously "circumscribed" by a racist determinism. See *The American Evasion of Philosophy* (Madison: University of Wisconsin Press, 1989), 60, 28–35. My reading of the Emerson-Burke-Ellison line of influence is offered, in part, to suggest alternatives to West's assessment of the political trajectory of pragmatic individualism.

8. Ralph Ellison, "Hidden Name and Complex Fate," in *CE*, 194–97; Ralph Ellison, *IM*, 41.

9. Ellison, *IM*, 44–45.

10. Ibid., 45, 191.

11. Alan Nadel, *Invisible Criticism: Ralph Ellison and the American Canon* (Iowa City: Iowa University Press, 1988), 115, 118, 116, 159.

12. Ibid., 86–89; James Livingston, *Pragmatism and the Political Economy of Cultural Revolution* (Chapel Hill: University of North Carolina Press, 1994), 225–55. Nadel's and Livingston's criticisms of Mumford's historical nostalgia are by no means representative of Mumford's reception—especially by critics on the Left. For an example of a more reverent reading of Mumford, see Casey Nelson Blake, *Beloved Community: The Cultural Criticism of Randolph Bourne, Van Wyck Brooks, Waldo Frank, and Lewis Mumford* (Chapel Hill: North Carolina University Press, 1990).

13. Lewis Mumford, *The Golden Day: A Study in American Experience and Culture* (New York: Boni and Liveright, 1926), 91, 183–93.

14. This line of argument is buttressed by Lawrence Buell's suggestion that Ellison's character Mr. Norton may allude to Charles Eliot Norton, as a "mocking echo of the late Victorian reduction of Emersonianism to personality gestalt" (*Emerson*, 315). For a discussion of the antiseptic, apoliticized version of Emerson promoted by figures like Charles Eliot Norton, see Charles E. Mitchell, *Individualism and Its Discontents: Appropriations of Emerson, 1880–1950* (Amherst: University of Massachusetts Press, 1997), 12–14 and 12–72 passim. Buell's suggestion can be extended further, since Charles Eliot Norton's father was the conservative Unitarian theologian Andrews Norton, who publicly blasted Emerson after his Divinity School address. The dual allusion to these two historical Nortons, then, would signify how the actual radicalism of Emerson's writings became obscured by the reductive version of "Emerson" promoted by intellectuals such as Charles Eliot Norton and Lewis Mumford.

15. Mumford, *The Golden Day*, 136; Ralph Ellison, "Twentieth-Century Fiction and the Black Mask of Humanity," in *CE*, 88. Recent scholarship has stressed that Emerson, though he felt that his talents and temperament made him ill-suited for politics, took an increasingly active role in voicing public support for the abolition movement throughout the 1840s and 1850s. See Len Gougeon, *Virtue's Hero: Emerson, Antislavery and Reform* (Athens: University of Georgia Press, 1990) and *Emerson's Antislavery Writings*, ed. Len Gougeon and Joel Myerson (New Haven, Conn.: Yale University Press, 2002).

16. Nadel, *Invisible Criticism*, 94–103, 113.

17. Ibid., 113.

18. Ralph Waldo Emerson, "Fate," in *E&L*, 952.

19. Ibid., 953.

20. Ibid., 958, 957.

21. See Michael Lopez, "The Anti-Emerson Tradition" and "De-Transcendentalizing Emerson" in *Emerson and Power: Creative Antagonism in the Nineteenth Century* (Dekalb: Northern Illinois University Press, 1996), 19–52, 165–89. For a discussion of the competing currents in Emerson's critical reception, see my chapter 2.

22. Ellison, "Hidden Name," 197, 208–9.

23. See my chapter 1 for a discussion of Emerson's relation to this pragmatic tradition, considered through the lens of William James, and chapter 4 for a discussion of Dewey's tribute to Emerson as "the philosopher of democracy."

24. In this section of chapter 6, I of necessity rehearse arguments—and discuss key passages—already discussed in a different context in chapter 2, which offers a fuller consideration of such themes in relation to Emerson's overall philosophy.

25. Ralph Waldo Emerson, "The Conservative," in *E&L*, 178; "Fate," 946.

26. Kenneth Burke, *A Grammar of Motives* (Berkeley: University of California Press, 1969 [1945]), 38–39.

27. Ralph Waldo Emerson, "Spiritual Laws," in *E&L*, 314; "Man the Reformer," in *E&L*, 140; "Self-Reliance," in *E&L*, 281; "Spiritual Laws," 311.

28. Emerson, "Self-Reliance," 260, 264; "Shakspeare; or, the Poet," in *E&L*, 710–11.

29. Emerson, "Self-Reliance," 274.

30. Ralph Waldo Emerson, "The Uses of Great Men," in *E&L*, 620.

31. For a discussion of Emerson's vision of community, see my chapter 2.

32. Kenneth Burke, *A Rhetoric of Motives* (Berkeley: California University Press, 1969 [1950]), 27, 30–31.

33. Burke's attitude toward technology here is firmly in the Jamesian pragmatic tradition. As Livingston cogently argues, it is ironic that Mumford should target pragmatism in his polemic against the modern threats to human agency, for one of James's central concerns is to reaffirm human will, belief, and action. As Livingston asserts, pragmatism did not "surrender the genuine self or the moral personality to the empiricists and positivists," but rather accepted the modern industrial order as an accomplished historical fact—as "the premise of their thinking about the meaning and moral stability of the human personality"—in order to appropriate the possibilities for future transformation inherent in that new order. Where "Mumford saw only symptoms of disease," pragmatists saw "attempted cures as well" (*Pragmatism and the Political Economy*, 278–89, 246). These are, of course, the same lines along which Dewey publicly rebutted Mumford's critique; see my chapter 5.

34. Burke, *A Rhetoric of Motives*, 146, 110, 72.

35. Kenneth Burke, *Attitudes toward History* (Los Altos, Ca.: Hermes, 1959 [1937]), 37–39, 107, 42, 107.

36. Ibid., 41.

37. Ibid., 107; Burke, *A Rhetoric of Motives*, 27–29.

38. Burke, *Attitudes toward History*, 5, 20, 3, 18, 19.

39. Ibid., 107.

40. Ralph Waldo Emerson, "Experience," in *E&L*, 484.

41. Ellison, "Address to the Harvard College Alumni," in *CE*, 418.

42. Ibid., 418–19.

43. Houston A Baker Jr., "To Move without Moving: An Analysis of Creativity and Commerce in Ralph Ellison's Trueblood Episode," *PMLA* 98 (October 1983): 844; Ralph Ellison, "The Novel as a Function of American Democracy," in *CE*, 760.

44. Ellison, "Address to the Harvard College Alumni," 419–20, 418.

45. Ibid., 420–21, 423.

46. Ibid., 425.

47. Ellison, "Novel as a Function," 760.

48. Ellison, "That Same Pain," 80.

49. Ellison, "Hidden Name," 208.

50. Ralph Ellison, introduction to *Shadow and Act*, in *CE*, 57.

51. Ralph Ellison, "Working Notes for *Invisible Man*," in *CE*, 344.

52. In contrast to Baker's description of Trueblood as a trickster figure of phallic power, Hortense Spillers stresses that the socioeconomic forces splintering the black family make the Western Oedipal myth inapplicable to African-American fathers and daughters. See "'The Permanent Obliquity of the In(pha)llibly Straight': In the Time of the Daughters and the Fathers," in *Changing Our Own Words: Essays on Criticism, Theory, and Writing by Black Women*, ed. Cheryl A. Wall (New Brunswick, N.J.: Rutgers University Press, 1989), 127–49.

53. Baker, "To Move without Moving," 832.

54. Ralph Ellison, "Change the Joke and Slip the Yoke," in *CE*, 103.

55. For examples of readings that stress the importance of the act of narration in *Invisible Man*, see John F. Callahan, "Frequencies of Eloquence: The Performance and Composition of *Invisible Man*," in *New Essays on Invisible Man*, ed. Robert O'Meally (New York: Cambridge University Press, 1988), 55–94; Robert B. Stepto, "Literacy and Hibernation: Ralph Ellison's *Invisible Man*," in *Speaking for You*, 360–85; and Valerie Smith, "The Meaning of Narration in *Invisible Man*," in *New Essays on Invisible Man*, 25–53.

56. Ellison, "The Art of Fiction," 215; "Change the Joke," 111; *IM*, 541, 13, 567–68, 556. This paralysis, Burke might suggest, reflects tragedy's tendency to associate insight with punishment and even death, while comedy, in contrast, tends to symbolize insight as rebirth in which the "mistaken" blindnesses of the old self are left behind (*A Grammar of Motives*, 39). Accordingly, in his short essay on *Invisible Man*, Burke describes Ellison's novel as a kind of bildungsroman, tracing the narrator's successive transformations as he develops a more complex comic consciousness in response to the complexities of race relations he encounters.

57. Ellison, *IM*, 556, 497, 557, 560, 496.

58. Ellison, "That Same Pain," 79–80.

59. For example: Valerie Smith discusses how Bledsoe, Brother Tarp, Rinehart, Trueblood, and Tod Clifton represent model identities for the narrator to emulate, models that place Ellison's protagonist "in a tradition of Afro-American letters" whose writers "name themselves before a culture that had denied their full humanity" ("The Meaning of Narration," 27); Stepto in "Literacy and Hibernation" places Ellison's novel in the rhetorical tradition of slave narratives; and Callahan in "Frequencies of Eloquence" argues that the political themes of Ellison's narrator reflect the particular experiences of southern blacks, and that the rhetoric of the narrator's speeches reflects the communal call-and-response form of African-American worship.

60. Ellison, "World and the Jug," 178, 218–19.

61. In addition to illuminating the narrator's hibernation, Burke's comic ethics inform a scene from chapter 14 of the novel, where the narrator, at a Brotherhood cocktail party, is asked by a white (and intoxicated) member of

the organization to sing a spiritual. While Brother Jack angrily denounces the request as racist, the narrator responds with laughter that defuses the situation. The narrator's subsequent reflection—"Shouldn't there be some way for us to be asked to sing? Shouldn't the short man have the right to make a mistake without his motives being considered consciously or unconsciously malicious?"—is a clear echo of Burke's comic frame, and suggests how consciously Ellison was patterning his protagonist's development along Burkean lines.

62. Ralph Ellison, "An Extravagance of Laughter," in *CE*, 647; Burke, *Attitudes toward History*, 171; Ellison, *IM*, 568.

63. Ellison, *IM*, 13. Strictly speaking, the narrator performs another confrontational act in his "hibernation": as described in the novel's prologue, he assaults and almost kills a white man who insults him with a racial epithet. Though, in temporal terms, both acts occur during the narrator's hibernation, in terms of the novel's structure this confrontation from the prologue provides a symmetrical contrast to the narrator's confrontation of Norton in the novel's epilogue. Ellison thus seems to offer rhetorical confrontation as an alternative to violent confrontation, which again aligns him with Burke, who argues in *Attitudes toward History* and *A Rhetoric of Motives* that the comic and rhetorical attitudes advocate persuasion and compromise instead of violence.

64. Ellison, *IM*, 564–65.

65. Ibid., 560.

66. Ibid., 566–67.

67. Ibid., 497–98, 16.

68. Ellison, "Twentieth-Century Fiction," 89–90, 88, 89, 91.

69. Ibid., 92–96, 88.

70. Ellison, *IM*, 568.

71. William James, "The Moral Philosopher and the Moral Life," in *W1878*, 614.

72. John Dewey, *Reconstruction in Philosophy*, in *MW*, 12:191; *The Public and Its Problems*, in *LW*, 2:329, 356.

73. Ellison, "Hidden Name," 208.

74. John Dewey, *Individualism Old and New*, in *LW*, 5:80.

75. John Dewey, *Human Nature and Conduct*, in *MW*, 14:215.

76. As Dewey writes: "conditions are not fixed. . . . By becoming conscious of their movements and by active participation in their currents, we may guide them to some preferred possibility. In this interaction, individuals attain an integrated being. The individual who intelligently and actively partakes in a perception that is a first step in conscious choice is never so isolated as to be lost nor so quiescent as to be suppressed" (*Individualism Old and New*, 112).

77. Emerson, "Self-Reliance," 260, 275.

Index

Addams, Jane, 314n23
Adell, Sandra, 365n6
Adventures of Huckleberry Finn (Twain), 305
Albrecht, James M., 321n45, 338n49
Allen, Danielle, 366n6
American Renaissance (Matthiessen), 282
Appiah, Kwame Anthony, 313n15
Aquinas, Thomas, 79
Arieli, Yehoshua, 328n104
Aristotle, 197, 229
Arvin, Newton, 325n27

Baker, Houston A., Jr., 295, 298–89, 369n52
Bartlett's Familiar Quotations, 43
Bellah, Robert, 13–15, 313n21, 314n23
Bercovitch, Sacvan, 107–8
Blake, Casey Nelson, 366n12
Bloom, Harold, 29
Bourne, Randolph, 249, 315n29, 357n11, 358n12
Brooks, Van Wyck, 26, 316n8
Buell, Lawrence, 364n4, 367n14
Burke, Kenneth: comic ethics, 291–94, 296, 369n61; doctrine of compensation, 65, 294; frames of acceptance, 293–94; and Ellison, Ralph, 296–304, 370n61; on Emerson, Ralph Waldo, 291–95; identification, 291, 293, 299, 302, 305; and James, William, 293–94; on transcendentalism, 39, 46.
Burke, Kenneth (works): *Attitudes toward History*, 65, 231–32, 292–94, 302, 321–22n58, 370n63; *A Grammar of Motives*, 39, 64–65, 289, 369n56; "I, Eye, Ay—Emerson's Early Essay 'Nature,'" 317n11; "Ralph Ellison's Trueblooded Bildungsroman," 365n6; *A Rhetoric of Motives*, 231–32, 291–93, 343n128, 370n63

Calhoun, John C., 114
Callahan, John F., 370nn55, 59
Campbell, James, 315n33, 333–34n5, 342n125, 344n3, 356n4
Capital (Marx), 98–99, 199, 328–29n110
Carlyle, Thomas, 43
Carpenter, Frederic, 29, 32, 318n18
Cavell, Stanley, 29–30, 48, 288, 322n63
Cherokee Nation, 123
Chesterton, G.K., 25
communitarianism, versus individualism, 12–15, 314n27
Compromise of 1850, 113
Coon, Deborah, 333n1
Cotkin, George, 333n2

D'Amico, Alfonso J., 356n4
Democracy in America (Tocqueville), 2, 12–13, 311n1, 313n17
Deutsch, Leonard J., 364n4
Dewey, John: character as "interpenetration of habits," 204; character in moral selfhood, chapter 4, *passim*; community, 240, 260; community as inherently local, 267–68; community threatened by global capitalist order, 247–51; democracy as community, 5–6, 239–41; democracy and education, 237–39; democracy as pragmatic ideal, 241–43; democracy as "way of life," 5, 194; dualisms of Western philosophy, 3–5, 198–99; egoism versus altruism, 222–26; ends-in-view, 210; experience, pluralistic model of, 3, 197–99; great society versus great community, 247, 267–68, 356n5; habit, compared to Emerson, 200, 203–4; habits, 198–99; habits as constituting the self 201, 204; habits, in deliberation, 206–10; habits and plasticity of self,

199–214; happiness, 220, 227; individual
responsibility for liberty, 270–271;
integrated individuality, 268–69;
and James, William, 18, 143–44,
156–57, 162–63, 184–85,189–90, 244,
271–72, 335n9, 337n44, 342n125; liberal
individualism, critique of, 6–8, 256–65;
liberty, 5–6, 230–31; means and ends,
208–214; meliorism, compared to
Emerson and James, 212–14; morals and
moral theory, 214–32; moral selfhood,
chapter 4, *passim*; moral self, compared
to Burke and Ellison, 231–32, 276–77;
moral self, dynamism of, compared to
Emerson 231–32; moral self, habits of,
218–32; Mumford, Lewis, debate over
"pragmatic acquiescence," 249–51,
358n12; public, defined, 251; public,
experimentalist theory of, 251–56;
pluralism, in metaphysics, 196–97;
reform, approach to, 232–43; reform,
compared to Emerson, 235–36; reform,
versus standard individualist or
collectivist approaches, 234–35, 259–65;
state, experimentalist theory of, 251–56;
tragic sensibility, 209
Dewey, John (works): *Art as Experience*,
191; *A Common Faith*, 362–63n60;
Democracy and Education, 104, 164,
191, 210, 223–24, 238, 346n25, 351n87;
"The Development of American
Pragmatism," 336–38; "Emerson—The
Philosopher of Democracy," 52, 191,
193–94, 344n5; *Ethics*, 152, 213–14,
217–23, 227–31, 259–60, 266–67,
346n30, 350n77, 351n88, 352–53n95,
362n51; *Experience and Nature*,
196–98, 321n45, 347n43, 352n92;
Freedom and Culture, 191; "From
Absolutism to Experimentalism,"
337n43; *Human Nature and Conduct*,
5, 16–17, 37, 41, 130, 133, 137–38,
156–57, 173, 199–213, 218–20, 226,
231, 233–38, 262, 309–10, 345n15, 23,
351n89, 352n94, 353n97, 354n104;
Individualism Old and New, 6, 190,
195, 232, 234, 240, 244–46, 248, 250–51,
256, 259, 261–66, 268–69, 271–73, 308,
311n1, 361n40, 370n76; *Liberalism and
Social Action*, 191, 362n41; "Philosophy
and Democracy," 316n2; *The Public
and Its Problems*, 15, 191–92, 195,

232, 234–35, 240, 243–48, 251–59,
261, 263–68, 272–76, 307, 312n9,
355n106, 360nn30–31; "The Pragmatic
Acquiescence," 187; *Reconstruction in
Philosophy*, 5, 197–98, 211–12, 238–39,
258, 260–61, 307, 321n45, 353n97;
"Three Independent Factors in Morals,"
214–15, 348–49nn61, 63–64; "Time and
Individuality," 156–57; "The Vanishing
Subject in the Work of William James,"
163, 335n9, 337–38n44; "William James
and the World Today," 333n4, 355n2;
"William James as Empiricist," 337n43;
"William James in Nineteen Twenty—
Six," 244.
Diggins, John Patrick, 315n28, 353n99
Du Bois, W.E.B., 281, 283, 314n23

Eldridge, Michael, 312n2
Eliot, T.S., 26, 316n8
Ellison, Ralph: and African-American
cultural traditions, 301; on American
literature's representations of African-
Americans, 304–5; Burke, Kenneth,
influenced by, 289, 295–306, 369n61;
Emersonian individualism, relation
to, chapter 6, *passim*; individuality,
necessary to society, 297–98, 307–8;
tragicomic ethics, 297–306; Wright,
Richard, critique of, 282, 363–64n2.
Ellison, Ralph (works): "Address to the
Harvard College Alumni," 295–97, 232;
"The Art of Fiction: An Interview,"
299; "Change the Joke and Slip the
Yoke," 299; "The Essential Ellison,"
365n6; "An Extravagance of Laughter,"
370n62; "Going to the Territory," 364n3;
"Hidden Name and Complex Fate," 283,
288, 307–8; "Introduction" to *Shadow
and Act*, 297; *Invisible Man*, 19–20, 232,
276–77, 232, 282–86, 288–89, 297–308;
"The Novel as a Function of American
Democracy," 296–97; "Richard Wright's
Blues," 364n2; "That Same Pain, That
Same Pleasure," 282, 297, 301, 363–64n2;
"Twentieth-Century Fiction and the
Black Mask of Humanity," 286, 304–5;
"Working Notes for *Invisible Man*," 298;
"The World and the Jug," 302, 364n2.
Emerson, Ralph Waldo: abandonment,
versus concentration in vocation,
70–76, 109, 231; and abolition

movement, 109, 118, 123–24, 367n15; action, versus thought, 76–78; active versus mental self-reliance (Kateb), 75–76; antagonism, in community, 88–89; antagonism, in metaphysics, 54–55; community, 86–97; community, nonconformist individuality in, 90–92; community, and pluralistic affirmation of individuality, 93–97; friendship, and influence of others on the self, 86–89, 93–94; idealism, pragmatic, 56–57; metaphysics, limitation and power in, 56–65; monism, versus pluralism, 34–42, and chapter 1, *passim;* monism, William James' view of in Emerson, 36–42; morality of our universe, 61–65; and Nietzsche, Friedrich, 78–86; pluralism, and egalitarianism, 94–96; reform and politics, approach to, 107–24; renunciatory morality, critique of, 78–86; self, as relational and social, 65–67; self, as socially indebted, 55; self-culture, ethics of, chapter 2, *passim;* self-reliance, and political engagement, 109–10, 118–19, 123–24; slavery and abolition, 113–22; social division of labor, 97–107; sublimation, 84–86; tragic sensibility, 56–65; transcendentalism, 54, 56, 59; vocation, 67–70; 102–4

Emerson, Ralph Waldo (works): "Address on the Emancipation of the Negroes in the British West Indies," 117–21; "American Scholar," 35, 49, 60, 65, 69, 74, 77; "Circles," 57, 59, 61, 64, 68, 71, 87–88, 121; "Compensation," 61–65, 68, 79, 88, 93, 102–3, 121–22, 203, 248, 294; *The Conduct of Life,* 219; "The Conservative," 56, 72, 101, 289; "Considerations by the Way," 84–85, 121; "Culture" 69, 74–75, 85–86; Divinity School Address, 34–35, 295; "Experience," 64, 92, 294, 362n59; "Fate," 33, 54, 62, 64, 121, 287, 289, 294, 325n43; "The Fortune of the Republic," 328n102; "Friendship," 54, 87; "The Fugitive Slave Law," 121–22; "History," 47–51, 56, 66, 68, 322nn65–66, 360–61n33; "Lecture on Slavery," 117–18; "Man the Reformer," 100–102, 104–5, 112, 289–90; "The Method of Nature," 102, 329; *Miscellanies: Embracing*

Nature, Addresses, and Lectures, 32; *Nature* (1836), 34, 39, 44, 57–58, 61, 64, 110–12, 324n10; "Nature" (1844), 44, 324n10; "New England Reformers," 85, 96, 99, 111; "Nominalist and Realist," 45–47; "Ode, Inscribed to W. H. Channing," 98; "The Poet," 34, 59, 76, 325n55; "Politics," 112–13, 116–17, 235–36, 253; "Power," 60, 73; "Self-Reliance," 32, 43–45, 49, 58, 60–61, 66–68, 70, 72–73, 76–77, 80–83, 89–92, 103, 123, 204, 219, 290–91, 310, 326n71, 327n90, 363n61; "Shakspeare; or, the Poet," 72–73, 290; "Spiritual Laws," 44, 60, 64, 67, 203, 289–90; "The Transcendentalist," 58; "Uses of Great Men," 44, 66, 69–70, 86–88, 94–95, 101, 155, 200, 291, 361n33; "Wealth," 74, 104

Everett, Edward, 113

Fesmire, Steven, 214, 348n60, 349n64
Fourier, Charles, 106, 237
Freedom and Fate (Whicher), 27, 288
Freud, Sigmund, 187, 225–26, 350–51nn84–85, 353n99, 354n105
Fugitive Slave Law, 108, 113–14, 119, 121
Fuller, Margaret, 106, 237

Gale, Richard M., 335n5, 341–42n115
Giamatti, A. Bartlett, 26, 317n8
Gilman, Charlotte Perkins, 314n23
Gilroy, Paul, 364n3
Goethe, Johann Wolfgang von, 106, 237
The Golden Day (Mumford), 249, 282, 284–85, 289, 315n29, 357–58nn11–12
Goodman, Russell, 317n11
Gougeon, Len, 108, 119, 330nn132, 134, 332nn149, 151, 367n15
Gouinlock, James, 348n60, 360n27

Habits of the Heart (Bellah), 13–15, 314n23
Hook, Sidney, 325n27
Howe, Irving, 26, 316n8, 365n5
Hughes, Gertrude Reif, 325n27

individualism, dominant model of, *see liberalism, classic*
individualism, pragmatic, overview of, 8–11

James, Henry, 26, 316n8, 318n17
James, Henry, Sr., 31

James, William: "bigness," critique of
183–84; community, and individuality
in morals 171–74; and Dewey, John,
18, 143–44, 156–57, 162–63, 184–85,
189–90, 244, 271–72, 335n9, 337n44,
342n125; education, and plasticity
of human nature 157–65; Emerson,
Ralph Waldo, influenced by, 31–32;
Emerson's works, James' marginalia
in, 32, 318nn16, 18; on Emerson as
philosopher, 47–49; on Emerson's
essay "History," 47–51; experience,
pluralistic model of, 3–4, 129–31;
individualism, and pragmatism,
137–42; habit, 157–65; individuality,
and community in morals, 171–74;
individuality, as creative catalyst,
146–56; meliorism, 41, 137–40, 151;
monism, 36–38, 137; monism, in
Emerson, 36–42; moral self, 148–53,
173–83; morals, theory of 167–75;
pluralism, 134–35, 137–40; pluralism,
versus monism, 36–39, 137; politics,
185, 189; pragmatism, of James,
overview; 36–37, 129–43; radical
empiricism, 32, 48, 134–35; reform,
James' approach compared to Dewey's,
183–90; theism, and pluralism, 180,
341n115; theory of truth, pragmatic,
132–36; vagueness in mental life, 150;
vocation, individualized ethic of,
175–80; will 150–52
James, William (works): "Address at the
Centenary of Ralph Waldo Emerson,"
39–42, 45, 47–48; "Brute and Human
Intellect," 338n51; "Dilemma of
Determinism," 37–38, 137–38, 341n102,
347n57; "Does 'Consciousness' Exist?,"
134; "Emerson" (*Manuscript Essays
and Notes*), 40–41, 320n44; *Essays
in Radical Empiricism,* 32; "Great
Men and Their Environment," 147,
153–55, 339n70; "The Importance of
Individuals," 146, 152, 338n58; *The
Meaning of Truth,* 335n10; "The Moral
Equivalent of War," 124, 144, 167,
186–90, 236; "The Moral Philosopher
and the Moral Life," 16, 131, 146,
156, 166–76, 180, 306; "On A Certain
Blindness in Human Beings," 50, 131,
146, 150, 166, 181; "The One and the
Many" (*Pragmatism*), 45; *A Pluralistic
Universe,* 134–35, 337n35; *Pragmatism,*
3, 17, 25–26, 36–38, 42, 48, 51, 53, 127–
28, 132–33, 135–38, 140, 146–47, 149,
175–76, 186, 271, 313n15, 319–20nn32,
34, 337n35, 345–46n24; "Pragmatism
and Religion" (*Pragmatism*), 42,
142, 156, 170, 175–180, 230, 244, 271;
Principles of Psychology, 18, 131, 134,
142, 144–65,175, 178, 182, 321n54,
340n86; *Psychology, Briefer Course,*
165; "Remarks on Spencer's Definition
of Mind as Correspondence," 134;
"Sentiment of Rationality," 41–42,
138–42, 177, 180, 321n54, 336n13, 25;
Some Problems of Philosophy, 137–38;
"The Stream of Thought" (*Principles
of Psychology*), 149–50, 152, 182; *The
Varieties of Religious Experience,* 39;
"What makes a Life Significant," 50,
149, 166, 180–81; *The Will to Believe*
(book), 127; "The Will to Believe,"
(essay), 127, 138–39; "A World of Pure
Experience," 134
Jehlen, Myra, 61, 317n10, 330n134

Kallen, Horace, 355n2
Kant, Immanuel, 201–2, 218, 221, 224
Kateb, George, 33–35, 48, 75–77, 109, 118,
123–24, 314n27, 325n53, 330n137
Kloppenberg, James T., 312n2, 334n5

Lasch, Christopher, 314n27
Lawrence, Abbott, 114
Lee, Kun Jong, 364n4
Lehrer, Jonah, 339n63, 340n80
Lenin, V.I., 359n21
liberalism, classic, 6–7, 128, 130–31, 174,
181, 192, 221, 226, 234–35, 246, 253,
256–65, 306, 307–8, 310, 313n11
Lippmann, Walter, 255, 360n32
Livingston, James, 285, 316n7, 359n14,
366n12, 368n33
Locke, John, 3, 6, 17, 313n11, 353n99
Lopez, Michael, 26–27, 35, 316n8, 318n23,
324n18, 325n27, 326n58, 367n21
Lysaker, John, 319n30, 323n3, 327n80, 331n145

MacIntyre, Alasdair, 314n27
Magee, Michael, 365n4
Marr, David, 26

Marx, Karl, 98–99, 199, 328n106–107, 328–29n110
Matthiessen, F.O., 282
McDermott, John, 318n12, 320n39, 322n62
McKenna, Erin, 355n114
Mead, George Herbert, 128
Melville, Herman, 26, 249–50, 285–86
Milder, Robert, 317n10
Mill, John Stuart, 156, 313n15, 360n27
Mitchell, Charles E., 26–27, 36, 316n8, 330n132, 367n14
Mumford, Lewis, 17, 26, 187, 249–50, 282–83, 285, 288–89, 292, 315n29, 343n130, 357n11, 358n12, 359n14, 366n12, 368n33
Myers, Gerald E., 334n5, 343n128

Nadel, Alan, 284–88, 364n4
Native American Party, 95
Nelson, Dana, 317n10
Newfield, Christopher, 317n10, 366n7
Nichols, William W., 364n4
Niebuhr, Reinhold, 17, 315n28, 353n99
Nietzsche, Friedrich: and Emerson, Ralph Waldo, 78–86; *The Gay Science*, 80, 83, 85, 326n63; *On the Genealogy of Morals*, 79–80, 83–84, 85, 326n59–60, 327n95; "self-overcoming," and sublimation, 74, 84, 85–86, 326n73; *The Twilight of the Idols*, 64
Norton, Andrews, 367n14
Norton, Charles Eliot, 367n14

Obama, Barack, 312n2
O'Meally, Robert, 366n6
Otto, M.C., 184–85, 188–89, 315n33, 333n5, 342n122

Pappas, Gregory, 348n60, 349n67, 350n77
Parrish, Timothy L., 366n6
Pawelski, James, 335n5, 341n115
Pease, Donald, 366n6
Peirce, Charles Sanders, 192
Perry, Ralph Barton, 318n15
Phillips, Wendell, 113
Poirier, Richard, 29–30, 48, 50, 91, 150, 288, 327n90
Porte, Joel, 327n79
pragmatism: overview of 3–6; enduring political appeal of, 15–18; view of philosophy, 25–26, 315–16n2

Reed, Sampson, 56
Richardson, Robert D., 128, 311n1, 319n26, 328n107, 333n1
Robinson, David, 318n12, 319n27, 333n159
Roosevelt, Theodore, 356n5
Rorty, Richard, 330n137
Rossi, William, 319n28, 327n80
Rovit, Earl H., 364n4
Royce, Josiah, 320n39
Ryan, Alan, 344n2, 360n32
Ryan, Paul, 312n2

Sandel, Michael, 314n27
Santayana, George, 26, 316n8, 320n39
Seigfried, Charlotte Haddock, 342n116
Second Treatise on Civil Government (Locke), 6, 17, 313n11, 353n99
Smith, John E., 129
Smith, Adam, 3, 7, 9, 350n81, 353n99
Smith, Valerie, 369nn55, 59
Spencer, Herbert, 134, 141, 336–37n
Spillers, Hortense, 369n52
Stepto, Robert B., 369nn55, 59
Stack, George, 326n58
Stuhr, John J., 344–45n8
Swedenborg, Emanuel, 56
Swift, Morrison I., 127, 333n1

Taft, William Howard, 356n5
Taylor, Charles, 314n27
Teichgraeber, Richard F., III, 28, 106
Thayer, H.S., 334n5
Thoreau, Henry David, 98, 101, 106, 173, 213, 250, 285–86, 329n126, 330n129, 347n58
Tocqueville, Alexis de, 2, 12–13, 311n1, 313n17
Tufts, James H., 344n4
Turner, Jack, 365n4
Twain, Mark (Samuel L. Clemens), 305

Updike, John 26, 316n8

Van Buren, Martin, 123
Virtue's Hero (Gougeon) 108, 330nn132, 134, 332nn149, 151, 367n15

Walden (Thoreau), 101, 329n126, 347n58
Wallas, Graham, 356n5
Walzer, Michael, 314n27
Watts, Jerry Gafio, 365n5

Webster, Daniel, 113, 119
Welchman, Jennifer, 348n60
West, Cornel, 107–8, 315n33, 318n12,
    328n101, 333n5, 342n125, 344n7, 364n4,
    366n7
Westbrook, Robert B., 343n2, 351n85,
    359n12, 359–60n21

"What's the use of calling Emerson a
    Pragmatist?" (Cavell), 30
Whicher, Stephen E., 27, 288.
Woman in the Nineteenth Century
    (Fuller), 106, 237
Worley, Sam McGuire, 330n129
Wright, Richard, 282, 365n5, 364n2

AMERICAN PHILOSOPHY
Douglas R. Anderson and Jude Jones, series editors

Kenneth Laine Ketner, ed., *Peirce and Contemporary Thought: Philosophical Inquiries.*

Max H. Fisch, ed., *Classic American Philosophers: Peirce, James, Royce, Santayana, Dewey, Whitehead, second edition.* Introduction by Nathan Houser.

John E. Smith, *Experience and God, second edition.*

Vincent G. Potter, *Peirce's Philosophical Perspectives.* Edited by Vincent Colapietro.

Richard E. Hart and Douglas R. Anderson, eds., *Philosophy in Experience: American Philosophy in Transition.*

Vincent G. Potter, *Charles S. Peirce: On Norms and Ideals, second edition.* Introduction by Stanley M. Harrison.

Vincent M. Colapietro, ed., *Reason, Experience, and God: John E. Smith in Dialogue.* Introduction by Merold Westphal.

Robert J. O'Connell, S.J., *William James on the Courage to Believe, second edition.*

Elizabeth M. Kraus, *The Metaphysics of Experience: A Companion to Whitehead's "Process and Reality," second edition.* Introduction by Robert C. Neville.

Kenneth Westphal, ed., *Pragmatism, Reason, and Norms: A Realistic Assessment— Essays in Critical Appreciation of Frederick L. Will.*

Beth J. Singer, *Pragmatism, Rights, and Democracy.*

Eugene Fontinell, *Self, God, and Immorality: A Jamesian Investigation.*

Roger Ward, *Conversion in American Philosophy: Exploring the Practice of Transformation.*

Michael Epperson, *Quantum Mechanics and the Philosophy of Alfred North Whitehead.*

Kory Sorrell, *Representative Practices: Peirce, Pragmatism, and Feminist Epistemology.*

Naoko Saito, *The Gleam of Light: Moral Perfectionism and Education in Dewey and Emerson.*

Josiah Royce, *The Basic Writings of Josiah Royce.*

Douglas R. Anderson, *Philosophy Americana: Making Philosophy at Home in American Culture.*

James Campbell and Richard E. Hart, eds., *Experience as Philosophy: On the World of John J. McDermott.*

John J. McDermott, *The Drama of Possibility: Experience as Philosophy of Culture.* Edited by Douglas R. Anderson.

Larry A. Hickman, *Pragmatism as Post-Postmodernism: Lessons from John Dewey.*

Larry A. Hickman, Stefan Neubert, and Kersten Reich, eds., *John Dewey Between Pragmatism and Constructivism.*

Dwayne A. Tunstall, *Yes, But Not Quite: Encountering Josiah Royce's Ethico-Religious Insight.*

Josiah Royce, *Race Questions, Provincialism, and Other American Problems, expanded edition.* Edited by Scott L. Pratt and Shannon Sullivan.

Lara Trout, *The Politics of Survival: Peirce, Affectivity, and Social Criticism.*

John R. Shook and James A. Good, *John Dewey's Philosophy of Spirit, with the 1897 Lecture on Hegel.*

Douglas R. Anderson and Carl R. Hausman, *Conversations on Peirce: Reals and Ideals.*

Rick Anthony Furtak, Jonathan Ellsworth, and James D. Reid, eds., *Thoreau's Importance for Philosophy.*

James M. Albrecht, *Reconstructing Individualism: A Pragmatic Tradition from Emerson to Ellison.*

Mathew A. Foust, *Loyalty to Loyalty: Josiah Royce and the Genuine Moral Life.*

Cornelis de Waal and Krysztof Piotr Skowroński (eds.), *The Normative Thought of Charles S. Peirce.*